Reader Comments on *What Dwells Beyond*

"I finished this nearly 500 page read today. I give it [5 out of 5] stars. ...I will save you a long review but I want to tell you that this is THE best book on this subject, bar none. ... I cannot recommend it highly enough. This goes on my list of automatic 'CLASSICS'. I believe every serious Bible student, especially those who believe the Book [*King James Bible*], ought to read this book as a help to understanding the times in which we live. ... It really is that THICK with great insights from the author.

Pastor Greg Miller
Bible Believer's Fellowship
Worthington, OH

"I've just finished reading one of the most astonishing books I have ever read in my lifetime. That is no exaggeration. This is one that Gary Stearman will read with great interest, a study for the ages into things you will most definitley never hear in church! Author Jeffrey Mardis has taken a deep look at the secret things of the cosmos and reached some startling conclusions about the events of the past, things that have changed the world forever. Get ready to understand UFOs like never before. You're not going to believe some of the things you are about to read. This is a work led no doubt by the Holy Spirit. Every now and then you find a gem full of new and exciting ideas that make such perfect sense. One chapter is more spectacular than the last."

Bob Ulrich, COO
Prophecy Watchers
Oklahoma City, OK

"Your latest book, *What Dwells Beyond*, is an absolute must-read for all Believers. So much information, crammed between the covers of one book, and wrote in a way that you make one not want to put it down. Excellent book, from cover to cover. God has truly blessed you. And your chapter on darkness? Awesome. Never have I read so much meat on this topic. Thank you, once again, and may God continually bless you and your ministry."

Chester Edward Kiluk Sr.
Southgate, MI

"If you want a clear understanding about extraterrestrials and UFO's, you won't get it by listening to George Noory and his guests. 'The Truth Is Out There', and it's revealed in *What Dwells Beyond*. ...I'm reading it through the second time already (before I start loaning it out). Excellent all the way through with massive use of the KJV."

Byron Smith
Camby, IN

"Espionage, History, Science, Philosophy, Paleontology, the Bible, Satanism, Angelology, Ufology and comic-book characters, this book has it all. At nearly five-hundred pages, a treasure-chest of spiritual truth, I highly recommend adding Jeffrey W. Mardis' book *What Dwells Beyond* to your library. A King James Only Bible advocate, brother Jeffrey has come up with many Bible-based answers to the questions we all ponder when we gaze across the sky wondering, "what does dwell beyond?"

Dr. Bob Leib
Pensacola, FL

WHAT DWELLS
BEYOND

WHAT DWELLS
BEYOND

The Bible Believer's Handbook to Understanding Life in the Universe

Jeffrey W. Mardis

THIRD EDITION

DEFENDER
Crane, Missouri

WHAT DWELLS BEYOND:
The Bible Believer's Handbook to Understanding Life in the Universe

Defender
Crane, Missouri 65633

First Edition 2009, (Titled: *Aliens, Angels & Outer Space*)
Second Edition 2013, Revised and Expanded (Sword-In-Hand Publishing)
Third Edition 2015, Revised (Defender Publishing)

All scripture quotations taken from the Authorized King James Version of the Holy Bible. Word-capitalization is added by the author for emphasis and does not represent an alteration of the text. Any other deviations therefrom are not intentional and do not represent an alteration of the text. All images are in the public domain unless noted otherwise. Some of the works referenced in this material were cited from the internet and were current at the time of publication. Neither the publisher nor the author are responsible for dead web links or any inaccessible references cited online.

ISBN 13: 978-0-9904974-6-2

A CIP catalog record of this book is available from the Library of Congress.

Cover design and interior layout by Jeffrey W. Mardis

A very special thanks to Cody Watters, Greg Miller, Moriah Miller, Mark Brown, John Adelmann and Thomas Horn.

Printed in the United States of America

"He revealeth the deep and secret things:
he knoweth what is in the darkness,
and the light dwelleth with him."

DANIEL 2:22

CONTENTS

PART III **Conclusions on Extraterrestrialism**

Closing Thought & Theories
on the Concept

SPECIAL CONTENT

PREFACE

As a child growing up in the 70s and 80s, I was introduced to the concept of life outside of Earth at an early age. This exposure came primarily through science fiction films and books on the "unexplained". One of the first movies I ever remember seeing was *STAR WARS*. It was part of a double feature at a local drive-in shown in 1977 (I was 6 years old). During my grade school, junior and high school years I remember going to the library many times and checking out books on UFOs and other unexplained phenomena. I was always extremely fascinated by those types of books, but I also remember that they were never able to provide any definite answers, only more questions.

Oddly enough, while I was never interested in horror movies and things (*Dracula*, *Frankenstein*, etc.) As a young child, I grew up scared and frightened. Easily scared – easily frightened. I remember having frequent nightmares from which I would wake up in the middle of the night and be terrified. I just knew that whatever was hiding itself in my darkened room would see me. I would lay motionless beneath my covers as sweat dripped down my face.

Running parallel with this on-and-off lifelong interest in UFOs and aliens (primarily UFOs – I never liked the alien aspect of the phenomenon), was my exposure to the Holy Bible (Praise the Lord). I was raised in a church-going, Christian family, and became a born-again Christian myself on April 29, 1979 after trusting and receiving the Lord Jesus Christ as my Saviour (I was 8 years old).

While I've retained a keen interest in the subject of UFOs and life beyond Earth for many years, through the protection of the Holy Spirit, my relationship with the Lord Jesus Christ, and my love and interest in His written word, I've been kept grounded and able to find answers in His Book which were not readily available elsewhere, including my own church. The Lord also took those things which scared me as a child and turned them into a strong passion and drive for scriptural knowledge. I knew that it was only *in the Bible* where I would find the truth and comfort from my fears (Jn. 16:13).

What Dwells Beyond is aimed primarily towards individuals with interests such as myself; Born-again, Bible-believing Christians who are not satisfied with the current low-key, run-of-the-mill, and even non-existent Christian education regarding this subject.

This book attempts to collect into one volume all biblical information relevant to life in the Universe. The book is written from a *King James Bible* angle, treats the Holy Bible as a *literal supernatural history book*, and deals with such fascinating subjects as: extraterrestrial life, outer space, the structure of the Universe, space travel, angels, devils, cherubim, celestial creatures, giants, dinosaurs, hybrid monsters, aliens, science fiction, evolution, witchcraft, end-times technology and more. The primary purpose of this study is to *provide Bible-based answers for Christian edification* and to *strengthen your faith in God's word*. I wish I would've had access to a book such as this when I was young. It would've helped me immensely in understanding the "big picture" sooner, while reinforcing the truths of the Bible. It is my prayer that the reader will receive such a blessing, and come away with a deeper knowledge and love for the Lord Jesus Christ and appreciation for the final authority of the *King James Bible*.

Even so, come, Lord Jesus. (Rev. 22:20)

Jeffrey W. Mardis

INTRODUCTION

This book is not primarily about modern "space aliens". This book is primarily about the Bible, what it says regarding INTELLIGENT LIFE and what we can learn from it regarding life beyond Earth. As a matter of fact, only the 16th chapter addresses the alien subject directly. The first five chapters chronicle the history of the belief, and the next ten chapters are designed to build a methodical Bible-based case for understanding its position on the subject. This is a detailed study. It delves into Bible authority, cosmology, angelology, demonology, technology, prophesy, witchcraft, dinosaurs and more. You will discover that the book contains many studies and lists regarding these individual subjects, each one being important to the Christian in and of itself.

Although the first edition of this book was acceptable (self published by the author in 2009, by Sword-In-Hand Publishing and titled *Aliens, Angels & Outer Space*), I was not 100% satisfied with the work. There was still much more to be said. It was my plan all along to offer to the Christian a detailed Bible resource on the subject. This expanded edition from Defender Publishing, I believe, gives a much more complete package along those lines. The book has been completely revised with the addition of seven all-new chapters, with several chapters from the first edition having been either rewritten or eliminated. The book has also been retitled in an effort to communicate the expansion of the material. The information presented builds a step-by-step case for understanding the Bible's position on intelligent life in the Universe. It is an "apologetics" resource. That does not mean I'm "apologizing" for the content, but a modern term used to describe a reasoned argument in accord with scripture and offered to the Christian for spiritual growth and edification. The premise for the book is based on the assumption that the *King James Bible is true and without error*. And because of that, it will act as our Final Authority, regardless of the ideas and opinions of modern philosophy, psychology, science or theology. I take every word of the Bible *literally*, as it stands, unless other scriptures dictate that it absolutely cannot be taken that way. This allows us to enter each verse in a mind-set of *belief*, and not *doubt* (1 Thess. 2:13).

It is my intension for this study to teach two important things to the reader: (1) that the *King James Bible* can be trusted to divulge Truth; and (2) that the Bible has the answer to the age-old question of extraterrestrial life. While several Christian books on the subject have been offered in the past, I believe you will find this work unique. And I believe that you will find it addresses and says several things that have not been addressed or said until now.

The subject of aliens and UFOs is not going away any time soon. Men will continue to ask the question, "Is there life out there?" And history shows, for various reasons, the subject continues to strengthen and grow on a yearly basis. However, the good news is that the *King James Bible* isn't going anywhere either. It's here to stay. And it will not only outlast any and all "aliens", it will outlast anything and everything thrown in its path (Matt. 24:35). In the end, the Christian needs a source rooted in the eternal scriptures which can help him defend his faith against a stubborn subject which refuses to die. *What Dwells Beyond* is little more than an organization and commentary on the scriptures which address the question. It is my prayer that the work will edify the saints while uplifting and honoring the Lord Jesus Christ and His word.

Jeffrey W. Mardis
Sword-In-Hand Publishing
www.swordinhandpub.com

PART I
CHAPTERS 1 - 5

The History of
Extraterrestrialism

A Chronological Survey
from Genesis to the Present

"So they read in the book in the law of God distinctly, and gave the sense, and caused them to understand the reading." Nehemiah 8:8

1

The Alien Paradigm Begins
Its Origin & History in Scripture

"Is there any thing whereof it may be said, See, this is new? it hath been already of old time, which was before us." Ecclesiasties 1:10

O ver the years much speculation has been offered up concerning the apparent puzzle of what dwells beyond the reaches of our planet. For the 21st century Christian, a large chunk of this conjecture has resulted from popular and fictional scientific theories which propose thousands, if not millions, of other worlds could possibly exist which support advanced alien life. While many Christians have an interest in this subject, and rightfully so, the larger part of church leaders today completely ignore the issue. It's unknown whether this mass shunning is a result of fear, ignorance, or willful disregard, but the fact remains that Bible-believing Christian education, on the whole, is woefully behind on establishing a firm Bible-based foundation regarding one of the great realities of the Universe. This first chapter will examine the scriptural origins of this fascinating issue, and set the stage for a phenomenon that has endured throughout the ages – the belief in intelligent life beyond Earth.

Capturing the Minds of Men

The thought of the possibility of intelligent life beyond Earth has been around for millennia. For the Bible-believing Christian its origins can be traced back to the days following the Great Flood around 4,360 years ago. This was the era which witnessed the rise of the heathen cults of old. Pagan religions which focused their worship on the heavenly bodies, and the beings which they now supposed dwelt there. As Bible-believing Christians, it's imperative to keep in mind that the written word of God contains the true accounts which outline THE HISTORY OF MANKIND. The Bible not only contains the history of man, but its revelation lies outside of time and space itself. The Lord Jesus Christ, who is the Word incarnate, is the Beginning, the End, and even more so, the Eternal, Everlasting God:

> "I am Alpha and Omega, the beginning and the ending, saith the Lord, which is, and which was, and which is to come, the Almighty." Revelation 1:8

> "Before the mountains were brought forth, or ever thou hadst formed the earth and the world, even from ever-lasting to everlasting, thou art God." Psalms 90:2

> "The LORD reigneth, he is clothed with majesty; the LORD is clothed with strength, wherewith he hath gird-ed himself: the world also is stablished, that it cannot be moved. Thy throne is established of old: thou art from everlasting." Psalms 93:1-2

Because scripture encompasses time and space, reaching even beyond those bounds, and because it contains the true record of the earliest exploits of the human race, it should be no real problem locating where the first thoughts of the belief in extraterrestrial life emerge. Because of this, it's important to always remember the following:

1.) The human race began with the creation of one man (Adam).

2.) Man's original relationship with God was good (monotheistic), and there were no false cults or religions.

3.) Man was highly intelligent at the time of his creation, with wisdom imputed directly from God Himself (super-intelligent by today's standards).

4.) Man's fall into sin.

5.) The history of man's early succeeding generations.

The reason for emphasizing these 5 points is when stepping back and viewing them as a whole, it's equally important to grasp what captured the minds of the first generations of man, leading him away – en masse – from his Creator. Was it merely a rapid progression of man's new "sin nature" (Rom. 5:12) that caused his early ancestry to apostatize so abruptly, or did he have help? Remember, the generations which followed Adam were much closer to "innocence" and "goodness" than the man of today. Their hearts did not have a record of thousands of years of history of rebelling against the Almighty on which to build. Even early man's relation to the animal world was different. There were no "wild animals", for the Creator did not instill their "fear of man" until *after* Noah's Flood (Gen. 9:1-2). So, recognizing that the world was much different then, this begs the question: _Do the scriptures point to some critical event from man's past which could account for such a sudden departure from God?_ If so, why and for what reasons? The scriptures indicate that some sort of major paradigm shift – a major change in man's thinking – took place at some point AFTER the fall of Adam, but BEFORE the Flood of Noah. Between the approximate years of 4000 BC and 2344 BC – an interval of around 1,656 years. However, the New Testament describes a future time of apostasy which will parallel _"the days of Noe"_ (Matt. 24:37, Lk. 17:26), indicating that the entire ancient downfall was within the pre-Flood lifetime of Noah (2944-2344 BC). An interval of only 600 years (Gen. 7:6). This early transformation in global thinking is not mentioned explicitly by scripture. But its fruits are clearly seen, resulting in God's wrath being judiciously poured out on a young mankind. Note and contrast the following scriptures which were both indicative of a time period which preceded the Great Flood:

> _"[27] So God created man in his own image, in the image of God created he him; male and female created he them. [28] And GOD BLESSED THEM ... [31] And God saw every thing that he had made, and, behold, IT WAS VERY GOOD. ..." Genesis 1:27, 28 & 31_

> _"[5] And God saw that the WICKEDNESS OF MAN WAS GREAT in the earth, and that every imagination of the thoughts of his heart was ONLY EVIL continually. [6] And it repented the LORD that he had made man on the earth, and it grieved him at his heart. [7] And the LORD said, I will destroy man whom I have created from the face of the earth; both man, and beast, and the creeping thing, and the fowls of the air; for it repenteth me that I have made them." Genesis 6:5-7_

IMAGE/Foster Bible Pictures, 1897   The Days of Noah (c. 2944-2344 BC)

The Gospels specifically point to the *"days of Noe"*, a period of 600 years preceding the Flood, as an era represented by a global transformation in man's thinking towards God. This change resulted in God describing man's heart as *"very good"*, to God describing man's heart as *"only evil continually"*. What factors could contribute to such an abrupt change that resulted in God destroying nearly all life on the planet?

AUTHOR'S NOTE: To learn more about how this book established the dates of early man and the events which surrounded him, see *Appendix A: The Bible Timeline of Early Man from Adam to Abraham*, on page 493.

The hearts of men changed from being *"very good"*, to being *"only evil continually"* in God's eyes. Man went from being *"blessed"* by God, to being the object of the Creator's grief. God went from instructing mankind to *"replenish the earth"* (Gen. 1:28), to destroying mankind *"from the face of the earth"*. Those are huge differences. What could have accounted for such a sudden spread and worldwide saturation of sin and evil? The scriptures point primarily to one event, and that singular event DIRECTLY PRECEDES the statement of God's indictment (Gen. 6:5). Because of this chronology in wording, I believe it's safe to conclude that THESE VERSES CONTAIN THE ANSWERS to man's rapid, early descent into wickedness:

> *"[1] And it came to pass, when men began to multiply on the face of the earth, and daughters were born unto them, [2] That the sons of God saw the daughters of men that they were fair; and they took them wives of all which they chose. [3] And the LORD said, My spirit shall not always strive with man, for that he also is flesh: yet his days shall be an hundred and twenty years. [4] There were giants in the earth in those days; and also after that, when the sons of God came in unto the daughters of men, and they bare children to them, the same became mighty men which were of old, men of renown."*
> *Genesis 6:1-4*

The expression *"it came to pass"* is used 457 times in the *King James Bible*. The Lord uses the phrase to point out something important that is about to happen. Note the usage, "it" came to pass. And the readers response should be, "what" came to pass? The Bible then proceeds to define the "it". The first time this phrase is used is found in Genesis 4:3 where a contrast is drawn between the offering of Cain and Abel (an important event). The second time the phrase appears (Gen. 4:8) marks the first murder in recorded history (an important event). Genesis 6:1 contains the third use of the expression. This third usage is at a time "when" Earth's population was on the increase. Man was fulfilling his command to *"replenish the Earth"* (Gen. 1:28), and the third *"it came to pass"*, more specifically, highlights a time when beings from beyond took notice of Earth's budding female population. Here's what the Bible points out:

> *"...MEN began to multiply on...EARTH, and DAUGHTERS were born unto them...the SONS of God saw the DAUGHTERS OF MEN... and they took them wives ..."*

Sounds simple and quaint enough, doesn't it? Note particularly the words (1) men, (2) earth and (3) daughters of men. Why not simply use the phrase "sons of men" in conjunction with "daughters of men"? Because the scriptures are highlighting a difference. The unique phraseology *"daughters of men"* is found nowhere else in scripture. When used in context with men multiplying *"on the face of the earth"*, it implies that the *"sons"* which were taking these *"daughters"* were somehow not born of earthly fathers. The origin of these *"sons"* is from somewhere else. While a seemingly insignificant and innocent event on the surface (sons marrying daughters), the scriptures go on to show that it was *this series of radical occurrences that marked the beginning of worldwide apostasy*, eventually incurring the wrath of God (Gen. 7). Much more will be said about these interesting verses later in the book, as we delve into the details and look specifically at life forms created by God, and other types of life. This is simply an introduction.

The First Visitors & the Seeds of Corruption

When dealing with the subject of "extraterrestrial" life, this book takes the word at its literal meaning; intelligent life forms "of or from outside the earth or its atmosphere". Unless otherwise noted, the use of this word does not imply, in any way, the more colloquial idea of the term, that of "little green men from Mars". That is a definition which has hijacked the term over the past century. According to the scriptures, the first extraterrestrial "close encounters" take place in the sixth chapter of Genesis. This marks the first account of extraterrestrial invaders, both biblically and in recorded history, and it triggered a detrimental change in mankind's attitude and thinking towards God. The influences of these alien visitors helped exacerbate the new sin nature of man to such a degree (Gal. 5:19-21), that it not only helped shape the thinking of much of the world prior to the days of the Great Flood, but also afterward. Pre-Flood peoples had direct, firsthand access to these things, their Earth-born children (the giants), and the corrupt higher wisdom which they espoused. There was no real need at the time for cultic and sorcerous religious type systems which sought to delve into the "Hidden Mysteries", because the beings which embodied such beliefs were right there in their midsts. Graven images, idols and rituals came later. Such close contact between a young, more-innocent man and a race of beings which had no conscience regarding their gross evils, placed man's sin nature on the fast-track and on a collision course with God. Sins which not only affected mankind, but according to the Bible, somehow affected the world's animals as well. God proceeded to JUDGE THE WHOLE EARTH because *"both man and beast"* no longer represented the *"very good"* condition in which they were originally made. It is the Bible itself which names both life forms as joint offenders, and not some unfounded pretext:

> *"[5] And God saw that the wickedness of man was great in the earth, and that every imagination of the thoughts of his heart was only evil continually. [6] And it repented the LORD that he had made man on the earth, and it*

grieved him at his heart. [7] And the LORD said, I will destroy man whom I have created from the face of the earth; <u>BOTH MAN, AND BEAST</u>, <u>and the creeping thing, and the fowls of the air; for it repenteth me that I have made THEM</u>." Genesis 6:5-7

Post-Flood memories of these encounters manifested themselves in the form of paganism and witchcraft, giving rise to the world of the occult and the ancient "Mystery Religions". Cultic sects which utilized, graven images and forbidden practices in an effort to rediscover and reproduce the lost wisdom of an evil world now past. Devilish wisdom which revered the "creature" (men-like gods, giants, animals and mongrelized hybrid monsters) more than the Creator. This was A NEW CONCEPT FOR MAN. After being mindful of the Truth (whether in writ, word or deed) from the patriarchs of mankind (Adam, Abel, Seth, Enoch, Noah etc.), the Earth took a turn for the worse. In the post-Flood world, this type of belief was one of the major reasons why God called out a people unto Himself in the person of Abram. Had the Lord not done this, it is the belief of this author that God would've soon judged the world again by major catastrophe much like He did in Genesis 1:2, and 7. But God had a plan. Instead of hitting the reset button and starting over again (for the third time), God separated a people unto Himself and formed an unbreakable covenant (Gen. 15:18). But let's not get ahead of ourselves. The beings which invaded the Earth in Genesis 6 had a MAJOR IMPACT on man's attitude towards his Creator. One man stood apart, however. The scriptures refer to Noah as *"a just man"* who *"walked with God"* (Gen. 6:8). God blessed this man (Gen. 9:1), and his beliefs helped form the foundation of the new world:

"And the LORD said unto Noah, Come thou and all thy house into the ark; for thee have I seen righteous before me in this generation." Genesis 7:1

IMAGE/Foster Bible Pictures, 1897   Tower of Babel (c. 2130 BC)

The memories of pre-Flood events were consolidated in the land of Shinar. Later, witchcraft and polytheism spread across the globe after the dispersal at Babel.

"And God blessed Noah and his sons, and said unto them,
Be fruitful, and multiply, and replenish the earth."
Genesis 9:1

The righteous influence of Noah did not last long, however. The memories of the pre-Flood sons of God and their unholy exploits were still fresh, and within a mere 362 years after the Great Flood, God calls Abram *"out of thy country, and from thy kindred, and from thy father's house"* (Gen. 12:1). The book of Joshua clarifies why the Lord required this separation:

"[2] And Joshua said unto all the people, Thus saith the LORD God of Israel, Your fathers dwelt on the other side of the flood in old time, even Terah, the father of Abraham, and the father of Nachor: and THEY SERVED OTHER GODS. [3] And I took your father Abraham from the other side of the flood, and led him throughout all the land of Canaan, and multiplied his seed, and gave him Isaac. [14] Now therefore fear the LORD, and serve him in sincerity and in truth: and put away THE GODS WHICH YOUR FATHERS SERVED on the other side of the flood, and in Egypt; and serve ye the LORD." Joshua 24:2-3 & 14

[NOTE: When Joshua mentioned *"the other side of the flood"*, he was not referring to the Flood of Noah, but to the land on the other side of the Jordan River.]

History points to Nimrod and his city and tower of Babel as the birthplace of the first concerted effort to organize the pre-Flood memory of "god-men from space" into a religious system under a new world order. The Lord put a stop to this, however, by confounding their language (Gen. 11:7). Unable to understand one another's speech, the Earth divided in the days of Peleg (around 101 years after Noah's Flood – Gen. 10:25). Each nation then went its separate way, carrying with it the generational stories and memories of the Genesis 6 "invasion". By the time of Abram's birth (Gen. 11:26), the concept of polytheism was operating globally in full force. The bulk of mankind now revered fallen beings from space and looked to them for truth and guidance, instead of their Creator. ⟍ *fallen angels*

These blasphemous budding beliefs were not simply an attempt to anthropomorphize the Sun, Moon and stars, but went way beyond such simplistic concepts as applying man-like qualities to the heavenly bodies. The truth ran much deeper. Remember, early mankind was not a bunch of ignorant, dumb thumps hauling around clubs and living in caves. According to the Bible, the human race started out as HIGHLY INTELLIGENT MONOTHEISTS. Men who worshiped and acknowledged the True Living God. But this truth was derailed by "something" that was literally witnessed. Something Earth's early ancestors literally SAW WITH THEIR EYES. An unexpected global event that shook and changed the foundations of mans beliefs at the core. Instead of listening to those men of their day who *"walked with God"* or were *"preachers of righteousness"* (men like Adam, Enoch and Noah – see Gen. 5:22-24 & 2 Peter 2:5); the larger part of humanity chose to judge this incident, like their mother Eve, according to the flesh and outward appearance (Gen. 3:6). The seeds of corruption had been sown, and through the new sin nature of man, grew and flourished into a world unidentifiable with its beginning – a beginning which was once referred to as *"very good"*. As time marched on, succeeding generations arose which knew nothing of the True God (Acts 17:30). The post-Flood return of the giants were also a reminder of the now-lost, pre-Flood "wisdom" after which the dominant pagan cults and mystery religions now sought (James 3:15). Further perusal of the Bible shows the link between the gods of the ancient cults and their connection with outer space and the stars.

Glorifying Men from the Stars

> *"But ye have borne the tabernacle of your Moloch and Chiun your images, the star of your god, which ye made to yourselves." Amos 5:26*

> *" [42] Then God turned, and gave them up to worship the host of heaven; as it is written in the book of the prophets, O ye house of Israel, have ye offered to me slain beasts and sacrifices by the space of forty years in the*

fallen angels / stars

wilderness? [43] Yea, ye took up the tabernacle of Moloch, and the star of your god Remphan, figures which ye made to worship them: and I will carry you away beyond Babylon." Acts 7:42-43

"[22] Then Paul stood in the midst of Mars' hill, and said, Ye men of Athens, I perceive that in all things ye are too superstitious. [23] For as I passed by, and beheld your devotions, I found an altar with this inscription, TO THE UNKNOWN GOD. Whom therefore ye ignorantly worship, him declare I unto you." Acts 17:22-23

IMAGE/public domain   Diana (c. 52 AD)

Diana of Ephesus, a fertility goddess, is associated with an image which came to Earth from Jupiter.

"And when the townclerk had appeased the people, he said, Ye men of Ephesus, what man is there that knoweth not how that the city of the Ephesians is a worshipper of the great goddess Diana, and of the image which fell down from Jupiter?" Acts 19:35

With subtle references to things like *"worship the host of heaven"*, *"the star of your god"*, *"the star of your god Remphan"*, devotions to gods on *"Mars' hill"* and an unidentified *"image"* coming to Earth *"from Jupiter"*, I propose there is more going on here than we probably realize. Because of their access to pre-Flood history, ancient peoples undoubtedly knew more about true extraterrestrial life than we do today. Firsthand accounts of the events that lead to the Great Flood were AVAILABLE FOR OVER 500 YEARS after the catastrophe (via word-of-mouth of Noah and his sons and their wives. Gen. 9:28-29 & 11:10-11). Scriptures also record that the *"giants"* somehow made a return following the Flood (Gen. 6:4). However, as Old Testament races of the creatures were eradicated (Deut. 2), and the memory of their off-world fathers forgotten, the history and knowledge of their existence became buried in legend and myth. Since that time, the belief in extraterrestrial life has waxed and waned from one century to the next, as philosophers, scientists and theologians have all contributed both for and against the argument. An argument which persists right up to the twenty-first century.

Chapter 1 Summary

Genesis chapter 6 reveals the first contact between man and "extraterrestrial" life forms. These first scriptural details are somewhat vague, and we've yet to address exactly "who" or "what" these beings are, but their impact on Earth's early ancestors and the outcome of their arrival turned man's thinking regarding his Creator upside-down. An event which set in motion a sharp rise in sin and evil, including the formation of groups and practices which regarded these things as "gods" and sought to establish their corrupt wisdom as the foundation for global spiritual thinking.

This first chapter has jumped into the subject rather abruptly. Further chapters will slowdown this thinking process and look at biblical details much more closely, as we investigate such topics as: the origins of outer space and its relation to darkness and the fall of Lucifer; an illustrated field guide and classification system to all

IMAGE/Bigstockphoto.com   Modern concept of the "Extraterrestrial" since 1961

The *New Oxford American Dictionary* defines the word "extraterrestrial" as *"of or from outside the earth or its atmosphere"*. This is the correct usage of the term. Yet today, many wrongly assume that the word always implies encounters with beings much like the ones shown above – highly evolved, saucer-flying "little green men from Mars". There's no real proof for this concept, only theories. In order to get the proper perspective and full truth regarding this subject, many readers may have to unlearn what they've unknowingly been conditioned to think.

life forms; a look at the little-known and rarely discussed mystery of counterfeit life; biblical cosmology and the Three Heavens; life in outer space and ancient space travel; angels, giants, devils and other strange creatures; science fiction and its role in the advancement of technology and end-times prophecy; and much more. The next 4 chapters will follow the historical evolution of the concept of extraterrestrial life, and examine the leading opinions, philosophies and movements which surround it up to the present day.

"Prove all things; hold fast that which is good."
1 Thessalonians 5:21

2

The Rise of Cosmic Pluralism
600 BC - 1600 AD

"There are infinite worlds both like and unlike this world...in all worlds there are living creatures..."
– Epicurus, Letter to Herodotus (341–270 BC)

T he belief in intelligent life on other planets did not begin in the twentieth century with the advent of the UFO phenomenon. To the contrary, variations of the concept have been around since nearly the beginning, growing more prominent within the last 550 years. In the previous chapter we looked very briefly at the biblical roots of the phenomenon and the incident which ultimately seeded the belief (Gen. 6:1-4). Chapter 2 will continue to follow this line of thinking, while looking at the most prominent ancient and historical positions up to the 17th century.

A Clash of Beliefs

When boiled down to their lowest commonalities it is discovered that two belief systems regarding the theory of extraterrestrial life have been in competition for over two-and-a-half millennia. Today, we would label these ideas as "Naturalism" and "Supernaturalism". While both of these belief systems have broad variances within themselves, their general concepts have remained basically unchanged. Naturalism is the foundation of philosophers, humanists, atheists and evolutionists. It teaches that extraterrestrial life is the accidental product of nature. Supernaturalism, while having its true roots in pre-Flood monotheism and the witness of the patriarchs of mankind (i.e. Adam, Enoch, Noah, et. al., see Gen. 2-6), later splintered into a polytheistic system (the belief in many gods) after post-Flood memories and stories gave way to new religious thought. Supernaturalism predates Naturalism by about 1,654 years (counting from the days of Noah after the Flood) and supports the belief that a Supreme Intelligence (or intelligences) represents, and/or is responsible for extraterrestrial life. One belief presupposes the interaction of a God (or gods), the other presupposes unguided natural forces of blind chance. These two basic belief systems were destined to clash after the birth of Greek Philosophy around the 6th century BC. The reason this battle continues today is because Greek Philosophy is responsible for the foundation of secular thought in much of Western civilization. These ideas undergird false sciences which Christians are warned to avoid (1Tim. 6:20).

Greek Philosophy & Atomistic Thought

Amid the preeminence of ancient polytheism, an alternate view began to emerge – Cosmic Pluralism. Cosmic Pluralism is an astronomical term used to describe the existence of more than one planet populated with intelligent life. Usually, the inference is more towards hundreds or millions of inhabited worlds. As we've noted, the kernel for such an idea originated with a belief in the "gods". A polytheistic, religious belief system which revered supernatural god-like men from the heavens, and other man-animal creatures. Cosmic

Pluralism is simply an attempt to separate from supernatural ideas via "rationalization" and "naturalism". It converts the ancient pagan gods into natural beings (aliens) and then places them on planets.

The earliest theories regarding Cosmic Pluralism began to circulate within philosophical circles around 600 BC (about 1,654 years after the Flood). This time was contemporaneous with the prophets Jeremiah, Daniel, Ezekiel and Obadiah, and with Israel's captivity under the King of Babylon. Incidentally, King Nebuchadnezzar also had a prophetic dream around this exact same time regarding the future mingling of *"the seed of men"* with something other than men (Dan. 2:43). The prophets of this era clearly demonstrated the dominance of polytheistic thought, showing it resulted in the apostasy of Judah and Israel:

> *"[13] For according to the number of thy cities were thy GODS, O Judah; and according to the number of the streets of Jerusalem have ye set up altars to THE SHAMEFUL THING, even altars to burn incense unto BAAL. [14] Therefore pray not thou for this people, neither lift up a cry or prayer for them: for I will not hear them in the time that they cry unto me for their trouble."*
> *Jeremiah 11:13-14*

> *"[17] If it be so, our God whom we serve is able to deliver us from the burning fiery furnace, and he will deliver us out of thine hand, O king. [18] But if not, be it known unto thee, O king, that we will not serve thy GODS, nor worship the golden image which thou hast set up."*
> *Daniel 3:17-18*

The father of Greek philosophy and founder of the philosophical school of naturalism, Thales of Miletus (624-545 BC), sowed the first seeds of life-on-other-planets after he proposed the idea that stars were not simply heavenly lights, but planets similar to Earth.[1] This thought led others to further theorize that perhaps these supposed new "planets" were also inhabited. Anaximander of Miletus (610-540 BC), a student of Thales, echoed his teacher's proposition, adding that an infinite number of other worlds may exist, not in outer space, but in "temporal succession".[2] Anaximander also believed that *"originally men were born from animals of a different kind"*, stating that man's forefathers were *"fish, or animals very like fish"*.[3] The belief continues today.

IMAGE/public domain
Thales of Miletus (624-545 BC)

Greek philosophers Xenophanes of Colophon (570-475 BC)[4] and Anaxagoras of Clazomenae (500-428 BC)[5&6] both theorized that the Moon was a harbor of life.

[1] Freitas Jr., Robert A. *2.1 Ancient Beginnings*. Xenology: An Introduction to the Scientific Study of Extraterrestrial Life, Intelligence, and Civilization, First Edition. Robert A. Freitas Jr., 2008. Xenology Research Institute. 18 Sept. 2012 <http://www.xenology.info/Xeno/2.1.htm>

[2] Darling, David. "Anaximander of Miletus". *The Extraterrestrial Encyclopedia*. New York: Three Rivers Press, 2000. p 19

[3] Barnes, Jonathan. *Early Greek Philosophy*. London: Penguin Books, 2001. p 20

[4] Freitas Jr., Robert A. *2.1 Ancient Beginnings*. Xenology: An Introduction to the Scientific Study of Extraterrestrial Life, Intelligence, and Civilization, First Edition. Robert A. Freitas Jr., 2008. Xenology Research Institute. 18 Sept. 2012 <http://www.xenology.info/Xeno/2.1.htm>

[5] Darling, David. "Anaxagoras of Clazomenae". *The Encyclopedia of Science*. Ed. David Darling. 17 Sept. 2012 <http://www.daviddarling.info/encyclopedia/A/Anaxagoras.html>

[6] Fragment 4 (H. Diels ed., *Die Fragmente der Vorsokratiker* [Berlin, 1952] II. 59).

The most popular ancient concept to advocate Cosmic Pluralism was conceived in the 4th and 5th centuries BC by the Greek philosophers Leucippus (c. 440 BC) and Democritus (460 - 370 BC). Known as "Atomism", it theorized that the Universe was ACCIDENTALLY MADE by tiny, indestructible, eternal particles known as "atoms". Its premise held that *"...life had developed out of a primeval slime, man as well as animals and plants. Man was a microcosm of the universe, for he contained every kind of atom."* [7] But original atomistic pluralism was more akin to "parallel universe" theories than with the modern idea of multiple populated planets all existing within the same Universe. Atomism advanced cosmic pluralism, but its supposed "other worlds" were impossible to see or reach. Regardless, the theory grew in popularity and evolved over time.

IMAGE/public domain
Epicurus (341-270 BC)

One strong early proponent of atomism was Epicurus (341–270 BC). Epicurus was atheistic at heart, but professed an outward form of deism for social conformity. He is the founder of the philosophical school of "Epicureanism", and was one of the first to propose the idea that atomism's "atoms" moved under their own power without any intelligent outside influences. He stated:

[7] Mason, S.F, *A History of the Sciences*, 1962, Macmillan Pub. Co., New York. p 33

> *"...the INHERENT POWER of the atom to move by its own weight, plus its power to cling together with other atoms both like and unlike itself, plus the LAW OF CHANCE, can and do account, of and by themselves, without the intervention of any outside force or guiding intelligence, for every form of being that can be observed by one or another of our senses."* [8]

This theory formed the basis for his belief in Cosmic Pluralism, and helped the popularity of Atomistic thought. Epicurus further theorized:

> *"There are infinite worlds both like and unlike this world of ours ... we must believe that in all worlds there are living creatures and plants and other things we see in this world".* [9]

Epicurus taught that the spaces between atomism's parallel worlds were inhabited by gods which had no interest or interaction with any of the inhabited planets.[10] This concept depicted a polytheistic form of deism which allowed gods, but blocked their interaction with the Universe. The scriptures show that Epicurus' beliefs survived for hundreds of years, manifesting themselves during the days of Paul:

> *"[18] Then certain PHILOSOPHERS of the EPICURIANS, and of the Stoicks, encountered him. And some said, What will this babbler say? other some, He seemeth to be a setter forth of STRANGE GODS: because he preached*

---

[8] Copley, F.O.,(tr.), Lucretius: *On the Nature of Things*, 1977, W.W. Norton & Co., New York. p xii

[9] Epicurus, *Epicurus to Herodotus*, trans. C. Bailey, in *The Stoic and Epicurean Philosophers, ed.* Whitney J. Oates (New York: Modern Library, 1957), p 13.

[10] Darling, David. "Epicurus", *The Extraterrestrial Encyclopedia.* New York: Three Rivers Press, 2000. p 128

unto them Jesus, and the resurrection. [19] And they took him, and brought him unto Areopagus, saying, May we know what this new doctrine, whereof thou speakest, is? [20] For thou bringest certain strange things to our ears: we would know therefore what these things mean. [21] (For all the ATHENIANS and strangers which were there spent their time in nothing else, but either to tell, or to hear some new thing.) [22] Then Paul stood in the midst of Mars' hill, and said, Ye MEN OF ATHENS, I perceive that in all things ye are too superstitious. [23] For as I passed by, and beheld your devotions, I found an altar with this inscription, TO THE UNKNOWN GOD. Whom therefore ye ignorantly worship, him declare I unto you." Acts 17:18-23

Metrodorus of Chios (c. 350 BC), a student of both Democritus and Epicurus, argued much like the secularists of today when he said:

> *"...to consider the Earth the only populated world in infinite space is as absurd as to assert that in an entire field sown with millet only one grain will grow."* [11]

The Roman poet and philosopher Lucretius (ca. 99-55 BC) wrote on the concept at length in his poem *De rearm nature* (*On the Nature of the Universe*):

> *"... it is in the highest degree unlikely that this earth and sky is the only one to have been created and that all those particles of matter outside are accomplishing nothing. This follows from the fact that our world has been*

[11] Darling, David. "Metrodorus of Chios." *The Encyclopedia of Science*. Ed. David Darling. 19 Sept. 2012 <http://www.daviddarling.info/encyclopedia/M/Metrodorus. html>

made by nature through the spontaneous and casual collision and the multifarious, accidental, random and purposeless congregation and coalescence of atoms whose suddenly formed combinations could serve on each occasion as the starting point of substantial fabrics – earth and sea and sky and the races of living creatures. ... You have the same natural force to congregate them in any place precisely as they have been congregated here. You are bound therefore to acknowledge that in other regions there are other earths and various tribes of men and breeds of beasts." [12]

It must be noted here, that these rising theories of the spontaneous creation of life on other worlds did not spread like wildfire. They were beliefs which initially circulated on the outer fringes, representing the "natural" side of polytheistic thought. As mentioned, they began around 600 BC and continued to percolate thereafter. Some may wonder "where was God" during this time, but the answer's quite simple. This was the time in history which God *"winked at"* (Acts 17:30), a time of global spiritual *"ignorance"* (Acts 17:30) in which God separated a people unto Himself (Abram was called out around 1981 BC. Israel became a nation around 1490 BC). While the Lord dealt with his special people, and gave them their first command; *"Thou shalt have no other gods before me."* (Ex. 20:3), He IGNORED the rest of the world. This was not only in an effort to separate the holy from the unholy (Lev. 20:7), but to bring forth a Chosen Seed to be the Saviour of the world (Gen. 3:15, Deut. 7:6, Jn. 4:42, Acts 13:16-23, etc.), a world now dominated by witchcraft and pagan philosophies. Had God not chosen to work in this manner, it is my

---

[12] Titus Lucretius Carus, *On the Nature of the Universe*, trans. and introduced by R. E. Latham (Middlesex: Penguin Books, 1975), 90-93.

opinion, that God would've DESTROYED THE WORLD AGAIN at the Tower of Babel or sometime soon thereafter.

Man lavishes much praise on the ancient Greek philosophers. But their philosophical guesswork contributes nothing to Christian knowledge. Firstly, one needs to remember that thoughts are not created in a vacuum. Thinkers or no, these men were raised in cultures where the idea of men or gods from the heavens was nothing new. It was simply a matter of perspective (naturalism vs. supernaturalism). But because they chose to ignore the idea that their religious mythology may actually be a stylized interpretation or refurbishing of real historical events, many wrongly assume that their speculations of cosmic life were original thoughts. They weren't. The only substantial thing that can be considered original is that their philosophies placed extraterrestrial life on planets. Secondly, it's the fear of the Lord that lays the proper foundation for knowledge and wisdom (Prov. 1:7 & 9:10). The Bible warns:

> *"Beware lest any man SPOIL YOU THROUGH PHILOSOPHY and vain DECEIT, after the TRADITIONS OF MEN, after the rudiments of the world, and not after Christ." Colossians 2:8*

Plutarch (45-120 AD), a famous philosopher who lived near the end of New Testament times, wrote in his *De Facie in Orbe Lunae* (*On the Face in the Moon*):

> *"...the men on the moon, if they do exist, are slight of body and capable of being nourished..."* [13]

When joined with Paul's encounter with the Epicurians (Acts 17:18-23), this quote illustrates that Cosmic Pluralism not only

---

[13] Plutarch, and Harold Cherniss. *Plutarch's Moralia. Vol. XII.* Harvard University Press, 1976.

existed hundreds of years before Christianity, but continued to grow throughout New Testament times and later. Ironically, just as the birth of Cosmic Pluralism began around a time when Jerusalem was in ashes (around 600 BC - 2 Kings 25:1-10), Plutarch was the last major philosopher to seriously comment on the subject before it revived in the late Middle Ages. His statement regarding lunar life was written in 70 AD, a time which, once again, paralleled Jerusalem being sacked and burned.

> **600 BC** (approx.) - Nebuchadnezzar burns Jerusalem/
> Cosmic Pluralism Begins
> **70 AD** - Rome burns Jerusalem/Cosmic Pluralism goes
> into hibernation until the Dark Ages

Interestingly, we find a third curious connection between Israel and Extraterrestrialism when they both pop up at the same time with the advent of the modern UFO/alien movement. Modern ufology and Extraterrestrialism began in 1947. Israel became a nation, again, exactly one year later, in 1948. I don't want to set up a straw dog if there's nothing here, but I find it very strange and *spiritually suspicious* for three historical dates to correlate such a volatile subject with Israel and/or Jerusalem. One date corresponds with the founding of Israel (1948), and two dates correspond with its destruction (600 BC and 70 AD). Is this pointing to some prophetic event connected with Jerusalem/Israel and Extraterrestrialism in the future? Maybe. The strange correlations do lead me to believe that *something of a spiritual nature is going on behind the scenes*. The Devil's up to something. History also shows that the more modern concept of extraterrestrial life began to grow around 1440 AD, a period of time *immediately prior* to the Protestant Reformation and the advent of the first English Bibles (1500s), just prior to the time the scriptures were getting into the hands of the common man.

IMAGE/public domain   Nicholas of Cusa, a.k.a. Nikolaus Krebs (1401-1464 AD)

The Catholic priest, cardinal, theologian and philosopher, Nicholas of Cusa, was the first man in history known to have placed alien life within the same Universe.

Cosmic Pluralism of the Dark Ages

No major events regarding the belief in life on other planets occur from about the first century AD to the mid 15th century. Although the philosophical theory of atomism was largely responsible for the early propagation of Cosmic Pluralism, it had yet to bridge the gap of placing any of these supposed "populated worlds" into a single Universe. Apart from the speculations of lunar life, the earliest writer who proposed the idea of actual higher-intelligences inhabiting planets within the *same* Universe, was the medieval Catholic theologian, Nicholas of Cusa. *The Vatican today is planning the arrival in the apples of a Christ by petigram for all the world to see*

Also known as Nikolaus Krebs (1401-1464 AD), Nicholas of Cusa *false* was schooled in philosophy, science, mathematics, theology and the arts. He took issue with the Aristotelian concept that the Earth is the only populated world, arguing that such an idea limited the actions of God. His concept proposed that because God COULD DO IT, God DID DO IT. In 1440, he wrote his *De Docta Ignorantia* (*On Learned Ignorance*) in which he proposed that not only were the Sun and Moon inhabited, but also Mars and all other planets:

> "Life, as it exists on Earth, in the form of men, animals and plants, IS TO BE FOUND, let us suppose, in a higher form in the solar and stellar regions. Rather than think that so many stars and parts of the heavens are uninhabited and that this earth of ours alone is peopled – and that with beings, perhaps, of inferior type – we will suppose that in every region there are inhabitants, differing in nature by rank and all owing their origin to God. ... And we may make parallel surmise of other stellar areas that NONE OF THEM LACK INHABITANTS, as being each, like the world we live in, a particular area of ONE UNIVERSE which contains as many such areas as there are uncountable stars." [14]

His reasoning behind these bold ascertains stemmed not from scripture, but from his theory that the Earth was an inhabited "star" emitting its own heat and light. Therefore other stars, being similar, harbored inhabitants as well.[15] The idea is not far from the original teachings of Thales of Miletus (Thales had theorized that stars were planet-like. Nicholas Of Cusa simply flipped the concept, stating that planets were star-like). Nicholas also theorized of solar and lunar life. One would think that such unorthodoxy would've encouraged excommunication or even worse. But surprisingly, the Roman Catholic Church pronounced Nicholas a cardinal-priest nine years

[14] Crowe, Michael J. *The Extraterrestrial Life Debate*. Notre Dame, IN: University of Notre Dame, 2008. p 31-32

[15] Ibid. p 29

later. Krebs' contribution to the modern concept of alien life should not be underestimated. Thomas Kuhn, 20th century physicist, historian, philosopher, and author of *The Copernican Revolution: Planetary Astronomy in the Development of Western Thought*, endorses Krebs, suggesting that his doctrine may have PLAYED A MAJOR ROLE in the development of astronomy.[16] It should also be noted here that while Rome was slapping a man on the back who played footsie with doctrines of life on other planets, the Catholic Church was also condemning and excommunicating others for translating Bibles into English (Wycliffe, 1428), and executing others who professed belief in the scriptures and Christ alone.

In the early-to-mid 1500s, a certain Polish astronomer and Roman Catholic Doctor of Canon Law had formulated a new theory regarding the structure of the solar system. At first, however, his findings were only transmitted orally due to his fear of public ridicule. In 1536, the Archbishop of Capua urged him to publish his findings. He refused. Finally, on the very day of his death, with

IMAGE/public domain   Nicolaus Copernicus

a dedication to *"His Holiness, Pope Paul III"*, Nicolaus Copernicus (1473-1543) was given the first two of six books regarding his new theory of a heliocentric solar system.[17] While these writings never

[16] Crowe, Michael J. *The Extraterrestrial Life Debate.* Notre Dame, IN: University of Notre Dame, 2008. p 34

[17] Hagen, John. "Nicolaus Copernicus." *The Catholic Encyclopedia.* Vol. 4. New York: Robert Appleton Company, 1908. 10 Feb. 2013 <http://www.newadvent.org/cathen/04352b.htm>.

mentioned a single word regarding extraterrestrial life, they are, nevertheless, credited by many as being the catalyst responsible for advancing the idea into the mainstream. And much like the theories of Nicholas of Cusa, the Roman Catholic Church never profusely opposed the theory. Short-lived opposition arose 73 years later after Galileo Galilei was condemned to house arrest for supporting it, but the 19th ecumenical council held at Trent (one of the greatest general councils in Roman Catholic history, 1545-1563), never mentions the issue. Regardless, Copernicus' heliocentric theory is responsible for removing the Earth as the literal center of the Universe, and, in the minds of many, as the center of importance and God's attention. The Earth was now seen as "just another planet" amongst a vast sea of stars – it was nothing special.

In 1584, the most fanatical ET views yet in print were proposed in Giordano Bruno's *De l'Infinito Universe e Mondi* (*On the Infinite Universe & Worlds*). In it he wrote:

> "Thus is the excellence of God magnified and the greatness of his kingdom made manifest: he is glorified not in one, but in countless suns; not in a single earth, a single world, but in a thousand thousand, I say in an infinity of worlds".[18]

Bruno went on to populate every heavenly body, and to "attribute souls not only to the planets, but also to stars, meteors, and the universe as a whole." [19] His argument echoed most pluralist theologians before him, stating that if God has the infinite "omnipotent" ability, then He logically must have created an infinite number of worlds. In 1600, Giordano Bruno was burned at the stake

---

[18] Crowe, Michael J. *The Extraterrestrial Life Debate.* Notre Dame, IN: University of Notre Dame, 2008. p 44

[19] Ibid. p 38

during the Roman Inquisition. But surprisingly, the ex-Dominican was not executed for his views on extraterrestrial life or pluralism. *The Catholic Encyclopedia* explains:

> *"Bruno was not condemned for his defence of the Copernican system of astronomy, nor for his doctrine of the plurality of inhabited worlds, but for his theological errors, among which were the following: that Christ was not God but merely an unusually skillful magician, that the Holy Ghost is the soul of the world, that the Devil will be saved, etc."* [20]

As Geocentrism slowly gave way to Copernicus' Heliocentric Theory, Extraterrestrialism began to encroach more and more upon society. According to the new discovery, the Earth was apparently no longer as exceptional as the scriptures taught, and any planet was now fair game as a harbor of life.

Chapter 2 Summary

After the global dispersion of polytheism at the Tower of Babel, the belief fragmented into separate national religious sects and mythologies. Because they were once part of a single, unified belief system, history shows these diverse nations all shared common origin themes (a judgement, a global flood, an ark, a family saved, etc.). Literally hundreds of Flood legends can be found in the roots of the world's cultures. Such consistency is exactly what one would expect to find if the scriptural record is true. However, about 1,600 years after Babel, a new theory began to be spread by early Greek philosophers. Today this theory is known as "Cosmic Pluralism". Purely a hypothetical concept, pluralism utilized the supposed

[20] Turner, William. "Giordano Bruno." *The Catholic Encyclopedia*. Vol. 3. New York: Robert Appleton Company, 1908. 11 Feb. 2013 <http://www.newadvent.org/cathen/03016a.htm>.

interaction of natural forces as the means of creation, instead of a guiding, supernatural intelligence. This theory inspired the creation of Atomism which became the popular philosophical stance for the next several centuries. After Copernicus placed the Sun at the center of the solar system, a slow tide began to build which favored life on other planets.

3

Post-Copernican Fallout
& the Occult Revival
1600 - 1900

"Creating other worlds, peopling them with our own eternal posterity...this is eternal life." – Kent Nielsen, LDS.org

The turn of 17th century witnessed several events which impacted the belief in extraterrestrial life. First, the replacement of the geocentric theory with Copernicus' heliocentric theory created a gradual groundswell in speculation regarding multiple inhabited solar systems. Secondly, after the invention of the telescope in 1608, the verification that the Moon had mountains, and what looked to be "seas", and that several other planets had "moons", simply obliged the idea that Earth-like similarities meant life on other planets was abundant. Finally, a subtle undercurrent of religious occult thought added much fuel to the fire. As a result, the next three centuries witnessed a rapid mushrooming of the belief in life on other planets. Regarding these influences, the Rev. John J. Cavanaugh, Professor Emeritus at the

University of Notre Dame, and a recognized world authority on the subject of the debate on extraterrestrial life, affirms that not only were astronomical technology and the heliocentric theory important contributing factors, but *"a supportive shift in the religious and philosophical mentality of the period was crucial."* [1]

The Shape of Things to Come

One of the first men to write about the physical appearance of aliens was Christiaan Huygens (1629-1695). Huygens was a Dutch physicist and astronomer who is noted for saying; *"The world is my country, science is my religion."* A strange statement for a man who also claimed to be a Protestant Christian. Published over 315 years ago, Huygens wrote the first work ever exclusively dedicated to the question of intelligent alien life and its possible physical appearance. The work appeared posthumously in 1698 and stated:

> *"But when we come to meddle with THE SHAPE OF THESE CREATURES, and consider the incredible variety that is even in those of the different parts of this Earth ... I must then confess that I think it beyond the force of Imagination to arrive at any knowledge in the matter, or reach probability concerning THE FIGURES of these PLANETARY ANIMALS. ... I make no doubt but that the Planetary Worlds have as wonderful a variety as we. ... NOT MEN perhaps LIKE OURS, but some CREATURES OR OTHER ENDUED WITH REASON."* [2]

However, Huygens' arrival at the conclusion that other planets may harbor men and animals that are not "like ours", was not based

---

[1] Crowe, Michael J. *The Extraterrestrial Life Debate.* Notre Dame, IN: University of Notre Dame, 2008. p 35

[2] Ibid. p 95

on a search of scripture (Acts 17:11, 1Thess. 5:21), but on assumption and human reason, a trait exhibited by nearly all pluralists.

Spirits from Other Worlds & the Kindling of the Occult Elite

In 1745, Cosmic Pluralism gave rise to a new paradigm. For the first time in history, spiritism, Extraterrestrialism and Christianity merged into a new system of thought. Its founder was a Swedish scientist, mathematician and false prophet, who was revered by many as one of the greatest mystics of all time. Emanuel Swedenborg (1688-1772) claimed to be "chosen by God" to unveil the scriptures. His

IMAGE/public domain
Emanuel Swedenborg (1688-1772)

contact came via "angels and spirits" which lived on Jupiter, Mars, Mercury, Saturn, Venus, and the Moon. He wrote:

> *"...it has been granted me of the Lord to DISCOURSE AND CONVERSE WITH SPIRITS AND ANGELS WHO ARE FROM OTHER EARTHS, with some for a day, with some for a week, and with some for months; and TO BE INSTRUCTED BY THEM concerning THE EARTHS, from which, and near which, they were; and concerning the lives, customs, and worship of THE INHABITNATS thereof, ..."* [3 & 4]

---

[3] Swedenborg, Emanual. *A Compendium of the Theological & Spiritual Writings of Emanuel Swedenborg.* Boston, NY: Crosby & Nichols, Publishers, 1853. p 349

Swedenborg admitted of these spirit guides: *"These are the spirits by which men are possessed."* [5]   And speaking of the inhabitants of Venus, he said, *"They are of two kinds; some are gentle and benevolent, others wild, cruel and of GIGANTIC STATURE."* [6] Adding that the Moon's Lunarians were *"small, like children".*[7] Swedenborg's otherworldly revelations not only resulted in the creation of a new "Christianity", but also captured the attention of occultists who formed both official and unofficial Masonic rites in honor of these new teachings. Prolific Masonic author Albert G. Mackey (33°) wrote of these influences when he said:

> *"...it was the Freemasons of the advanced degrees who borrowed from Swedenborg, and not Swedenborg from them."* [8]

Swedenborg also represents one of the cogs in the wheel of modern esotericism – a 19th and 20th century revival and repackaging of witchcraft into a "New Age" occult movement. Today, the Exeter Centre for the Study of Esotericism awards doctorates and master's degrees in Western Esotericism. Its program partner, the Blavatsky Trust, describes the course as follows:

> *"The modern revival of esotericism extends from Romantic Naturphilosophie to nineteenth-century*

[4] Bush, George. *Mesmer & Swedenborg: or, The Relation of the Developments of Mesmerism to the Doctrines & Disclosures of Swedenborg.* New York, NY: John Allen, 1847. p 174

[5] Spence, Lewis. *An Encyclopedia of Occultism.* Secaucus, NJ: Citadel Press & Carol Publishing Group, 1996 [reprint of a 1920 ed]. p 395

[6] Ibid.

[7] Ibid.

[8] A. G. Mackey, *Encyclopaedia of Freemasonry.* New edition revised and enlarged by W. J. Hughan and E. L. Hawkins. New York, 1929 p 997

occultism involving Swedenborgianism, Mesmerism, spiritualism, the ancient wisdom-tradition, and ceremonial magic and para-masonic orders. Today, Helena Blavatsky and the Theosophical Society, Rudolf Steiner and Anthroposophy, C.G. Jung and his archetypal psychology, and Fourth Way movements are among the major currents of modem esotericism, providing an inspiration to CONTEMPORARY THINKERS and practitioners in the arts, education and medicine. ... The purpose of the Master's programme in Western Esotericism is to introduce students to this new and EXPANDING FIELD OF ACADEMIC STUDY, providing an adequate grounding in its historical, theological, and philosophical aspects. ... Students begin with a historical survey course entitled The Western Esoteric Traditions (a compulsory core module) in order to appreciate the broad scope and common features of this SPIRITUALITY. The optional modules then provide more specialised studies in the component traditions and subjects of Hermeticism, Neo-Platonism, Theurgy, Astrology, Alchemy, Kabbalah, Theosophy, Rosicrucianism, Freemasonry, Romantic Natural Science, and Modern Esotericism." [9]

The Blavatsky Trust is an outgrowth and mission of the Theosophical Society, and is the primary sponsor of the doctorate program. Their objective is to promote *"study and research in the field of the laws of nature and the POWERS LATENT IN MAN."* [10]

---

[9] "Master of Arts course in Western Esotericism School of Humanities & Social Sciences, University of Exeter, UK." The Blavatsky Trust. Web. 19 Feb 2013. <http://www.blavatskytrust.org.uk/html/ma_exeter.htm>.

[10] The Blavatsky Trust. Web. 19 Feb 2013. <http://www.blavatskytrust.org.uk/html/nf_bt1.htm>.

IMAGE/public domain   Theosophical Society Logo (c.1875)

The Theosophical Society is a grooming ground for elitists who promote Antichrist philosophies. Its use of the Oroboros (the serpent biting its tail) and hexagram (star symbol) are telltale signs of its ominous spiritual roots.

"The Trust aims to accomplish this by promoting a knowledge of the essential nature of man and the Cosmos in which he lives and of which he forms a part. There is a tradition in many countries of an ANCIENT WISDOM or Wisdom Religion KNOWN TO MEN OF SUPERIOR

DEVELOPMENT AND POWER WHO REPRESENT THE ADVANCE GUARD OF HUMANITY (this Ancient Wisdom has latterly been referred to as Theosophy)." [11]

"Theosophy is a relatively recent name for the Ancient Wisdom known from time immemorial. It is variously known as the Wisdom Religion, the Ancient Wisdom, Esotericism, Occultism and is included in the Western Mystery Tradition. It was kept secret to preserve it from distortion, adulteration and misuse but as much of it as was thought wise was made public ... for the first time, at the end of the 19th century." [12]

This brief rabbit trail was important because it illustrates the dark spiritual link between Cosmic Pluralism and the occult arts. Emanuel Swedenborg was one of the first mystics to claim contact with beings from another world (one of the first "alien contactees"). His endorsement of extraterrestrial life, and the incorporation of that belief into a metaphysical religious system, helped revive its true connections with the ancient gods and Mystery Religions. Its recognition by nineteenth, twentieth and twenty-first century occult elitists as a system of wisdom conformable to their objectives, helped shape the modern concept that "aliens" are beings which impart advanced, higher knowledge (Jam. 3:15). To this very day, it's nearly impossible to separate alienism and ufology from occult overtones.

Other prominent men of the 1700s who contributed much to the growth of pluralism include: Voltaire, Benjamin Franklin, Thomas Wright, Immanuel Kant, Johann Lambert, David Rittenhouse, John Adams, Thomas Paine and Sir William Herschel. Needless to say,

[11] The Blavatsky Trust. Web. 19 Feb 2013. <http://www.blavatskytrust.org.uk/html/nf_bt1.htm>.

[12] Ibid. <http://www.blavatskytrust.org.uk/index.html>.

by the end of the 18th century, the belief in life on other planets was no longer an obscure concept. It had moved out of the circle of ancient philosophers, and into the labs of astronomers. One must remember, however, that much of modern science is founded on the Greek philosophical school of naturalism, so to pass from one field to the next (philosophy to astronomy) is not saying a whole lot. The change had more to do with its perception and general acceptance, than with any type of real physical evidence – like the witnessing of extraterrestrial life. What had basically happened was that the philosophers of the ancient past became the scientists of the present. No 18th century scientist had ever seen an alien, but that did not stop them from having faith in their reality. As the calendar turned over to the 19th century, the belief reached new heights.

Mansions of Intelligent Life

In the early 1800s, a new series of books were published which went a long way in helping to establish extraterrestrial life in the minds of many Christians. Published in Scotland and America simultaneously, the 1817 sermon series sold like hotcakes into the tens of thousands and launched its author into the public eye. Because of this (and later unrelated efforts), Presbyterian minister Thomas Chalmers (1780-1847) was dubbed *"Scotland's greatest nineteenth-century churchman"*. His main bone of contention was not that extraterrestrial life may exist, but that many secular astronomers and deists were using the argument to prove the Bible unreliable. While Chalmers' sermons were no doubt intended to uplift the scriptures and the Lord Jesus Christ, and in many ways did so, they also suggested that God had indeed placed life on other planets. When discussing the findings and speculations of modern astronomy, of which Chalmers was an enthusiast, he wrote:

"Why resist any longer the grand and interesting conclusion? That each of these stars may be a token of

a system as vast and as splendid as the one in which we inhabit. Worlds roll in these distant regions; and these worlds must be the mansions of life and intelligence." [13]

By now, Chalmers' argument in defense of alien life was cliché. Like many men before him (and after), he assumed that the supposed existence of similar, Earth-like solar systems, indicated life was equally peppered throughout the Universe.

The Man-god from the Kolobian Star System

Joseph Smith was truly a product of his time. Undoubtedly influenced by the growing social belief in extraterrestrial life, when coupled with his upbringing in witchcraft and interests in Freemasonry, he was later able to form one of the largest Christian cults in the history of the world (as of 2012, the official cult total was numbered at 14 million worldwide).[14] In 1830, much like Emanuel Swedenborg 85 years prior, Smith merged the three ideologies into a new "Christian" religion – The Church of Jesus Christ of Latter-Day Saints, better known as "Mormons". Former LDS President Spencer W. Kimball wrote, *"Is it not thrilling to know that the prophets knew long ago that the earth is but one of numerous planets created and controlled by God!"*[15] The popular Mormon hymn *If You Could Hie to Kolob* (c. 1850) vividly illustrates this doctrine:

---

[13] Chalmers, Thomas. *The Works of Thomas Chalmers*, D.D. Pittsburgh, PA: A. Towar, Hogan & Thompson, 1833. p 73

[14] Newsroom. "Worldwide Statistics." The Church of Jesus Christ of Latter-Day Saints. Intellectual Reserve, Inc. Web. 22 Feb 2013. <http://www.mormonnewsroom.org/facts-and-stats>.

[15] Kimball, Spencer W. "Seek Learning, Even by Study and Also by Faith." The Church of Jesus Christ of Latter-Day Saints. Intellectual Reserve, Inc. 1983. Web. 21 Feb 2013. <http://www.lds.org/ensign/1983/09/seek-learning-even-by-study-and-also-by-faith>.

If you could hie to Kolob
In the twinkling of an eye,
And then continue onward
With that same speed to fly,
Do you think that you could ever,
Through all eternity,
Find out the generation
Where Gods began to be?

The works of God continue,
And worlds and lives abound;
Improvement and progression
Have one eternal round.
There is no end to matter;
There is no end to space;
There is no end to spirit;
There is no end to race.

- William W. Phelps, 1792-1872

When I first read this so-called "Christian hymn", it gave me cold chills. However, it is by no means obscure to Mormon theology. To the contrary, it reflects their most fundamental teachings on the meaning of eternal life. The hymn line which speaks of *"Where Gods began to be"* is a reference to Mormonism's secret cosmic roots (notice the "G" in gods is capitalized). A religion which supposedly *"began to be"* in the Kolobian star system, on the planet of a man who progressed to godhood, and later seeded planet Earth with HIS OWN OFFSPRING. In other words, Mormonism's "god" is an exalted sinner who ascended *"above the heights of the clouds"* after becoming *"like the most high"* (Isa. 14:14) and his misguided worshipers are taught to do the same. One LDS teacher wrote:

"Nothing is more basic in the RESTORED GOSPEL than these truths that, because of recent events of space

IMAGE/LDS.org   From the Mormon *Book of Abraham*

According to Mormonism, both the *Book of Abraham* and ancient Egyptian artifacts reveal that Kolob is the home of God. The Egyptian artifact above is supposedly proof of this belief. Needless to say, neither scripture nor Egyptian historians agree with this supposition.

travel, are so timely. The great hope of the gospel for us is that we may come to a oneness with our Lord and our Father and partake of this same work and glory and GODHOOD. Being joint-heirs of all that the Father has, WE may then look forward to USING THOSE POWERS TO ORGANIZE STILL OTHER WORLDS from the unorganized matter that exists throughout boundless space. CREATING OTHER WORLDS, PEOPLING THEM with OUR OWN ETERNAL POSTERITY, PROVIDING A

SAVIOR for them, and making known to them the saving
principles of the eternal gospel, that they may have the
same experiences we are now having and be exalted with
us in their turn — THIS IS ETERNAL LIFE." [16]

Sorry, but no. That *is not* eternal life. Not even close. It's the delusions of a raving spiritual lunatic named "Joseph Smith", a man who no more feared God or the Bible than satanic rock star Marilyn Manson or German tyrant Adolf Hitler.

To the Mormon, the heavens are eternal *("There is no end to space")*. They demand an infinite existence, for without it, it would be impossible to house the multiple gods and universes of the past, present and future – including future gods like Mitt Romney, Harry Reid, Orrin Hatch and Glenn Beck. Newly commissioned god-men who will create their own worlds, populate them with their own spirit-children, hinder them with their own devils, and save them with their own saviors. Pure insanity. The official LDS website references its *Doctrine & Covenants* (D&C 132:19-24) as proof of this "truth". These occult overtones (to put it mildly) do not offend the Mormon, however. Instead, they see them as being proofs of a "restored gospel". A gospel within a gospel. Next only to the teachings of the Roman Catholic Church, the LDS cling to one of the world's most perverted forms of "Christianity". It is a masterpiece of demonic crafting, being nothing more than blatant occult doctrine, cleverly cloaked in an aura of Jesus, God and family values. One would be hard-pressed to find a more perfect example of satanic deception.

The doctrines of Smith's cult reveal its foundational need for Cosmic Pluralism. Their form of "eternal life" is dependent upon it. Smith was able to steal Christianity, turn it on its head, and then

---

[16] Nielsen, Kent. *People on Other Worlds*. The Church of Jesus Christ of Latter-Day Saints. Intellectual Reserve, Inc. Web. 21 Feb 2013. <http://www.lds.org/new-era/1971/04/people-on-other-worlds>.

turn it into a spiritual monstrosity of the most blasphemous sort. To understand how such a feat was possible, one must understand the ancient secrets hidden within Masonry, and how that philosophy came to bear on the professing Christian public of the 1800s.

The Hoodwinking of America

Between 1720 and 1835, a major work of the Holy Spirit swept through early America. Consisting of two "Great Awakenings", these revivals produced hundreds of thousands of born-again Christians who were the fruits of *King James Bible*-believers like John Wesley, George Whitfield, Jonathan Edwards, Charles Finney, Peter Cartwright and others. Satan was right there, however, and immediately began to sow tares among the wheat (Matt. 13:19, Mk. 4:15). One strategy used to usurp the gospel was in the guise of a seemingly benevolent fraternity know as "Freemasonry". Christians not rooted in good ground became easy targets for the Devil's seed-snatching ravens (Matt. 13:19-23, et. al.).

Freemasonry first began to grow in America in the early 1730s. It utilized a series of secret handshakes, tokens and rituals to teach secret doctrine. Curiosity of these secrets, and the possibility of economic or political success and advancement, drew many to join its ranks. However, because "the Craft" often used the *King James Bible* in its rituals, many wrongly assumed it was compatible with Christian doctrine. It wasn't. The truth was, the only reason American Freemasonry "used" the *King James Bible* is not because it revered or exalted the words of the Living God, but because it was the professed Book of the majority of American Masons. Had these men been of a different religious persuasion, the book on the altar would've been different as well. The belief of the candidate dictated the "holy book" placed on the altar. Freemasonry's "secret doctrine" was the Fatherhood of God and the Brotherhood of Man, a belief that revered the gods and teachings of ALL FAITHS, and sought

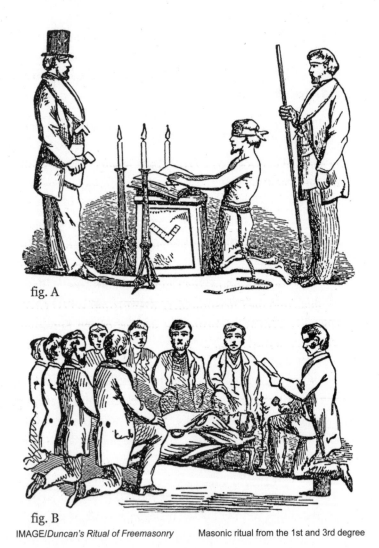

fig. A

fig. B

IMAGE/*Duncan's Ritual of Freemasonry*   Masonic ritual from the 1st and 3rd degree

FIG. A: In the first degree (Entered Apprentice) the candidate is taught that *he is his own* cornerstone upon which he may begin to build his spiritual temple (not Jesus Christ - 1Cor. 3:11). He is then made to kneel at the Masonic altar while half-naked and blindfolded, where he swears a blood oath to keep the secrets of the order, ending his oath with *"SO HELP ME GOD and keep me steadfast in the due performance of the same"*. The Bible is then kissed as a token of his sincerity. **FIG. B:** In the third degree (Master Mason) the candidate is symbolically murdered and then raised from the dead. This rebirth represents his new life in the secret doctrines of MASONRY – not Christ (1Tim. 1:3).

to UNITE THEM ALL under the fraternal umbrella of Masonry. The following quotation is from the official teaching monitor of the Grand Lodge of Kentucky. It reveals the true spiritual motives behind Lodge secrets:

> "It [Masonry] *makes no profession of Christianity, and wars not against sectarian creeds or doctrines, but LOOKS FORWARD TO THE TIME when ... there shall be but ONE ALTAR and but ONE WORSHIP; ONE COMMON ALTAR of Masonry, on which the Veda, Shastras, Sade, Zend-Avesta, Koran, and Holy Bible shall lie untouched by sacrilegious hands, and at whose shrine the Hindoo [sic], the Persian, the Assyrian, the Caldean, the Egyptian, the Chinese, the Mohammedan, the Jew, and the Christian MAY KNEEL and WITH ONE UNITED VOICE celebrate the praises of the Supreme Architect of the Universe."* [17]

The ignorance of this fact resulted in whole generations of Christian men and women becoming desensitized to the occult. This is because, even though all Blue Lodge Masons had first-hand experience in occult practice and ritual, they were, evidently, unaware of what they were witnessing, promoting and participating in. Ignorance may have been bliss, but it was no excuse. Regardless, such a ridiculous and profound lack of spiritual understanding showed that Bibles were not being believed or read, or that sermons were not being preached or listened to. This resulted in scriptural warnings going unheeded. The Bible reveals that a people can be *"destroyed for lack of knowledge"*, and this is exactly what happened (Hos. 4:6). This spiritual dropping-of-the-ball by pastors

---

[17] Pirtle, Henry. *The Kentucky Monitor: Complete Monitorial Ceremonies of the Blue Lodge.* Masonic Home, KY: Grand Lodge of Kentucky Free And Accepted Masons, 1990. p 95

and/or professing Christians allowed occult philosophy to make inroads into society and the political founding of America. Masonry, although by no means solely responsible, contributed much towards the destruction of Christian discernment. This was one of its MAJOR FRUITS. (NOTE: Wherever secret societies and rituals exist, they will always be used by Satan to advance his goals, regardless of the professions of the societies themselves). Masonry not only helped introduce many professing Christian men to the occult (in spite of their ignorance), but also helped lay the groundwork for New Age thought in America. Freemasonry was a powerful and destructive weapon in the Devil's arsenal of spiritual wrecking balls.

Masonry had been in America for nearly a century when the Mormon church was birthed in 1830. It represented the perfect hodgepodge of Extraterrestrialism, Masonism, occultism and Christianity. Its profession of polytheism was able to slide hand-in-glove with the secret mysteries taught by the Lodge. It also had many things in common with Emanuel Swedenborg's church founded nearly a century earlier. Both founders were involved in some form of witchcraft or mysticism; both religions were based on false angelic revelation; both felt called of God to spread a new Christianity; both espoused extraterrestrial life as gospel truth; and both systems grabbed the attention of occultists and Freemasons. All of this spiritual slop and refuse could've easily been avoided, however, had people simply read and believed the Bible:

> "But though we, or an ANGEL from heaven, PREACH ANY OTHER GOSPEL unto you than that which we have preached unto you, let him be accursed." Galatians 1:8

The Lunar Man-Bats of 1835

Perhaps no other event better illustrated the public's gullibility and acceptance of extraterrestrial life than the series of news stories

IMAGE/public domain   Lunar inhabitants of 1835

An illustrated panorama of the lively lunar landscape as supposedly reported by famous astronomer Sir John Herschel. The 1835 news story, originally reported by the *New York Sun*, caused a sensation.

printed by the *New York Sun* in August of 1835. For a short time, the articles resulted in the *Sun* becoming the world's best-selling newspaper. Nineteen thousand copies were initially sold, and sixty thousand copies were also later bought when the series was compiled into booklet form. The subject that so ignited this mad fury of newspaper-buying, was the brainchild of one Richard Adams Locke. Locke was a reporter with the *New York Sun* whose explosive story recorded the supposed observations of famous astronomer Sir John Herschel (1792-1871). John Herschel was the son of Sir William Herschel (1738-1822), an astronomer and avid telescope engineer. William Herschel, a strong proponent of pluralism, had previously affirmed that the possibility of lunar inhabitants was an *"almost absolute certainty"*, being also convinced of Solar and Martian life.[18]

[18] Darling, David. "William Herschel" *The Extraterrestrial Encyclopedia*. New York: Three Rivers Press, 2000. p 191

This, along with his official discovery of Uranus (1781), added much credibility to the story of his son's supposed lunar discoveries. In Locke's Sun series titled, *Great Astronomical Discoveries Lately Made By Sir John Herschel, L.L.D. F.R.S. &c., At The Cape of Good Hope*, he claimed that a variety of intelligent creatures had been spotted on the Moon, one of which was scientifically dubbed "Vespertilio-homo", or the Man-bat:

IMAGE/publicdomain   Vespertilio-homo or Man-bat

"...we beheld continuous herds of brown quadrupeds, having all the external characteristics of the bison... The next animal perceived would be classed on earth as a monster. It was of a bluish lead color, about the size of a goat, with a head and beard like him, and a single horn ... Of animals, he [Herschel] classified nine species of mammalian, and five of ovipara [egg-layers]. Among the former is a small kind of rein-deer, the elk, the moose, the horned bear, and the biped beaver. ...we were thrilled

A VIEW OF

THE INHABITANTS OF THE MOON,

AS SEEN THROUGH THE TELESCOPE OF SIR JOHN HERSCHEL.

IMAGE/public domain   From a pamphlet of the famous 1835 *Moon Hoax*

An illustrated close-up of lunar life depicting hairy, naked, bat-winged humanoids and bipedal beavers. A vision defended by many respected astronomers and "men of science" of 1835.

> *with astonishment to perceive four successful flocks of large winged creatures ... they were like human beings ... averaged four feet in height, were covered, except for the face, with short and glossy copper-colored hair. ... We could then perceive they possessed wings of great expansion, and were similar in structure to those of a bat, being semi-transparent membrane ... We scientifically denominated them the Vespertilio-homo, or man-bat; and they are doubtless innocent and happy creatures..."* [19]

As sensational as this story is, many people supported its claims, including many respected men of science, professors, theologians,

[19] Crowe, Michael J. *The Extraterrestrial Life Debate.* Notre Dame, IN: University of Notre Dame, 2008. p 282-287

and the faculty at Yale University. Edgar Allen Poe stated, *"Not one person in ten discredited it"*, claiming that the chief doubters were *"those uninformed in astronomy"*.[20] Although many later accused the writings of Locke as being a deliberate hoax, this was not the case. His objective was to simply poke fun at the growing belief in extraterrestrial life, especially resulting from the widely published claims of Scottish theologian and philosopher Thomas Dick, as well as German astronomers who claimed to have discovered a lunar fortification.[21] Instead, his sarcasm backfired, causing many to accept it as fact:

> *"If the story be either received as a veritable account, or rejected as a hoax, it is quite evident that it is an abortive satire; and, in either case, I am the best self-hoaxed man in the whole country."* [22]

It was a sign of the times, however, and I suppose in hindsight many astronomers, eager to discover life outside of Earth, were ashamed that they had walked away with egg on their faces. Rumor also has it that one American pastor considered soliciting funds for Bible donations to the Moon (although it's possible the comment was tongue-in-cheek).[23] Regardless, the *New York Sun* never admitted to anything or claimed any responsibility (a typical news media response).

---

[20] Clark, Jerome. *Unexplained!*. 2nd. ed. Canton, MI: Visible Ink Press, 1999. p 3

[21] Griggs, William N. *The Celebrated Moon Story, It's Origin And Incidents; With A Memoir Of The Author.* New York, NY: Bunnell & Price, 1852. p 8

[22] Griggs, William N. *The Celebrated Moon Story, It's Origin And Incidents; With A Memoir Of The Author.* New York, NY: Bunnell & Price, 1852. p 30

[23] Crowe, Michael J. *The Extraterrestrial Life Debate.* Notre Dame, IN: University of Notre Dame, 2008. p 274

To Knock on Wood

Running nearly parallel to the mid-1800s growing acceptance of alien life was the emerging phenomenon of Spiritism (or Spiritualism). Consisting of such things as automatic writing, mediumship, clairvoyance, psychic abilities, séances, mesmerism, hypnotism and channeling, Spiritism is based primarily around necromancy – communication with the dead. Modern Spiritism traces its roots to an 1848 event in Hydesville, New York, where three sisters (Leah, Margaretta and Kate Fox) are said to have communicated with the spirit of a murdered salesman calling itself "Splitfoot". Contact was made via rappings on wood. From this evolved the term "poltergeist" or "noisy-ghosts", from the German "poltern" (to make a racket), "geist" (ghost). Although the Fox sisters are revered as the pioneers of the modern religion, spiritists point to Emanuel Swedenborg (1688-1772), Franz Anton Mesmer (1734-1815), Charles Fourier (1772-1837) and Andrew Jackson Davis (1826-1910) as their true forefathers. Spiritism became increasingly popular in America in the last quarter of the 19th century. This growth undoubtedly resulted from persons trying to reestablish contact with loved ones lost during the Civil War. Probably the most famous spiritist events of the era were those of Mary Todd Lincoln. In an attempt to contact her son (William), history records she conducted numerous séances while living in the White House.

But for spiritists to point to recent events as the origin for their beliefs is an error. Much like the belief in extraterrestrial life, necromancy has ancient roots. It is a grievous sin which the Bible condemns, and the life of King Saul was ended for observing it (Deut. 18:10-12, 1Sam. 28:7, 1Chron. 10:13). Modern supposed alien "contactees" and "abductees" have many times been associated with these very same practices. Believe it or not, Lynn E. Catoe, former senior bibliographer for the Library of Congress, said it best in her 1969 report compiled for the U.S. Air Force Office of Scientific

Research; *UFOs and Related Subjects: An Annotated Bibliography*.
In its preface she wrote:

> *"A large part of the available UFO literature is closely
> linked with mysticism and the metaphysical. It deals with
> subjects like mental telepathy, automatic writing and
> invisible entities as well as phenomena like poltergeist
> manifestations and 'possession.'* [24] *...Many of the UFO
> reports now being published in the popular press* [c. 1969]
> *recount alleged incidents that are strikingly similar to
> demonic possession and psychic phenomenon which have
> long been known to theologians and parapsychologists."* [25]

While this *official report* has been cited many times by Christian
ufologists over the years, it bears repeating due to its profound
honesty and insight. For the Christian, such official disclosure of
the close connections between UFOs, alienism and the spirit world,
while not surprising, should be alarming. Agnostic John Keel came
to the same general conclusion in his book *UFOs: Operation Trojan
Horse* published the following year (1970).[26] The connections are no
accident, however, and they serve to help demonstrate that the gods
and spirits of old form the true basis for the belief in intelligent life on
other planets.

[24] Catoe, Lynn E. *UFO's & Related Subjects: An Annotated Bibliography.* 2. 19. Washington, DC: U.S. Printing Office, 1969. p iv. NOTE: Unsubstantiated claims state that the 1968 Condon Report had all the underlying documentation for this report destroyed. The full bibliography and Catoe's preface for the '69 printing survived, but not the collected evidential substance of those articles. In other words, they kept the book titles which comprised their report, but threw out the books. Why would they do that?

[25] Thomas, I.D.E. *The Omega Conspiracy: Satan's Last Assault On God's Kingdom.* Oklahoma City OK: Hearthstone Publishing, Ltd., 1986. p 73

[26] Alnor, William M. *UFO's in the New Age: Extraterrestrial Messages & the Truth of scripture.* Grand Rapids, MI: Baker Book House. 1992. p 80-81

Fifteen Billion Martians

In 1848, the same year marked by the birthing of the modern Spiritist movement, Scottish Presbyterian minister, Thomas Dick, published his most extravagant work. Persuaded by the general similarities of the planets (mountains, moons, supposed bodies of water, etc.), Dick took the presumption one step further and calculated the size of each planet's population, based on Earth's relative size to its own inhabitants. Much like fellow Scotsman Thomas Chalmers, Dick rightfully glorified God with the Heavens (Psa. 19:1), but added the following declaration:

> "...the doctrine of the plurality of worlds is more worthy of the perfections of the Infinite Creator, and gives us a more magnificent idea of his character and operations than to suppose his benevolent regards confined to the globe on which we dwell. ...There is an absurdity involved in the contrary supposition – namely, that the distant regions of creation are devoid of inhabitants" [27]

After declaring those who hold forth a special place for planet Earth as "absurd", Dick went on to make his own absurd statements. His book *Celestial Scenery* populates Mercury with over 8 billion inhabitants, Venus with 53 billion, Mars with 15 billion, Jupiter with 6 trillion, Saturn with 5 trillion, Saturn's rings with 8 trillion, Uranus with 1 trillion and the Moon with 4 billion. Dick also populated all the satellites, guesstimating the solar system to house a total of over 21 trillion souls.[28] The Bible-believer's response to such reckless supposition should be, *"But if any man be ignorant, let him be*

---

[27] Crowe, Michael J. *The Extraterrestrial Life Debate*. Notre Dame, IN: University of Notre Dame, 2008. p 260-261

[28] Crowe, Michael J. *The Extraterrestrial Life Debate*. Notre Dame, IN: University of Notre Dame, 2008. p 270

ignorant." (1Cor. 14:38) Thomas Dick's works were a success on both sides of the Atlantic, and they all addressed extraterrestrial life in some form or another, but *Celestial Scenery* was his masterpiece.

Like many of the early astronomers, Dick included God in his cosmogony. While this is admirable, arguments which favored pluralism were never postulated from a strong scriptural position. The stance, instead, was always argued from an astronomical position. That is, like many today, astronomers were distracted by the vast number of the stars, and argued from that position. Dick could've just as easily reasoned that all men are created by God, so God, therefore, MUST EQUALLY USE ALL MEN. After all, according to Dick, such a view would be "*more worthy of the perfections of the Infinite Creator*", and to believe otherwise would be "*an absurdity*". Why waste all those people? Its the THEOLOGICAL FALLACY of "God uses all parts of His creation equally." Later in the book we will address this argument in more detail, and show how the scriptural documentation of consistent patterns of God's behavior supports a much different position.

By the close of the 1800s, several other prominent pluralists made their mark on the public's conscience. Among them were Cardinal John Henry Newman (1801-1890), a highly lauded ex-Calvinist turned Roman Catholic, who stated that "*it almost amounts to blasphemy to doubt*" the plurality of worlds, and Ellen G. White (1827-1915), the founder of Seventh-Day Adventism, who proclaimed "*the sinless intelligences of other worlds*". [29 & 30] Science fiction was also beginning to have an impact on the belief with Jules Verne and H.G. Wells who published *From the Earth to the Moon* (1865) and *The War of the Worlds* (1897) respectively. The latter

[29] Crowe, Michael J. *The Extraterrestrial Life Debate.* Notre Dame, IN: University of Notre Dame, 2008. p 262

[30] White, Ellen G. *The Story of Patriarchs and Prophets* (Mountain View, CA; Pacific Press Publishing Association, 1913), p 68-70.

had a profound impact on the public and would translate into a radio play and multiple movie adaptations in the coming century. The first sentence of Wells' *The War of the Worlds* read:

> *"No one would have believed, in the last years of the nineteenth century, that human affairs were being watched keenly and closely by intelligences greater than man's."*

Wells also authored *The Island of Dr. Moreau* (1896), a novel which depicted the experimentation and cross-breeding of humans and animals, and the lesser known *The New World Order* (1940), where he writes of his desire of a socialist world society where *"armament should be an illegality everywhere, and some sort of international force should patrol a treaty-bound world."* And last, but certainly not least, was Charles Darwin (1809-1882), the man responsible for turning an amoeba into a man. Although Darwin never mentioned extraterrestrial life specifically, his theory of evolution *"by means*

IMAGE/public domain
Charles Robert Darwin (1809-1882)

of natural selection" was revered as the "Holy Grail" for cosmic pluralists. Like ancient atomism, it represented a means to an end. The means – *how to spontaneously create life.* The end – *to do away with the Creator.* That is, Darwin built the engine that powered the concept of atomism's autonomous moving atoms. This was the crucial steppingstone that helped move atomism from a purely speculative guess into a workable (albeit make-believe) biological "scientific theory". This new mystical force was dubbed "natural selection". It was a powerful universal influence which GUIDED THE CREATION OF INTELLIGENT LIFE, WITHOUT ANY INTELLIGENCE OR CONSCIENCE ITSELF – it was a paradox. If true, it meant that intelligent, thinking creatures were nothing more than meaningless accidents. The Universe was no better, or no worse, with or without them. If intelligence emerged by chance, then the issues of intelligent, thinking creatures (including intelligence itself) are illusions – morality, immorality, love, hate, good, evil, etc. If creation began with non-thinking nothingness, then life and death have no meaning. After all, an "accident" has no deliberate purpose. Every man is an island unto himself. Eat, drink and be merry, for tomorrow we die. In such a situation, the only "purpose" an intelligent creature may have, is the purpose it gives to itself. Which, in the grand scheme of things, means nothing at all. It's a worthless opinion – your word against mine. But, if creation began with a Holy God, then somewhere there's something more than an "opinion" – there's the WORD OF GOD.

Chapter 3 Summary

Major changes regarding the belief in intelligent life on other planets were ushered-in during the 17th, 18th and 19th centuries. What was once an ancient philosophical guess, became a mainstream theory. This mainstreaming, however, (for better or for worse) was not the result of one single event, but rather a combination of events in astronomy (heliocentrism), technology (the telescope) and religious thought (paganism and occult doctrine). By the advent of the 20th century, the belief in extraterrestrial life was viewed as a strong likelihood by the fields of astronomy and biology. This persuasion was spearheaded by the growing theory of evolution by means of natural selection.

4

The Rise of Science Fiction & the Birth of the Space Age
1900 - 1960

"Many of the pioneers in exobiology and SETI grew up on science fiction and were led to their careers by its imaginative lure." – Steven J. Dick, NASA Historian

B y the arrival of the 20th century the concept of intelligent life beyond Earth was no longer new. While the theories of 19th century astronomers, theologians and occultists helped settle the idea in the minds of many, there were yet many more who remained unconvinced. But the new century would bring with it a variety of influences which would help the theory become more popular than ever before.

Calling Mars Is Anyone There?

The 20th century was the first to witness radical measures taken by those who were convinced in the existence of extraterrestrial life. No longer content with simply viewing the stars, a new technology was emerging which would allow more innovative measures. Even though the study of radio waves was still in its infancy, there were those who saw its immediate potential for extraterrestrial communication, claiming it was *"destined to become the dominating idea of the century"*.[1] In 1901, *Collier's Weekly* carried an article titled, *Talking with the Planets*. Written by radio pioneer and electricity wizard Nikola Tesla (1856-1943), the piece related a recent incident where Tesla suspected he may have intercepted intelligent radio signals from another world:

IMAGE/public domain
Nikola Tesla (1856-1943)

"As I was improving my machines for the production of intense electrical actions ... I discovered those mysterious effects which have elicited such unusual interest. My first observations positively terrified me, as there was present in them something mysterious, not to say supernatural, and I was alone in my laboratory at night, but at that time the idea of these disturbances being intelligently controlled signals did not yet present itself to me. ... It was some time afterward when the thought flashed upon my mind that the disturbances I had observed might be due to an intelligent control. Although I could not decipher their

[1] Tesla, Nikola. "Talking with the Planets." Collier's Weekly. 7 Feb. 1901: p 4-5.

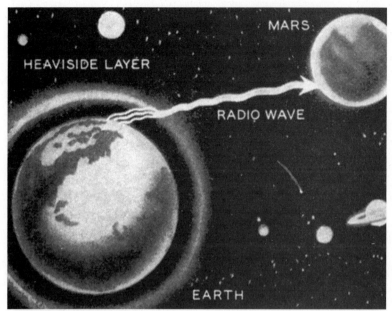

IMAGE/*Modern Mechanix*, 1934   Tesla's plan to communicate with the planets.

The July 1934 issue of *Modern Mechanix* carried an article by Nikola Tesla titled "Radio Power Will Revolutionize the World". The above image accompanied the story with the following caption: *"By using ultra-short waves, science expects to penetrate the heaviside layer, or gaseous medium surrounding the earth, and establish radio communication with Mars and other distant planets".*

> *meaning, it was impossible for me to think of them as having been entirely accidental. The feeling is constantly growing on me that I had been the first to hear the greeting of one planet to another."*[2]

It was later discovered that Tesla's "intelligently controlled signals" were merely radiation whistlings from the ionosphere. But the false assumption is irrelevant. The point is, how eager and convinced man was at the possibility of extra-planetary life. Tesla was not the first to consider communication with other planets, nor

[2] Tesla, Nikola. "Talking with the Planets." <u>Collier's Weekly</u>. 7 Feb. 1901: p 4-5.

the first to attempt such measures. But he *was* the first, however, to follow through on a practical and workable method for doing so. Along with other pioneers in the field (Hertz, Edison, Marconi) Tesla helped lay the groundwork for the future field of radio astronomy. But because Tesla was decades ahead of his time, that realization was still over half a century away.

Amazing Stories of Space Monsters & Supermen

Although the term "science fiction" did not exist at the time, fantasy authors like Jules Verne (1828-1905), H.G. Wells (1866-1946), and even Mary Shelley (1791-1851) were 19th century trailblazers for

IMAGE/public domain
One of the first "aliens" on the cover of a book or magazine (1916).

the genre. Their books made a huge impact on their generation and generations to follow, and included such famous works as: *Frankenstein* (1818), *Journey to the Center of the Earth* (1864), *Twenty Thousand Leagues Under the Sea* (1870), *The War of the Worlds* (1897), and *The First Men in the Moon* (1901). Edgar Rice Burroughs (1875-1950) also arrived in the early 1900s with his popular *John Carter of Mars* saga. Burroughs' *Thuvia, Maid of Mars*, in both pulp (1916) and novelization (1920), was one of the first widely read stories to portray an extraterrestrial life form on its cover. It was a green, spidery-like, humanoid creature with big eyes, fangs and six limbs (see image above). The book sold well. Soon after, with the birth of science fiction pulp (1926), readers were treated to literary "close encounters" on a regular basis.

The WAR of the WORLDS
By H. G. Wells
Author of "Under the Knife," "The Time Machine," etc.

IMAGE/public domain   *The War of the Worlds*, from *Amazing Stories*,1927

First published in 1897, H.G. Wells' *The War of the Worlds* is one of the most popular science fiction novels in the history of the world. The novel inspired a 1938 Halloween radio drama presented as a series of fake news bulletins. Some listeners in parts of the US and Canada were swept up in a wave of panic, after having mistook the broadcast as authentic.

The first pulp magazine devoted solely to the science fiction genre was *Amazing Stories*. Within a few months of its publication its circulation reached 100,000.[3] As science fiction came of age, it hit its golden age in the 1930s and 1940s. This caused a chain reaction in literature and entertainment, which set off two new "booms" – the sci-fi serial movie boom and the superhero boom. Also known as "cliffhangers", the science fiction movie serial included such titles as, *The Phantom Empire* (1935), *Undersea Kingdom* (1936), *Flash Gordon's Trip to Mars* (1938), *Buck Rogers* (1939), *The Purple Monster Strikes* (1945), *King of the Rocket Men* (1949), *Zombies of the Stratosphere* (1952) and *Radar Men From The Moon* (1952). This lead to the birth of the science fiction film genre. The sci-fi boom of the 1950s resulted in the golden age of the sci-fi film. The world was then hammered

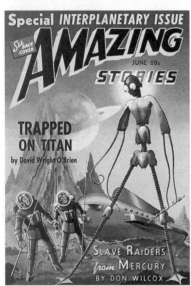

IMAGE/public domain   Cover from June 1940 *Amazing Stories* emerged in 1926 as the first science-fiction-only magazine.

with a nonstop barrage of "live action" imagery depicting beings from other worlds. Lasting a little over a decade, the era witnessed the production of nearly 300 science fiction films. Strangely enough, many of the posters for these pictures not only depicted aliens, robots and monsters lustfully carrying Earth women in their arms (more on this later), but also a variety of GIANT CREATURES hell-bent

[3] Nevins, Jess. *Where did science fiction come from? A primer on the pulps.* io9. Gawker Media, 10 Nov 2010. Web. 11 Mar 2013. <http://io9.com/5680191/where-did-science-fiction-come-from-a-primer-on-the-pulps>.

1953

1958

1955

1962

IMAGE/Graffix Multimedia Image Services

Golden-Age Science Fiction Movie Poster Gallery
Humanoids from space and monsters taking women

1959

1957

1958

1955

IMAGE/Graffix Multimedia Image Services

Golden-Age Science Fiction Movie Poster Gallery

Giant men, giant monsters and giant creatures ravaging the Earth

1940

1958

1940

1940

Golden-Age Comic Book Covers
Man-animal hybrids, demigods and giants

on man's destruction (giant monsters, dinosaurs, birds, animals, insects and humans – much more on this later).

The superhero boom, in many cases, merged science fiction, pagan mythology and Extraterrestrialism. These illustrated fantasy stories included the tales of alien demigods, or men with god-like powers (Superman, Captain Marvel, Thor, et.al.). Others would be either man-animal hybrids, scientifically created monsters or heroes with names which implied such (Spider-Man, Batman, Hulk, et. al.). Others still, would be humans who genetically evolved into advanced super-humans known as "mutants" (X-men, et.al.). The reverberation of this explosion is still being felt today. Some of the highest grossing films at the box-office continue to depict superheroes. And the obsession is showing no signs of slowing down.

For the last eight decades science fiction novels, comic books and movies have fueled the dreams of countless children who would aspire to be the teachers, entertainers, scientists and astronomers of their generation. What you get when you amass this voluminous output of fundamentally, anti-God, anti-Bible entertainment is this:

1.) Thousands of books and movies which replace the Bible in the hearts and minds of men and women worldwide.

2.) A subliminal, humanistic, atheistic COUNTERFEIT GOSPEL that preaches that man's past is nothing more than a coincidental series of accidents (evolution); and PROPHECIES (or dreams) that man's future will involve the arrival of super-beings from space, or man will evolve into super-humans, or will entail man himself creating a form of monster or super-being.

3.) The vehicles for spreading this gospel are evolution and science fiction. Evolution is the Devil's "creation story", science fiction is his "prophecy".

4.) The Devil tipping his hand to his involvement in ancient history by showing bits and pieces of truth – and this history will repeat itself.

The Coming of the Saucers & Hollywood Hype

Compounding the impact of the early science fiction movement was the arrival of the modern UFO phenomenon. This mystery, which continues to baffle to this very day, conveniently arrived in the middle of the early sci-fi/superhero explosion and one year after the government's institution of the secretive "Project Paperclip" (more on this later). All this was one year prior to the rebirth of the nation of Israel (1948).

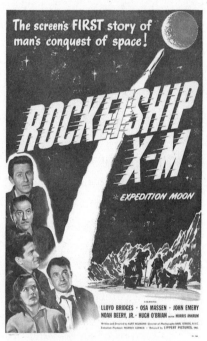

The screen's FIRST story of man's conquest of space!

ROCKETSHIP X-M

EXPEDITION MOON

LLOYD BRIDGES · OSA MASSEN · JOHN EMERY
NOAH BEERY, JR. · HUGH O'BRIAN and MORRIS ANKRUM

IMAGE/Graffix Multimedia Image Services
Rocketship XM (1950) was the first major
motion picture to show life on Mars.

On June 24, 1947 a civilian pilot named Kenneth Arnold was flying near Mount Rainier in Washington state when he unexpectedly encountered nine shiny objects flying in single file. Arnold later reported that the unidentified flying objects "flew like a saucer would if you skipped it across the water". He estimated their speeds at 1,600 miles per hour (nearly three times as fast as any known aircraft at that time). This famous incident would go down in history and mark the beginning of the modern age of "flying saucers". Only eight days later (July 2, 1947) the most famous/

infamous UFO incident in history would occur, as an alleged crashed saucer with accompanying "alien bodies" was supposedly recovered by the United States Military near Roswell, New Mexico.

By 1950, as UFO sightings erupted into a worldwide phenomenon, the exploitive nature of Hollywood promptly jumped on the bandwagon by showing the first two major motion pictures depicting flying saucers and alien life on another planet (*The Flying Saucer* and *Rocketship XM*).

Over the next six-plus decades Hollywood would crank out movie after movie showing aliens, saucers and "things" from other worlds, firmly ingraining in the minds of Americans, and the world, that intelligent life must indeed exist "out there somewhere". *The Internet Movie Database* (imdb.com) shows that between 1900 and 2013, over 64,000 individual TV and movie programs worldwide have addresses the subject of science fiction in one way or another. And 9,000 of those titles have dealt with the subject of "aliens" directly.[4] That averages to about 1.5 programs a day, 566 programs a year, for the past 113 years ("program" is a good name for it). To say that such a massive outpouring had (or has) no effect on the minds of the public or the minds of aspiring scientists would be ridiculous. Steven J. Dick, former NASA Chief Historian, writes; *"Many of the pioneers in exobiology and SETI grew up on science fiction and were led to their careers by its imaginative lure."* [5]

By the late 1930s and 1940s, with much thanks to science fiction, those interested in locating intelligent life beyond Earth were no longer as rare and obscure as they once were. The ongoing attempts to confirm Cosmic Pluralism would soon catapult itself into a branch

[4] "Most Popular Alien Sci-Fi Titles." IMDb. IMDb.com, Inc. . Web. 12 Mar 2013. <http://www.imdb.com/search/title?at=0&genres=sci_fi&keywords=alien&sort=movie meter,asc&start=1>.

[5] Dick, Steven J. *The Biological Universe: The Twentieth Century Extraterrestrial Life Debate and the Limits of Science*. Cambridge, UK: Cambridge University Press, 1996. p 266.

of national government: NASA, the National Aeronautics and Space Administration, with other nations forming their own space programs. Times had changed.

How to Build a Moon Rocket with a Paperclip

Many may be unaware of the dark side of the origins of the US government's NASA organization. But a quick historical review will help you get a better idea of its position when viewed from a spiritual perspective. Don't assume that man's drive to *"reach unto heaven"* (Gen. 11:4) is solely based on an innocent desire for space exploration. And don't assume that other reasons for pursuing such goals ended at the Tower of Babel. The scriptures show that *"the children of disobedience"*, whether they realize it or not, walk in accord with a spiritual principality who's *"the prince of the power of the air."* (Eph. 2:2)

The Bible clearly states that *"the Greeks seek after wisdom"* (1 Cor. 1:22). That is, the sons of Japheth (the one prophesied to be "enlarged", dwell in the tents of Shem, and have Ham as his servant - Gen. 9:27) eventually spread out and became the Indo-European peoples (among which are Romans, Greeks, Europeans and Germans). At the end of World War II, American Japhethites became interested in exploiting the knowledge and technology of their fellow German Japhethites. In 1945 the US intelligence agency (OSS) made the following observation:

> *"German technicians, cultural experts and undercover agents have well-laid plans to infiltrate into foreign countries with the object of developing economic, cultural and political ties. German technicians and scientific research experts will be made available at low cost to industrial firms and technical schools in foreign countries."* [6]

[6] Keith, Jim. *Mind Control & UFOs: Casebook On Alternative 3*. Lilburn, GA: IllumiNet Press. 1999. p 44

After inspecting the spoils of war, the US officials salivated at the proposition of learning from the wisdom of displaced Nazi scientists. Whether purely an attempt to prevent technology from falling into the wrong hands, or merely moved by the lust for wisdom (or both), plans were soon drawn up to inculcate these men into the US. In 1946, "Project Paperclip" was conceived to covertly fulfill this plan. The United States Holocaust Memorial Museum reports:

> *"The scene in Nordhausen provoked outrage among the occupiers; the US Army made a propaganda film that made the name of the city briefly infamous. But soon afterward came a different set of US Army personnel who were ONLY INTERESTED IN THE TECHNOLOGY. Before the Soviets could move forward into their prescribed occupation zone, US forces removed large numbers of missile parts and personnel. The operation to exploit German science and technology that came to be known as OPERATION PAPERCLIP had one of its most important origins here."* [7]

While outward restrictions against Nazi sympathizers was emphasized by the new technology-scavenging program, internal procedures were lax. The program operated under the pretense of strict security and screening, but the opposite was actually true. During the 27-year life of Paperclip (1946-1973), it is reported that nearly 70,000 Nazis were pardoned of their war crimes and granted citizenship in the US.[8] By the time the American public learned of

[7]   United States Holocaust Memorial Museum. "The Holocaust." Holocaust Encyclopedia. 3 June 2013. <http://www.ushmm.org/wlc/en/?ModuleId=10005143>.

[8] Keith, Jim. *Mind Control & UFOs: Casebook On Alternative 3.* Lilburn, GA: IllumiNet Press. 1999. p 50

this scheme the damage had been done. One of the major fruits of the project was the birth of NASA (NOTE: Paperclip is also responsible for the creation of the CIA). Of the 70,000 recruits, it is said that 600 "conceived and controlled" the American rocketry program.[9]

The man elected to head the new venture was former *"technical director of Nazi Germany's missile-development program"*, SS Major Wernher von Braun.[10] Von Braun would also become the mastermind behind the massive Saturn V rocket which propelled the first Americans into space and later to the Moon. Completed in 1967, the Saturn V was a monument to the achievements of man. It was a giant 363-foot tower of explosives, capable of 7.5 million pounds of thrust (the chemical equivalency of a small atomic weapon). During the war, while Von Braun was conducting his Nazi V-2 trials, it is said that *"one hundred slave laborers died per day"*.[11] Jean Michael, a survivor of the Dora-Mittelbau Nazi rocket factory said:

> *"I could not watch the Apollo mission without remembering that triumphant walk was made possible by our initiation to inconceivable horror."*[12]

In other words, much of the bedrock of the US space program owes a huge nod-of-the-head, not to American freedom, perseverance and exceptionalism, but to the deaths of countless Jews who met their fate in Nazi rocket factories at the behest of German scientists. It was

---

[9] Keith, Jim. *Mind Control & UFOs: Casebook On Alternative 3.* Lilburn, GA: IllumiNet Press. 1999. p 47

[10] Chaikin, Andrew. Air and Space: The National Air and Space Museum Story of Flight. New York: The Smithsonian Institute, and Little Brown and Company Inc. 1997. p 175

[11] Keith, Jim. Mind Control & UFOs: Casebook On Alternative 3. Lilburn, GA: IllumiNet Press. 1999. p 49

[12] Ibid. p 51

IMAGE/public domaim　　　　　　　　　　　American airmen at Dora-Mittlebau

The secret German rocket facility at Dora-Mittlebau (also known as Dora-Nordhausen or Nordhausen) was hidden underground. The *Holocaust Encyclopedia* of the United States Holocaust Memorial Museum reports that 12,000 prisoners were housed within its bowels during peak production in 1944. More than 200 prisoners were publicly hanged for attempting to sabotage German rocket efforts, and a much greater number (both Jews and non-Jews) were murdered while constructing the facility. Visit www.ushmm.org.

an industry conceived in blood – the blood of God's chosen people. After all, what's the death of a few Jews if it can get you to the Moon? The official NASA History Program website admits:

> *"Wernher von Braun (1912-1977) was one of the most important rocket developers and champions of space exploration during the period between the 1930s and the 1970s. As a youth he became enamored with the possibilities of space exploration by READING the SCIENCE FICTION of Jules Verne and H.G. Wells ... Von Braun is well known as the leader of what has been called the 'rocket team,' which developed the V-2 ballistic missile for the Nazis during World War II. The V-2s were manufactured at a FORCED LABOR FACTORY called Mittelwerk. Scholars are STILL REASSESSING HIS ROLE IN THESE CONTROVERSIAL ACTIVITIES. Before the Allied capture of the V-2 rocket complex,*

von Braun engineered the surrender of 500 of his top rocket scientists, along with plans and test vehicles, to the Americans. For fifteen years after World War II, von Braun would work with the United States army in the development of ballistic missiles. As part of a military operation called PROJECT PAPERCLIP, he and his 'rocket team' were scooped up from defeated Germany and sent to America where they were installed at Fort Bliss, Texas. In 1960, his rocket development center transferred from the army to the newly established NASA and received a mandate to build the giant Saturn rockets. Accordingly, von Braun BECAME DIRECTOR OF NASA's Marshall Space Flight Center and THE CHIEF ARCHITECT of the Saturn V launch vehicle, the superbooster that would propel Americans to the Moon. Von Braun also became one of the most prominent spokesmen of space exploration in the United States during the 1950s. In 1970, NASA leadership asked von Braun to move to Washington, DC, to HEAD UP THE STRATEGIC PLANNING effort for the agency." [13]

So what are Christians to make of all this conspiratorial kook-talk? First, they need to realize that, according to the Bible, "conspiracies" are a NORMAL PART of government operation when under the leadership of fallen man (more on this later). Secondly, stepping back and looking at this dark spiritual aspect of the US space program will help put it in perspective when considering its legitimacy in the eyes of God. Does God approve of NASA or any of the things it does? What about its programs to search for intelligent

---

[13] Dick, Steven J. "Wernher von Braun (1912-1977)." NASA History. National Aeronautics & Space Administration, 25 May 2006. Web. 14 Mar 2013. <http://history. nasa.gov/sputnik/braun.html>.

life in space? Consider the root of the tree – roots nourished by the corpses of those beloved of the Father:

> "As concerning the gospel, they [Israel] are ENEMIES for your sakes: but as touching the election, they are BELOVED for the fathers' sakes." Romans 11:28

Questionable Connections to the Dark Side

However, the hiring of hundreds of men historically proven to have belonged to a group openly committed to the total destruction and genocide of the Apple of God's eye (Deut. 32:10), is not the only questionable link illustrating the spiritual underpinnings of NASA. There's more. The evidence suggests that the occult revival of the 18th and 19th centuries, after finding its way into the 20th century, may have, in part, infiltrated the halls of NASA. Not only does much mystery and lore swirl around the occult ties of the Third Reich with its secret Vril and Thule Societies (groups with which NASA's "Paperclip" scientists were undoubtedly aware), but other encounters with occultism have reared their ugly heads as well.

Like many of the events we've covered, it is a matter of history that one of the founding members of NASA's Jet Propulsion Laboratory (JPL) was a high ranking American occultist and sex pervert. Marvel Whiteside Parsons (1914-1952), better known as "Jack Parsons", was the brains behind NASA's solid fuel technology. He was also a strong adherent and pupil of Aleister Crowley's occult "Thelema" philosophy. In 1952 Parsons died at the young age of 37 after having blown himself up in his garage in Pasadena, California. Some researchers allege the explosion was the result of his regular practices in black magic sex rituals, while others contend he simply

[14] Marrs, Texe. "Leviathan In Space." Power of Prophecy. 08 August (2003). p 1

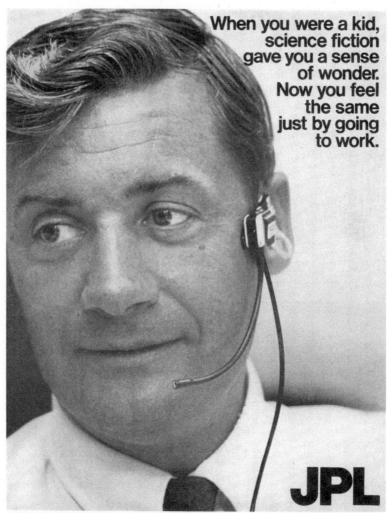

When you were a kid, science fiction gave you a sense of wonder. Now you feel the same just by going to work.

JPL

In fact, you've got what the great science-fiction heroes never had so good: the excitement of discovery. If you want to be part of the action, we can help.

Right now openings exist in: Spacecraft Structural Design · Temperature Control Materials & Processing · Application of Microelectronics & Transistors · Guidance & Control Systems · Electro Optics · Propulsion Systems Analysis · Space Vehicles Design · Trajectory Design & System Analysis · Systems Design & Integration · Deep Space Support Systems · Electromechanical Spacecraft Instrumentation · Scientific Programming · TV Image Processing and Electronic Packaging.
Send your resume to:
JET PROPULSION LABORATORY
California Institute of Technology
4802 Oak Grove Drive,
Pasadena, California 91103
Attn: Professional Staffing Dept. 11

"An equal opportunity employer." Jet Propulsion Laboratory is operated by the California Institute of Technology for the National Aeronautics and Space Administration.

IMAGE/public domain   A 1960s job ad for NASA's JPL

Early ads for NASA's Jet Propulsion Laboratory illustrate how science fiction is often the primary motivating factor for many of those interested in space exploration and the concept of life beyond Earth. This holds true for many modern cutting-edge sciences.

dropped a container of Mercury(II) fulminate.[14 & 15]   Either way, Parsons' involvement in the black arts is well documented.

Another bizarre and maybe lesser known fact is the establishment of the 1969 "Tranquility Lodge 2000". The official website states:

> *"On July 20, 1969, two American Astronauts landed on the moon of the planet Earth, in an area known as Mare Tranquilitatis , or 'Sea of Tranquility'. One of those brave men was Brother Edwin Eugene (Buzz) Aldrin, Jr., a member of Clear Lake Lodge No. 1417, AF&AM, Seabrook, Texas. Brother Aldrin carried with him SPECIAL DEPUTATION of then Grand Master J. Guy Smith, constituting and appointing Brother Aldrin as Special Deputy of the Grand Master, granting unto him full power in the premises to represent the Grand Master as such and authorize him to claim Masonic Territorial Jurisdiction for The Most Worshipful Grand Lodge of Texas, Ancient Free and Accepted Masons, on The Moon, and directed that he make due return of his acts. Brother Aldrin certified that the SPECIAL DEPUTATION was carried by him to the Moon on July 20, 1969. Tranquility Lodge 2000 was Chartered by The Grand Lodge of Texas for the purpose of promoting, encouraging, conducting and fostering the principles of Freemasonry..."* [16]

The sheer audacity of an occult organization to grant "full power" and to "claim Masonic Territorial Jurisdiction" (on the Moon no less) in the name of a man with the title "Grand Master" (Matt. 23:8-10)

[15] Duncan, Michael. "Cameron." Cameron-Parsons Foundation. Cameron-Parsons Foundation, Inc. Web. 15 Mar 2013. <http://cameron-parsons.org/>.

[16] Hammers, Danny. "The Story of Tranquility Lodge No. 2000." Tranquility Lodge 2000. TL2K & The Grand Lodge of Texas. Web. 18 Apr 2013. <http://tl2k.org/history.htm>.

is absolutely outrageous. Where was the mass of people demanding such a measure? Nowhere. The act was carried out in subterfuge by the Grand Lodge of Texas with the full cooperation of "brother" Buzz Aldrin (33°). I wonder why a "claim" wasn't staked in the name of the Lord Jesus Christ or the *King James Bible*? Easy, the world would never accept such a claim. But the world loves its own (John 15:19), so it's okay for Freemasonry to do it. The Grand Lodge of British Columbia and Yukon states:

> *"Freemasons have always been in the forefront of the scientific community; from the founding of the British Royal Society to today's NASA programme in the United States."* [17]

A partial list of NASA Freemasons includes: Kenneth Kleinknecht (Mercury Project Manager), Clark McClelland, James Webb (NASA Administrator, 1961-1968), Buzz Aldrin, Gordon Cooper, John Glenn, Gus Grissom, Edgar D. Mitchell, Wally Schirra and others. [18]

Anyone who's done even the smallest amount of research into the authorities endorsed by every Grand Lodge, knows that Freemasonry is the religious home of deists, polytheists and pagans – not Bible-believing Christians. Those who are led by the Holy Spirit will eventually leave the organization (2Cor. 6:14). Those who remain, will join in the grand scheme of Masonry, as they unite with the world under one god and one religion. The philosophy of Freemasonry is the religion of the Antichrist, and that is the long and short of it. However, the majority of people see it as "no big deal" because *"the god of this world hath blinded the minds of*

[17] "Freemasons in Space." Grand Lodge of British Columbia & Yukon. Grand Lodge of British Columbia and Yukon A.F. & A. M.. Web. 18 Apr 2013. <http://freemasonry. bcy.ca/biography/spacemason/#1>.

[18] The New Age Magazine. Supreme Council 33° A.&A. Scottish Rite of Freemasonry of the Southern Jurisdiction, Washington, D.C.: November 1969. pp. 14-30.

NATIONAL AERONAUTICS AND SPACE ADMINISTRATION
MANNED SPACECRAFT CENTER
HOUSTON, TEXAS 77058

IN REPLY REFER TO: September 19, 1969

Illustrious Luther A. Smith, 33°
Sovereign Grand Commander
Supreme Council, 33°
Southern Jurisdiction, U.S.A.
1733 16th Street, N.W.
Washington, D.C. 20009

Dear Grand Commander:

   It was a great moment in my life to be so cordially welcomed
to the House of the Temple on September 16, 1969, by you and Grand
Secretary General Kleinknecht, 33°, and also the members of your
staffs. My greatest pleasure, however, was to be able to present
to you on this occasion the Scottish Rite Flag which I carried on
the Apollo 11 Flight to the Moon--emblazoned in color with the
Scottish Rite Double-headed Eagle, the Blue Lodge Emblem and the
Sovereign Grand Commander's Insignia.

   I take this opportunity to again thank you for the autographed
copy of your recent book, entitled "Action by the Scottish Rite,
Southern Jurisdiction, U.S.A.," which is filled with a wealth of
information about your Americanism Program sponsored by the Supreme
Council, participating activities and related activities of the
Rite.

                        Cordially and fraternally,

                        Edwin E. Aldrin, Jr.
                        NASA Astronaut

IMAGE/Grand Lodge of British Columbia and Yukon A.F. & A. M

The official 1969 letter from US astronaut, (Buzz) Edwin E. Aldrin, Jr., to the
Sovereign Grand Commander, Supreme Council, 33°, Southern Jurisdiction, U.S.A.,
acknowledging the return of the Masonic flag from the Moon. Note in the letter that
Aldrin freely admits *"...the Scottish Rite Flag which I carried on the Apollo 11 Flight to
the Moon...".* By doing so, occultism had exercised its supremacy and authority over
that which the scriptures typify as the Bride of Christ.

To view this letter online visit:
http://freemasonry.bcy.ca/biography/spacemason/aldrin_letter.jpg

IMAGES/miscellaneous sources   Freemasonry and the Moon

TOP CENTER: The official Masonic flag which traveled to and from the Moon. **BOTTOM LEFT:** The official lodge apron of Tranquility Lodge 2000 which honors the symbolic establishment of a Masonic Lodge on the Moon. **BOTTOM RIGHT:** A 10th anniversary commemorative coin (1979) remembering *"our flags on the Moon"* – the American flag and the Masonic flag.

Flag: http://freemasonry.bcy.ca/biography/spacemason/flag.jpg
Apron: http://tl2k.org/aprons.htm
Coin: conspiracyarchive.com

them which believe not". (2Cor. 4:4) This also explains why the vast majority of "Christian" Freemasons are such spiritual lunkheads with zero spiritual discernment (You'll know what I'm talking about if you've ever had to deal with a Mason on the issue of salvation or the conflicts between scripture and the Lodge).

So how has NASA dealt with its historical connections with anti-Christian philosophies, Masonry, Nazism, Satanism and occultism? It ignores them, pretending that they are without significance in its pursuit in reaching the stars. What NASA doesn't realize, however, is that when man steps off planet Earth and enters the dark, deadly realm of outer space, he *exits his sphere of dominion*, and *enters the domain of another* (much more on this later).

Equations for Life

In 1931 the radio telescope was invented. Not only could scientists put their "eyes in the skies", but now they had the technical know-how of putting their ears there as well. As a result, radio astronomy was born. In 1960, Dr. Frank Drake conducted the first organized search for intelligent radio signals in space. Known as "Project OZMA", this search was based on the assumption that there were possibly many other extrasolar civilizations. *"For all we knew, practically every star in the sky had a civilization that's transmitting* [alien signals]*."* Drake said.[19] In 1961, Dr. Drake devised an equation for *"estimating the number of technological civilizations that may exist in our galaxy"*. Known as "The Drake Equation", this series of mathematical factors has become generally accepted by many scientists as a valuable tool in the search for life in the Universe. Some scientists believe that the Drake Equation could someday be as important as Einstein's E=mc2 theory.

---

[19] Sarah Scoles and Sue Ann Heatherly, "The Drake Equation: 50 Years of Giving Direction to the Scientific Search for Life Beyond Earth." astrosociety.org, The Universe in the Classroom, No. 77, Winter 2011. Astronomical Society of the Pacific. p1 pdf.

THE DRAKE EQUATION

$$N = R_* \times f_p \times n_e \times f_l \times f_i \times f_c \times L$$

N = The number of civilizations in The Milky Way Galaxy whose electromagnetic emissions are detectable.

R* =The rate of formation of stars suitable for the development of intelligent life.

fp = The fraction of those stars with planetary systems.

ne = The number of planets, per solar system, with an environment suitable for life.

fl = The fraction of suitable planets on which life actually appears.

fi = The fraction of life bearing planets on which intelligent life emerges.

fc = The fraction of civilizations that develop a technology that releases detectable signs of their existence into space.

L = The length of time such civilizations release detectable signals into space.

Communicate

Dr. Frank Drake was born in 1930 and admits to belief in alien life since the age of eight.[20] Today he is the Director of the SETI Institute's Carl Sagan Center for the Study of Life in the Universe, and Emeritus Professor of Astronomy and Astrophysics at the University of California at Santa Cruz. Regardless of all the modern Hollywood

[20] Venton, Danielle. *Frank Drake: Undetected Worlds.* The University of California Santa Cruz. Regents of the University of California, 17 May 2011. Web. 12 Mar 2013. <http://scicom.ucsc.edu/publications/essays-profiles-pages/profile-venton.html>.

hype, the existence of the Drake Equation tells us that scientists (like Tesla six decades earlier) are very serious about searching for life in space. And the ambitions of Drake are not unique, for modern science has an extensive history of programs aimed at such ideas.

Dawning of the Space Age

One year after its inception, NASA funded its first project to locate life in space (1959). The following year, it established its official "Exobiology Program":

> *"NASA's Exobiology and Evolutionary Biology Program, an element of the Astrobiology Program, supports research into the origin and early evolution of life, the potential of life to adapt to different environments, and the implications for life elsewhere. Exobiology and evolutionary biology research is conducted in the context of NASA's ongoing exploration of our stellar neighborhood and efforts to detect and identify biosignatures – that is, clear signs of life – by in-situ and remote sensing methods. Areas of research emphasis in the Exobiology and Evolutionary Biology Program are: planetary conditions for life, prebiotic evolution, early evolution of life and the biosphere, and evolution of advanced life."* [21]

In short, for the first time in history (and running nearly parallel with the Soviet's military-based space programs), a government had established a proactive "ongoing effort" to locate intelligent life in space. Sitting back and casually looking at the stars through

[21] Fletcher, Julie, ed. "About Astrobiology." *Astrobiolog: Life in the Universe.* National Aeronautics & Space Administration, 15 Aug 2012. Web. 16 Mar 2013. <https://astrobiology.nasa.gov/about-astrobiology/>. Author's note: In the context, the latin phrase "in situ" means to study an organism in its natural environment.

IMAGE/public domain   *Roswell Daily Record*, Tuesday, July 8, 1947

The claims of many astronauts and NASA officials seem to substantiate the idea that "flying saucers" are not of earthly origin.

a telescope was no longer acceptable. <u>Mankind decided, instead of letting the heavens come to us, that it was time for us to actively</u> *"reach unto heaven"* (Gen. 11:4) – <u>the Space Age had begun.</u>

Although man had yet to set foot on the surface of another planet, the new technological era brought with it the testimonies of many astronauts who assured us of the reality in extraterrestrial life. Likewise, the belief in evolution, when coupled with multiple sightings of UFOs, drove many to accept the ET hypothesis:

> *"I believe that these extra-terrestrial vehicles and their crews are visiting this planet from other planets..."*
> - Major Gordon Cooper (astronaut)

> *"All Apollo and Gemini flights were followed, both at a distance and sometimes also quite closely, by space vehicles of extraterrestrial origin – flying saucers, or*

UFOs, if you want to call them by that name. Every time it occurred, the astronauts informed Mission Control, who then ordered absolute silence." - Maurice Chatelain (former chief of NASA Communications Systems)

"We all know that UFOs are real. All we need to ask is where do they come from, and what do they want?" - Captain Edgar Mitchell (astronaut)

"I believe, and I scientifically am certain, that there are endless other living forms out there, including intelligent sentient beings." - Dr. Story Musgrave (astronaut)

"I've been convinced for a long time that the flying saucers are interplanetary. We are being watched by beings from outer space." - Albert M. Chop, (Deputy Public Relations Director, NASA, and former US Air Force Spokesman – True Magazine, January 1965)

"In my official status, I cannot comment on ET contact. However, personally, I can assure you, we are not alone!" - Dr. Charles J. Camarda (astronaut)

Chapter 4 Summary

The first half of the 20th century experienced some of the most radical changes regarding the concept of extraterrestrial life. A shift took place which moved the idea from a side-issue, background type of a setting, to the forefront of national superpower initiatives. One of the primary catalysts for igniting this shift was the birth of science fiction. The other mover and shaker motivating the change will be addressed in the next chapter as we follow the concept up to the present day.

5

Into the Final Frontier
1960 - Present

"I really feel that Darwinian evolution is a defining feature of all life. ...[and it] will define the range of planets that can support life – at least Earth-like life."
– Dr. John Baross, Astrobiologist

NASA was conceived through the "National Aeronautics and Space Act of 1958", and with the arrival of the Space Age, the world's superpowers (USA and USSR) were now involved in a race to achieve space supremacy. This was a milestone in the history of the world, and it was inevitable that mankind would soon be scouring the stars for signs of life in an effort to supposedly learn more about the "origins" of life on Earth. Man now lived in a post-space world. Since that time, succeeding generations would see the efforts surrounding space exploration as a normal part of everyday life. A lot had happened in the last 50 to 100 years, and the remainder of the 20th century would see a concentrated effort in the search for extraterrestrial life.

To Boldly Go Where No Man has Gone Before

As mentioned previously, Dr. Frank Drake is seen by many as the father of modern radio astronomy and the search for communications from alien civilizations. His 1960 "Project Ozma" was the first systemic attempt to detect artificial radio signals from nearby stars. The program was based on the worn-out assumption that solar systems with Earth-like planets were candidates for life. The underlying theory was not new, however, only the technology in use. Nicholas of Cusa, the Roman Catholic Cardinal, had written over 500 years earlier:

> *"We may make PARALLEL SURMISE OF OTHER stellar*
> *areas that NONE OF THEM LACK INHABITANTS, as*
> *being each, LIKE THE WORLD WE LIVE IN, a particular*
> *area of one universe which contains AS MANY SUCH*
> *AREAS as there are uncountable stars."* [1]

But the Cardinal's statement wasn't all that original either. It was a mixture of earlier theories by Thales, Anaximander, Epicurus and others. This makes one wonder that if any of these early men would've had the technology, perhaps they would've pioneered SETI instead of Drake. The point is, technology doesn't necessarily make one smarter. Drake's generation may have had more sophisticated stuff, but their theories on extra-planetary life were really no more advanced than those of a half-millennia earlier. Despite the inference of the high-sounding "Space Age", the era was plagued by those *"Ever learning, and never able to come to the knowledge of the truth."* (2Tim. 3:7). This intellectual epidemic, especially when viewed in the context of LIFE ORIGINS, continues on a mass scale to this very day (1Cor. 3:19).

---

[1] Crowe, Michael J. The Extraterrestrial Life Debate. Notre Dame, IN: University of Notre Dame, 2008. p 31-32

"But God hath chosen the foolish things of the world to confound the wise; and God hath chosen the weak things of the world to confound the things which are mighty;"
1 Corinthians 1:27

"[18] Let no man deceive himself. If any man among you seemeth to be wise in this world, let him become a fool, that he may be wise. [19] For the wisdom of this world is foolishness with God. For it is written, He taketh the wise in their own craftiness. [20] And again, The Lord knoweth the thoughts of the wise, that they are vain."
1 Corinthians 3:18-20

After the invention of space rocketry (V-2, 1942), orbital satellites (Sputnik, 1957), and radio astronomy (Project Ozma, 1960), new doorways were opened for proactive efforts in the search for alien life. Mankind was now boldly going "where no man had gone before" – or so he thought.

Since that time, research has continued on a worldwide scale. Between 1960 and 2011, space probes have been placed near, in orbit around, or on the Moon, Mercury, Venus, Mars, Jupiter, Saturn, Uranus, Neptune, Titan, four asteroids (Eros, Vesta, Itokawa and Steins), and three comets (Halley, Tempel 1 and P/ Wild 2). Other extreme "contact" measures have included beaming messages into space, and launching LP records with photos, music and Earth "greetings" to aliens. Despite decades of worldwide research and hundreds of billions of dollars spent, it has only served to demonstrate that the hopeful dreams and wishes of "Cosmic Pluralism" are FALSE. No one's there, at least not on the planets.

In spite of this failure, one strong fact remains: *Mankind is SERIOUS about finding life in space.* What motivates this mad drive to constantly risk human life and throw away untold billions of dollars? Why is mankind so adamant that sooner or later "something" will be found? On the 150th anniversary of the publication of Charles Darwin's *On the Origin of Species*, oceanographer and astrobiologist, Dr. John Baross stated:

> *"I really feel that Darwinian evolution is a defining feature of all life. ... [and it] will define the range of planets that can support life – at least Earth-like life. ... there are many different ways for non-Earth-like life to [evolve and] not use [sun] light or chemical energy but use some other form like radiation energy, wave energy, or ultraviolet energy. ... the need for water may not be universal. [Life may exist] in an organic solvent rather than liquid water on Titan, or... at temperatures of minus 100 degrees Celsius — there are a lot of ways to think of this because those conditions exist on other planetary bodies."* [2]

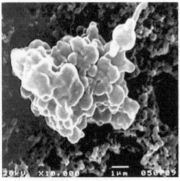
IMAGE/public domain
Microorganism

Although thousands of scientists undoubtedly view this statement as gospel, it has major problems. Essentially, the idea that Darwinian evolution will define the range of planets that can support *"Earth-like life"*, is broadly aimed at the hopeful discovery of intelligent Earth-like ANIMAL LIFE or HUMAN LIFE. Yet, what most people miss

[2] Chivers, Tom C. *Darwinian evolutionary theory will help find alien life, says Nasa scientist.*The Telegraph. Telegraph Media Group Limited, 04 Nov 2009. Web. 18 Mar 2013. <http://www.telegraph.co.uk/science/space/6500471/Darwinian-evolutionary-theory-will-help-find-alien-life-says-Nasa-scientist.html>.

is that the next part of the statement is where the fantastical leap in logic takes place. The doctor jumps from discussing intelligent *"Earth-like life"*, to discussing life which does not require sunlight or water to survive. How is this a jump? The explanation for this other type of life is not aimed at research which supports intelligent animal or human type life, but instead, is aimed at INVISIBLE MICROORGANISMS LIKE BACTERIA, VIRUSES AND GERMS.

IMAGE/public domain   The modern astrobiologist

"By Jove, it's a Martian!"

Which, according to scripture, is no life at all (more on this later). When Baross states that life may exist *"in an organic solvent...or... at temperatures of minus 100 degrees Celsius"*, he's thinking of MICROORGANISMS – not people or animals. He then assumes that these brainless microbes have the capacity to "evolve" into thinking creatures. The propaganda is that finding microscopic BACTERIA in extreme environments means that he's somehow on the trail of finding INTELLIGENT LIFE in space. He's found no such thing. He's found germs – he's found nothing. I shouldn't have to explain that the intelligence and sophistication-gap between a microbe and a man is so great, that to unjustly pair the two in the same sentence, when casually discussing *"planets that can support life"* is to mislead the reader into believing something that isn't so.

> *"O Timothy, keep that which is committed to thy trust* [the scriptures], *avoiding profane and vain babblings, and oppositions of science falsely so called". 1Tim. 6:20*

Evolution: The Great Biological Boondoggle

Today, the search for intelligent life in space is nonexistent on a true biological level. That may sound shocking at first, but Radio Astronomy is really the only field in which intelligent life is being sought out. The primary research for finding life in space is actually not about finding life in space. It's about searching for space microorganisms, germs and bacteria. The reasoning behind this is based on the ancient theory of atomism, the idea that all ordered creation is the fruit of purposeless "particles of matter" (see chapter 2). Atomism is a precursor to evolution, and it explains why modern science continues to search for supposed "life" in such unconventional places as thermal vents, lava and sub-zero ecosystems. An essay published in 1973 by *The American Biology Teacher* stated:

> *"...species are produced NOT BECAUSE THEY ARE NEEDED for some purpose but simply because there is an ENVIRONMENTAL OPPORTUNITY and GENETIC WHEREWITHAL to make them possible."* [3]

---

[3] Dobzhansky, Theodosius. *Nothing in Biology Makes Sense except in the Light of Evolution*. American Biology Teacher. Vol. 35. No. 3 (1973): p 125-129.

Train Up a Child in the Way of UFOs

IMAGE/screen capture   British school children participating in UFO crash drills

Scriptures teach us to *"Train up a child in the way he should go: and when he is old, he will not depart from it."* (Prov. 22:6) While the Bible outlines the proper way to raise children, government schools in the UK have a different idea. Since 2008, a growing trend in primary education is to hold mock UFO crash-site drills, complete with fake spacecraft, debris and alien bodies. Through the joint efforts of local school officials, law enforcement and forensic scientists, the drills are perpetrated on *unsuspecting 6 to 10-year-olds* in order to *"stimulate creative writing"* and teach proper investigative skills. Why not just take the children to the zoo to teach creative writing, why all this outrageous propaganda? Clearly, children are being brainwashed into believing in life on other planets.

Hardy, Clare. "Sight of crash-landed UFO greets Buckhurst Hill schoolchildren." Guardian. Newsquest, 27 Wed. 2013. Web. 20 Apr 2013. <http://www. guardianseries.co.uk/news/10254610.Sight_of_crash_landed_UFO_greets_ schoolchildren/>.

Endorsed by the NABT (National Association of Biology Teachers) and written by Russian Orthodox Christian, Theodosius Dobzhansky, the article went on to state:

> *"It is a matter of opinion, or of definition, whether viruses are considered living organisms or peculiar chemical substances. The fact that such differences of opinion can exist is in itself highly significant. It means that THE BORDERLINE BETWEEN LIVING AND INANIMATE MATTER IS OBLITERATED."* [4]

In other words, there's *no real difference between life and death*! If evolution cannot distinguish between something DEAD and something ALIVE, it obviously cannot know the meaning of "life" . The truth is, there are only four possibilities regarding the reality of what you see outside your window:

I.   The Universe is *ETERNAL*. It has always existed and always will exist.

II.   The Universe is *NOT ETERNAL*, but *began from nothing accidentally*, via natural spontaneous processes *INSIDE* the Universe.

III. The Universe *does not exist* – we just *think* it exists.

IV.   The Universe is *NOT ETERNAL*, but *was created from nothing via supernaturally guided, self-existing Intelligence, OUTSIDE* the Universe. [5]

If you've never been taught these four basic theories, then someone has shortchanged you regarding the truth. These four origin theories

---

[4] Dobzhansky, Theodosius. *Nothing in Biology Makes Sense except in the Light of Evolution.* <u>American Biology Teacher</u>. Vol. 35. No. 3 (1973): p 125-129.

[5] Ruckman, Peter S. *The Christian's Handbook of Science & Philosophy.* Pensacola, FL: Bible Baptist Bookstore, 1985. p163

Evolutionary Theory Applied to the Broomstick

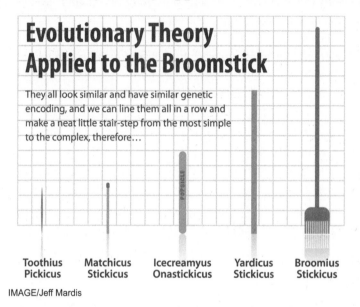

Evolutionary Theory Applied to the Broomstick

They all look similar and have similar genetic encoding, and we can line them all in a row and make a neat little stair-step from the most simple to the complex, therefore...

| Toothius Pickicus | Matchicus Stickicus | Icecreamyus Onastickicus | Yardicus Stickicus | Broomius Stickicus |

IMAGE/Jeff Mardis

Suppose an evolutionist had never seen a toothpick, matchstick, popsicle stick, yardstick or broomstick, and yet dug these five items out of the ground. If treated as life forms, what do you suppose would be his scientific conclusion? Would he not conclude that all five specimen are related, even though there are no transitional forms? After all, the items are of similar appearance and makeup. And when viewed with an evolutionary, stair-step chart, is not the relationship obvious? Now all we need find are the "missing links". When compared with the functional broom, it would take a substantially more advanced level of sophistication to create a man. And yet science tells us that intelligence is behind the design and creation of one (the broom) but not the other (man)? Or that evolution is behind the formation of one but not the other? Unbelievable.

are not taught in any public school or university. The reason is, by the time the second theory gained popular acceptance, science had already exposed two of the theories as false:

> *"The demonstrable laws of thermodynamics not only prove that theories I and II are nonscientific jokes, but the demonstrable laws of biogenesis add their weight. These laws show that life comes from life. Every living organism came from a living organism and no Russian, German, English or American scientist has ever DEMONSTRATED EMPIRICALLY ... that a living thing came from a dead thing. ... Now having eliminated their own 'faith' by empirical data, the scientists are faced with theory No. III and theory No. IV. God has given them the 'options' of believing Genesis 1:1 or losing their minds."* [6]

Notwithstanding, the theorizing goes on. And with it comes the studies of astrobiology, exobiology, xenobiology and bioastronomy, a motley crew of "space sciences" dedicated to promoting evolution as the genesis of all life. However, the supposed accidental spontaneity of life is not the only madness contained within the theory. On their website *Understanding Evolution*, the University of California, Berkeley states:

> *"Biological evolution, simply put, is descent with modification. Through the process of descent with modification, the common ancestor of life on Earth gave rise to the fantastic diversity that we see documented in the fossil record and around us today. Evolution means that WE'RE ALL DISTANT COUSINS: HUMANS and OAK TREES, HUMMINGBIRDS and WHALES."* [7]

---

[6] Ruckman, Peter S. *The Christian's Handbook of Science & Philosophy*. Pensacola, FL: Bible Baptist Bookstore, 1985. p165-167 [Emphasis in the original]

The official website of America's largest public media enterprise, the Public Broadcasting System (PBS), reiterates:

> *"One of Darwin's most revolutionary ideas was that all living things on Earth are related, connected to each other like branches on a giant 'tree of life.' At the root of the tree of life lies a single-celled organism, the 3.8-billion-year-old ancestor that gave rise to all subsequent life forms. All living things are descendants of that ancestor. That includes you, your cat, your potted plant, the fruit you ate for lunch, the last mosquito that bit you, and the cotton that's woven into your shirt. On the surface, it may not look like all living things are related. But looks can be deceiving."* [8]

Evidently, when traced back far enough on the so-called "Evolutionary Tree", all life on Earth is related to each other – BY BLOOD. All life shares the same "ancestor". The dictionary defines "ancestor" as *"a person, typically one more remote than a grandparent, FROM WHOM ONE IS DESCENDED."* Man is not simply a brother to the monkey, but a long lost cousin of tapeworms, cockroaches and house flies. The Public Broadcasting System even suggested to its watching children that man cannibalizes his kinfolk (*"... the fruit you ate for lunch..."*) on a regular basis. Imagine such an "education" system trying to teach the Bible-believing Christian what's "deceiving" and what's not. *"Be not deceived: evil communications corrupt good manners."* (1Cor. 15:33)

---

[7] "An introduction to Evolution." *Understanding Evolution: Your One-Stop Source for Information on Evolution.* University of California Museum of Paleontology (UCMP) and the National Center for Science Education. Web. 26 Mar 2013. <http://evolution.berkeley.edu/evolibrary/article/0_0_0/evo_02>.

[8] "Evolution: All in the Family." PBS.org. WGBH Educational Foundation and Clear Blue Sky Productions, Inc. Web. 26 Mar 2013. <http://www.pbs.org/wgbh/evolution/change/family/>.

The Mad Ravings of a Modern Monkey-Man

In 1983, the January/February issue of the secular humanist magazine *The Humanist* published an essay by John Dunphy titled '*A Religion for a New Age*'. In it he stated: "*I am convinced that the battle for humankind's future must be waged and won in the public school classroom by teachers who correctly perceive their role as the proselytizers of a new faith: a religion of humanity that recognizes the spark of what theologians call divinity in every human being. There teachers must embody*

IMAGE/public domain
The Rabid Evolutionist

the same selfless dedication of the most rabid fundamentalist preacher, for they will be ministers of another sort, utilizing a classroom instead of a pulpit to convey humanist values in whatever subject they teach, regardless of the educational level -- preschool, daycare, or large state university. The classroom must and will become an arena of conflict between the old and the new -- the rotting corpse of Christianity, together with all its adjacent evils and misery, and the new faith of humanism, resplendent in its promise of a world in which the never-realized Christian ideal of 'love thy neighbor' will finally be achieved." After the comment exploded on the Christian scene, Dunphy later reaffirmed; "*Have I mellowed over the past 11 years? Of course, who hasn't? But have I repudiated or even questioned the basic tenets of 'A Religion For A New Age'? No, nor can I envision myself ever doing so.*"

Schlafly, Phyllis. "Secular Humanists Give Dunphy Another Platform." Eagle Forum. 1994. Web. 11 May 2013. <http://www.eagleforum.org/educate/1995/nov95/dunphy.html>.

But like the purposeless particles of atomism, there is nothing unique about Darwin's "tree of life" (a title plagiarized from scripture). It dates even further back than Greek philosophy's pluralism. In his workbook, *Buckland's Complete Book of Witchcraft*, author and lifetime practitioner, student and authority on the occult arts, Raymond Buckland writes:

> *"The Craft is a religion of love and joy. It is not full of the gloom of Christianity, with its ideas of 'original sin' ... Early people lived hand-in-hand with nature, not separate from it. An animal was a brother or sister, as was a tree. Woman and Man were a part of the natural order of things, not separate from it. Not 'above' it."* [9]

So there it is. Choose either source, and regardless, all life on Earth has a familial kinship to one another. Evolution says man, animals and plants are *"distant cousins"*. Witchcraft says man, animals and plants are *"brothers and sisters"*. Their theories are the same – their RELIGIOUS BELIEFS are the same. The Holy Bible teaches no such relationship:

> *"[27] So God created man in his own image, in the image of God created he him; male and female created he them. [28] And God blessed them, and God said unto them, Be fruitful, and multiply, and replenish the earth, and subdue it: and have dominion over the fish of the sea, and over the fowl of the air, and over every living thing that moveth upon the earth." Genesis 1:27-28*

> *"[26] And hath made of one blood all nations of men for to dwell on all the face of the earth, and hath determined*

---

[9] Buckland, Raymond. *Buckland's Complete Book of Witchcraft*. St. Paul, MN: Llewellyn Publications, 1998. p 8

the times before appointed, and the bounds of their habitation; [27] That they should seek the Lord, if haply they might feel after him, and find him, though he be not far from every one of us". Acts 17:26-27

"For a man indeed ... is the image and glory of God: but the woman is the glory of the man." 1 Corinthians 11:7

"[19] They made a calf in Horeb, and worshipped the molten image. [20] Thus they changed their glory into the similitude of an ox that eateth grass. [21] They forgat God their saviour, which had done great things in Egypt". Psalms 106:19-21

"[26] As the thief is ashamed when he is found, so is the house of Israel ashamed; they, their kings, their princes, and their priests, and their prophets, [27] Saying to a stock [e.i. stump of a tree], *Thou art my father; and to a stone, Thou hast brought me forth: for they have turned their back unto me, and not their face: but in the time of their trouble they will say, Arise, and save us. [28] But where are thy gods that thou hast made thee? let them arise, if they can save thee in the time of thy trouble: for according to the number of thy cities are thy gods, O Judah."* Jeremiah 2:26-28

"[21] Because that, when they knew God, they glorified him not as God, neither were thankful; but became vain in their imaginations, and their foolish heart was darkened. [22] Professing themselves to be wise, they became fools, [23] And changed the glory of the uncorruptible God into an image made like to corruptible man, and to birds, and fourfooted beasts, and creeping things." Romans 6:21-23

These scriptures teach five very important facts concerning the so-called "science" of how life supposedly arose and is all interrelated:

1.) Man was created a separate being from the animal, not related to it.

2.) Man's *"one blood"* kinship extends only to his fellow man, not the animal world.

3.) Man is the *"image and glory"* of God, to suggest otherwise is blasphemy against the personage and likeness of God Himself.

4.) To claim you originate from trees or animals is to *"turn your back"* to God; *"forget God"* and to *"change"* His Glory (i.e. His image).

5.) Those professing a kinship to the animal are unthankful, godless fools, who raise their vain imagination above the words of God.

The modern search for life in space is built squarely upon Darwin's theory of a mindless force of fate which is supposedly responsible for all LIFE and INTELLIGENCE in the Universe. As revealed in the previous chapter, NASA's exploratory space programs admit to this by their support of *"research into the origin and early evolution of life"*.[10] But as we also covered earlier, a tree is known by its fruit. And some of the primary fruits of Darwin's "Tree of Life" are Communism, Fascism and Atheism. All communist governments are built on Evolutionism. Many evolutionists hate this fact, and vainly try to distance themselves from it, but the truth remains that the most deadly, evil and vile governments in the world today are, run by "monkey-men" (those that believe that men and apes share a "common ancestor" - and this includes the Vatican). Why this

[10] Fletcher, Julie, ed. "About Astrobiology." Astrobiology: Life in the Universe. National Aeronautics & Space Administration, 15 Aug 2012. Web. 26 Mar 2013. <https://astrobiology.nasa.gov/about-astrobiology/>.

upsets so many evolutionists is a mystery, for many seem genuinely horrified when witnessing the raw "standards of life" they've fought so hard to champion. Regardless, when it comes to the blind chance of Darwin's "natural selection", there is no moral high ground. One man's choice and decision-making is just as good (or evil) as another. After all, if all life is an unguided, meaningless accident, as evolution so clearly teaches, then what in the world is "wrong" with applying its principals of life to the principals of social government? Nothing. And because of that, the "morals" of Karl Marx, Mao Tse Tung, Pol Pot, Vladimir Lenin, Che Guevara, Ho Chi Minh, Kim Il Sung, Benito Mussolini, Slobodan Milosevic, Francisco Franco, Saddam Hussein, Osama bin Laden, Barack Hussein Obama and Adolph Hitler are all "as good as" the morals of Santa Claus, Mother Teresa or even the Lord Jesus Christ. In a godless evolutionary world, "morality" is a pipe dream. The ruling standard is set by "natural selection" and the "the survival of the fittest", not by right or wrong – *because there is no right or wrong*. And if that so-called "standard" includes killing babies, killing the elderly, killing blacks, killing the disabled, killing the less fortunate, and killing the Jews, then who's to argue? Killing, after all, is an act of nature – *an act of animals and the evolutionary process*. So any monkey-man who opposes Communism or Fascism needs to "suck it up" and shut his stupid mouth. Those are HIS PRINCIPLES in action. What did the fool expect, cotton candy and cupcakes with sprinkles?

> *"Even so every good tree bringeth forth good fruit; but a corrupt tree bringeth forth evil fruit. A good tree cannot bring forth evil fruit, neither can a corrupt tree bring forth good fruit." Matthew 7:17-18*

The ET Hypothesis & Alien Disclosure

Beginning as early as 1896 and continuing up to the present day, hundreds of thousands, if not millions of eyewitness accounts have peppered the globe regarding sightings of strange humanoid-type beings. These sightings gave rise to the modern "Extraterrestrial Hypothesis" (ETH), a belief system which purports that *"intelligent beings from other planets are visiting Earth."* [11] This theory has come about due to several concurring factors:

1.) The sightings coincide with the arrival and growth of evolution.

2.) The sightings coincide with the arrival and growth of science fiction.

3.) The sightings coincide with the arrival and growth of the Space Age and related technologies.

4.) Nearly all sightings were embroiled with the modern UFO phenomenon.

5.) Many of the alleged beings actually claim to be from outer space.

6.) These sightings gave rise to both the "contactee" and "abductee" movements.

When you add all these simultaneous events together (Evolutionism, science fiction, modern space exploration, Space Age technology, the UFO phenomenon, and alleged "alien encounters") you come away with the Extraterrestrial Hypothesis. This popular theory has had a HUGE IMPACT on the general belief in Cosmic Pluralism. However, for the most part, it is a SEPARATE MOVEMENT altogether from the movement within academia. Cosmic Pluralism is primarily a theory of evolutionary science which says that life on other planets is PROBABLE, but not proven. While the Extraterrestrial Hypothesis says aliens are here, NOW. While many evolutionists,

---

[11] Story, Ronald. The Encyclopedia of Extraterrestrial Encounters. New York: New American Library, 2001. p 173. AUTHOR'S NOTE: A modern outgrowth of this theory is the belief in "ancient aliens". The idea that beings from other planets have monitored, manipulated or seeded all life on Earth, and have been around for eons. This theory purports that Earth is basically an alien experiment, and humans are little more than "lab rats".

astronomers and astrobiologists have sat in their laboratories for decades (centuries even), and *never* seen nor heard a "peep" from any "little green men", today a whole faction of mankind insists that the aliens are knocking on Earth's door, and have been for centuries. In the eyes of many, the modern ETH movement is now poised to completely absorb the differing facets of Extraterrestialism worldwide. The reason for this is because the movement now claims to be on the verge of official ALIEN DISCLOSURE – *government revelation to the world that non-human extraterrestrial life is a reality*. Two of the leading institutions at the vanguard of the 21st century ETH movement are The Disclosure Project (also known as "Sirius Disclosure" at siriusdisclosure.com) and the Exopolitics Institute. The official website for The Disclosure Project states:

> *"The Disclosure Project is a research project working to fully disclose the facts about UFOs, extraterrestrial intelligence, and classified advanced energy and propulsion systems. We have over 500 government, military, and intelligence community witnesses testifying to their direct, personal, first hand experience with UFOs, ETs, ET technology, and the cover-up that keeps this information secret."* [12]

The project descriptions of both the *Disclosure Project* and the *Sirius Disclosure* project are identical and read as follows:

> *"- To hold open, secrecy-free hearings on the UFO/ Extraterrestrial presence on and around Earth.*
> *- To hold open hearings on advanced energy and propulsion systems that, when publicly released, will provide solutions to global environmental challenges.*

[12] The Disclosure Project. Web. 28 Mar 2013. <http://www.disclosureproject.org/index.shtml>.

- To enact legislation which will ban all space-based weapons.
- To enact comprehensive legislation to research, develop and explore space peacefully and cooperatively with all cultures on Earth and in space." [13]

Founded in 2005, the Exopolitics Institute is a 501 (c) (3) non-profit educational organization dedicated to the study, promotion and support of extraterrestrial life. For $1200 - $1500 one can acquire a "Galactic Diplomacy Certificate" which includes "Ambassador Training" to help assist in the coming post-disclosure paradigm shift. Its official website states:

"The Institute seeks to PREPARE HUMANITY FOR INTERACTION WITH EXTRATERRESTRIAL CIVILIZATIONS whose existence is supported by credible evidence, and supports full public disclosure by government authorities of all evidence concerning the extraterrestrial presence. The Institute supports THE VISION OF AN INTERCONNECTED GLOBAL HUMAN SOCIETY that interacts with extraterrestrial civilizations in a peaceful, harmonious and mutually respectful manner." [14]

While this movement is composed of credible testimony from high-ranking government and military officials worldwide, and outwardly appears to be moving towards some sort of major climax, the movers and shakers behind the scenes who use such testimony to advance their objectives, render the movement suspect. Not suspect in the

[13] Sirius Disclosure. Web. 19 April 2013. <http://siriusdisclosure.com/about-us/project-description/>.

[14] Exopolitics Institute. "Goals/Missions." Web. 28 Mar 2013. <http://exopoliticsinstitute.org/?page_id=814>.

legitimacy of the witnesses, but suspect in the motivating spiritual ties undergirding many of those at the forefront of the movement.

Dr. Steven M. Greer, the founder of the high-profile Disclosure Project (and several other ET disclosure initiatives), is a 30-year student and teacher of the Sanskrit Vedas and mantra meditation. His self-prescribed motto is *"One Universe. One People."* In his 2006 book *Hidden Truth: Forbidden Knowledge,* Dr. Greer teaches how we can have our own ET "close encounters" simply through self-induced astral projection or "remote viewing".[15] Likewise, Angelika Whitecliff, the Coordinator of the Citizen Diplomacy program of the Exopolitics Institute, *"has been a conscious clairvoyant and telepath since childhood",* as well as having *"professionally taught classes and seminars in developing clairvoyance, the energetic healing arts, retrieving past/future life memories and communicating with spiritual guides, angels and extraterrestrial visitors."* [16]

These disclosure organizers represent the same type of spiritist sympathizers that popped up during the mid 18th and 19th centuries. They subscribe to much of the same occult beliefs which first motivated men like Emmanuel Swedenborg and those involved in the early spiritist movement (see chapter 3). What this means is that those today who are the most enthused about making "contact" with alien life (NASA and SETI notwithstanding), are the same people the scriptures connect with those that *"hath a familiar spirit"* (Lev. 19:31, et.al.). Is there a reason why unclean spirits would have an interest in promoting the belief in extraterrestrial life?

Modern alien disclosure projects have been prominent in varying degrees for over a decade (since about 2001). They represent a

---

[15] Masyk-Jackson, Janis. "How to Meditate to Make Space Alien Contact." Suite101. com. Suite101 Media Inc., 09 Feb. 2010. Web. 27 Mar 2013. <http://suite101.com/article/how-to-meditate-to-make-space-alien-contact-a199091>.

[16] Exopolitics Institute. "Board of Directors." Web. 28 Mar 2013. <http://exopoliticsinstitute.org/?page_id=818>.

Alien Corpse from a Catholic Ghost Town

IMAGE/S.T.A.R. Research   Alleged humanoid found in an abandoned ghost town.

Well known in the area for its "paranormal activity" and its mass of unkempt and open graves, La Noria, Chile was once a salt mining town, but died-out in late 1950s. In 2003, a local relic hunter who frequented the area, allegedly dug up a tiny body wrapped in *"white cloth tied with a purple ribbon"* buried near the church. The man kept the remains, but eventually sold it to a local shopkeeper. Since its discovery, rumors have swirled around the find implying that it's the body of a creature of off-world origins. Over the next several years the remains found their way to the founder of the Disclosure Project, Dr. Steven Greer. On April 22, 2013, Dr. Greer's SIRIUS organization released a documentary regarding the find. According to on-going DNA testing, the tiny carcass is not an alien or an unborn infant, but *a bizarre, 6-inch, hyper-diminutive HUMAN, 6 to 8 years old.* Regardless of its earthly origins, and the dashed hopes of finding ET, Greer's filmmakers claimed the disclosure would *"completely change the reality of human existence."*

Huneeus, Antonio. "Background of UFO documentary's humanoid alien revealed." OpenMinds. Open Minds Production, LLC, 8 Apr 2013. Web. 19 Apr 2013. <http://www.openminds.tv/background-of-ufo-documentary-humanoid-alien-revealed-964/>.

dangerous movement that threatens an already fragile spiritual state in mankind, a mind-set that's ready to completely cast-off any vestiges of belief in a Holy God, and embrace fallen alien beings as galactic co-equals or saviors of the Earth. One such disclosure report given in 2011 by a professor at the University of New Hampshire and a member of CSETI stated in part:

"Intelligent beings from other star systems have been and are visiting our planet Earth. They are variously referred to as Visitors, Others, Star People, ETs, etc. ... They are visiting Earth NOW; this is not a matter of conjecture or wistful [sic] thinking. ... In this paper open Disclosure means that governments of the world and the media totally accept and publicly

IMAGE/exopolitics.org   Galactic Diplomacy Published in May 2013 and authored by the director of the Exopolitics Institute (Michael Salla), *Galactic Diplomacy* details the secret history of supposed "diplomatic relations" between alien civilizations and governments around the world since 1952.

discuss the reality of ETs, the fact that we are and have been visited by them and the time has come to interact with them in a peaceful manner. Once open Disclosure has occurred and these facts become widely accepted on Earth, there will be dramatic and rapid change in many areas of human endeavors. ... Once open Disclosure has taken place, humans will want very much to learn about the spiritual nature of the ETs, THEIR VIEW of the role of GOD in their various cultures (for there are many), and the nature of consciousness and intelligence." [17]

Spiritual Guidance for the 21st Century

In May of 2008, the Vatican newspaper, *L'Osservatore Romano* reported that the Vatican Observatory's head Jesuit, Father Jose Funes, was claiming that, based on evolution, it was difficult to exclude the possibility of intelligent life on other planets. Citing God's "creative freedom" as a backbone to his argument, Father Funes contended that life in space may be just as varied as life on Earth. He also argued that such creatures may be sinless, not needing a pastor or redeemer, and could logically be embraced as mankind's *"extraterrestrial brother".* But *"if needed"*, he said, God's mercy could extend to aliens as well:

> *"God became man in Jesus in order to save us. So if there are also other intelligent beings, it's not a given that they need redemption. They might have remained in full friendship with their creator. We who belong to the human race could really be that lost sheep, the sinners who need a pastor."* [18]

The Jesuit also repudiated scripture as a means of educating the Christian on the reality of outer space and extraterrestrial life.

---

[17] Loder, Theodore C. "ET Contact: The Implications for Post Contact Advancement in Science and Technology." PDF Document. Mutual UFO Network, 27 May 2011. Web. 28 Mar 2013. (All-caps emphasis added)

[18] Thavis, John. "Vatican astronomer says if aliens exist, they may not need redemption." catholicnews.com. Catholic News Service, 14 May 2008. Web. 28 Mar 2013. <http://www.catholicnews.com/data/stories/cns/0802629.htm>.

Father Funes said that it was *"wrong"* to expect a scientific answer from the Bible:

> *"The Bible is not fundamentally a work of science. It is a letter of love that God has written to his people, in a language that was used 2,000-3,000 years ago. Obviously, at that time a concept like the big bang was totally extraneous."* [19]

The Catholic director has just taught the Christian to throw out the Bible when wanting to learn the truth about aliens. According to him, God's *"letter of love"* will teach error if you choose to believe it as a literal *"work of science"* (never mind the fact that Christ could walk on water, stop the rain, heal the blind, or raise Himself from the dead – all real events which illustrate the futility of science). However, for the Catholic Church to endorse evolution should come as no real surprise. Pope Benedict XVI reported on the official Vatican website:

> *"Currently, I see in Germany, but also in the United States, a somewhat fierce debate raging between so-called 'creationism' and evolutionism, presented as though they were mutually exclusive alternatives ... This antithesis is absurd because, on the one hand, there are so many scientific proofs in favour of evolution which appears to be a reality we can see and which enriches our knowledge of life and being as such."* [20]

---

[19] Thavis, John. "Vatican astronomer says if aliens exist, they may not need redemption." catholicnews.com. Catholic News Service, 14 May 2008. Web. 28 Mar 2013. <http://www.catholicnews.com/data/stories/cns/0802629.htm>.

[20] Benedict, Pope. "MEETING OF THE HOLY FATHER BENEDICT XVI WITH THE CLERGY OF THE DIOCESES OF BELLUNO-FELTRE AND TREVISO." vatican.va. Libreria Editrice Vaticana, 24 Jul 2007. Web. 28 Mar 2013. <http://www.vatican.va/holy_father/benedict_xvi/speeches/2007/july/documents/hf_ben-xvi_spe_20070724_clero-cadore_en.html>.

In 2009, the Vatican sponsored "a five-day conference to mark the 150th anniversary of the publication of Charles Darwin's *Origin of Species*."[21] Later that same year, the Pontifical Academy of Sciences and the Vatican Observatory held a week-long conference on astrobiology to further investigate the subject of life on other planets. Earlier that same decade (2005), US Jesuit Guy Consolmagno wrote a 48-page booklet on the subject titled *Intelligent Life in the Universe? Catholic Belief and the Search for Extraterrestrial Intelligent Life.* The book is published through the British-based Catholic Truth Society. And finally, the late Vatican theologian and demonologist, Monsignor Corrado Balducci (1923-2008), made five appearances on Italian television discussing the issue. His conclusions regarding the UFO-related "close encounters" were that such events "are not demonic" and "are not a case of entity attachment". The demonologist encouraged further investigation into the phenomenon.[22]

Chapter 5 Summary

For the Christian, history is not just built around the open news stories and political events popularized by the press or taught in public school systems. History has a spiritual side which the Holy Bible takes for granted, a side which follows the workings of the Holy Spirit through history, as well as the hidden (and many times not-so-hidden) workings of the Adversary (Eph. 6:12). This is true for the belief in Extraterrestrialism. Having began in the book of Genesis and traveled to the 21st century, we have now covered a fairly

[21] ABC News "Vatican sponsors Darwin anniversary conference." ABC.net.au. ABC, 03 Mar 2009. Web. 28 Mar 2013. <http://www.abc.net.au/news/2009-03-03/vatican-sponsors-darwin-anniversary-conference/1607566>.

[22] Boylan, Ph.D, Richard. "Vatican Official Declares Extraterrestrial Contact Is Real." UfoDigest. UFODIGEST.COM. Web. 28 Mar 2013. <http://www.ufodigest.com/balducci.html>.

detailed history of the belief in alien life. I felt this history necessary in order to provide the Christian with the most outstanding ideas and circumstances which helped shape the theory into what it is today. This chronology has revealed several interesting facts:

1.) The belief in alien life on other planets was not caused by pre-Flood monotheism (4000 - 2344 BC). The scriptures show that the fathers of mankind (Adam, Seth, Enoch, Noah, et.al.) all knew and acknowledged the true God, the Creator of the Universe (Gen. 1-5).

2.) The first extraterrestrial invasion (Gen. 6:4) initiated polytheism after Noah's Flood (around 2344 BC). Through the early influences of philosophy (600 BC), the false belief in MANY GODS splintered into the naturalistic concept of "Cosmic Pluralism" – the belief that INTELLIGENT LIFE populated MANY PLANETS.

3.) One of the first major religious systems that helped mainstream Extraterrestrialism was the Roman Catholic Church. Their early approval of the idea was not so much an *overt acknowledgement of extraterrestrial life*, but rather, a lack of scriptural utilization in a effort to *judge the concept* (1 Thess. 5:21, Acts. 17:11). Silence was consent, however. The ideas and concepts of several of their Dark Age cardinals, priests and doctors of cannon law played a MAJOR ROLE in the revival and promotion of life on other planets. Twenty-first century Vatican astronomers have also encouraged the concept by proposing that aliens should be received as fellow "brother and sisters" and co-created beings of God. The former Pope Benedict XVI privately called the denial of theistic evolution "absurd", thus giving credence to the secular machine of blind, happenstance-creation, once known as "atomism". The important thing to get here is that the Roman Catholic Church has *never opposed the idea*. Instead, history shows their tentacles have subtly been at the spiritual forefront of the issue for the last five and a half centuries. However, for those familiar with church history this is not surprising. The Roman Church has a long history of compromise with pagan philosophies.

4.) In the early days of Heliocentrism (late 16th century), the idea of planetary similarities lead many to accept the possibility of life on other planets. This meant that planets which appeared to have very general Earth-like qualities (mountains, seas, moons, etc.) were assumed to be candidates for life. Today this search for life continues, yet no planets with Earth-like atmospheres have ever been found.

5.) For many, the vast size of the Universe, with its seemingly endless supply of stars and other planetary bodies, presents a major stumbling block. This is the hurdle that many CANNOT GET OVER without drawing the conclusion that God (or evolution) must have placed life elsewhere. To think otherwise would be nonsense. This concept will be addressed later in the book.

6.) Another major cog in the wheel of Extraterrestrialism, is the mid-twentieth century advent of the baffling UFO phenomenon (1947). This mystery helped birth the "Extraterrestrial Hypothesis". The idea that highly evolved beings from other planets are piloting spacecraft to Earth. This has never been proven.

7.) And finally, the stimulation of the imagination of man (Rom. 1:21, 2Cor. 10:5, et.al.) through the medium of SCIENCE FICTION has played a MAJOR ROLE in the modern advancement of the idea. For more than a century, novels, magazines, comic books, movie serials and films have fed a continuous line of "alien life" propaganda. Many underestimate the power of science fiction, but history proves it to be a HEAVY HITTER when influencing this field. Many of the most outstanding scientists of the last century were motivated by it as a child. This subject will continue to be examined as the book progresses.

Now that a foundation of the history of Extraterrestrialism has been laid, it's time to get into the *meat* of scripture (This will not be a study for the "milkshake" Christian. Heb. 5:13-14).

Whether it be from TV, movies, magazines, newspapers or the internet, Christians today are inundated from all sides by the concept of life on other planets. While the Bible certainly hints at the fact that early man recognized that "something" (other than God) was indeed out there, modern science continues to search for life based upon its theory of evolution. Some claim aliens created mankind, while others theorize that aliens are our godly "brothers". When faced with questions such as these, can you give a doctrinally-sound answer with the Bible? Is the Earth "just another planet" floating aimlessly adrift in space, or something more? Do intelligent civilizations inhabit other planets, or are we alone? What about God's "creative freedom"? Would God create other inhabited planets? Why or why not? What about the supposed modern sightings of unexplained life forms? Are these real? Are they fake? Are they demons? WHAT ARE THEY? In the chapters that follow, we will build solid, scripture-based answers to these questions and many others. Chapter 6 will lay the cornerstone of our continued search for answers.

PART II
CHAPTERS 6 - 15

The Scriptures & Extraterrestrialism

Biblical Insights Regarding
Outer Space & Life Beyond Earth

"Study to shew thyself approved unto God, a workman that needeth not to be ashamed, rightly dividing the word of truth." 2Tim. 2:15

6

The Limits of an All-Powerful God

A t the end of the previous chapter we discovered that the Roman Catholic Vatican Observatory's official stance on the alien is that life on other planets is difficult to exclude. According to Jesuit Director, the Rev. Jose Gabriel Funes, if such beings exist, then they are very possibly our sinless *"brothers"*, and denying that possibility is akin to putting limits on God's creative freedom. This conclusion sounds very reasonable. Who would dare want to limit the creative freedom and power of God? After all, God *is* omnipotent. God can do whatever He wants, in any manner He wants, at any time He wants:

> *"And I heard as it were the voice of a great multitude, and as the voice of many waters, and as the voice of mighty thunderings, saying, Alleluia: for the Lord GOD OMNIPOTENT reigneth." Revelation 19:6*

The scriptures leave no question regarding the Creator's all-powerfulness. But the fact that God is all-powerful does not mean he can't, or doesn't, practice restraint (Job 26:9). The idea that God exercises His power like a cocky man with a chip on his shoulder, and flaunts it like He needs to "prove something", or does something simply "because He can" is a carnal idea of God. God is not only a God of ORDER, but a God of RESTRAINT. Anyone who doesn't know that has forgotten His great mercy and longsuffering:

> "...The LORD God, merciful and gracious, longsuffering, and abundant in goodness and truth," Ex. 34:6

> "Know therefore that the LORD thy God, he is God, the faithful God, which keepeth covenant and MERCY with them that love him and keep his commandments to a THOUSAND GENERATIONS". Deut.y 7:9

What this means is if there *are* any "limits" placed upon God, they must obviously be limits He has placed there Himself.

God and a Book

I think it can be stated, with a fair amount of accuracy, that most people do not fully grasp the ramifications of a God-breathed Book. Even for Christians, the reality has become cliché. Think about it, however. The very idea that the same God who created the Universe, would give His very words to men to put into a Book, should fill us with an overwhelming sense of awe and fear. We should be beating down the bushes to find such a Book, and pouring over it day and night, holding each and every word with the utmost importance. Have you ever really thought about how significant and crucial it is to actually hold a Book in your hands that was written and preserved by God Himself? If it helps, walk outside at night with your *King James Bible* and look up at the sky. See all those stars? The Lord made each and every one of those stars (even the ones you can't see). Now, open the scriptures and look at the words. The same God who made all those stars, preserved each and every one of those words:

> *"[16] ALL SCRIPTURE IS GIVEN BY INSPIRATION OF GOD, and is profitable for doctrine, for reproof, for correction, for instruction in righteousness: [17] That the man of God may be perfect, thoroughly furnished unto all good works." 2 Timothy 3:16*

But the amazement doesn't stop there. When the Creator manifested Himself in the flesh (in the form of the Lord Jesus Christ), can you guess what He did? He called Himself after THE SAME NAME as the Bible you hold in your hands: ***the Word of God.***

The incarnate "Word of God"

The written "word of God"

On the one hand there's God (the Word of God - John 1:1, etc.), and on the other hand there's a Book (the word of God - Isa. 34:16, Lk. 4:4, etc.). God and a Book. When God-incarnate began His earthly ministry, what did He do? HE CONFINED HIS EVERY MOVE, by choice, TO WORDS WRITTEN IN A BOOK. God Himself did this.

The actions of the Lord Jesus Christ reflect the actions of God and show that the Creator of the Universe has a deliberate way of doing things. A method of operation. This method of operation is to

LIMIT HIMSELF TO WRITTEN WORDS. Words which are written in a Book which share His very name. A Book which He Himself has EXALTED ABOVE His very name:

> *"I will worship toward thy holy temple, and praise thy name for thy lovingkindness and for thy truth: for thou hast magnified thy word above all thy name." Psa. 138:2*

The truth is this, no one is "limiting God" or "putting God in a box". God limits Himself and puts Himself there, and that "box" is His written word – the *King James Bible*.

Bound by His Words

Modern man is so accustomed to lying and liars that a man's "word" no longer holds any real significance. However, this is not so with the Lord. God not only binds Himself to His word, GOD IS HIS WORD. Consider the following salient Bible references:

> *"[1] In the beginning was the Word, and the Word was with God, and THE WORD WAS GOD. [2] The same was in the beginning with God. [3] All things were made by him; and without him was not any thing made that was made." John 1:1-3*

> *"[1] That which was from the beginning, which WE HAVE HEARD, which WE HAVE SEEN with our eyes, which we have LOOKED UPON, and OUR HANDS HAVE HANDLED, of THE WORD of life; [2] (For the life was manifested, and we have seen it, and bear witness, and show unto you that eternal life, which was with the Father, and was manifested unto us;) [3] That which we have seen and heard declare we unto you, that ye also may have fellowship with us: and truly our fellowship is*

with the Father, and with his Son Jesus Christ."
1John 1:1-3

"And THE WORD WAS MADE FLESH, and dwelt among us, (and we beheld his glory, the glory as of the only begotten of the Father,) full of grace and truth."
John 1:14

"Then said I, Lo, I come: IN THE VOLUME OF THE BOOK it is written of me". Psalms 40:7 & Heb. 10:7

"[23] Then the soldiers, when they had crucified Jesus, took his garments, and made four parts, to every soldier a part; and also his coat: now the coat was without seam, woven from the top throughout. [24] They said therefore among themselves, Let us not rend it, but cast lots for it, whose it shall be: THAT THE SCRIPTURE MIGHT BE FULFILLED, which saith, They parted my raiment among them, and for my vesture they did cast lots. These things therefore the soldiers did." John 19:23-24

"After this, Jesus knowing that all things were now accomplished, THAT THE SCRIPTURE MIGHT BE FULFILLED, saith, I thirst." John 19:28

"[33] But when they came to Jesus, and saw that he was dead already, they brake not his legs: [34] But one of the soldiers with a spear pierced his side, and forthwith came there out blood and water. [35] And he that saw it bare record, and his record is true: and he knoweth that he saith true, that ye might believe. [36] For these things were done, THAT THE SCRIPTURE SHOULD BE

FULFILLED, A bone of him shall not be broken. [37] And again another scripture saith, They shall look on him whom they pierced." John 19:33-37

"[23] And he answered and said, He that dippeth his hand with me in the dish, the same shall betray me. [24] The Son of man goeth AS IT IS WRITTEN OF HIM..." *Matthew 26:23-24*

"Then saith Jesus unto them, All ye shall be offended because of me this night: for IT IS WRITTEN, I will smite the shepherd, and the sheep of the flock shall be scattered abroad." Matthew 26:31

"[55] In that same hour said Jesus to the multitudes, Are ye come out as against a thief with swords and staves for to take me? I sat daily with you teaching in the temple, and ye laid no hold on me. [56] But all this was done, THAT THE scriptures OF THE PROPHETS MIGHT BE FULFILLED. Then all the disciples forsook him, and fled." Matthew 26:55-56

"[15] And when he had made a scourge of small cords, he drove them all out of the temple, and the sheep, and the oxen; and poured out the changers' money, and overthrew the tables; [16] And said unto them that sold doves, Take these things hence; make not my Father's house an house of merchandise. [17] And his disciples remembered that IT WAS WRITTEN, The zeal of thine house hath eaten me up." John 2:15-17

"[14] And Jesus, when he had found a young ass, sat thereon; AS IT IS WRITTEN, [15] Fear not, daughter of Sion: behold, thy King cometh, sitting on an ass's colt. [16] These things understood not his disciples at the first: but when Jesus was glorified, then remembered they that THESE THINGS WERE WRITTEN OF HIM, and that they had done these things unto him." John 12:14-16

"But this cometh to pass, that THE WORD MIGHT BE FULFILLED THAT IS WRITTEN in their law, They hated me without a cause." John 15:25

"[30] And many other signs truly did Jesus in the presence of his disciples, which are not written in this book: [31] But these are written, that ye might believe that Jesus is the Christ, the Son of God; and that believing ye might have life through his name." John 20:30-31

"[29] And when they had FULFILLED ALL THAT WAS WRITTEN OF HIM, they took him down from the tree, and laid him in a sepulchre. [30] But God raised him from the dead: [31] And he was seen many days of them which came up with him from Galilee to Jerusalem, who are his witnesses unto the people. [32] And we declare unto you glad tidings, how that the promise which was made unto the fathers, [33] God hath fulfilled the same unto us their children, in that he hath raised up Jesus again; AS IT IS ALSO WRITTEN in the second psalm, Thou art my Son, this day have I begotten thee. [34] And as concerning that he raised him up from the dead, now no more to return to corruption, he said on this wise, I will give you the sure mercies of David. [35] Wherefore

he saith also in another psalm, Thou shalt not suffer thine Holy One to see corruption." Acts 13:29-35

"[44] And he said unto them, These are the words which I spake unto you, while I was yet with you, that ALL THINGS MUST BE FULFILLED, WHICH WERE WRITTEN in the law of Moses, and in the prophets, and in the psalms, concerning me. [45] Then opened he their understanding, that they might understand the scriptures". Luke 24:44-45

"[27] And with him they crucify two thieves; the one on his right hand, and the other on his left. [28] And THE SCRIPTURE WAS FULFILLED, which saith, And he was numbered with the transgressors." Mark 15:27-28
"[22] Now ALL THIS WAS DONE, THAT IT MIGHT BE FULFILLED which was spoken of the Lord by the prophet, saying, [23] Behold, a virgin shall be with child, and shall bring forth a son, and they shall call his name Emmanuel, which being interpreted is, God with us." Matthew 1:22-23

"[4] And when he had gathered all the chief priests and scribes of the people together, he demanded of them where Christ should be born. [5] And they said unto him, In Bethlehem of Judaea: for THUS IT IS WRITTEN by the prophet, [6] And thou Bethlehem, in the land of Juda, art not the least among the princes of Juda: for out of thee shall come a Governor, that shall rule my people Israel." Matthew 2:4-6

"[13] And when they were departed, behold, the angel of the Lord appeareth to Joseph in a dream, saying,

Arise, and take the young child and his mother, and flee into Egypt, and be thou there until I bring thee word: for Herod will seek the young child to destroy him. [14] When he arose, he took the young child and his mother by night, and departed into Egypt: [15] And was there until the death of Herod: THAT IT MIGHT BE FULFILLED which was spoken of the Lord by the prophet, saying, Out of Egypt have I called my son." Matthew 2:13-15

"[17] Then was FULFILLED that which was spoken by Jeremy the prophet, saying, [18] In Rama was there a voice heard, lamentation, and weeping, and great mourning, Rachel weeping for her children, and would not be comforted, because they are not." Matthew 2:17-18

"And he came and dwelt in a city called Nazareth: THAT IT MIGHT BE FULFILLED which was spoken by the prophets, He shall be called a Nazarene." Matthew 2:23
"[13] And leaving Nazareth, he came and dwelt in Capernaum, which is upon the sea coast, in the borders of Zabulon and Nephthalim: [14] THAT IT MIGHT BE FULFILLED which was spoken by Esaias the prophet, saying, [15] The land of Zabulon, and the land of Nephthalim, by the way of the sea, beyond Jordan, Galilee of the Gentiles; [16] The people which sat in darkness saw great light; and to them which sat in the region and shadow of death light is sprung up."
Matthew 4:13-16

"[16] When the even was come, they brought unto him many that were possessed with devils: and he cast out the spirits with his word, and healed all that were sick: [17]

THAT IT MIGHT BE FULFILLED which was spoken by Esaias the prophet, saying, Himself took our infirmities, and bare our sicknesses." Matthew 8:16-17

"[16] And charged them that they should not make him known: [17] THAT IT MIGHT BE FULFILLED which was spoken by Esaias the prophet, saying, [18] Behold my servant, whom I have chosen; my beloved, in whom my soul is well pleased: I will put my spirit upon him, and he shall show judgment to the Gentiles. [19] He shall not strive, nor cry; neither shall any man hear his voice in the streets. [20] A bruised reed shall he not break, and smoking flax shall he not quench, till he send forth judgment unto victory. [21] And in his name shall the Gentiles trust." Matthew 12:16-21

"[34] All these things spake Jesus unto the multitude in parables; and without a parable spake he not unto them: [35] THAT IT MIGHT BE FULFILLED which was spoken by the prophet, saying, I will open my mouth in parables; I will utter things which have been kept secret from the foundation of the world." Matthew 13:34-35

"[1] And when they drew nigh unto Jerusalem, and were come to Bethphage, unto the mount of Olives, then sent Jesus two disciples, [2] Saying unto them, Go into the village over against you, and straightway ye shall find an ass tied, and a colt with her: loose them, and bring them unto me. [3] And if any man say ought unto you, ye shall say, The Lord hath need of them; and straightway he will send them. [4] ALL THIS was done, THAT IT MIGHT BE FULFILLED which was spoken by the prophet, saying, [5] Tell ye the daughter of Sion, Behold, thy King cometh

unto thee, meek, and sitting upon an ass, and a colt the foal of an ass." Matthew 21:1-5

"The Son of man goeth AS IT IS WRITTEN of him: but woe unto that man by whom the Son of man is betrayed! it had been good for that man if he had not been born." Matthew 26:24

"[52] Then said Jesus unto him, Put up again thy sword into his place: for all they that take the sword shall perish with the sword. [53] Thinkest thou that I cannot now pray to my Father, and he shall presently give me more than twelve legions of angels? [54] But how then shall THE SCRIPTURES BE FULFILLED, that thus it must be?" Matthew 26:52-54

"[55] In that same hour said Jesus to the multitudes, Are ye come out as against a thief with swords and staves for to take me? I sat daily with you teaching in the temple, and ye laid no hold on me. [56] But ALL THIS was done, THAT THE SCRIPTURES OF THE PROPHETS MIGHT BE FULFILLED. Then all the disciples forsook him, and fled." Matthew 26:55-56

"[9] Then was FULFILLED that which was spoken by Jeremy the prophet [i.e. Jeremiah], saying, And they took the thirty pieces of silver, the price of him that was valued, whom they of the children of Israel did value; [10] And gave them for the potter's field, as the Lord appointed me." Matthew 27:9-10

"And they crucified him, and parted his garments, casting lots: THAT IT MIGHT BE FULFILLED which

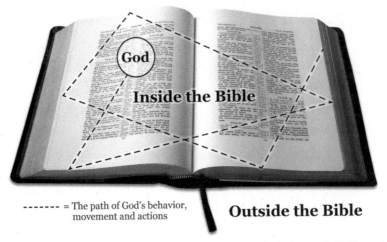

God

Inside the Bible

------- = The path of God's behavior, movement and actions

Outside the Bible

IMAGE/Jeff Mardis

God moves and behaves in accord with His word.

was spoken by the prophet, They parted my garments among them, and upon my vesture did they cast lots."
Matthew 27:35

"Seek ye out of THE BOOK OF THE LORD, and read..."
Isaiah 34:16

Chapter 6 Summary

So why is all this so important, and what does it have to do with our study of extraterrestrial life? These passages illustrate how high of a regard the Creator holds for His written word. An estimation that is so high, in fact, that He will go out of His way to see that those words are adhered to. If you were to take all the words of the Holy Bible and shape those words into the figure of a man, that Man would be the Lord Jesus Christ – the Word Incarnate. What the Christian needs to get here is that when God moves and works, it's ALWAYS IN ACCORD with the written words of His Holy Bible. God can always be counted upon to adhere to what He has said and written. For Him to act outside of these SELF-IMPOSED BOUNDS, would be against His very nature. As we continue to build the case of a Bible-based answer regarding life beyond Earth, many readers may find themselves asking; "But, but, – But what about God's creative freedom? What about all that space and and all those stars? What about this, what about that ...?" And my answer will simply be, "Yeah, but what about the scriptures?" It might be a neat thing to consider what *might happen* if God exercised His "creative freedom" and did a few things wildly chaotic or unrehearsed, but God is much more concerned with mankind *believing, learning and trusting in His word* than stepping outside of those words to do something spectacular or something we would've done if we were God.

> *"Have not I WRITTEN TO THEE excellent things in counsels and knowledge, That I might MAKE THEE KNOW THE CERTAINTY OF THE WORDS OF TRUTH; that THOU MIGHTEST ANSWER the words of truth to them that send thee?" Proverbs 22:20-21*

> *" So they read in THE BOOK in the law of God distinctly, and gave the sense, and caused them to understand the reading." Nehemiah 8:8*

> *"For whatsoever things were WRITTEN aforetime were WRITTEN FOR OUR LEARNING, that we through patience and comfort of THE SCRIPTURES might have hope." Romans 15:4*

> *"To the law and to the testimony: if they speak not ACCORDING TO THIS WORD, it is because there is NO LIGHT in them." Isaiah 8:20*

God gave us His Book so that we can know the *"certainty"* of truth. God gave us His Book so that we can learn and take comfort in the fact that He will do what He has said, and that what He has written will come to pass. This premise represents the CORNERSTONE upon which all our answers will be built. God's Book was given to us to answer such questions. As a matter of fact, it's the Christian's duty to *"prove all things"* with God's Book (1 Thess. 5:21). It's the Christian's duty to search *"the scriptures daily"* (Acts 17:11). Don't ever let anyone tell you to throw out God's Book when seeking truth. Don't ever let anyone tell you that the Bible is inept, and that you can only depend on "science". The Bible is above science, for unlike science, God has exalted it above His very name. It's anybody's guess as to why a highly educated Roman Catholic Jesuit can't answer a simple question regarding extraterrestrial life. But appealing to God's "creative freedom" is not an answer – it's a cop-out, a willful avoidance of clear scriptural evidence that shows God's creative freedom is a moot issue. Never mind God's "creative freedom", and never mind those who would suggest such things. God is not concerned with FREEDOM FROM HIS WORDS, for His words are eternally established:

"For ever, O LORD, THY WORD IS SETTLED in heaven."
Psalms 119:89

"God is not a man, that he should lie; neither the son of man, that he should repent: HATH HE SAID, and shall he not DO IT? or HATH HE SPOKEN, and shall he not MAKE IT GOOD?" Numbers 23:19

"Heaven and earth shall pass away: but MY WORDS SHALL NOT PASS AWAY." Mark 13:31

7

Operation: Discrimination

I n a failed attempt at comedy, some modern evolutionists and pluralists have asked, *"Is there intelligent life on Earth?"* This question is meant to ridicule the Christian. Nevertheless, this chapter will use the Bible to demonstrate how the centuries-old assumption of both scientists, and many theologians, wrongly assumes that "all that extra space", and "all those stars" means God must have placed life elsewhere in the Universe. This oft-used line of reasoning is based on the fallacy that GOD USES ALL THINGS IN EQUAL MEASURE. It is a wrong assumption. Those who make such assumptions regarding the decisions of God will come to wrong conclusions. The Bible says that God's ways are not the ways of man:

> *"For my thoughts are not your thoughts, neither are your ways my ways, saith the LORD. For as the heavens are higher than the earth, so are my ways higher than your ways, and my thoughts than your thoughts." Isa. 55:8-9*

Despite the musings of 18th century men like Samuel Pye, who, in an attempt to defend both God and pluralistic thought, suggested that God had inspired a "Genesis Account" for every planet (i.e. "*In the beginning God created the heaven and Jupiter*.").[1] But we're not going to get off the hook quite that easily. Searching for Bible answers to the question of extraterrestrial life is one of those subjects that require a little more digging.

Since God is eternal and unchanging, one of the best places to start our search is with the character of God. The cornerstone of that groundwork was laid by the previous chapter where we discovered that the Creator will not act outside of His written word. Instead, it is the Lord's nature to act in concert with His word. God did this for our learning and benefit. To move forward, however, we need to ask ourselves: "*Is it within God's character to indiscriminately populate planets with intelligent life, or does He pick and choose? Does God operate 'at random' like some mindless natural process, or does He deal in ordered specifics?*" By observing how God works in other matters, we can discover His method of operation. If the Bible reveals a distinct pattern and consistency to God's behavior, we can then apply this standard to the question of life on other planets.

Those familiar with the Bible will already know that in many cases God has special preferences. God chooses some things to the exclusion of others. And although "discrimination" may be the "unforgivable sin" of our modern global society, if true, it will provide the first important piece to our puzzle. Please note the following biblical examples of Godly discrimination:

1.) One Man to Populate a Planet - When God created mankind, He did not create groups and pockets of men and women all over the world. He began, instead, with

---

[1] Crowe, Michael J. *The Extraterrestrial Life Debate*. Notre Dame, IN: University of Notre Dame, 2008. p 201

IMAGE/public domain   An ancient stargazer.

Many ancient astronomers were convinced that the heavens were populated with Earth-like life simply due to the "vast number of the stars", but does such a number have any real bearing on the number of populated worlds? Even today, this same theory is touted.

the creation of only one man. And if you'll remember, the woman was created from the man (Gen. 2:22). So, in essence, the entire human race started with the direct creation of ONLY ONE MAN.

"This is the book of the generations of Adam. In the day that God created man, in the likeness of God made he him; Male and female created he them; and blessed them, and called their name, Adam, in the day when they were created" Genesis 5:1-2

2.) One Man Saved from Destruction - When God uses a global flood to wipe every living thing from off the face of the Earth, ONLY ONE man's family is saved. God deliberately ignores all the others.

"And the Lord said, I will destroy man whom I have created from the face of the earth; both man, and beast, and the creeping thing, and the fowls of the air; for it repenteth me that I have made them. But Noah found grace in the eyes of the Lord. And, behold, I, even I, do bring a flood of waters upon the earth, to destroy all flesh, wherein is the breath of life, from under heaven; and every thing that is in the earth shall die. But with thee will I establish my covenant; and thou shalt come into the ark, thou, and thy sons, and thy wife, and thy sons' wives with thee." Genesis 6:7-8 & 17-18

3.) One Man to bring forth a Nation - When God wants to raise up a great nation, He selects ONLY ONE man with which to do so. Not a dozen, not a hundred or a thousand "potential candidates" – only one.

300 Sextillion Inconsequentials

The exact number of the stars has always been a detail which has eluded science. Every few years the number seems to climb higher. The current estimation is already so colossal it's difficult to comprehend. In a recent joint study by Harvard and Yale (2010), it was discovered that our

IMAGE/public domain   ESO's La Silla Observatory

initial estimation of 100 sextillion, is only one third the number of what we have now found – 300 sextillion stars (that's the number three followed by 23 zeros, or three trillion times 100 billion). When the Bible records the creation of the stars, it sums up their extraordinary number in five short words; *"... he made the stars also."* (Gen. 1:16) To modern man, discounting this vast number in five mere words is nearly as mind-boggling as the number itself. Some may even see it as a borderline "sin" against astronomy. But there it is. Clearly, what appears significant to man, is not always significant to God. It is the ultimate example of Godly discrimination:

"For my thoughts are not your thoughts, neither are my ways your ways, saith the Lord. For as the heavens are higher than the earth, so are my ways higher than your ways, and my thoughts than your thoughts." Isaiah 55:8-9

"Now the Lord had said unto Abram, Get thee out of thy country, and from thy kindred, and from thy father's house, unto a land that I will show thee: And I WILL MAKE OF THEE A GREAT NATION, and I will bless thee, and make thy name great; and thou shalt be a blessing: And I will bless them that bless thee, and curse him that curseth thee: and in thee shall all families of the earth be blessed." Genesis 12:1-3

"Thou art the LORD the God, who didst CHOOSE ABRAM, and broughtest him forth out of Ur of the Chaldees, and gavest him the name of Abraham; And foundest his heart faithful before thee, and madest a covenant with HIM to give the land of the Canaanites, the Hittites, the Amorites, and the Perizzites, and the Jebusites, and the Girgashites, to give it, I say, TO HIS SEED, and hast performed thy words; for thou art righteous". NEHEMIAH 9:7-8

4.) One Chosen People - After God calls out a people unto Himself, ONLY ONE nation of people is selected – Israel. God has no direct, one-on-one dealings with any other nations of the world. It is written:

"And what ONE NATION in the earth is like thy people, even like Israel, whom God went to redeem for a people to himself, and to make him a name, and to do for you great things and terrible, for thy land, before thy people, which thou redeemedst to thee from Egypt, from the nations and their gods?" 2 Samuel 7:23

"And ye [Israel] shall be holy unto me: for I the Lord am holy, and have SEVERED YOU FROM OTHER PEOPLE, that ye should be mine" Leviticus 20:26

"For thou [Israel] art an holy people unto the Lord thy God: the Lord thy God hath chosen thee to be a special people unto himself, ABOVE ALL PEOPLE that are upon the face of the earth." Deuteronomy 7:6

God has no love or interest for global-political organizations like the United Nations. Such institutions are Satan's business. On rare occasions, however, there *are* nations that actually "fear God" (Psa. 33:12). But in a few short generations the fear of those nations fades away and apostasy and rebellion takes over. Compare God's special love for Israel to what He says about the nations of the world:

"All nations before him are as nothing; and they are counted to him less than nothing, and vanity" Isaiah 40:17

5.) The Land of God - When God declared a piece of earthly real estate as His own, that tract of land was nowhere to be found on the North American continent. Africa, Antarctica, Europe, Australia and South America were never candidates either. God chose ONLY ONE piece of literal dirt as His own – the land of Israel. Note these verses of scripture showing God literally speaking to a piece of ground:

"Also, thou son of man, PROPHESY UNTO THE MOUNTAINS of Israel, and say, YE MOUNTAINS OF ISRAEL, HEAR THE WORD OF THE LORD: Thus saith the Lord God; Because the enemy hath said against you, Aha, even the ancient high places are ours in possession: Therefore prophesy and say, Thus saith the Lord God; Because they have made you desolate, and swallowed you up on every side, that ye might be a possession unto

the residue of the heathen, and ye are taken up in the lips of talkers, and are an infamy of the people: Therefore ye mountains of Israel, hear the word of the Lord God; Thus saith the Lord God to the mountains, and to the hills, to the rivers, and to the valleys, to the desolate wastes, and to the cities that are forsaken, which became a prey and derision to the residue of the heathen that are round about; Therefore thus saith the Lord God; Surely in the fire of my jealousy have I spoken against the heathen, and against all Idumea, which have appointed my land into their possession with the joy of all their heart, with despiteful minds, to cast it out for a prey." Ezekiel 36:1-5

6.) One Saviour - God chose ONLY ONE man to be the Saviour of mankind. Billions and billions of people have walked this earth, and many counterfeit "saviors" have been offered by man, but God chose only *one man* to be the true Saviour of the world. That man is the Lord Jesus Christ – God manifest in the flesh. Mary, Mohammed, Allah, Joseph Smith, Buddha, Krishna, the Pope and all the other fakers don't win, place or show.

"Jesus saith unto him, I am the way, the truth, and the life: no man cometh unto the Father, but by me." John 14:6

"For there is one God, and one mediator between God and men, the man Christ Jesus." 1 Timothy 2:5

"Wherefore God also hath highly exalted him, and given him a name which is above every name: That at the name of Jesus every knee should bow, of things in heaven, and

things in earth, and things under the earth; And that
every tongue should confess that Jesus Christ is Lord, to
the Glory of God the Father." Phillippians 2:9-11

These six outstanding examples clearly illustrate that God discriminates. It shows that God will often pick ONLY ONE to the exclusion of the vast majority. Many times the vast majority being left out can number into the billions, trillions or sextillions. Not only that, the cases in which God selects ONLY ONE are highly important, crucial events, such as: (1.) Populating a planet; (2.) Saving an inhabited world from total destruction; (3.) Creating a nation; and (4) providing a Saviour. None of these situations are trivial. All PLAY A MAJOR ROLE, and have a PROFOUND IMPACT on the history of mankind. In the following examples of godly discrimination, take into consideration the large number of those being excluded:

- God started the human race with only **ONE MAN**.
- God saved only **ONE MAN'S FAMILY** from a global flood.
- God chose only **ONE MAN** from which to raise up a nation.
- God picked only **ONE NATION** to be his chosen people.
- God chose only **ONE PIECE OF LAND** as His own.
- God chose only **ONE MAN** as the Saviour of the world.

Chapter 7 Summary

Contrary to both popular belief and wishful thinking, God does not treat everyone and everything the same. God separates, divides, differentiates, draws distinctions and discriminates in many cases. The word "selectivity" is defined as "the quality of carefully choosing someone or something as the best or most suitable." The Bible reveals that God's character exhibits this quality. It is the attribute of "godly discrimination". And believe it or not, on the other hand, there's *only one real example* of God demonstrating the use of equal-measured treatment across the board.

"[9] That if thou shalt confess with thy mouth the Lord Jesus, and shalt believe in thine heart that God hath raised him from the dead, thou shalt be saved. [10] For with the heart man believeth unto righteousness; and with the mouth confession is made unto salvation. [11] For the scripture saith, WHOSOEVER believeth on him shall not be ashamed. [12] For THERE IS NO DIFFERENCE between the Jew and the Greek: for the same Lord over ALL is rich unto ALL THAT CALL UPON HIM. [13] For WHOSOEVER shall call upon the name of the Lord shall be saved." Romans 10:9-13

In the scriptures quoted above, note especially the *rare use* of the words *"there is no difference"* (see also Rom. 3:22). Over the years, whether through scriptural ignorance, infidelity or political and religious expediency, men have extrapolated this one-time, indiscriminate behavior of God and wrongly applied it to all or most of his actions. The Rev. Billy Graham is reported as saying:

"Our solar system is just one of billions in God's colossal Creation – and I find it very hard to believe He would have created only one living planet, Earth." [2]

However, this instance of God proclaiming, *"there is no difference"* is a *singular unique event* (that's why it's called "salvation" – it's offered to all that will receive it). Yet, as our examples have shown, there's no real reason why any Bible-reader should find the act of God creating only one inhabited world as *"very hard to believe"*. The Creator's behavior of discrimination, along with special selection and separation, sets the precedent for understanding the truth behind the question of other inhabited worlds.

[2] Stewart, Josh. "Billy Graham on ET." Chronicles of the Voyager. Blogger, 30 Jun 2011. <http://voyager-chronicles.blogspot.com/2011_06_01_archive.html>.

8

Earth:
God's Chosen Planet

"When I consider thy heavens, the work of thy fingers, the moon and the stars, which thou hast ordained; What is man, that thou art mindful of him? and the son of man, that thou visitest him?" Psalms 8:3-4

"The LORD looketh from heaven; he beholdeth all the sons of men. From the place of his habitation he looketh upon all the inhabitants of the earth." Psalms 33:13-14

I n chapter seven we discovered, much to the chagrin of our politically correct society, that God discriminates. However, this is not the unjust or "prejudicial" type of judgement that the modern news media so often loves to inflame. God does not unjustly pre-judge anything. God IS the judge. As it is written; *"Shall not the Judge of all the earth do right?"* (Gen. 18:25) When God selects only one to the exclusion of billions (or pick your own colossal number), this baffles modern man. But, as we have learned, rejecting the "many" while receiving the "few" is standard operating procedure for God in many cases. Clearly, as we've already emphasized, the ways of God are not the ways of man.

> *"Enter ye in at the strait gate: for wide is the gate, and BROAD IS THE WAY that leadeth to DESTRUCTION, and MANY there be which go in thereat: Because strait is the gate, and NARROW IS THE WAY, which leadeth unto LIFE, and FEW there be that find it." Matthew 7:13-14*

When we look at the Universe we see that it is literally filled with an incalculable number of stars and planets (science has supposedly numbered the current visible stars at 300 sextillion – 3 followed by 23 zeros). Seeing this great expanse and all this "extra room" we think to ourselves, *"Surely there must be someone or something else out there."* Some even consider the possibility that God could have placed intelligent life on other planets – life drastically different than that found on Earth. Is any of this possible? When dealing with funny-bunnies like "evolution by means of natural selection" (the spontaneous and meaningless self-generation of life), I guess anything *is* possible. But when dealing with Bible truth a few facts need to be taken into consideration before jumping to conclusions:

> **FACT 1** - God *limits his actions* to the confines of His written word. This means that there's no need to entertain thoughts of God's "creative freedom" (see chapter 6).

> **FACT 2** - God, in many important instances, *chooses only one* in exclusion to the vast majority (see chapter 7).

> **FACT 3** - The scriptures reveal that God is favorably predisposed towards planet Earth.

Regardless of whether outer space is filled with other heavenly bodies, the Earth is unquestionably God's favorite. This partiality towards our planet is made evident by the following Bible proof texts:

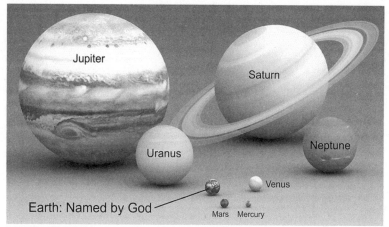

Jupiter

Saturn

Uranus

Neptune

Venus

Earth: Named by God

Mars   Mercury

IMAGE/public domain   God named the Earth, but man named the other planets.

PROOF 1 - The First Planet: Earth was the first planet created by God. According to the scriptures, the Earth was even created before the Sun, Moon or any of the stars.

"In the beginning God created the heaven and the earth."
Genesis 1:1

"And God made two great lights; the greater light to rule the day, and the lesser light to rule the night: he made the stars also." Genesis 1:16

PROOF 2 - Named by God: It is God Himself who names this planet "Earth". God did not name Mercury; God did not name Venus; God did not name Mars; God did not name Jupiter; God did not name Saturn; God did not name Uranus; God did not name Neptune, and God did not name the now-defunct "planet" of Pluto (now labeled a plutoid "Dwarf Planet"). All the other planets in our solar system were named by man in honor of false gods.

"And God called the dry land Earth; and the gathering together of the waters called he Seas" Genesis 1:10

PROOF 3 - Created to be Inhabited: The Earth was intentionally created to be inhabited by man. The Earth's breathable atmosphere, distance from the Sun, etc., did not come about by chance or *"the multifarious, accidental, random and purposeless congregation and coalescence of atoms"*.[1]

"For thus saith the Lord that created the heavens; God himself that formed the earth and made it; he hath established it, he created it not in vain, HE FORMED IT TO BE INHABITED; I am the Lord; and there is none else." Isaiah 45:18

"The heaven, even the heavens, are the Lord's: but the earth hath he given to the children of men." Psalms 115:16

PROOF 4 - The Stars are Ours: The Sun, Moon and all the stars in the Universe – that is, ALL THE STARS in the Universe – were created only for the benefit of the Earth. Any other planets which may consequently soak-in a sunbeam, moonbeam or grab some passing starlight are simply profiting from rewards designed exclusively for planet Earth. Modern science hates this concept, and anyone professing such is viewed as a "mad man". Who cares? Fret not brethren, we're in good company (Acts 26:25).

[1] Titus Lucretius Carus, On the Nature of the Universe, trans. and introduced by R. E. Latham (Middlesex: Penguin Books, 1975), 90-93.

The Secret Name of the Stars

IMAGE/Jeff Mardis

The scriptures clearly teach that God named the stars (Psa. 147:4). However, this naming of the stars is not as important as God's naming of the Earth. This is apparent for a couple of reasons:

First, after the waters are divided in Genesis, the Earth is intentionally singled-out and named by God, *"And God called the dry land Earth..."* (Gen. 1:10). Yet, an incalculable number of stars are relegated to a sort of footnote status, *"... he made the stars also"* (Gen. 1:16). Ironically, while it's clear that the Lord has named the stars (Psa. 147:4), no star-names are mentioned in Genesis or anywhere else (other than names given to them by men – see Job 9:2-10 & 38:31-33).

Secondly, Psalms 147:4 has a double meaning. The word "stars" can also refer to "angels" (Rev. 1:20), and according to Judges 13:17-18, angel names can be "secret". In other words, BOTH STARS AND ANGELS HAVE NAMES, but the vast majority of those names have never been revealed to man. The multitude of stars is simply a typology of the *"innumerable company of angels"* (Heb. 12:22):

"...so many as the stars of the sky in multitude, and as the sand which is by the sea shore innumerable." Heb. 11:12

"And God said, Let there be lights in the firmament of the heaven to divide the day from the night; and let them be for signs, and for seasons, and for days, and years: And let them be for lights in the firmament of the heaven to GIVE LIGHT UPON THE EARTH: and it was so. And God made two great lights; the greater light to rule the day, and the lesser light to rule the night: he made the stars also. And God set them in the firmament of the heaven to GIVE LIGHT UPON THE EARTH, And to rule over the day and over the night, and to divide the light from the darkness: and God saw that it was good."
Genesis 1:14-18

Notice that "light" is not the only purpose for the Sun, Moon and stars. Genesis 1:14-18 shows that they were also designed for "signs, seasons, days, years," and to act as "dividers".

PROOF 5 - Home of God's Eternal Kingdom: The Earth is destined to become the home of God's eternal Kingdom. This is one of the most powerful biblical proof texts explaining God's partiality and favoritism towards this planet.

"And in the days of these kings shall the God of heaven set up a kingdom, which shall never be destroyed: and the kingdom shall not be left to other people, but it shall break in pieces and consume all these kingdoms, and it shall stand for ever." Daniel 2:44

"And I John saw the holy city, new Jerusalem, coming down from God out of heaven, prepared as a bride

adorned for her husband. And I heard a great voice out of heaven saying, Behold, the tabernacle of God is with men, and he will dwell with them, and they shall be his people, and God himself shall be with them, and be their God. And the nations of them which are saved shall walk in the light of it: and the kings of the earth do bring their glory and honour into it." Revelation 21:2-3 & 24

"Behold, the days come, saith the Lord, that I will raise unto David a righteous Branch, and a King shall reign and prosper, and shall execute judgement and justice in the earth. In his days Judah shall be saved, and Israel shall dwell safely: and this is his name whereby he shall be called, THE LORD OUR RIGHTEOUSNESS." Jeremiah 23:5-6

"And the Lord shall be KING OVER ALL THE EARTH: in that day shall there be one Lord, and his name one. And it shall be, that whoso will not come up of all the families of the earth unto Jerusalem to worship the King, the Lord of hosts, even upon them shall be no rain." Zechariah 14:9 & 17

God Himself plans one day to literally, physically and permanently set His throne upon planet Earth. When this is done, this will make Earth the headquarters and home of the Creator of the Universe. The Universe will become "geocentric" (spiritually speaking). Now how do you think the "aliens" and "saucer-men" feel about that? I mean, after all, what's wrong with THEIR planet? Isn't it "just as good" as planet Earth? No, as a matter of fact it's not. God did not choose planet Earth because it is "special", the Earth is "special" because it is chosen by God. To blazes with Mars, Jupiter and Planet-X. God is not concerned with them. Mankind has a really bad problem, a severe "hang-up" with the fact that God does not treat everything the same. Mankind *demands* that God see things the way they see things, but this is not possible. God is holy and man is not. To insist that "all things are equal" is madness. The root of man's fear lies in the fact that one day all men will be judged, and it is God Himself who will declare some of those men "righteous" while the others will be condemned to eternal damnation. Man's obsession with "equality" (especially the unsaved man's obsession) is rooted in the fact that God will choose the born-again, blood-bought Christian for salvation to the exclusion of all others. God is resented for making this "unfair" choice and thus man demands the equality of all things. Mars IS as good as Earth. The only reason life showed up here is because of "random chance" and a fortunate "fluke of nature". Life could've just as easily appeared anywhere on a million different worlds – right? Sure, why not. If you completely ignore God's words, what makes the Earth any different? It's just one grain of sand on the shorelines of the Universe.

The following is a breakdown of biblical word usage concerning stars, planets and other heavenly bodies comparing the number of times these words appear in the scriptures:

- **Mercury** - appears zero times in the Bible. However, the word "Mercurius" appears once in Acts 14:12 in reference to the Roman god "Mercury".

- **Earth** - appears 982 times.

- **Mars** - appears one time. This one-time appearance is in reference to an Athens landmark to the Roman god "Mars", not a direct reference to the planet (Acts 17:22).

- **Jupiter** - appears three times. Two of these occurrences refer to the Roman god "Jupiter" (see Acts 14:12-13), and the other is a direct reference to the planet (Acts 19:35).

- **Sun** - appears 159 times.

- **Moon(s)** - appears 63 times .

- **Star(s)** - appears 66 times.

The words *Venus, Saturn, Uranus, Neptune,* and *Pluto* appear nowhere in the Bible, while the word "planets" (which includes every planet in the Universe except the Earth) appears only once. The Book of Job mentions four star constellations; Pleiades, Orion, Mazzaroth and Arcturus.

> *"Canst thou bind the sweet influences of Pleiades, or loose the bands of Orion? Canst thou bring forth Mazzaroth in his season? or canst thou guide Arcturus with his sons? Knowest thou the ordinances of heaven? canst thou set the dominion thereof in the earth?" Job 38:31-33*

The final analysis is: The Bible only mentions two planets directly by name; one is Earth and the other is Jupiter. The Earth is mentioned 982 times, while Jupiter is mentioned only once (How's that for a lopsided figure? 982 to 1). All the other planets in the Universe are summed up in one word – "planets" (2 Kings 23:5). Other heavenly bodies like the Sun, Moon, stars and star constellations appear a total of 280 combined times. This should be expected, however, for as we have discovered, it is consistent with God's behavior of CHOOSING ONLY ONE over the majority. Just as God did not interact personally with any other nation other than Israel (His chosen people), so too, *God does not interact personally with any other planet* in the Universe other than planet Earth. And as the Lord said of Israel; *"And ye shall be holy unto me: for I the Lord am holy, and have severed you from other people, that ye should be mine.";* it is also written of the Earth; *"The earth is the Lord's, and the fulness thereof; the world, and they that dwell therein"* (see Lev. 20:26 & Psa. 24:1). So much for the "Martians".

Earth: Compass of the Universe

The fact that planet Earth is the focal point of God and the sky and atmosphere surrounding the Earth are classified as the "first heaven", anchors the Earth in space as the center of the entire Universe. In relation to Earth, Heaven, the Home of God, is located "up" (Jer. 51:53, Amos 9:2, Matt. 14:19, John 3:13, Rev. 11:12, etc.). You can point "up" with your finger. The direction

IMAGE/public domain

Circumpolar image appearing to circle the North Star. North is the absolute direction of God and Heaven.

of God is not only "up" from Earth, but "north" (Job 26:7, Psa. 48:2, Isa. 14:13, Psa. 75:6-7, etc.). The Earth's North Pole points northward through outer space towards the dwelling place of God (an imaginary line stretching the breadth of the three heavens). Contrary to popular thought that direction in space is relative, North is an absolute direction which can only be located by using the Earth as a universal compass. If you walk outside at night and find the North Star, THAT is the direction of Heaven. True "North", the direction of God, is only found by locating planet Earth. In other words, to find God Himself, you must first find planet Earth.

Chapter 8 Summary

The old clichéd argument is that the vast size of the Universe renders the Earth so infinitesimally small, that it's impossible, and even absurd, to believe that God would be concerned with this planet alone. The point the Christian must understand, however, is that vast numbers are meaningless to God. While God rightfully understands that such numberings impact man (Gen. 13:16, 15:5, 32:12, Jer. 33:22, Hos. 1:10, etc.), when it comes to God, astronomical numbers have no significance when placed alongside ETERNITY. In science, huge mind-bending numbers thrown about in a effort to prove that God is or is not concerned with something is a moot point. In other words, one cannot argue that 300 sextillion stars and planets "proves that the Earth holds no significance to God". It proves no such thing. It proves there are a lot of stars – that's it. The apostle Peter gave us an example of comparing large numbers with the Lord when he wrote:

> *"But, beloved, be not ignorant of this one thing, that one day is with the Lord as a thousand years, and a thousand years as one day."* 2Peter 3:8

For man, much of the time large numbers hold significance and meaning, and God knows this (Gen. 15:5). One book of the Bible is even called "Numbers". But, as chapters 7 and 8 have demonstrated, huge numbers DO NOT IMPACT GOD'S ACTIONS OR BEHAVIOR. Many times the Lord utilizes such vastness to simply *"confound the wise"* (1Cor. 1:27). The truth is, God is going to work with whatever He chooses (Earth, mankind, Israel, etc.). *That's* what makes a thing significant. *God* makes a thing significant, for it is God Himself that created innumerable heavenly bodies, and yet it is the same Holy God that *chose only one* upon which to focus His attention.

"When I consider thy heavens, the work of thy fingers, the moon and the stars, which thou hast ordained; What is man, that thou art mindful of him? and the son of man, that thou visitest him?"
Psalms 8:3-4

9

Outer Space:
No Man's Land

T he Holy Bible does not contain the words "outer space", nor does it contain the words "universe" or "cosmos". For many, this is an obvious indicator that God has nothing to say on the matter. The problem, however, is that most people have no understanding of the biblical wording used to describe the Universe. And with over 200 English Bibles on the market since the publication of the *King James Bible* (NIV, NKJV, QJV, etc.), the confusion surrounding exact wording grows on a daily basis. If we truly desire God's word to teach us its Truth, it's incumbent upon us that we realign our thinking to match its words (John 8:47). For the modern twenty-first century, English-speaking man, those "words" can be found in a *King James Bible*. Sure, we may not be able to find outer space, Universe or cosmos, but there are other words.

> *"[6] And God said, Let there be a FIRMAMENT in the MIDST of the waters, and LET IT DIVIDE the waters from the waters. [7] And God made the firmament, and divided the waters which were under the firmament*

from the waters which were above the firmament: and it was so. [8] And God called the FIRMAMENT HEAVEN. And the evening and the morning were the second day. [9] And God said, Let the waters under the HEAVEN be gathered together unto one place, and let the dry land appear: and it was so. [10] And God called the dry land Earth; and the gathering together of the waters called he Seas: and God saw that it was good. [11] And God said, Let the earth bring forth grass, the herb yielding seed, and the fruit tree yielding fruit after his kind, whose seed is in itself, upon the earth: and it was so. [12] And the earth brought forth grass, and herb yielding seed after his kind, and the tree yielding fruit, whose seed was in itself, after his kind: and God saw that it was good. [13] And the evening and the morning were the third day. [14] And God said, Let there be LIGHTS in the FIRMAMENT of the HEAVEN to divide the day from the night; and let them be for signs, and for seasons, and for days, and years: [15] And let them be for lights in the firmament of the heaven to give light upon the earth: and it was so. [16] And God made two great lights; the greater light to rule the day, and the lesser light to rule the night: he made the stars also. [17] And God SET THEM IN the FIRMAMENT of the HEAVEN to give light upon the earth, [18] And to rule over the day and over the night, and to divide the light from the darkness: and God saw that it was good. [19] And the evening and the morning were the fourth day." Genesis 1:6-19

This stretch of 14 verses reveals that God placed a "firmament" in the midst of covering waters. A firmament is an open expanse of empty SPACE. This firmament then divided the waters, resulting in bodies of water both "under" and "above" (Gen. 1:6-7). God called this firmament "Heaven" (Gen. 1:8), and placed a Sun, Moon, planets and stars WITHIN IT. We now have our biblical word for outer space – Heaven. But that's not all. The scriptures also show that Heaven is divided into THREE DISTINCT LEVELS:

"And God said, Let the waters bring forth abundantly the moving creature that hath life, and fowl that may fly above the earth in the OPEN FIRMAMENT OF HEAVEN." Genesis 1:20

Since it's not possible for birds to fly in the cold void of space, this can only mean that the Earth's atmosphere, located directly *"above the earth"*, is the first and lowest level of Heaven. This fact is verified by other scriptures which state that "clouds" are also located in "heaven".

"Look unto the HEAVENS, and see; and behold the CLOUDS which are higher than thou." Job 35:5

"Sing unto the LORD with thanksgiving; sing praise upon the harp unto our God: Who covereth the HEAVEN with CLOUDS, who prepareth rain for the earth, who maketh grass to grow upon the mountains." Psalms 147:7-8

"And then shall appear the sign of the Son of man in HEAVEN: and then shall all the tribes of the earth mourn, and they shall see the Son of man coming in the CLOUDS of HEAVEN with power and great glory." Matthew 24:30

Identifying the immediate atmosphere surrounding this planet as the first heaven is not without great significance. The designation establishes Earth as the center of the Universe. Not so much a "center" in terms of location, but in terms of importance. The first heaven belongs to the Earth. No other planet in the Universe can lay claim to this privilege.

The scriptures also describe a second and third heaven. Immediately beyond the Earth's atmosphere is outer space. Outer space is the "second heaven" and it encompasses the entire Universe. Even in modern times, outer space is frequently referred to as "the heavens". When the word "heavens" is placed in a biblical context, for many it conjures mental images of clouds and winged women strumming on harps. For the Bible-believer, however, this should not be the case. The Bible never literally labels outer space as a "second" heaven, yet the fact that the scriptures identify a first and "third heaven" logically indicates there is a second.

"The third heaven" is a biblical title which the apostle Paul attributes to the dwelling place of God. Like the first and second heavens, the third heaven is a literal, physical location containing (among other things) the Throne of God, the Lord Jesus Christ, and the giant cube city of New Jerusalem (see Chapter 13 for more information on the giant cube city):

> "I knew a man in Christ above fourteen years ago, (whether in the body, I cannot tell; or whether out of the body, I cannot tell: God knoweth;) such an one caught up to the THIRD HEAVEN." 2 Corinthians 12:2

Clearly, the Bible shows that there is a third level to heaven. King Solomon's prayer at the dedication of the House of the Lord best illustrates the fact that this "third" location is the actual dwelling place of God Almighty.

> "And hearken thou to the supplication of thy servant, and of thy people Israel, when they shall pray toward

this place: an hear thou in HEAVEN thy dwelling place: and when thou hearest, forgive." *1 Kings 8:30*

"Then hear thou in HEAVEN thy dwelling place, and forgive, and do, and give to every man according to his ways, whose heart thou knowest; (for thou, even thou only, knowest the hearts of all the children of men;)" *1 Kings 8:39*

"Hear thou in HEAVEN thy dwelling place, and do according to all that the stranger calleth to thee for: that all people of the earth may know thy name, to fear thee, as do thy people Israel; and that they may know that this house, which I have builded, is called by thy name." *1 Kings 8:43*

"Then hear thou their prayer and their supplication in HEAVEN thy dwelling place, and maintain their cause" *1 Kings 8:49*

"Hearken therefore unto the supplications of thy servant, and of thy people Israel, which they shall make toward this place: hear thou from thy dwelling place, even from HEAVEN; and when thou hearest, forgive." *2 Chron. 6:21*

"Then hear thou from HEAVEN thy dwelling place, and forgive, and render unto every man according unto all his ways, whose heart thou knowest; (for thou only knowest the hearts of the children of men:)" *2 Chron. 6:30*

"Then hear thou from the HEAVENS, even from thy dwelling place, and do according to all that the stranger

The Three Heavens Diagram

◄ The Third Heaven

The "Third Heaven" is a biblical term used by the apostle Paul in the second book of Corinthians (2Cor. 12:2). It is defined as the literal "dwelling place" of God. The Lord Jesus Christ, Moses, Elijah and Enoch are there right "now" in the flesh, as well as cherubim, angels, the spirits of the saved, and the giant city of New Jerusalem. It is the home of sinless life forms.

◄ The Second Heaven

The second level of Heaven begins at the rim of the Earth's atmosphere and continues into "outer space". This heaven, consisting mostly of darkness and sub-zero temperatures, is also filled with star constellations, planets and galaxies. The absence of a breathable atmosphere makes it impossilbe for life to dwell here without artificial means. It is a deadly realm for most all forms of life.

◄ The First Heaven

The first and lowest level of Heaven consists of the atmosphere surrounding planet Earth. It is an atmosphere unique from all other planets. Birds, clouds and men dwell here. The fact that it is considered the "first" heaven, anchors the Earth as the center of the universe. It is the home of fallen life forms.

calleth to thee for; that all people of the earth may know thy name, and fear thee, as doth thy people Israel, and may know that this house which I have built is called by thy name."   2 Chron. 6:33

"Then hear thou from the HEAVENS, even from thy dwelling place, their prayer and their supplications, and maintain their cause, and forgive thy people which have sinned against thee."   2 Chron. 6:39

Heaven thy dwelling place, heaven thy dwelling place, heaven thy dwelling place. Over and over again the Bible uses these words to describe the physical home of the Creator of the Universe. Earlier verses revealed that the "Heavens" can also contain birds, clouds, stars and planets. We can now say with authority that "heaven" is the biblical word for "outer space". And these heavens, as a whole, extend from the northern surface of the Earth all the way up to God's Throne. When the word "heaven" (singular) appears in scripture, it can refer to any one of these three levels. The context of the verse will dictate which of the three levels are being addressed. When the word "heavens" (plural) appears, it can be referring to any combination of two or more heavens. Again, the verse context will decide.

"Behold, the heaven and THE HEAVEN OF HEAVENS is the LORD's thy God, the earth also, with all that therein is."   Deuteronomy 10:14

Thou, even thou, art LORD alone; thou hast made heaven, the heaven of heavens, with all their host, the earth, and all things that are therein, the seas, and all that is therein, and thou preservest them all; and the host of heaven worshippeth thee."   Nehemiah 9:6

"To him that rideth upon the heavens of heavens, which were of old; lo, he doth send out his voice, and that a mighty voice." Psalms 68:33

"Praise him, ye heavens of heavens, and ye waters that be above the heavens." Psalms 148:4

At the Edge of the Universe

Like those educated in the public school system, I grew up thinking the Universe was infinite. I thought outer space was eternal in size and went on forever. I no longer believe that. As I began to read and study the Bible, and to conform my thinking to the words of God's Book, (instead of assuming that everything taught by man concerning science and astronomy was the truth), I started seeing scriptural hints that indicated otherwise. First, provided that the theory of an infinite Universe is true, if *"the whole creation groaneth and travaileth in pain"* (Rom. 8:22), it means that sin and the curse are infinite. Is sin endless in size? Does the curse go on forever? Nowhere in the Bible do we find such an implication. A holy, everlasting God can occupy eternity, but sin and death cannot. It, therefore, like the Universe which it has cursed, must have some sort of RESTRICTED SIZE:

"Of old hast thou laid the foundation of the earth: and the heavens are the work of thy hands. They shall perish, but thou shalt endure: yea, all of them shall wax old LIKE A GARMENT; AS A VESTURE shalt thou change them, and they shall be changed". Psalms 102:25-26

"Bless the LORD, O my soul. O LORD my God, thou art very great; thou art clothed with honor and majesty. Who coverest thyself with light as with a garment: who stretchest out the HEAVENS LIKE A CURTAIN". Psalms 104:1-2

"And, Thou, Lord, in the beginning hast laid the foundation of the earth; and the heavens are the works of thine hands: They shall perish; but thou remainest; and they all shall wax old as doth a GARMENT; And AS A VESTURE shalt thou FOLD THEM UP, and they shall be changed: but thou art the same, and thy years shall not fail." Hebrews 1:10-12

"And all the host of heaven shall be dissolved, and the heavens shall be ROLLED TOGETHER as a scroll: and all their host shall fall down, as the leaf falleth off from the vine, and as a falling fig from the fig tree." Isaiah 34:4

"And the heaven departed as a scroll when it is rolled together; and every mountain and island were moved out of their places." Rev. 6:14

"It is he that sitteth upon the circle of the earth, and the inhabitants thereof are as grasshoppers; that stretcheth out the HEAVENS AS A CURTAIN, and spreadeth them out AS A TENT to dwell in". Isaiah 40:22

Modern science many times uses the phrase "the fabric of space" or the "space-time fabric" in an attempt to define the construct of the Universe. But Bible-believers knew about this "fabric" way before they did. We're working backwards from *Special Revelation*, while they're working forwards from hypothesis and speculation. The Lord knows that most men can't understand the physics of space, so He uses scriptural similes to teach us the truths of reality. The scriptures say that the heavens are stretched out *"like a curtain"* or spread out *"like a tent"*. I can get that, and I know you can, too. Also note the above biblical wording; *"stretchest out the heavens like a curtain"*; *"as a vesture shalt thou fold them up"* and *"stretcheth out the heavens as a curtain, and spreadeth them out as a tent to dwell in"*. Have you seen any infinite-sized curtains or tents lately? No. Curtains and tents occupy a fixed, measurable amount of space. When the Lord created the Second Heaven (outer space) He spread them out *"as a tent"*. Without question the heavens are large. A size so immense that it's difficult to grasp. But God simplifies the matter by giving us something we can work with. We can't comprehend the size of the Universe, but we can easily understand the functions of a "tent". Tents are not infinite. Tents can be folded up and put away. Tents have tops, bottoms and sides. Tents can get old and wear out. The scriptures say of the heavens; *"as a vesture shalt thou fold them up"*. An infinite object cannot be folded up, it has no center point, and no edges. Garments, vestures, curtains, scrolls and tents, however, are another matter. A further detailed description of the garment-like construct of the cosmos is found is Isaiah where we find:

> *"I CLOTHE the heavens with BLACKNESS, and I make SACKCLOTH their covering." Isaiah 50:3*

This interesting passage reveals several nuggets of truth concerning Bible-based cosmology. It compares the black garment or "clothes" of heaven with that of a "sackcloth". These details will be examined much more closely in the next chapter.

Death Trap Outer Space

On July 20, 1969 NASA astronauts Edwin E. Aldrin Jr. and Neil A. Armstrong landed their Apollo 11 "Eagle" lunar module on the surface of the Moon. It was a mind-boggling feat, and a pinnacle in the history of mankind. However, no one ever thought to ask the question; "Should we go there?" Because most people are influenced by public education and television (and not scripture), they see nothing wrong with mankind going to the Moon (and this includes

The World's Deadliest Occupation

In order for man to set foot even on the nearest celestial body, it is required that he wear a specially made suit. A self-contained atmosphere, without which he would instantly suffocate, freeze and die. Not including other dangers related to the job, statistics show that the fatality rate of astronauts is unparalleled in the job world. The 2010 Bureau of Labor Statistics stated that the *"average*

IMAGE/NASA   Buzz Aldrin on the Moon (1969 AD)

rate of fatalities per 100,000 full-time equivalent workers is 3.5". That equals about 1 death for every 28,500 people. For the astronaut however, that number is many times greater. Since the beginning of the space age there have been about 540 astronauts worldwide (this number includes government and military trained astronauts, as well as commercial astronauts and spaceflight participants). Of those 540 spacefarers, there have been 18 recorded deaths. That equals 1 death for every 30 people – it's the world's deadliest occupation.

Cessna, Abby. "Astronauts." *Universe Today.* N.p., 30 Dec. 2009. Web. 23 Apr 2013. <http://www.universetoday.com/49018/astronauts/>.

most professing Christians). While there is no direct scriptural command or verse indicating whether man should physically explore the Moon (or any other planet for that matter), there *are scriptural indicators* showing God's view on the matter (NOTE: The majority of subjects to which we seek answers from the Bible will not have direct verse references – i.e. *"Thou shalt not smoke cigarettes"*, etc.).

The first thing to observe is where God has placed man's dominion, and the scriptures are clear, man's dominion is strictly relegated to the land, sea and air of PLANET EARTH (Gen. 1:26 & 28). As far as these three are concerned, man is free to explore them to his heart's content. Outer space, however, is a different matter.

Another important fact to consider is that WITHIN THE REALM OF MAN'S DOMINION, God has placed an atmosphere that's congruent to life (man, beasts, fowl, fish). That is, man can "breathe" (for the most part) when in his designated domain. And although man cannot breathe when under water, God has still, in no uncertain terms, declared that the oceans of Earth are under his authority. The same cannot be said for outer space. Most have never really considered the fact that God did not create outer space with an environment in agreement with life. Instead, outer space (which consists mostly of empty space) has a mean temperature of about -459° degrees Fahrenheit, an extreme temperature known as "Absolute Zero". Needless to say, anyone without a significant amount of protection and self-contained breathing equipment will immediately die. This is by design. This dark, deadly area IS PART OF THE ORIGINAL *"firmament"* PLACED BETWEEN THE WATERS in Genesis 1:6-7. While this may not be able to be read as an explicit "no" from the Lord, at the very least, it most certainly makes it more dangerous and more difficult for man. It is a very good indicator as to where our Creator does not want us to go.

Man became a *"living soul"* after God *"breathed into his nostrils the breath of life"* (Gen. 2:7). This too, is by design. Whenever man's breath is removed, the spirit leaves, and the body dies (Job 34:14-15, Psa. 104:29). When man enters outer space, this is exactly what happens. To say that such an extreme effect on man is insignificant, is to ignore one of its designed purposes. Outer space kills, and first and foremost by REMOVING man's "breath of life". However, lack of oxygen and temperature extremes are only a few of the problems man encounters when entering the realm outside of his established domain. According to research, three to five percent of body mass is lost during the first three to five days in space, a result of decreased fluid intake, metabolic imbalances and muscle atrophy.

> "There are many repercussions due to the lack of gravity, but the most serious effect on the human body is the deterioration of bones. With the removal of pressure on the skeletal structure, the body needs less calcium to support itself. ... The future possibilities for living in space for periods longer than six months are severely limited because of the EVENTUAL DETERIORATION of the skeletal structure. Research is ongoing to combat this LETHAL side effect to weightlessness." [1]

As stated, man is currently working to overcome these health risks. And the approaching mainstream of modern science is considering techniques that many view as taboo.

> "Why let a little thing like 'near-inhospitability of a planet' crush our dreams of solar system stretching Manifest Destiny? That...is where GENETIC ENGINEERING comes in. Human enhancement—CREATING a pre-adapted colonist—may be the only way to survive the initially hostile terrain of other planets." [2]

[1] "Space Flight: The Dangers of Weightlessness." 123HelpMe.com. 02 Dec 2012 <http://www.123HelpMe.com/view.asp?id=24488>.

When discussing the human colonization of Mars, Reason.com reports:

> *"A future for humans on Mars requires us to clear a conceptual hurdle, to accept that THE HUMAN FORM IS NOT A NORM or an ideal or even a default. It's how INTELLIGENT LIFE ADAPTED, with MANY INEFFICIENCIES, to a particular place. ... Looking around the solar system, we see nothing but worse planets. If we want to live there, we're going to need better humans."* [3]

In other words, to guarantee his survival, man must do one of two things if he wishes to explore space or go to another planet: (1.) artificially RECREATE EARTH'S ATMOSPHERE, or (2.) artificially RECREATE MAN. This not only includes breathable air and livable temperatures, but gravity, protection from speeding meteors, clouds of deadly "space dust" and cancer-causing cosmic rays. The longer man remains in space, the greater his chances of death. Prolonged activity in a weightless environment promotes muscle atrophy and loss of bone mass (this includes a weakened heart and the onset of osteoporosis). Currently, an astronaut's survival is entirely dependent upon his man-made equipment, inventions designed by man to counteract an environment designed by God. Eventually, science may decide to take the alternate route of RECREATING MAN (i.e. If the shoe doesn't fit – create a new foot). Regardless, for mankind, outer space remains a vast DEATH TRAP, a cosmic realm of environments created so extreme, that man is essentially

[2] Wlizlo, Will. "GMAs: Genetically Modified Astronauts." UTNE Reader. Ogden Publications, Inc., 16 2012. Web. 4 Jan 2013. <http://www.utne.com/Science-Technology/Genetically-Modified-Astronauts-Future-Of-Space-Colonization.aspx>.

[3] Cavanaugh, Tim. "Human Martians." Reason.com. Reason Foundation, 12 Feb. 2012. Web. 22 Mar 2013. <http://reason.com/archives/2012/01/27/human-martians>.

IMAGE/NASA Oficial Apollo 11 mission patch

This is the official NASA illustration of the Apollo 11 mission patch. It is a graphic representation of mankind's first successful venture to a realm outside of his established domain. However, most Christians are unaware that the scriptures actually prophesied of this event nearly 3,000 years ago. The prophecy is a virtual description of this image. It explicitly mentions the Eagle, the making of a nest and being among the stars (see Obadiah 1:4).

"quarantined" to the surface of planet Earth. The mystery of WHY GOD CREATED IT THIS WAY is a subject that will be addressed in the next chapter. Interestingly, when NASA's lunar module, the "Eagle", landed on the Moon, the prophet Obadiah had written nearly 3,000 years earlier:

> "Though thou EXALT THYSELF as the EAGLE, and though thou set thy nest AMONG the STARS, thence will I bring thee down, saith the Lord." Obadiah 1:4

"The heaven, even the heavens, are the LORD's: but the earth hath he given to the children of men." Psalms 115:16

As mentioned, there are no explicit scriptures forbidding manned space exploration. But there is *strong evidence to suggest otherwise.* While I believe in freedom and would be against any national laws forbidding such things, I also recognize that, for the Christian, the scriptures reign supreme, and we should be mindful of what it says regarding the matter. Really, it's only natural for fallen man to want to go there. After all, being without God and Christ, mankind has no hope (Eph. 2:12). And fallen man's desires are a reflection of THEIR FATHER'S DESIRES (Jn. 8:44, Isa. 14:13). Speaking of rocket design and manned space travel, Wernher von Braun, former Nazi Rocket Scientist, and chief architect of NASA's Saturn V rocket, said;

> *"It* [space travel] *will free man from his remaining chains, the chains of gravity which still tie him to this planet. It will open to him the gates of heaven. ... Don't tell me that man doesn't belong out there* [in space]. *Man belongs wherever he wants to go – and he'll do plenty well when he gets there."* [4]

This was the spirit and attitude which helped pioneer the modern space program. Sound familiar?

> *"...I will ascend into heaven, I will exalt my throne above the stars of God: I will sit also upon the mount of the congregation, in the sides of the north: I will ascend above the heights of the clouds; I will be like the most High." Isaiah 14:13-14*

But the Lord has an answer to this kind of arrogance and pomposity.

---

[4] Miller, Ron. *Extreme Aircraft.* Irvington, NY: Harper Collins Publishers, 2007. p 201

*"[1] Why do the heathen rage, and the people imagine
a vain thing? [2] The kings of the earth set themselves,
and the rulers take counsel together, against the LORD,
and against his anointed, saying, [3] Let us break their
bands asunder, and cast away their cords from us. [4]
He that sitteth in the heavens shall laugh: the Lord shall
have them in derision." Psalms 2:1-4*

Waters of Death, Waters of Life

Two features mark planet Earth as being unique among all
planets: (1) God *"formed it to be inhabited"* (Isa. 45:18); and (2)
God gave man *"dominion"* over it (Gen. 1:28). In contrast, no such
directive is found anywhere in scripture for outer space. Nowhere
is it found that the Lord formed outer space *"to be inhabited"*, and
nowhere do we find the Lord giving man dominion over it. Despite
this fact, some may still question the evidence that suggests that
outer space was primarily designed to kill (never mind the fact that
it's easily demonstrated), reasoning that the waters of planet Earth
are an equally deadly environment.

The official website for the Centers for Disease Control
and Prevention (CDC) states that *"about ten people die from
unintentional drowning"* every day.[5] For the US, that equals about
3,650 deaths annually. Considering those numbers, the position
seems legitimate. But when examined further, in light of scripture
and other outstanding facts, the argument has problems. There's
no dispute that the Earth's water environments *can* be dangerous
for man. They cover over 70% of the Earth's surface, occupy 99%
of its living space, and kill thousands of people annually. But to

---

[5] "Unintentional Drowning: Get the Facts." CDC. Centers for Disease
Control and Prevention, May 30, 2012. Web. 2 Jan 2013. <http://www.cdc.gov/
homeandrecreationalsafety/water-safety/waterinjuries-factsheet.html>.

IMAGE/Bigstockphoto.com   Man has dominion over all the seas and waterways of Earth.

While the environmental conditions of water are similar to that of outer space, in that they have the potential of removing man's "breath of life", the waterways of Earth are also drastically different. Seas and oceans are not only a part of man's proper domain, but they provide recreation, food and jobs, and an element vital to man's existence – water.

equate this danger with the hazards of space is to stretch the facts. Traveling into space puts man at much greater risk than traveling the high seas. Most importantly, the scriptures show that when man travels the oceans he is still WITHIN HIS PROPER DOMAIN. The seas and oceans are an environment sanctioned by God and specifically created for the inhabitants of planet Earth. Furthermore, the Lord commanded life to *"fill the waters in the seas"* (Gen. 1:22). No dominion is given to man beyond the First Heaven, and no such directive as *"fill the planets in the firmament"* is ever made regarding life for outer space. Was this an oversight on God's part, or was it simply consistent with its design? Some may argue that outer space only became deadly after the fall of man (Gen. 3), but that doesn't answer the question of why man's dominion and multiplication were restricted to the Earth BEFORE HE TRANSGRESSED (Gen. 1).

> *"[21] And God created great whales, and every living creature that moveth, which the waters brought forth abundantly, ... [22] And God blessed them, saying, Be*

fruitful, and multiply, and FILL THE WATERS IN THE
SEAS, and let fowl multiply in the earth. [23] And the
evening and the morning were the fifth day. ...[28] And
God blessed them, and God said unto them, Be fruitful,
and multiply, and replenish the earth, and subdue it:
and have DOMINION OVER the fish OF THE SEA, and
over the fowl of the air, and over every living thing that
moveth upon THE EARTH." Genesis 1:21-23 & 28

The oceans and seas not only provide an ideal environment suitable to pleasure-viewing and recreation (fishing, swimming, boating, etc.), but they also provide food (fish, etc.), minerals (salt, etc), natural resources (oil, natural gas, etc.), economic endeavors (fishing, real estate, entertainment, transportation, etc.) and, most of all, water, an element necessary to life. The main human danger shared by the two environments is their ability to kill by suffocation. Regardless of that fact, the waters of Earth offer mankind much more than death, and in most instances provide just the opposite.

Chapter 9 Summary

The Bible's word for outer space is "heaven". It is the Second Heaven within a three-tiered structure known collectively as the "Heavens". For man to step into outer space means certain death. Zero gravity, temperature extremes, cosmic rays, space dust, muscle atrophy, bone deterioration and an absence of oxygen represent some of its more severe threats. This deadly realm did not exist *"in the beginning"* (Gen. 1:1), but only arrived after a universal restructuring – after the arrival of darkness and the deep (Gen. 1:2-31). Why would God create outer space in such a way, and what significance does this hold for our study on extraterrestrial life? The answers to these questions will be uncovered in the next chapter.

"And the earth was without form, and void; and darkness was upon the face of the deep. And the Spirit of God moved upon the face of the waters."
Genesis 1:2

10

The Mystery & Origins of Darkness

"He revealeth the deep and secret things: he knoweth what is in the darkness, and the light dwelleth with him."
Daniel 2:22

I f readers can get a hold of the enormity and profoundness of the subject this chapter is about to tackle, it will go a long way in helping them to understand biblical cosmology and man's current place in the Universe. As far as I'm aware, there is no Bible study anywhere like the one you're about to read, especially when it comes to dealing with the reality of outer space and why it is the way it is. The study is simple, really, but its effects are far-reaching. After making this discovery, it helped reposition my thinking on the cosmos as a whole, and further helped to open other biblical truths and mysteries.

One of the classic questions many children ask their parents is, *"Why is the sky blue?"* And many parents rightfully respond, *"Because God made it that way."* The answer is short, sweet and right on target, and within the grasp of a simple child-like faith. The child understands that the power needed to create a blue sky is profound, and that that profundity can only be satisfied by an Almighty Creator. Likewise, an equally baffling question many children may ask is, *"Why is the sky black at night?"*. And just as the answer to the blue sky, many respond, *"Because God made it that way."* And yes, God did *"make it that way"*. But this chapter is going to tell you WHY God made it that way. The answer will probably change your impression of the Universe forever.

Darkness: King of the Universe

Have you ever considered the most prevalent condition in the Universe? Is it gravity? No. Is it light? No. Is it coldness? No, but you're getting "warmer". If your guess is "darkness" you are correct. Darkness, by far, is the most prevalent condition in the Universe. It has no competitors. You may be thinking to yourself, so what. But think about it for a moment. If it were not for the light of the Sun and stars, we would live in complete darkness. Have you ever realized that when nighttime falls, that *that* is the way things really are – THAT'S THE NORMAL STATE OF THE UNIVERSE? It is a condition which modern science describes as extending from Earth into the visible horizon, some 14 billion known light years in every direction (and undoubtedly farther). One "light year" is the distance light can travel in a year. Now try traveling at the speed of light for 14 billion years in ONE DIRECTION, and then you'll reach the "edge" of where our current technology extends. What this means is that, as far as our current technology allows us to see, DARKNESS EXTENDS FOR NEARLY 30 BILLION LIGHT YEARS from one side of the Universe to the other. It is all-consuming.

We only have 12 hours of sunlight by the mercy and grace of God. That being true, did you know that even though darkness is easily the dominant state of the Universe, God is never referred to as a

"Father of Darkness"? In light of the overwhelming facts, doesn't that seem kind of strange? Instead, the Bible states:

> *"Every GOOD gift and every PERFECT gift is from above, and cometh down from THE FATHER OF LIGHTS, with whom is no variableness, neither shadow of turning."*
> James 1:17

Note the words "good" and "perfect" are connected with God and light. God never calls the darkness "good" anywhere in the Bible. Even in Genesis 1:4-5 God only refers to the light as "good", and then it is SEPARATED FROM THE DARKNESS. Darkness is the one common denominator that's consistent throughout the Universe. It is everywhere and permeates everything. Light, on the other hand, must originate from a source. Sunlight comes from a source. Moonlight comes from a source. Starlight comes from a source. Any form of light, whether natural or artificial, in the current construct of this Universe, must originate from a source. Remove that source, and darkness reigns. Darkness has no source. Darkness just "is". The truth is, in spite of the Creator being a *"Father of lights"* (Jam. 1:7) in whom is *"no darkness at all"* (1Jn. 1:5), we live in PERPETUAL DARKNESS. That is reality and a very frightening thought.

Have you ever wondered why outer space is black, why it's consumed by darkness? Was it originally created that way "just because", or is there more going on here? If darkness was not created *"in the beginning"* (Gen. 1:1), where did it come from, and why? Do the scriptures portray darkness as something good? Why or why not? The remainder of this chapter will delve into more detail on this fascinating subject, how it relates to God, and the circumstances which surround its existence. This is an amazing and profound study, but once complete, you will have a better understanding of biblical cosmology, and why darkness is currently the ruling king of the Universe.

IMAGE/Bigstockphoto.com
Like the bruise of a wound, night is the open manifestation of a fallen Universe.

Did you ever consider that when the Sun goes down, you enter the true state of the Universe? Darkness permeates its entirety, making the light of the Sun, Moon and stars, insignificant by comparison. Although the scriptures reveal a lot regarding this condition, unfortunately, many fail to ever discover its purpose or meaning.

Seemingly Out of Nowhere

It may come as a surprise, but there is no biblical record of the direct "creation" of darkness. When light is created in Genesis 1:3, it is recorded; *"And God said, Let there be light: and there was light."* No such creative act is recorded for darkness. When darkness first appears in Genesis 1:2, it is just "there" and it is accompanied by "water". Why? We know that these two elements were not just always there, they had to have some sort of beginning. But from where does the water and darkness come, and why are they not the end result of a scriptural passage which reads:

> *"And God said let there be a great deep, and let darkness cover the deep: and it was so. And God saw the darkness and the deep, that they were good. And the evening and the morning were the first day."*

The reason the "darkness" of Genesis 1:2 is so important to our study, is because IT IS THE SAME DARKNESS which fills the firmament of Heaven in Genesis 1:6-8. IT IS THE SAME DARKNESS which currently pervades our Universe. And IT IS THE SAME DARKNESS into which the Lord, out of necessity, places the Sun, Moon and stars (see Gen. 1:14-18). There's a very good reason why such a passage explaining its origin does not exist. But the answer is not found in Genesis chapter 1. It can only be found by doing a biblical word-study of HOW, WHEN and WHY God uses the word "darkness". HOW does God use the word darkness? WHEN does God use the word darkness? WHY does God use the word darkness? By searching the scriptures and looking at *other instances* of how, when and why this word is used (i.e. by comparing scripture with scripture), we will then be able to determine why there is no biblical record of the "creation" of darkness, and why the word seemingly appears "out of nowhere" in the first book of the Bible. When this is done, we will have an answer to the meaning behind the existence of outer space, and in turn, a significant head start to understanding the kinds of life (if any) which dwell there.

Dark Matters in the Light of Scripture

"I form the light, and create darkness: I make peace, and create evil: I the LORD do all these things." Isaiah 45:7

While this verse is not a record of the creation of darkness, it does testify that God is its Author. The darkness of Genesis 1:2 was placed there for a reason. But the fact is, that reason is not immediately given. The question we need to ask ourselves is not does God create darkness, but under what circumstances does God use darkness. Do the scriptures use the word to signify the beginning of something, or does it mean something different? After all, "God is light", and only He existed in unrecorded eternity past. Perhaps darkness pictures something other than a beginning? If so, how would the Bible show this? Consider the following 30 salient verses and note the context, and other words used in conjunction with "darkness". This study will help demonstrate the Lord's consistent use of the word.

> **1.** - *"[21] And the LORD said unto Moses, Stretch out thine hand toward heaven, that there may be DARKNESS over the land of Egypt, even DARKNESS which may be felt. [22] And Moses stretched forth his hand toward heaven; and there was a thick DARKNESS in all the land of Egypt three days: [23] They saw not one another, neither rose any from his place for three days: but all the children of Israel had light in their dwellings." Exodus 10:21-23*

- Literal "darkness" is used as a judgement upon the enemies of God. Darkness is also used as divider between the people of God and the enemies of God.

2. - *"[19] And the angel of God, which went before the camp of Israel, removed and went behind them; and the pillar of the cloud went from before their face, and stood behind them: [20] And it came BETWEEN the camp of the Egyptians and the camp of Israel; and it was a cloud and DARKNESS to them, but it gave light by night to these: so that the one came not near the other all the night." Exodus 14:19-20*

- God uses darkness as a divider.

3. - *"And when they cried unto the LORD, he put DARKNESS BETWEEN you and the Egyptians, and brought the sea upon them, and covered them; and your eyes have seen what I have done in Egypt: and ye dwelt in the wilderness a long season." Joshua 24:7*

- Darkness is used as a divider and is associated with the judgment of God's enemies - especially a judgment of covering waters. Also note that, Pharaoh is a type of the Devil, and Egypt a type of the world (see Ezk. 29:3).

4. - *"Before I go whence I shall not return, even to the land of DARKNESS and the shadow of death; A land of DARKNESS, as DARKNESS itself; and of the shadow of death, WITHOUT ANY ORDER, and where the light is as DARKNESS." Job 10:21-22*

- Darkness is associated with "death" and being "without any order" (also see Gen. 1:2 for a cross reference).

5. - *"When I looked for good, then evil came unto me: and when I waited for light, there came DARKNESS." Job 30:26*

- Darkness is equated with "evil", and is shown as being the OPPOSITE of light and goodness.

6. - *"[21] For his eyes are upon the ways of man, and he seeth all his goings. [22] There is no DARKNESS, nor shadow of death, where the workers of iniquity may hide themselves." Job 34:21-22*

- Darkness is connected with death and the workers of iniquity.

7. - *"Thou hast laid me in the lowest pit, in DARKNESS, in the deeps." Psa. 88:6*

- Darkness is associated with "the pit" and "the deeps".

8. - *" [14] LORD, why castest thou off my soul? why hidest thou thy face from me? [15] I am afflicted and ready to die from my youth up: while I suffer thy terrors I am distracted. [16] Thy FIERCE WRATH goeth over me; thy terrors have cut me off. [17] They came round about me daily LIKE WATER; they compassed me about together. [18] Lover and friend hast thou put far from me, and mine acquaintance into DARKNESS." Psa. 88:14-18*

- Darkness is associated with God hiding his face from the guilty, affliction, death, terror, the "fierce wrath" of God pictured as covering "water", and the absence of friends and lovers.

9. - *" [10] Such as sit in DARKNESS and in the shadow of death, being bound in affliction and iron; [11] Because they REBELLED AGAINST THE WORDS of God, and contemned the counsel of the most High:" Psa. 107:10-11*

- Those that *"sit in darkness"* are associated with death, being bound and afflicted and *"because they rebelled against the words of God"*.

10. - *"The way of the wicked is as DARKNESS: they know not at what they stumble." Prov. 4:19*

- Darkness is likened unto "the way of the wicked".

11. - *"Woe unto them that call evil good, and good evil; that put DARKNESS for light, and light for DARKNESS; that put bitter for sweet, and sweet for bitter!" Isa. 5:20*

- Again, darkness is equated with "evil", and is shown as being the OPPOSITE of light and goodness.

12. - *"[1] I am the man that hath seen affliction by the rod of HIS WRATH. [2] He hath led me, and brought me INTO DARKNESS, but NOT INTO LIGHT. [3] Surely AGAINST ME is he turned; he turneth his hand AGAINST ME all the day." Lamentations 3:1-3*

- Darkness is intricately connected with God's wrath. Note the important statement; *"Surely against me is he turned; he turneth his hand against me all the day"*. For the full effect read the entire third chapter of Lamentations.

13. - *"[18] Woe unto you that desire the day of the LORD! to what end is it for you? the day of the LORD is DARKNESS, and not light. [19] As if a man did flee from a lion, and a bear met him; or went into the house, and leaned his hand on the wall, and a serpent bit him.*

[20] Shall not the day of the LORD be DARKNESS, and not light? even very DARK, and no brightness in it? [21] I hate, I despise your feast days, and I will not smell in your solemn assemblies. [22] Though ye offer me burnt offerings and your meat offerings, I will not accept them: neither will I regard the peace offerings of your fat beasts. [23] Take thou away from me the noise of thy songs; for I will not hear the melody of thy viols. [24] But LET JUDGEMENT RUN DOWN AS WATERS, and righteousness as a mighty stream." Amos 5:18-24

- Darkness is equated with the judgment of God, being hated by God, and being rejected by God. Note that the judgement of God is shown in the verse as running down *"as waters"*.

14. - *"But with an OVERRUNNING FLOOD he will MAKE AN UTTER END of the place thereof, and DARKNESS shall pursue HIS ENEMIES." Nahum 1:8*

- Again, this verse contains both darkness and water. Note the words *"make an utter end"*, and that darkness is associated with the *"enemies"* of God. This verse points to a clear answer surrounding the darkness of Genesis 1:2.

15. - *"That day is a day of wrath, a day of trouble and distress, a day of wasteness and desolation, a day of DARKNESS and gloominess, a day of clouds and thick DARKNESS" Zeph 1:15*

- Darkness is associated with wrath, trouble, distress, wasteness and desolation.

IMAGE/Bigstockphoto.com

Over and over again, we find the scriptures associating darkness with death, sin, evil, and other extremely negative aspects and conditions both physical and spiritual.

16. - *"Then said the king to the servants, Bind him hand and foot, and take him away, and cast him into outer DARKNESS; there shall be weeping and gnashing of teeth." Matthew 22:13*

- Darkness is connected with a "servant" being separated from the "king" – separation from God. The first servant to ever rebel against the Creator was Lucifer – not Adam.

17. - *"And cast ye the unprofitable servant into outer DARKNESS: there shall be weeping and gnashing of teeth." Matt. 25:30*

- Again, darkness is connected with casting out an *"unprofitable servant"*. Lucifer was the first (Ezk. 28:15).

18. - *"[45] Now from the sixth hour there was DARKNESS over all the land unto the ninth hour. [46] And about the ninth hour Jesus cried with a loud voice, saying, Eli, Eli, lama sabachthani? that is to say, My God, my God, why hast thou FORSAKEN ME?" Matthew 27:45-46*

- This is one of the most powerful, salient verses in all the Bible regarding this subject. Here is a clear, stark passage demonstrating that darkness represents being *"forsaken"* by God. The verse shows, from the mouth of the Lord Jesus Christ no less, that at the exact moment the Lord was bearing the sins of the world, SUPERNATURAL DARKNESS covered the land as God forsook Christ.

19. - *"[33] And when the sixth hour was come, there was DARKNESS over the whole land until the ninth hour. [34] And at the ninth hour Jesus cried with a loud voice, saying, Eloi, Eloi, lama sabachthani? which is, being interpreted, My God, my God, why hast thou FORSAKEN ME?" Mark 15:33-34*

- Mark reiterates the lessons of Matthew in showing that "darkness" appeared upon the land at the same instant the Lord Jesus Christ was "forsaken" by God. This was not just any kind of darkness, however. It was not the darkness of nightfall, for the scriptures are clear that this darkness appeared between the sixth and ninth hours, from 12 noon to 3 PM, *the brightest part of the day!* It was not a celestial eclipse, but something more profound.

20. - *"[52] Then Jesus said unto the chief priests, and captains of the temple, and the elders, which were come to him, Be ye come out, as against a thief, with swords and staves? [53] When I was daily with you in the temple, ye stretched forth no hands against me: but this is your hour, and the power of DARKNESS." Luke 22:52-53*

- This another one of the most salient verses in scripture regarding this subject. Darkness can signify a betrayal of God or Christ. Note especially in this context, that Christ refers to *"hands against me"* as being related to *"the power of darkness"*. The word "against" is used twice in the verse, meaning "in opposition to" or "hostile towards". Darkness signifies being "against" Christ.

21. - *"[44] And it was about the sixth hour, and there was a DARKNESS over all the earth until the ninth hour. [45] And the sun was darkened, and the veil of the temple was rent in the midst. [46] And when Jesus had cried with a loud voice, he said, Father, into thy hands I commend my spirit: and having said thus, he gave up the ghost." Luke 23:44-46*

- An outstanding verse showing darkness is connected with death. When Christ died on the cross, supernatural darkness covered the land for three hours.

22. - *"And this is the condemnation, that light is come into the world, and men loved DARKNESS rather than light, because their deeds were evil." John 3:19*

- Darkness is equated with evil.

23. - *"To open their eyes, and to turn them from DARKNESS to light, and from the POWER OF SATAN unto God, that they may receive forgiveness of sins, and inheritance among them which are sanctified by faith that is in me."* Acts 26:18

- Darkness is associated with being turned from light, and *"the power of Satan"*.

24. - *"[15] Be ye not unequally yoked together with unbelievers: for what fellowship hath righteousness with unrighteousness? and what communion hath light with DARKNESS? [16] And what concord hath Christ with Belial? or what part hath he that believeth with an infidel?"* 2 Cor. 6:14-15

- Darkness is connected with unbelief, unrighteousness, false gods, and infidelity. Note also that darkness and light have no *"communion"* – no common union. This is why God separates the two in Genesis 1:4.

25. - *"For we wrestle not against flesh and blood, but against principalities, against powers, against the rulers of the DARKNESS of this world, against spiritual wickedness in high places."* Eph. 6:12

- Darkness is associated with *"spiritual wickedness in high places"*. Another salient window into the big picture.

26. - *"[4] But ye, brethren, are not in DARKNESS, that that day should overtake you as a thief. [5] Ye are all the children of light, and the children of the day: we are not of the night, nor of DARKNESS. [9] For God hath not appointed us to wrath, but to obtain salvation by our Lord Jesus Christ."* 1Thess. 5:4,5&9

- Note how this verse shows the children of "darkness" are those "appointed" to God's wrath, while the "children of light" are not. Darkness has a direct connection to the wrath of God.

27. - *"For if God spared not the angels that sinned, but cast them down to hell, and delivered them into chains of DARKNESS, to be reserved unto judgment." 2 Peter 2:4*

- Darkness is associated with sin, judgment and hell.

28. - *"This then is the message which we have heard of him, and declare unto you, that God is light, and IN HIM IS NO DARKNESS AT ALL." 1 John 1:5*

- Another outstanding verse. God is light and not darkness. This means that wherever God dwells, there is no darkness – literal or spiritual. *"And the city had NO NEED OF THE SUN, neither of the moon, to shine in it: for THE GLORY OF GOD DID LIGHTEN IT, and THE LAMB IS THE LIGHT thereof." Revelation 21:23*

29. - *"And the angels which kept not their first estate, but left their own habitation, he hath reserved in everlasting chains under DARKNESS unto the JUDGMENT of the great day." Jude 1:6*

- Darkness is associated with rebellion against God, and the judgment of God.

30. - *"[13] Raging waves of the sea, foaming out their own shame; wandering stars, to whom is reserved the*

*blackness of DARKNESS for ever. [14] And Enoch also,
the seventh from Adam, prophesied of these, saying,
Behold, the Lord cometh with ten thousands of his saints.
[15] To execute judgment upon all, and to convince all
that are ungodly among them of all their ungodly deeds
which they have ungodly committed, and of all their hard
speeches which ungodly sinners have spoken against
him." Jude 1:13-15*

- Darkness is associated with ungodliness and the
judgment of God.

These 30 salient references represent only a partial list of the Bible's
total revelation on the subject. But I think it's fair to surmise that the
negative message surrounding the usage of the word is clear. While
these various meanings may not apply all at once, at least one or two
will apply in nearly all appearances of the word. To summarize, here
are the following reasons why God uses the word "darkness":

1. - To denote *death* or *a place of death*
2. - To denote *evil, sin, wickedness, hatred, unbelief,
   unrighteousness, infidelity* and *ungodliness*
3. - To denote *a place of judgment for sins*
4. - To denote *the Lord's wrath or judgment*
5. - To denote *a place of the enemies of God*
6. - To act as *a divider between the holy and unholy,*
   or *clean and unclean*
7. - To denote *being forsaken by God*
8. - To denote *betrayal against God or Christ*
9. - To denote *something secret or hidden*

When we lay down to sleep at "night" and close our eyes, we
symbolically enter the darkness in our vision and in our minds.
Because of this, according to the Lord Jesus Christ, "sleep" is a picture

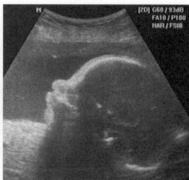

IMAGES/Bigstockphoto.com   LEFT: Man sleeping. RIGHT: Baby in womb
The Bible teaches that "sleeping" (especially at night in the darkness) is a type and
picture of death (Matt. 9:24, Mk. 5:39, Lk. 8:52). Likewise, a child in the womb is
submerged in water and darkness (Gen. 1:2) – a type and picture of sin and death
(Psa. 51:5). When the child is born, it enters the light – a type and picture of life.

of "death" (Matt. 9:24, Mk. 5:39, Lk. 8:52). A picture of entering
the darkness. When we awake with the morning Sun, it is a picture
of resurrection and life. A picture of EXITING THE DARKNESS
and ENTERING THE LIGHT. This is why Christ is called the *"day
star"* in 2 Peter 1:19. Every night we sleep, and then awake in the
morning, we show forth a constant picture of death and resurrection.
A picture of the Christian's Hope.

> *"...Lazarus SLEEPETH; but I go, that I may awake him
> out of SLEEP. ...Howbeit JESUS SPAKE OF HIS DEATH:
> but they thought that he had spoken of taking of rest in
> SLEEP." John 11:11-13*

> *"Then spake Jesus again unto them, saying, I am the
> light of the world: he that followeth me shall not walk in
> darkness, but shall have the LIGHT of LIFE." John 8:12*

So what does all this mean when dealing with outer space?
Does the blackness of space hold that big of a significance? Yes,
apparently. I believe when you understand WHY outer space is the

way it is, and understand HOW the Lord uses the word "darkness", and how God relates to "darkness" and "blackness", it opens up a whole new level of scriptural understanding. The truth is, regardless of how you may feel about it, regardless of what any evolutionist or creationist may think about it, *darkness always connotes something bad* (see the 9-point summary on page 212). This especially includes the circumstances of Genesis 1:2, since that is the first appearance of the word. Do you realize that when Genesis 1:31 states; *"And God saw every thing that he had made, and, behold, it was very good."* that this is NO REFERENCE to Genesis 1:2? How do you know, you ask? Because seven times in Genesis 1 the Lord blesses or declares what is "good" AS IT IS BEING MADE. Genesis 1:2 is not a record of the creation of darkness (And God said, let there be..."), but only a record of it's prior existence. It is therefore not a part of the "good". You now have a good foundation for understanding why that's so. But, we're not finished quite yet. To further undergird and strengthen our findings, consider the next biblical study regarding "sackcloth".

Sackcloth: The Covering of Heaven

"I clothe the heavens with blackness, and I make sackcloth their covering." Isaiah 50:3

This is a fascinating passage. It shows the reason the heavens are black is connected to THE SAME REASON sackcloth is used as a covering. A brief perusal of the Bible concerning the word "sackcloth" should reveal rich truths regarding the blackness of outer space, and help answer the question of "why" it is black. We are not going to reprint a large number of salient verses regarding "sackcloth" like we did with "darkness". You are free to search the scriptures yourself.

The word "sackcloth" appears 46 times in the *King James Bible*. All 46 references can be categorized under one or more of the following three headings:

1. - Mourning because of death (Gen. 37:34, 2 Sam. 3:31)

2. - Seeking mercy from judgment or repentance from sin (usually the judgment of God, chastening or imminent death). 1 Kgs. 20:31-32, 1 Kgs. 21:27, 2 Kgs. 6:30, 2 Kgs. 19:1-2, 1 Chr. 21:16, Est. 4:1-4, Job 16:15, Psa. 30:11, Psa. 35:13, Psa. 69:11, Isa. 3:24, Isa. 15:3, Isa. 20:2, Isa. 22:12, Isa. 32:11, Isa. 37:1-2, Isa. 58:5, Jer. 4:8, Jer. 6:26, Jer. 48:37, Jer. 49:3, Lam. 2:10, Ezk. 7:18, Ezk. 27:31, Dan. 9:3, Joel 1:8 & 13, Amos 8:10, Jon. 3:5-6, Jon. 3:8, Matt. 11:21, Lk. 10:13, Rev. 11:3

3. - Blackness or darkness due to the wrath of God (Isa. 50:3, Rev. 6:12)

With these scriptures in hand, we can now start to build a solid scripture-based answer regarding the reason darkness is the hallmark of outer space. When the heavens are *"clothed with blackness"* in Genesis 1:2, we learn by comparing scripture with scripture, that this is likened unto being covered with *"sackcloth"* (Isa. 50:3). Being covered with sackcloth, scripturally speaking, always carries with it a *negative connotation*. What these studies have pushed us to conclude, is that the reason outer space is black, is either because of *mourning, death, judgment, repentance from sin, or the wrath of God*. There are no other reasons. Your or my opinion means absolutely nothing next to the weight of God's words. This is what the scriptures teach, regardless of any preconceived ideas or how anyone feels about it. A few salient verses showing when and how God uses the word "sackcloth" include:

> *"Hear, O LORD, and have mercy upon me: LORD, be thou my helper. Thou hast turned for me my mourning into dancing: thou hast put off my SACKCLOTH, and girded me with gladness" Psalms 30:10-11*

Here the Psalmist shows that those wearing sackcloth are in "mourning", and are seeking "mercy" from the Lord. Note that the verse also reveals that being girt with "gladness" is the opposite of being clothed in sackcloth. This verse helps us to understand why the Lord never refers to darkness as something "good" in the first chapter of Genesis. God calls the light "good", but then separates it from the darkness (Gen. 1:3-4). Psalms 30:11 shows that the Lord will be "glad" with the heavens (i.e. the Second Heaven of outer space) only after it's sackcloth is put off – after the darkness is gone.

> *"For this gird you with SACKCLOTH, lament and howl:*
> *for the fierce anger of the LORD is not turned back from*
> *us." Jeremiah 4:8*

The prophet Jeremiah clearly shows the major reason for being girt with sackcloth: *"for the fierce anger of the LORD"*. In other words, those clothed in sackcloth are under the imminent judgment of God. So what else could it possibly mean when the Bible likewise states that "sackcloth" is the covering of heaven?

> *"[3] And I set my face unto the Lord God, to seek by prayer*
> *and supplications, with fasting, and SACKCLOTH, and*
> *ashes: [4] And I prayed unto the LORD my God, and*
> *made my confession, and said, O Lord, the great and*
> *dreadful God, keeping the covenant and mercy to them*
> *that love him, and to them that keep his commandments;*
> *[5] We have sinned, and have committed iniquity, and*
> *have done wickedly, and have rebelled, even by departing*
> *from thy precepts and from thy judgments". Dan. 9:3-5*

Note that Daniel was seeking mercy and wearing sackcloth when he stated; *"We have sinned, and have committed iniquity, and have done wickedly, and have rebelled, even by departing from thy precepts and from thy judgments"* (Dan. 9:5).

Another very important thing to consider, is when Judas came to betray Christ, do you know what the Lord Jesus said?

"When I was daily with you in the temple, ye stretched forth no hands against me: but this is your hour, and THE POWER OF DARKNESS." Luke 22:53

Note here that hands of betrayal were stretched forth against the Lord Jesus Christ, not *"daily"* during the light, but at night in the darkness (compare with Jn. 3:19-21). This event also mentions *"the power of darkness"*, a condition that God connected with *"the power of Satan"*, who is also said to wield *"the power of death"* (Acts 26:18, Heb. 2:14). This does not mean that Satan has the power to *create darkness*, but it does indicate that whenever the Lord FIRST INSTITUTED THE CONDITION, its purpose was in some way connected to the Devil. The fact that the Bible constantly uses the word in association with such negative things as sin, evil, wickedness, death, God's judgment, etc., helps us to understand this.

One profound point to remember is that the Bible depicts the Lord's Eternal Personage as exhibiting two primary features; *fire* and *light* (1Jn. 1:5, Heb. 12:29). This means that these two conditions existed in God in eternity-past, BEFORE THE CREATION of Heaven and Earth. Yet, when Genesis 1:2 appears, we are shown two conditions that are the EXACT OPPOSITE; *water* and *darkness*. Why?

In Genesis 1:1, only one Heaven and the Earth are present. At that time, God had direct fellowship with the Earth and HIS OWN LIGHT was predominant. Now, however, there are three Heavens and an Earth, with DARKNESS BETWEEN the Earth and the sinless Light of God. The standing of Earth changed from having only one Heaven and being near *"the glory of God"* (as in Rev. 21:23), to having three Heavens, dominant darkness, and the need for God to CREATE LIGHT apart from the eternal Light of Himself (Gen. 1:3).

IMAGE/Bigstockphoto.com   There's a purpose to the darkness of outer space, but what?

In the beginning the Heaven and Earth became part of a reality where the eternal, sinless Light of God had filled eternity-past (1John 1:5, Gen. 1:1). But something happened that changed everything (Gen. 1:2). This change set in motion God's plan to see that it would never happen again (1John 3:8, Gen. 1:3-31).

> "Bless the LORD, O my soul. O LORD my God, thou art very great; thou art clothed with honor and majesty. Who COVEREST THYSELF WITH LIGHT as with a garment: who stretchest out the HEAVENS LIKE A CURTAIN". Psalms 104:1-2

God covers Himself with Light. He is known as "the Father of lights" in whom is "no darkness at all" (Jam. 1:17, 1John 1:5). Between the Father of Lights and planet Earth is a veil of darkness, an outspread garment known in modern times as "outer space" or "the heavens". This garment is likened unto a tent, or the mourner's sackcloth which *separates a Holy God from a Universe under a curse.* Any living being on planet Earth which exits man's proscribed domain and enters this darkness, immediately encounters its power – *death!* When the Lord Jesus Christ died on the cross and was *"made to be sin"* and forsaken by God, he was surrounded by darkness for six hours (2Cor. 5:21, Matt. 27:46). Christ did this so that *"he might destroy him that had THE POWER OF DEATH, that is, the devil."* (Heb. 2:14) The veil of the temple was then rent from top to bottom, showing, among other things, that God had now provided mankind a Way back to the Home of God, *a Land of Light* which dwelt *on the other side of the veil of separation* (Glory to God!).

Events which lead up to this condition began long ago (the Bible is not specific on how long), at a time when Lucifer had a *"throne"* and held a position of authority in planet Earth (Isa. 14:13, Ezk. 28:5-18). After he sinned the first sin, and *"iniquity was found"* in him (Ezk. 28:15-16), he was deposed and his kingdom was judged by a massive flood of waters (Gen. 1:2). This region was then *separated from God, and replaced by DARKNESS.* A typological *"curtain"* or *"veil"* which DIVIDED a Holy God from a realm now marred by sin. This is why darkness and waters appear seemingly out of nowhere in Genesis 1:2. They are the *aftermath of the judgement* of Lucifer's former kingdom. This is also why it is recorded of the Lord:

> *"...he knoweth what is in the DARKNESS, and THE LIGHT DWELLETH WITH HIM." Daniel 2:22*

Today, Satan still has access to the Third Heaven, but *his primary dwelling place is in outer space*, a lifeless place marked by perpetual darkness. During the six days of Genesis, God must now CREATE LIGHT and *"replenish the earth"* (Gen. 1:3 & 28). But direct physical access to the Creator is now *blocked*. The darkness and judgmental remains of Genesis 1:2 becomes the deadly *"firmament"* into which outer space (the Second Heaven) is placed (see Gen. 1:6-19). *The*

Earth, with its new atmosphere (the First Heaven)**,** *becomes a solitary* **BUBBLE OF LIFE** *floating in a black lifeless sea of space and darkness.* Because of this, it is written:

> *"For we wrestle not against flesh and blood, but against principalities, against powers, against the RULERS OF THE DARKNESS of this world, against SPIRITUAL WICKEDNESS IN HIGH PLACES." Ephesians 6:12*

That is why outer space is perpetually dark. The same can also be SPIRITUALLY SAID of this world of sin. It is SIN that is predominant, and righteousness, truth and light must be PROVIDED. That "light" is the Lord Jesus Christ and His written word. Without the light of the word, the world would dwell in eternal darkness.

> *"We have also a more sure word of prophecy; whereunto ye do well that ye TAKE HEED, AS UNTO A LIGHT THAT SHINETH IN A DARK PLACE, until the day dawn, and the day star arise in your hearts".*   *2 Peter 1:19*

Chapter 10 Summary

Yes, both spiritual and physical darkness are currently the most prevalent condition in the Universe. It is a fallen Universe which resides *"in a dark place"*, cursed by sin, under the sway of *"the rulers of the darkness of this world"* and under the thumb of the one who betrayed Christ and who holds *"the power of darkness"*. Outer space is not simply pitch black for no reason. It is not simply pitch black "just because". It is not simply pitch black because God likes its decorative aesthetic when used in conjunction with glowing nebula and stars. No! The reason is much more profound than that. There is a *reason* and a *meaning* to the darkness, a reason put there by a God of design and order. Darkness is much more than simply the absence of light. *It is a type and picture of sin, death, betrayal, judgement*

IMAGE/Bigstockphoto.com   Scripture is the light that illuminates the darkness.

and being God-forsaken. And any living creature that steps out into this darkness (outer space) immediately dies (that's a demonstrable scientific fact – see chapter 9 for more information).

Regarding this issue, here's one last thing to think about: Many children, if not most (especially very young children 1-4 years old), are NATURALLY AFRAID OF THE DARK. Think about it. While parents simply excuse this attitude as childish foolishness, (or simply an unnecessary "fear of the unknown") could it be that these young children – those still in a state of "innocence" before God to whom sin has not yet been imputed – actually almost have a "sixth sense" of what darkness really is – something connected with evil. Only after they get older and more acquainted with sin, do they become accustomed to the darkness and no longer fear it. Maybe we have something to learn from this child-like fear of the dark?

Not to trivialize a serious matter, but an old black-and-white British thriller from 1957 makes similar sentiments regarding children and darkness. In the picture it is stated:

Deep Thoughts on the Deep

Although not covered specifically in this book, the scriptures reveal that there exists between the Second and Third Heavens a giant barrier of water known as "the Deep" (see Gen. 1:2&6, Job 38:30, Rev. 4:6). It is described directly by the Psalmist as *"waters that be above the heavens"* (Psa. 148:4). An immense body of water, the Deep is nearly all that remains of a catastrophic act of God that originally covered *"the world that then was"* (2Ptr. 3:6). Today, this past judgment is often referred to as "The Gap" – meaning *a gap of unspecified time* between the first two verses of Genesis. Much like our study on darkness, these details can be discovered by searching the scriptures for answers to WHY the earth is a formless void and a deep, black body of water is found in Genesis 1:2. When this is done, and scripture is compared with scripture, it is discovered that pitch-black, covering waters are not consistent with a CONSTRUCTIVE ACT of God, but a DESTRUCTIVE ACT of God. Things submerged under water are always a picture of God's judgment, and many times have a direct connection with darkness, death and the pit (This is not difficult to discover – see especially Gen. 1:2, 6:17, Psa. 36:6, Psa. 69:1-2 & 14-15, 88:6-7 & 16-17, Ezk. 26:19, Nah. 1:8, Jonah 2:2-5 and 2 Ptr. 3:5-7). Genesis shows this giant body of water is DIVIDED and a "firmament" (i.e. the known Universe) is placed BETWEEN the two parts (Gen. 1:6-17). The waters ABOVE the firmament become a partially-frozen *"sea of glass"* (Rev. 4:6), and the waters BELOW the firmament become the oceans and seas of planet Earth (Gen. 1:9-10). The biblical doctrine of "the Deep" is a deep subject, but such a study will reveal rich scriptural truths, not only on the structure of the Universe, but also on birth, baptism, sin and salvation.

"You could learn a lot from children. They believe in things in the dark until we tell them it's not so. Maybe we've been fooling them." – Night of the Demon, 1957

I believe that. When viewed through the lens of scripture the statement is true. The Lord knows *"what is in the darkness"* (Dan. 2:22). Many young children seem to sense it, but the majority of grown-ups ignore it (John 3:19, Eph. 6:12).

IMAGE/Bigstockphoto.com
Many young children have a natural fear of the dark. Could there be a legitimate reason? Scripture sure seems to support the idea.

Did you realize that there are easily four times as many scriptures which support the doctrine of darkness, as discussed here, than scriptures which support the Virgin Birth? There are approximately sixteen primary verses which undergird the doctrine that the Lord Jesus Christ was born of a virgin (Gen. 3:15, Isa. 7:14, Matt. 1:18-23, Luke 1:26-31, Lk.1:34-35, et. al.). But there are easily over 60 verses (and undoubtedly many more) which support the negative doctrine of darkness. Does this mean that the doctrine of darkness is "more important" than the Virgin Birth? No. It simply shows that some doctrines have more witnesses than others. But suppose I were to find a verse of scripture that appeared to put "darkness" in a positive context? Should I overthrow the weight of the majority of the other negative scriptures, simply because one verse may seem to be positive? Or should I interpret the majority of verses in the light of a single verse which may seem to point the opposite direction? I wouldn't recommend it. Trying to learn the meaning of a verse in a stand-alone context can invite *"private interpretation"* (2Ptr. 1:20). That is, reading a verse "privately", divorced from the light of the rest of scripture, can easily create doctrinal error. Instead, if the meaning of the context of a word or phrase is not readily apparent, it's much better to interpret that word or phrase in light of other verses dealing with the same word or phrase (scripture with scripture).

> *"[9] Whom shall he TEACH KNOWLEDGE? and whom shall he MAKE TO UNDERSTAND DOCTRINE? them that are WEANED from the MILK, and drawn from the breasts. [10] For precept must be upon precept, precept upon precept; line upon line, line upon line; here a little, and there a little". Isaiah 28:9-10*

> *"[13] For every one that useth MILK is UNSKILFUL in THE WORD of righteousness: for he is a BABE. [14] But strong meat belongeth to them that are of full age, even those who by reason of USE have their senses exercised TO DISCERN both good and evil.". Hebrews 5:23-14*

When dealing with Bible cosmology, the doctrine of darkness goes a long way in helping to explain the current state of the Universe. The doctrine helps explain WHY space is the way it is. And helps bring a reality to the Bible that makes the truths of scripture more real. It helps to show that darkness is not simply an "accident" or simply the "opposite of light", because we can witness its effects whether on earth (the darkness of nighttime) or in outer space (instant death without proper protection). And the frequency of verses which support the doctrine show that *the Lord is trying to teach us something* by having it appear again, and again, and again. The next chapter will cover the seven life classes found in scripture, as we continue our Bible study in search of what dwells beyond.

11

The Illustrated Field Guide
to Life Forms

"[16] For by him were all things created, that are in heaven, and that are in earth, visible and invisible, whether they be thrones, or dominions, or principalities, or powers: all things were created by him, and for him: [17] And he is before all things, and by him all things consist." Colossians 1:16-17

L ife is a complex issue. And because it deals with both the visible and invisible, it's not the easiest subject to understand. The scriptures clearly teach that God is the original Author. However, to better understand what we're about to cover, it's best to keep in mind that THINGS HAVE CHANGED since *"the beginning"* (Gen. 1:1). Things have changed since God *"ended his work"* and then *"rested"* (Gen. 2:2-3). A lot has changed as a matter of fact. The difference lies with the entry of sin. Not only the sin and fall of man (Gen. 3), but also the fall of the Adversary (Ezk. 28:14-17, Isa. 14:12-14, Gen. 1:2). Those who refuse to make distinctions where the Bible makes distinctions run the risk of error. In this case, error regarding that all modern things *"were created by him"* (John 1:3, Col. 1:16). What do I mean? God did not create sin. And because of that, God did not create the Devil IN HIS CURRENT STATE. God did not create man IN HIS CURRENT STATE. Things have changed. Yes, the Lord created *"all things"*, but only as they were in the beginning. We're no longer at the beginning. Times have changed. Sin and corruption have entered the creation, and as a result, other things have entered as well. Things pertaining to life forms with no original ties to a Holy God. Those who insist that "anything" and "everything" was created by the Lord AS IT IS TODAY (6 millennia after Genesis 3), have failed to make the distinction that God is Holy. The scriptures show that God *"ended"* His work when His creation was in a state which pleased Him (Gen. 2:2-3). However, those pleasing conditions have long since past (Gen. 1:31, 1 Jn. 5:19, Gal. 1:4), and many tend to forget this.

The information presented in this chapter represents the *core purpose* of this book. It was written specifically as a reference for Bible-believing Christians, and is a breakdown and analysis showing the KINDS OF LIFE FORMS outlined by scripture. It is the Bible's "field guide" to life forms, and constitutes the primary starting point for discerning the extraterrestrial phenomenon.

God: The Pattern for Life

God is the Eternal, Holy Creator and has no beginning. In Him rests the mysteries of life itself. He IS life, and without Him there would be no reality. The Bible says; *"...by him all things consist."* (Col. 1:17) He is the "Glue" of the Universe, and by His word the Universe and everything contained therein is held together. His great mercy and longsuffering withhold His hand from a world which continues to wax worse (2Tim. 3:13). The scriptures show He is a tripartite Being. One God consisting of three parts: a Spirit, a Soul and a Body (the

Holy Spirit, God the Father, and the Word; the Lord Jesus Christ – 1Jn. 5:7, 1Tim. 3:16). Because of this, life also follows this three-in-one pattern. Facts and functions of the tripartite life form are as follows:

THE SPIRIT - A spirit is an invisible, wind-like, living energy which originates from God. Its Greek roots come from the word "pneuma", meaning "that which is breathed or blown". It is the inhabitant, driver and life-giving-force of its "house" or "temple" – the physical body (Matt. 12:43-44, 1 Cor. 3:16-17, 2 Cor. 5:1-4, 6:16). If an organism has no spirit, it is technically (and scripturally) NOT ALIVE (trees, plants, micro-organisms, etc.). The Bible lists four different kinds of spirits:

1.) The Spirit of God (Holy Spirit or Ghost - 1John 5:7, etc.)
2.) The spirit of man (Ecc. 3:21)
3.) The spirit of beasts (Ecc. 3:21)
4.) The spirit of devils (unclean spirits - Matt. 10:1, etc.)

The spirits of men return to God at death, while the spirits of beasts go *"downward to the earth"* (Ecc. 3:21 & 12:3&7). The scriptures show that unclean spirits exist in a raw spectral or ghost form, without the benefit of a physical body (the Devil excluded). These spirits are constantly in search of living bodies to possess, whether it be man, animal or some other type being. The spirit, is the KEY COMPONENT OF ALL LIFE. It is what makes a living thing "alive". It is the difference-maker, in conjunction with the blood, between dead matter and living beings. The spirit is not scientifically testable, and therefore, not recognized by biological science. It is the stumbling block for all modern life sciences.

THE SOUL - A soul is defined by its Greek equivalent, the "psyche". It is connected with the seat of intellect and emotion (the heart), as well as the conscious mind (Matt. 22:37, Mk. 12:30,

Acts 4:32, et. al.). According to scripture, *"a living soul"* is created
only when A SPIRIT UNITES WITH THE BODY FOR WHICH IT
WAS CREATED (Gen. 2:7). This union (a body and spirit) creates
the spark which makes a soul. The soul then takes on an invisible
shape comparable to the body it inhabits (Lk. 16:22-24). The soul
is eternal. It represents YOU as an individual, and goes to Heaven
or Hell upon the death of the physical body (Psa. 16:10. Rev. 20:4).

THE BODY - A body is a physical, visible manifestation of life,
inhabited and powered by a spirit. Since this part of the tripartite
nature is visible and scientifically testable, it is the part to which we
can relate best. And just as there are differing spirits, the scriptures
teach there are different types of physical bodies. Not only physical
bodies of men, beasts, birds and fish, but mortal and immortal
bodies as well.

*"[39] All flesh is NOT THE SAME flesh: but there is one
kind of flesh of men, another flesh of beasts, another
of fishes, and another of birds. [40] There are also
celestial bodies, and bodies terrestrial: but the glory
of the celestial is one, and the glory of the terrestrial is
another." 1 Corinthians 15:39-40*

*"[51] Behold, I shew you a mystery; We shall not all
sleep, but we shall all be changed, [52] In a moment, in
the twinkling of an eye, at the last trump: for the trumpet
shall sound, and the dead shall be raised incorruptible, and
we shall be changed. [53] For this corruptible must put on
incorruption, and this mortal must put on immortality. [54]
So when this corruptible shall have put on incorruption,
and this mortal shall have put on immortality, then shall
be brought to pass the saying that is written, Death is
swallowed up in victory. [55] O death, where is thy sting?
O grave, where is thy victory?" 1 Corinthians 15:51-55*

THE BLOOD - And finally, as one might guess, the blood contributes some sort of mysterious and major part to life. In a way that I can't exactly explain or understand, it seems that the blood may not only be the "glue" responsible for tying the spirit, soul and body together, but it may also be the vehicle which perpetuates the sin nature of the flesh. In conjunction with the spirit, it is THE BLOOD THAT GIVES LIFE to the flesh, and the flesh, in turn, manifests the sin nature. Note the words of the following scriptures:

"For THE LIFE OF THE FLESH IS IN THE BLOOD: and I have given it to you upon the altar to make an atonement for your SOULS: for it is THE BLOOD that maketh an atonement for THE SOUL." Leviticus 17:11

"[19] Now the works of THE FLESH are manifest, which are these; Adultery, fornication, uncleanness, lasciviousness, [20] Idolatry, witchcraft, hatred, variance, emulations, wrath, strife, seditions, heresies, [21] Envyings, murders, drunkenness, revellings, and such like: of the which I tell you before, as I have also told you in time past, that they which do such things shall not inherit the kingdom of God." Galatians 5:19-21

"Among whom also we all had our conversation in times past in the LUSTS OF OUR FLESH, fulfilling the DESIRES OF THE FLESH and of the mind; and were BY NATURE THE CHILDREN OF WRATH, even as others." (Eph. 2:3)

"Then when LUST hath CONCEIVED, it BRINGETH FORTH SIN: and sin, when it is finished, BRINGETH FORTH DEATH." James 1:15

An interesting thing to consider, is that when the Lord Jesus Christ died on the cross, he had to SHED HIS BLOOD – he had to GET RID OF his blood – he had to REMOVE THE BLOOD FROM HIS BODY (the sinless blood of God - Acts 20:28, Eph. 1:7, Heb. 10:19). When this was done Christ said, *"It is finished: and he bowed his head, and gave up the ghost."* (John 19:30) Later, when the Glorified Body of the Lord Jesus Christ appeared, he spoke the following:

> *"Behold my HANDS and my FEET, that it is I myself: handle me, and see; for a spirit hath not FLESH AND BONES, AS YE SEE ME HAVE." (Luke 24:39)* Christ now made no profession of having blood. His holy blood was shed in our place that he might *"give his life a ransom for many" (Matt. 20:28, Mk. 10:45, et. al.).*

> *"For this is my BLOOD of the new testament, WHICH IS SHED for many for the remission of sins." Matthew 26:28*

> *"And he said unto them, This is my BLOOD of the new testament, WHICH IS SHED for many." Mark 14:24*

> *"Likewise also the cup after supper, saying, This cup is the new testament in my BLOOD, WHICH IS SHED for you." Luke 22:20*

> *"And almost all things are by the law purged with blood; and without SHEDDING OF BLOOD is no remission [of sins]." Hebrews 9:22*

Note how many times the words "shed" and "blood" come together when dealing with salvation from sin. All the Old Testament animal sacrifices were a picture of this. A picture of POURING BLOOD OUT OF A BODY. The point is, for some reason, the scriptures point to the fact that the blood must be emptied from the body in order to defeat the sin nature. And yet, on the same hand, blood is tied to our LIFE. The Lord Jesus Christ, the one who IS LIFE (John 1:4, 11:25, 14:6, et. al.), when it came time to give His life a *"ransom for many"*, He did not put his Holy Blood INTO His body to save us, He took it OUT. The average man cannot shed his own sinful blood and live – he will die. Only the Lord Jesus Christ could accomplish such a feat. Christ arose without blood, because His blood was shed for us:

> *"But now in Christ Jesus ye who sometimes were far off are MADE NIGH BY THE BLOOD of Christ." Eph. 2:13*

> *"And, having made peace THROUGH THE BLOOD of his cross, by him to reconcile all things unto himself; by him, I say, whether they be things in earth, or things in heaven." Colossians 1:20*

The spirit, soul, body and blood comprise a series of deep, mysterious subjects. The exact nature of their intricacies, and how they interrelate remain difficult to understand. Nevertheless, the light of scripture has revealed truth which science, up till now, can only partially provide (barely even half of the total picture). Although we've only scratched the surface, this quick overview was necessary in order to lay a proper foundation for the study and meaning of life.

The Seven Classes of Life

Each life form listed in the following section represents a separate and distinct class of life. Each class is known as "strange flesh" in relation to the other. Any cross-mixing of the groups produces a counterfeit form of life, at variance with the Creator's original guidelines as found in the first chapter of Genesis. This taboo boundary between the life classes is seen in such scriptures as: Gen.

6:1-7, Ex. 22:19, Lev. 18:23, Lev. 20:15-16 and 1Cor. 11:9-10. The counterfeit classification does not necessarily have to be the product of a PHYSICAL PROCREATIVE UNION, but a forced genetic mixing between the groups and sub-groups, such as those found in modern laboratories, will apply as well (more on this in chapter 14).

Instead of seeing man as being separate and distinct from the animal, modern science erroneously classifies him as being part of a long, unbroken chain of "evolved" life with supposed "missing links" in-between. This hypothetical view immediately puts modern science at a disadvantage. Because it merges life groups that are NOT THE SAME, any scientific research or conclusion built upon this false theory is automatically wrong. The bottom line is this: God created SEPARATE AND DISTINCT classes and sub-classes of life – man should not try to UNITE what God has DIVIDED. The end result always equals confusion and disaster, and in this case will eventually trigger the wrath of God.

On the pages which follow is an illustrated guide to life forms as outlined by the revelation of Holy Scripture. All seven life classifications are organized by the following six categories:

1.) CLASSIFICATION: Name of group to which the life form belongs.

2.) ORIGINS: Tells whether the life form is a creation of God or made by some other means. ALL LEGITIMATE LIFE FORMS were originally direct creations of God (Gen. 1). Now, however, legitimate life can arise in only one of two ways: (1) Direct Creation, or (2) After its Kind. A Being that is a "Direct Creation" has no parents, but is manifest by a direct command by the word of God (i.e. "Let there be angels." or some similar spoken directive). Examples of the Creator's ability to "speak" things into existence is found numerous times throughout the first chapter of Genesis. A Being made "After it's Kind" has a male and female parent, and is a life form indigenous to Earth. *"After its kind"* was the process of life-creation put in place by God during the six-days of Genesis. A being classified as "Other", is neither a direct creation, nor a being having been created after its kind. It is a unique life form outside of the sanctioning of God.

3.) RESIDENCE: Location where the life form currently resides (i.e. Earth, Hell, first heaven, second heaven or third Heaven). Many life forms may dwell in multiple locations at once.

4.) RELATION TO GOD: Refers to a fallen or just state before God. "Fallen" life forms were once in a just standing, but are currently under the curse of sin and separated from God. "Just" life forms are in a righteous, sinless state and are in fellowship with God. A third appellation to life forms regarding their stance before God, is "illegitimate". An illegitimate life form cannot be classified in a "fallen" state because neither it, nor its progenitors (if it has any), were ever in a justified state before God. It had no justified state to fall from, and therefore, cannot be described as "fallen". It is an illegal form of life which falls outside the sanctions of God.

5.) REDEEMABLE: States in a "yes", "no" or "n/a" (not applicable) fashion whether the redeeming blood of the Lord Jesus Christ extends to cover the cursed sin nature of the life form.

6.) ABOUT: Describes a few unique characteristics and details of the life form.

Fowl

Fowl or Flying
Creeping Thing

Beast

Creeping Thing

Fowl or Flying
Creeping Thing

Life in
the Waters

Beast or
Creeping Thing

IMAGE/Jeff Mardis

CREATURE

Classification: Creature

Origin: After Its Kind

Residence: Earth

Relation to God: Fallen

Redeemable: Yes and No

About: The word "creature", in a broad sense, can refer to ANY LIVING THING "created" by God – hence the word relationship of "creature" and "create". Sometimes the word may refer to man (2 Cor. 5:17 or Gal. 6:15, etc.) and on occasion may refer to cherubim (see Ezekiel 1). But the most common, most used reference, is to the animal. The word "animal" is not found in the Bible. The biblical class of "Creature" (animal) can be broken-down into 4 subclasses categorized primarily by size and ability:

> **1.) CREEPING THINGS** - Creatures which belong to the "Creeping Things" subclass are small. The name indicates the small size allows the creature to move about by "creeping" along. The class consists of such creatures as bugs, mice, weasels, ferrets, moles, turtles, chameleons, lizards, creatures that *"goeth upon the belly"*, and a whole host of animals not named (see Lev. 11).

> **2.) BEASTS** - The "Beast" subclass is of medium to large size, and includes such creatures as cows, goats, sheep and oxen; as well as dogs, cats, lions, tigers, camels, deer, pigs, rabbits and more (see Lev. 11 & Deut. 14:4-8).

> **3.) FOWL** - Includes birds and all flying things.

> **4.) LIFE IN THE WATERS** - All life that lives in water.

Because animal size and ability varies greatly, occasionally these 4 classes will overlap. Such as the *"fowls that creep"* or *"flying creeping things"* which include: bats, locusts, grasshoppers, beetles and all such small flying creatures (Lev. 11:20-23). There are also Creeping Things and Beasts which cross over into the Life in the Waters class. Each of these 4 subclasses can also be further broken down into "kinds". It is at the boundary of the "kind" where the cross-mixing is forbidden. For example, all dogs belong to the "Dog Kind". All cats belong to the "Cat Kind." Both kinds vary greatly, but dogs are still dogs and cats are still cats, and neither are to be bred with the other.

All creatures were originally docile plant-eaters (herbivores). In the beginning there were no meat-eaters (carnivores) and no blood-eaters (hemovores). Their inherent fear of man and "wild" behavior did not exist until after the Flood of Noah (see Gen. 1:30 & 9:1-3). The fact that THEY ARE NOW DIFFERENT means something significant happened to their behavior and/or genetic makeup after their creation. The causes for these differences can include, God (God made a change in them), sin (sin caused a change in them) and in some cases, possibly other circumstances (something else may have made a change in them).

Creatures are like organic robots, powered by a spirit and programmed to do what they do. For example, many birds do not fly south for the winter because they were taught to do so, but because their brains are intentionally "hard-wired" that way. A more common term for this God-instilled programming is known as "instinct". It is an innate, fixed type of behavior. Animals instinctively do what they do because that's how they were made – not how they "evolved". Each animal was created to do a particular task, and their size was proportionate to that job under the dominion of man.

The spirits of animals *"goeth downward to the earth"* (Ecc. 3:21). Those creatures who reside on the Earth during the millennial reign of the Lord Jesus Christ will be RESTORED to a pre-fallen

Dragon: The Ultimate Animal

IMAGE/Bigstockphoto.com   The Dragon fits in all animal subclasses.

There is only one historical animal which falls into ALL ANIMAL SUBCLASSES – the dragon. It is classified among the cattle, so it falls in the Beast Class (Gen. 3:14). It is also classified as a serpent which now *"goeth upon the belly"*, so it fits into the Creeping Things Class (Gen. 3:14 & Lev. 11:42). It has wings, so it falls into the Fowl Class (Isa. 14:29). And it can also dwell in the sea, so it's grouped with the Life-in-the-Waters Class (Isa. 27:1 et.al.). It is the ultimate animal.

condition. That is, they will be DIFFERENT again. A major change will affect their behavior and/or genetic makeup. The Bible indicates this change will come about *because of God*. This means that the creature will once again become docile, having no fear of man, and revert to a herbivorous diet (excluding serpents - Isa. 11:6-8, 65:25).

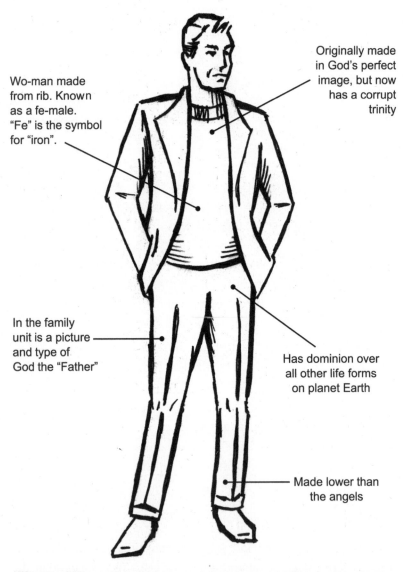

Wo-man made from rib. Known as a fe-male. "Fe" is the symbol for "iron".

Originally made in God's perfect image, but now has a corrupt trinity

In the family unit is a picture and type of God the "Father"

Has dominion over all other life forms on planet Earth

Made lower than the angels

IMAGE/Jeff Mardis

MAN

Classification: Man

Origin: After Its Kind

Residence: Earth

Relation to God: Fallen

Redeemable: Yes

About: The word "man" refers to mankind as a whole, but in a more general sense, the "male" gender. Man was originally created in the "image" and after the "likeness" of the Creator, with the female gender being made "of" and "for" the man (1 Cor. 11:8-9). Modern science refers to man as a "Homo Sapien", falsely classifying him with the "primate" (or monkey-like) species of animal. MAN IS NOT AN ANIMAL, but an entirely separate form of life which has been given complete sovereign control over the Earth and the animal world. To classify man as an "animal" and to declare that his physical appearance is simply an inconsequential fluke of evolution is to spit in the face of God Almighty. It is a blasphemy of the worst sort. Man looks the way he does because GOD LOOKS THE SAME WAY – but in a much more perfect form (Heb. 1:1-3). Currently, man is in a state of sin and has lost the perfect, tripartite image of God. That "image", composed of a spirit, soul and physical body, is only regained through the imputed righteousness of the Creator. Of the six classes of life created by God, the "man" class is the only one redeemable from a fallen state. The spirits of all men return unto God at death (Ecc.12:7), it is the soul which goes to either Heaven or Hell. Animals cannot be saved; angels cannot be saved; and cherubim cannot be saved. When the scriptures testify that, *"For God so loved the world, that he gave his only begotten Son, that whosoever believeth in him should not perish, but have everlasting life."* (John 3:16), the word "world" is not a reference to the planet itself, but to the nations and races of "men" who reside upon it.

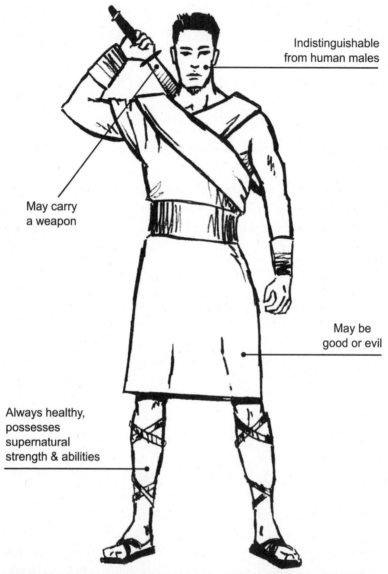

Indistinguishable
from human males

May carry
a weapon

May be
good or evil

Always healthy,
possesses
supernatural
strength & abilities

IMAGE/Jeff Mardis

ANGELIC

Classification: Angel

Origin: Direct Creation

Residence: Third Heaven (angels of God), Second Heaven/Earth (vagabond angels of Satan), locked away in Hell (angels that sinned)

Relation to God: Just (angels of God); Fallen (angels of Satan and the angels that sinned)

Redeemable: No

About: According to the scriptures, angels existed before the foundation of the Earth, and comprise an *"innumerable company"* (see Job 38:7 and Heb. 12:22). Also known as heavenly host, ministering spirits, stars and sons of God, these beings appear identical to human men, but possess supernatural abilities like super strength, invisibility, wingless-flight, healing, telekinesis, the ability to control animals, and the ability to control certain elements such as fire, water and air. Angels also exist in military-like ranks (archangels, king angels, prince angels), with certain angels having authority over others, and "Michael" being the only known "archangel" (see Dan. 10:13, 20 & 12:1, Jude 1:9, and Rev. 9:11 & 12:7).

By far, the most common attribute the Bible prescribes to angels is not relaying messages, as many teach, but carrying out the judgments of God by dispensing the sword, pestilence, famine, plagues, etc. Known as destroying angels (1Chron. 21:9-15) or "evil angels" (Psa. 78:42-49), the scriptures also list a variety of other angelic tasks such as those performed by messenger angels (Lk. 1:19 & 26, Zech. 1-6, etc.), reaper angels (Matt. 13:39-42 & 49-50, Rev. 14:14-16) and guardian angels (Psa. 91:1-15 & Heb. 1:14). In contrast to the righteous and just *"angels of God in heaven"*, there exists a

IMAGE/public domain   Melchior Paul von Deschwanden, 1859

Angels are often depicted as being effeminate or as women with wings. While such depictions may make for charming works of art, such ideas have no place in Bible doctrine (see Zechariah 5:7-9).

group of fallen angels under the command of Satan. Not all fallen angels are currently running around loose with the Devil, however. An unknown number are locked away in Hell under *"chains of darkness"* awaiting judgment (2 Peter 2:4); another four are *"bound"* in the Euphrates River (Rev. 9:14); and one, a king angel known as *"Abaddon"* or *"Apollyon"*, reigns over monsters of the Bottomless Pit which will be loosed during the Great Tribulation (Rev. 9:11).

Because angels appear identical to human men (Heb. 13:2), and because there are no female angels, certain *"angels that sinned"* became physically attracted to Earth women and sired illicit children by them. This union between two distinct classes of life (the Angelic Class and Man Class) created the *"giant"* (see Gen. 6:2-4), a "strange" form of life not sanctioned by God. Sin, however, is a one-way street for angels. Once an angel transgresses against God, it cannot be redeemed. Instead, *"everlasting fire"* has been prepared for them (Matt. 2:41).

Four faces:
(1) Man
(2) ox
(3) eagle
(4) lion

Four to six wings

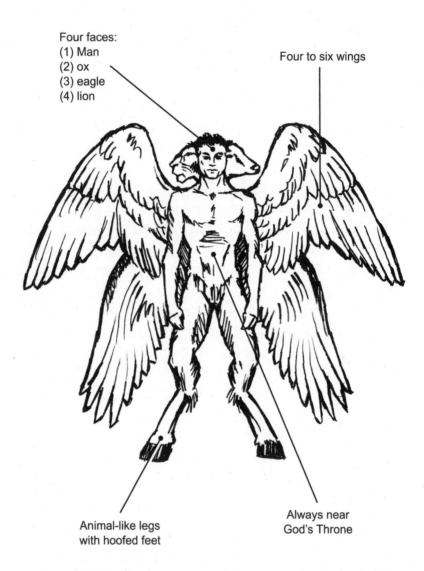

Animal-like legs
with hoofed feet

Always near
God's Throne

IMAGE/Jeff Mardis

CHERUBIC

Classification: Cherub

Origin: Direct Creation

Residence: Third Heaven (heavenly cherubim), Second Heaven/Earth (Lucifer)

Relation to God: Just (heavenly cherubim), Fallen (Lucifer)

Redeemable: No

About: The cherub is undoubtedly the most bizarre life form of all Bible-based life classes. Cherubim can be described as "humanoid" type creatures, with two arms, two legs, hands, feet and head, but their appearance is much more extraordinary than that of an ordinary man. Also known as "beasts", Cherubim are multi-winged creatures which have a human-like torso with arms and hands, but their legs are calf-like with two cloven feet. Their heads, which are most unusual, project four different faces on all four sides. Front (man), left (ox), back (eagle) and right (lion – see Ezk. 1:5-10). While the cherub outwardly appears to be a *mixture* of human and animal life forms, in reality, it is not. No humans or animals were used to create the cherubim class. The cherub is NOT A MIXTURE of other life forms, but, like the other six classes of life created by God, a separate and distinct life form unto itself. The cherub is very often confused with the angel, or depicted as a young, naked child with wings, but neither idea is supported by scripture. While the Bible describes an *"innumerable company of angels"* (Heb. 12:22), only five cherubim are mentioned. Ezekiel refers to *"four living creatures"*, and Revelation refers to *"four beasts"* (see Ezk. 1:5, Rev. 4:6-8, 5:6, 8&14, 6:1&6, 7:11, 14:3, 15:7 and 19:4). The fifth cherub, known as "Lucifer", was once *"the anointed cherub that covereth"*, but sin and iniquity caused this being to lose his position of authority.

May be used as transportation
for angels or heavenly saints.
May also be used in battle

Supernatural
immortal body

IMAGE/Jeff Mardis

CELESTIAL CREATURE

Classification: Celestial Creature

Origin: Direct Creation

Residence: Third Heaven

Relation to God: Just

Redeemable: n/a

About: The title "Celestial Creature" is found nowhere in scripture, but it is used to describe the biblical class of supernatural creatures which reside, *not in outer space*, but *exclusively* in the Third Heaven. These life forms have a just, non-fallen state before God (they're not under the curse of sin) and evidently appear *identical* to certain Earth-based animals (as if some of the animals of Earth were made "in the image" of a heavenly counterpart). The only Celestial Creature named directly by scripture is the horse. Their first recorded appearance is in 2 Kings chapter 2. Referred to once as *"horses of fire"* (2 Kings 2:11), these unearthly, supernatural creatures exhibit the powers of flight, and are impervious to fire and the adverse effects of outer space. The Bible lists *no direct interaction* between man and this form of life. Only an indirect, second-hand type of relationship is mentioned. Elijah rides in a chariot pulled by the creatures; Elisha reveals the beings standing in battle array; and the Lord Jesus Christ and His saints descend from heaven on their backs. It is not known whether any other type of celestial animal exists in the third heaven, but an educated guess would suggest it is probable (see Acts 10:11-12 & 11:5-6). Due to its title, some Christians who believe in life on other planets may be tempted to force the "alien" into this category. But the fact that the Bible clearly demonstrates that this class *dwells nowhere in outer space* and is identical to animal life found on Earth, quickly dispels that notion.

When in this configuration,
all cherubims share
their spirit with inorganic,
mechanical parts

All wheels
contain the spirits
of cherubims

IMAGE/public domain

SYMBIOTIC

Classification: Symbiotic

Origin: Direct Creation

Residence: Third Heaven

Relation to God: n/a

Redeemable: n/a

About: The sixth life classification is the most rare and mysterious form of life mentioned in the entire Bible. Being THE ONLY ONE OF ITS KIND, this living machine of sorts, exhibits a correlation between mechanical flying "wheels" and cherubim. The scriptures reveal a symbiotic relationship so intricate that it states, *"the SPIRIT of the living creature was IN THE WHEELS"* (Ezk. 1:20-21). The implication here is that the machine itself is somehow alive. Not alive in and of itself, but due to an unknown relationship with the cherubim which causes the spirits of the cherubim to also *act within the wheels.* Four cherubim are each standing next to *"a wheel in the middle of a wheel"*, and a cherubic spirit resides *"in the wheels"*. That's what the scriptures state.

Further reading shows this thing to be the flying Chariot Throne of God – a living, flying, wheeled machine, powered by four heavenly creatures. Nothing like this exists anywhere else in the Universe. Because this life classification results due to the shared spirits of cherubim acting upon inorganic matter, I hesitate to add this life group to the other primary 5 biblical life classes. This is because without the spiritual influence of the cherubim, *the flying wheels would have no life at all*. Its "life" is totally dependent upon the spiritual life force of *another living creature*. I have called this class "Symbiotic". A word which *The Merriam-Webster Dictionary*

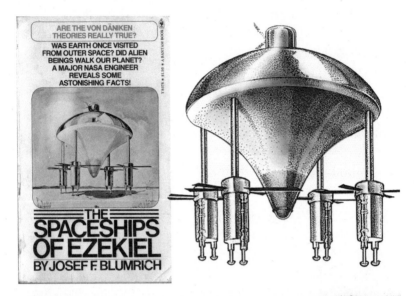

IMAGES/copyright of their respective owners   New Age interpretation of Ezekiel's Wheel.

All the opinions of those New Age/UFO sympathizers who like to cherry-pick the Bible, and claim that the prophet "did not know what he was looking at" can be thrown in the dumpster where they belong. Ezekiel described EXACTLY what he was witnessing, and it had nothing to do with "flying saucers" or "spaceships" from another planet. When you read the description of the thing on the previous page, it was not an "interpretation", but simply believing the Bible as it is written. An "interpretation" can be found in the images above.

defines as, *"The living together in more or less intimate association or close union of two dissimilar organisms."* Such a relationship is evidenced nowhere else in scripture.

Perhaps certain modern UFOs are SATANIC COUNTERFEITS of this particular Bible life form. A situation where *the spirits of living creatures are being shared with flying machines.* If true, it would explain how so many such objects seem to move and react with intelligence. But if this is the case, it should come as no big surprise to the Bible believer (For more information read Ezekiel chapters 1, 10, & 11:22, Daniel 7:9, 2 Samuel 22:7-11, and Psalms 18:6-10).

May appear as
an amalgam
of various
legitimate animals,
but not always

Artist's interpretation
of the Pit Locust

May be under
the headship of
a fallen angel

May be an image, cybernetic
or genetic organism created
via science, sorcery or both

IMAGE/Jeff Mardis

COUNTERFEIT

Classification: Counterfeit

Origin: Other

Residence: Earth and possibly other undisclosed locations

Relation to God: Illegitimate

Redeemable: No

About: The Counterfeit life class consists of beings which are neither direct creations of God, nor sired by any same life forms previously in existence. These mysterious beings are misfits whose origins come about through other means. The majority of those which fall into this classification can have the appearance of mixtures and amalgamations of life forms already in existence. There is no scriptural evidence for their direct classification into any of the 6 God-ordained life classes. For the most part, their physical appearance dictates that they are something different. The primary beings in scripture which fall into the Counterfeit classification include Giants, Winged-Women, Pit Locusts (pictured at left) and the Horsemen Army of the Killer Angels. These life forms are probably the product of the joining of "strange flesh" (i.e. united life forms of differing kinds and makeup) and are associated with "confusion" (Lev. 18:23). The scriptures show that "confusion" is never associated with anything good. It is associated with shame, envy, strife, sin and *"every evil work"* (Jam. 3:16), and God is not its author (1 Cor. 14:33). The Giants have a direct connection with the fallen sons of God (Gen. 6-4); the Winged-Women have a direct connection with wickedness (Zech. 5:7-9); the Pit Locusts have a direct connection with the angel of the Bottomless Pit (Rev. 9:11); and the Horsemen Army is spearheaded by four killer angels (Rev.

Another author suggests the weird, animal-like, creatures were & are results of the fallen angels efforts to be and do all that God is and does; so, in their efforts to create mankind, these weird creatures have been created, They have not been able to duplicate God's creation of humankind.

9:13-19). Disturbingly, others in the Counterfeit Class can appear as EXACT DUPLICATES of legitimate life forms (Ex. 7:11-12 & 8:7). These, evidently, are not "clones", whose creation must have access to original genetic materials, but are somehow raw replicas not attained through procreation or scientific methods. This rarely-discussed phenomenon of counterfeit-life-creation is scheduled to rear its ugly head primarily during the Great Tribulation. Its purpose? Deception and destruction. (A detailed scriptural examination of this life class will be conducted in Chapter 14).

The Satyr

The Cockatrice

Secondary beings which may also fall into this outcast group include satyrs (half goat, half man) and cockatrices (half rooster, half serpent). However, since the physical appearance of neither the satyr nor the cockatrice is mentioned in scripture (we only have mythological records upon which to base their appearance), their classification into the "counterfeit" class cannot be stated with 100% accuracy. There is simply too little scriptural information to draw a definite conclusion. However, there may be paleontological evidence

of their bad creation included possible dinosaurs & many other beasts of antiquity. This isn't going on or isn't in Noah's Day + part of the reason God destroyed by flood. Today: mans renewed efforts to destroy all life + create life (which antichrist will form) if trans human going on today

IMAGE/Bigstockphoto.com   An Archaeopteryx or a Cockatrice?

pointing to the fact that the "cockatrice" was once a legitimate creature. The so-called "Archaeopteryx", a lizard-like bird whose fossilized remains were first discovered in 1861, may very well be the Bible's cockatrice. Why the similar imagery between the two has never really been connected, I don't know. But if this is the case, the cockatrice may simply be one of God's extinct creatures, and not a mongrelized monster or a transitional life form jumping the imaginary "evolutionary gap" between dinosaurs and birds. The scriptures describe the creature as a flying reptile connected to *"a fiery flying serpent"*, which implies the cockatrice is dragon-like (see Isa. 14:29). Likewise, the creature has classically been depicted as a reptile-like bird, which is exactly what scientists claim the Archaeopteryx to be – a feathered serpent.

But whether or not these two life forms are counterfeit monsters, or legitimate extinct creatures, the Bible testifies to their existence. The Bible names the satyr in 2 verses (Isa. 13:21 & 34:14). The Bible names the cockatrice in 4 verses (Isa. 11:8, 14:29, 59:5 & Jer. 8:17).

Chapter 11 Summary

The purpose of this chapter has been to COLLECT and ORGANIZE all the scriptural information available on differing life forms. As a result, we have learned that there are SEVEN PRIMARY CATEGORIES OF LIFE outlined by scripture: (1.) Creature Class; (2.) Man Class; (3.) Angelic Class; (4.) Cherubic Class; (5.) Celestial Creature Class; (6.) Symbiotic Class; and (7.) Counterfeit Class (with an actual eighth life category being *God Himself*). Recognizing differences between these life forms has helped divide the classes into their respective groups. This was done because many times people confuse and intermix some of the forms.

Without exception, ALL LIFE IN THE UNIVERSE, within or without the Bible, will fall into one of these groups. There are no other options. Even unclean spirits and devils (beings which once inhabited physical bodies) may be classified somewhere within this Bible-based system. Since the modern alien phenomenon deals with eyewitnesses who claim to have apparently encountered "life", the Christian must determine WHERE WITHIN THESE SEVEN GROUPS the mysterious creature fits. Future chapters will examine this question in more detail.

demons are the disembodied spirits of the Nephilim / fallen angels

12

What Dwells Beyond

ow that we've established that outer space is the "Second Heaven" (chapter 9), and the diverse types of life forms created by God (chapter 11); we can combine these two studies and begin our search of the scriptures to locate extraterrestrial life. Since the previous chapter covered ALL THE CATEGORIES OF LIFE in existence, it will obviously overlap some of the information presented here. This is not done to be unnecessarily redundant, but to focus on the life which *actually does* dwell beyond Earth.

Man interacts with life in the First Heaven on a daily basis. Birds, bugs and such things are seen there every day. Just over a century ago, man himself even gained the ability of flight after the airplane was invented (1903). We now travel the heavens nonstop, as giant passenger jets zip back and forth around the globe (Dan. 12:4). Space shuttles and a space station orbit the Earth regularly. But what about the Second or Third Heaven? The scriptures show that the Earth is the only inhabited planet in the Universe, if anything did live or move through space, who or what would it be? According to the Bible, the heavens are filled with "hosts". Part of this host consists of dead, inorganic matter.

"And lest thou lift up thine eyes unto heaven, and when thou seest the sun, and the moon, and the stars, even all the HOST OF HEAVEN, shouldest be driven to worship them, and serve them, which the LORD thy God hath divided unto all nations under the whole heaven."
Deuteronomy 4:19

"And he put down the idolatrous priests, whom the kings of Judah had ordained to burn incense in the high places in the cities of Judah, and in the places round about Jerusalem; them also that burned incense unto Baal, to the sun, and to the moon, and to the planets, and to all the HOST OF HEAVEN." 2 Kings 23:5

The above scriptures show that the term "host of heaven" can often refer to the planetary type of celestial bodies – suns, moons, stars and planets. However, this is not always the case. Another type of "heavenly host" refers to something quite different.

"And he said, Hear thou therefore the word of the LORD: I saw the LORD sitting on his throne, and all the HOST OF HEAVEN standing by him on his right hand and on his left." 1 Kings 22:19 also see 2 Chron 18:18

Obviously suns, stars, moons and planets are incapable of "standing" around the throne of God. What is seen here is life in the Third Heaven. If there really are beings that exist that are more advanced and more intelligent than man, the word of God would surely say so. And it does. What follows is a detailed biblical summary of that life – the official biblical record of *WHAT DWELLS BEYOND*.

ANGELS – God's written word lists 297 references to "angels". Most of these angels are *"the angels of God in heaven"*, but an undisclosed number are servants of the Devil. The angels of Satan are often referred to as "fallen angels", although the Bible never uses the phrase. A Bible study will reveal that angels are also called: *the Bible was uses "Nephilim & Rephaim & the world's gods, enemies.*

1.) Heavenly Host - (Luke 2:13-15, Psa. 148:2 & Neh. 9:6) This title not only refers to all the Host of Heaven, but in a more specific context it refers to the angels – both good and evil. Satan and his angels' access to the Third Heaven is not permanently cut off until sometime in the future (see Rev. 12:7-12 and note that verse 8 says "their place"). Until that time, however, the angels of the Devil will also be known as "heavenly host".

2.) Spirits - (Heb. 1:7 & Psa. 104:4) This title reveals that angels are spirit beings. Many Christians misread this to imply that angels are "spirits only", but this is not so. Like their Creator, angels are tripartite, having a spirit, soul and physical body. Their physical body is immortal. It is not a "natural body" like fallen man, but a supernatural "spiritual body" (1 Cor. 15:44) with the powers of flight, invisibility, super strength, etc.

3.) Stars - (Rev. 1:20, 6:13, 9:1, 12:4, Dan. 8:10-11) Stars can refer to both those tiny points of light in the night sky or angels. Job 38:7 says that the *"stars sang together"* when the foundation of the Earth was laid. From this we can know that the angels were here BEFORE the earth was created. Celestial stars and angels have several things in common:

> **a.)** Both are innumerable. (Gen, 15:5, Jer. 33:22 & Heb. 12:22)

b.) Both can radiate light. (Gen. 1:14-17, Psa. 148:3, Luke 2:9, Acts 12:7 & 10:30)
c.) Both have names. (Psa. 147:4, Jude 1:9, Luke 1:19 & Rev. 9:11)
d.) Both occupy the heavens (Second or Third).

When the heathen (and Israel) were driven to worship the host of heaven, they often used the symbol of a star to represent their false god (see Amos 5:26 & Acts 7:43, also see chapter 16 for more information). Likewise, when the first "stars" came to Earth, both they and their offspring became famous. The scriptures say *"mighty men ... men of renown"* (Gen. 6:4). Because of this precedent, modern vernacular many times labels "famous" or "high profile" individuals with the same title: Stars, Movie Stars, or Hollywood Stars.

4.) Men - A careful study of scripture will reveal that angels look exactly like human men, and are often misidentified as being such. As a matter of fact, it is a common practice found in scriptures to use the word "men" or "man" as a substitute for the word "angel":

a.) The angels who appeared to Lot both appeared to be men. (Gen. 19:1-16)
b.) The angel which appeared to Manoah and his wife (Samson's parents) appeared as a man. (Judges 13:2-21)
c.) The angel who appeared to Balaam appeared as a man. (Num. 22:22-35)
d.) The angel who appeared to Gideon looked like a man. (Judges 6:11-21)
e.) The angel who appeared to Hagar looked like a man. (Gen. 16:7-8)

f.) The angel who appeared to Cornelius appeared to be a man. (Acts 10:2-4)

g.) The angel sent to destroy Israel looked like a man. (1 Chron. 21:16)

h.) The angels which rolled back the stone at the sepulcher of Christ both appeared to be men. (Matt. 28:2-6, Mark 16:2-7, Luke 24:2-4 & 23)

i.) The angel Gabriel appears as a man. (Luke 1:11-38)

j.) The angel who loosed Peter from prison appeared as a man. (Acts 12:6-10)

k.) Michael the Archangel appears as a man. (Jude 1:9 and Rev. 12:7)

l.) The angel that binds the Devil and casts him into the bottomless pit is pictured as a man. (Rev. 20:1-3)

The appearance of angels and men match so closely, the Bible even warns us that we may even encounter "angels" without even realizing it.

"Be not forgetful to entertain strangers: for thereby some have entertained angels unawares." Hebrews 13:2

An angel that visits earth, whether good or evil, would simply appear as a human man with superhuman powers – super strength, the power of flight, the power to control certain elements like fire, water and wind, invisibility, telekinesis, etc. All of these angelic abilities, and more, are found in the scriptures. The Bible has no female angels, and no angel is ever depicted as having wings (wings are useless when flying through outer space). Surprisingly, winged female creatures are identified with *"wickedness"*, not the angels of God (see Zech. 5:7-9). If an angel had wings, it would be impossible to mistake it for a human being.

5.) Sons of God - (Job 1:6, 2:1 & 38:7 and Gen. 6:2-4) The final alternate name for the angels (and the most controversial) is that of "sons of God". Controversial or not, however, the word of God reveals that the born-again Christian is not the only "son of God" found in the Bible. Specifically, three different types are described:

A.) The Only Begotten [Conceived] Son of God - The Lord Jesus Christ was given this title because He was born of a woman. All angels are known as sons of God, but none were born of a woman. *None were conceived. Angels were created.*

"I will declare the decree: the LORD hath said unto me, Thou art my Son; this day have I begotten thee." Psalms 2:7

"For unto which of the angels said he at any time, Thou art my Son, this day have I begotten thee? And again, I will be to him a Father, and he shall be to me a Son?" Hebrews 1:5

"In this was manifested the love of God toward us, because that God sent his only begotten Son into the world, that we might live through him." 1 John 4:9 *(His own inner being He gave to Jesus.)*

Also see John 1:14 & 18, 3:16-18, Acts 13:33 et al.

B.) Adopted sons of God - Before Christians are born-again by the Spirit of God, they are the unsaved children of the Devil (see Matt. 13:38-39 & 1 John 3:10). Once saved, the lost sinner becomes a spiritually adopted son of God.

"For as many as are led by the Spirit of God, they are the sons of God. For ye have not received

"Because" (the reason that) we are God sons is that God has shed His love abroad in our hearts; making us to look like Him in love actions

IMAGE/Foster Bible Pictures, 1897   The Angel of Death at the Passover (c. 1487 BC)

While the angel's "wings" in this image are a misrepresentation, it does illustrate the primary job of angels, that of executing the judgments of God. Plus, without the added artistic embellishment of the wings, it is difficult to illustrate the idea of an angel without it simply looking like a man (even though that's exactly how angels look). I have no problem with drawing angels in this manner, so long as the viewer is aware of the truth. Which, unfortunately, most are not.

> the spirit of bondage again to fear; but ye have received the Spirit of adoption, whereby we cry, Abba, Father." *Romans 8:14-15*

> "But when the fulness of the time was come, God sent forth his Son, made of a woman, made under the law, To redeem them that were under the law, that we might receive the adoption of sons." *Galatians 4:4-5*

C.) Created sons of God - Created sons of God have no earthly parents, but are direct creations made in His image (i.e. they look like men). It is this category into which both Adam and the angels belong (see Gen. 1:27, 2:7 and Luke 3:38

concerning Adam, and Gen. 6:-2-4 and Job 2:1 & 38:7 concerning angels). Note the verse below showing created sons of God (angels) standing before God's throne in the third heaven:

"Now there was a day when the sons of God came to present themselves before the Lord and Satan came also among them." Job 1:6

Contemporary thinking teaches that all angels are "messengers". This narrow description of angels is arrived at by looking up the Hebrew and Greek words for the meaning (*mal'ak* and *aggelos* respectively) instead of relying upon the scriptures to interpret themselves. A thorough search of the Bible will reveal that the role of the angel far outreaches any simplistic description than that of a "messenger". Many angels never relay any message at all. Instead, the primary purpose for the angel as shown by scripture is to carry out the judgments of God. Also referred to as destroying angels or "evil angels", these beings are responsible for dispensing the sword, pestilence, famine, plagues, etc. upon man as directed by the Lord (see Gen. 19:13, 2 Sam. 24:16, 2 Kings 19:35, 1 Chron. 21:12-16, 2 Chron. 20:9, Psa. 78:42-49, Isa. 37:36, 45:7, Ezk. 14:21-22, Jonah 3:4&10, Rev. 8:7-12, 9:1-15, 15:1-8 et al.).

CHERUBIM – The Bible lists 94 references to the words "cherub" (singular) and "cherubims" (plural). For whatever reason, cherubim remain one of the most misrepresented creatures in the word of God. Many believe that cherubim and angels are basically the same, but other than the fact that each can reside in the Third Heaven with God, no proof of this exists anywhere. As a matter of fact, the scriptures give such a clear physical description of the two, that it would be impossible to get them confused. Only a reader woefully blinded to the clear Bible wording could ever believe the two were "the same". Apples are not oranges; bananas are not carrots; and cherubim are not angels. Note the following major differences:

1.) The cherub is nearly always associated with God's Throne. Angels are not. If you come across the word "cherub" or "cherubim" in the Bible, somewhere nearby is the Throne of God. When God designed the Ark of the Covenant (a type of God's Throne) two cherubim were placed on either side of the "Mercy Seat" to give us a picture of this truth. The real cherubim and Throne are seen in Ezekiel chapters 1 and 10 and Revelation chapter 4. (see Ex. 25:17-22, Num. 7:89, 2 Sam. 22:7-11, 1 Kings 9:6-7, Psa. 99:1, Ezk. 1 & 10, Rev. 4:6-8, etc.)

2.) The angel is referred to as a "man". The cherub is referred to as a "creature" or "beast". Cherubim are called "beasts" because they possess several animal-like attributes.

"Also out of the midst thereof came the likeness of four living creatures. And this was their appearance; they had the likeness of a man. And every one had four faces, and every one had four wings. And their feet were straight feet; and the sole of their feet was like the sole of a calf's foot: and they sparkled like the color of burnished brass. And they had the hands of a man under their wings on their four sides; and they four had their faces and their wings. Their wings were joined one to another; they turned not when they went; they went every one straight forward. As for the likeness of their faces, they four had the face of a man, and the face of a lion, on the right side: and they four had the face of an ox on the left side; they four also had the face of an eagle." Ezekiel 1:5-10

IMAGE/Foster Bible Pictures, 1897   Ezekiel's vision of God on His Chariot Throne (c. 590 BC)

3.) The cherub has four or six wings, angels do not have any wings (see Ezk 1:6 & 10:21).

"And the four beasts had each of them six wings about him; and they were full of eyes within: and they rest not day and night, saying, Holy, holy, holy, LORD God Almighty, which was, and is, and is to come." Rev. 4:8

4.) The cherubim have four faces; the face of a man, the face of a lion, the face of an ox, and the face of an eagle. Angels only have one face.

"As for the likeness of their faces, they four had the face of a man, and the face of a lion, on the right side: and they

four had the face of an ox on the left side; they four also had the face of an eagle." Ezekiel 1:10

Without question, this cherubic quality is one of the most bizarre and disturbing. To think of a creature with four faces (!?) and then one of those faces being that of a man and the other three faces being the faces of animals is just too weird. But there it is. As professing Christians, we can't just throw out the verse because we don't like or understand it. The word of God testifies that cherubim have four faces with each face facing one of the four cardinal directions. What can we do with it? Nothing. It says what it says, just believe it and go on.

5.) The Bible depicts a total of four cherubim (with a fifth cherub that "sinned" found in Ezk. 28:14-17). The prophet Ezekiel describes four (and only four) cherubim (see Ezk. 1:5). The prophet John describes four (and only four) cherubim (see Rev. 4:6&8, 5:6, 8 &14, 6:1&6, 7:11, 14:3, 15:7 and 19:4). That's four cherubim, in contrast with *"an innumerable company of angels"* (Heb. 12:22). Angels and cherubim are not the same and never have been.

The Bible clearly shows major differences between the angel and the cherub. Those differences are easily ascertained by simply reading the text and comparing the descriptions. A few more notes are in order, however, before we move on.

It's the belief of this author that cherubim have the ability to CHANGE THEIR APPEARANCE. More specifically, the cherub seems to have the ability to physically transform into one of its four representative faces; that of a winged ox, lion, eagle or man. This theory is based on the following biblical facts:

FACT 1: The prophet Ezekiel says that "they four" had the face of a man, a lion, an ox and an eagle. That is, each of the four creatures had each of the four faces. Ezekiel 10:21 clearly states; *"Every one had four faces apiece"*. Ezekiel even describes on which sides of the head the faces appear (see Ezk. 1:10).

FACT 2: The book of Revelation describes the four cherubic faces as being four separate individual creatures:

"And the first beast was like a lion, and the second beast like a calf, and the third beast had a face as a man, and the fourth beast was like a flying eagle." Revelation 4:7

FACT 3: The Bible shows that Satan is a fallen cherub and not a fallen angel. Satan has the ability to TRANSFORM HIMSELF into the appearance of an angel. The only difference between a true angel and the Devil's counterfeit angelic appearance is that Satan's "angel" would have wings. If you compare Revelation 4:7 & 8 you'll see that cherubim can appear as MEN WITH WINGS:

"And the first beast was like a lion, and the second beast like a calf, and THE THIRD BEAST had a face as a MAN, and the fourth beast was like a flying eagle. And the four beasts had each of them SIX WINGS about him; and they were full of eyes within: and they rest not day and night, saying, Holy, holy, holy, Lord God Almighty, which was, and is, and is to come." Revelation 4:7-8

"And no marvel; for Satan himself is transformed into an angel of light." 2 Corinthians 11:14

These 3 facts lend credence to the theory that cherubim have the ability to transform their physical appearance. Now it may be that each cherub can only change into one of the four faces, or it could be that each cherub has the ability to change into any four of the faces. The Bible's not clear on this detail. In the end, however, the theory of "cherubic transformation" remains sound.

SERAPHIM – The scriptures reveal very little about seraphim (the word only appears in two verses – Isa 6:2 & 6). I believe that "seraphim" is simply another word for "cherubim". This may not be true, but I do not believe that the scriptures draw enough distinction to claim that the two are COMPLETELY DIFFERENT life forms:

> *"In the year that king Uzziah died I saw also the LORD sitting upon a throne, high and lifted up, and his train filled the temple. Above it stood the SERAPHIMS: each one had SIX WINGS; with twain he covered his face, and with twain he covered his feet, and with twain he did fly. And one cried unto another, and said, Holy, holy, holy, is the LORD of hosts: the whole earth is full of his glory."*
> *Isaiah 6:1-3*

Apparently, cherubims and seraphims have much in common. Both are associated with God's Throne. Both cry, *"Holy, holy, holy"*. Yet, unlike cherubims (Ex. 25:18-22, Num. 7:89, 1Kgs. 6:23-35, Psa. 99:1, Heb. 9:5, etc.), seraphims are not mentioned nor depicted anywhere else in the Bible. This is why I believe the two are the same.

THE 24 ELDERS – The *"four and twenty elders"* are only found in 6 verses in the book of Revelation. It's unclear who or from where these elders come. Are they Old Testament saints, New Testament saints or something different? The fact that they have crowns on their heads leads me to believe that they are saints of some kind. But if they are saints, why are there only twenty four of them? The Bible doesn't say. What is known, however, is that these 24 gold-crowned, white-garbed elders worship God from 24 seats which surround the Throne. Very little is revealed beyond this:

> *"And round about the throne were four and twenty seats: and upon the seats I saw four and twenty elders sitting, clothed in white raiment; and they had on their heads crowns of gold. And the four and twenty elders, which sat before God on their seats, fell upon their faces, and worshipped God". Revelation 4:4 & 11:16 Also see Revelation 4:10, 5:8 & 14 and 19:4*

THE WATCHERS – Also known as *"holy ones"*, these mysterious beings only appear in 2 books of the Bible. King Nebuchadnezzar had a dream of these things coming *"down from heaven"*. In the context of the four verses in which *"watcher"* and *"watchers"* are found (see Jer. 4:16, Dan. 4:13, 17 & 23), some sort of negative message is being declared against the enemies of God. In Jeremiah, this negative message is aimed at Jerusalem (see Jer. 4:14-17). In Daniel, a *"decree of the Most High"* is aimed at the King of Babylon (see Dan. 4:13-24). Evidently, watchers are used to relay the words of God. When God entrusts His word to the watchers, the words of God become known as *"the word of the holy ones"* (Dan. 4:17). Comparing scripture with scripture, it's probably safe to assume that "watchers" are the angels of God in heaven – not fallen angels. They're referred to as *"holy ones"* and act as an extension of God Himself by conveying His words. Angels can also perform these types of tasks. We can also conclude that watchers "watch" – perhaps they act as the eyes of God?

> *"The eyes of the LORD are in every place, beholding the evil and the good." Proverbs 15:3*

UNCLEAN SPIRITS – The subject of unclean spirits, or devils, is too huge, really, to just simply mention in passing. But that's what we're going to do here nevertheless. The Bible records 38 verses where the Lord Jesus Christ spoke of the reality of unclean spirits and the Devil. The word *"devils"* is mentioned 54 times in the Bible. *"Unclean spirit"* and *"unclean spirits"* are mentioned 21 times. *"Evil spirit"* and *"evil spirits"* are mentioned 14 times. *"Familiar spirit"* and *"familiar spirits"* are named 16 times. The book of Luke has the word *"devil"* or *"devils"* appear 31 times (this is easily over 25% of the Bible's entire references to these two words). Some of the more salient facts concerning unclean spirits include:

1.) Unclean spirits are known by a number of other biblical names including: familiar spirits, evil spirits, foul spirits, principalities, powers, spiritual wickedness, devils and rulers of the darkness (see Mt. 10:1, Lev. 19:31, Luke 7:21, Rev. 18:2, Eph. 6:12, 1 Tim. 4:1, Luke 4:33, et. al.).

2.) All devils believe in God and know who Jesus Christ really is (God incarnate). Devils major in deception. They attend church, worship Jesus, quote scripture, tell the truth (at times), work miracles, impart wisdom and prophesy (see Jas. 2:19, Matt. 4:3-6, Rev. 12:9, 1 Tim. 4:1-3, Lk. 4:33-34, Mk. 5:1-8, Acts 16:16-18, Rev. 16:14, Jas. 3:15, 1 Sam. 18:10, etc.).

3.) With the exception of the Devil himself, there is absolutely no record in the Bible of an unclean spirit being able to manifest in a physical form. Devils must "possess" (i.e. dwell inside the physical body of) humans or animals in order to be at rest. That is, they prefer to possess someone or something, rather than to simply remain disembodied spirits (see Matt. 4:24, Mk. 5:12-13, Lk. 11:24, etc.).

4.) Unclean spirits have an affinity (natural liking or sympathy) for death and/or dead bodies (man or animal). The term "unclean" not only refers to their affinity for death, but also to their state – that of an *"unclean thing"*. The first example of the word *"unclean"* is found in Leviticus 5:2. Here we learn that an *"unclean thing"* is directly associated with *"carcasses"* of DEAD THINGS. What this implies is that *"unclean"* spirits became *"unclean"*, BECAUSE THEY ORIGINATE FROM DEAD BODIES. Yet, for whatever reason, these spirits did not return unto God at death (see page 227). Unclean spirits enjoy dwelling in cemeteries and may cause homicidal or suicidal tendencies. They also promote insanity, self-mutilation and nakedness in those they possess. They can also cause those they possess to do all the things listed in point #2 listed above. (see Matt. 8:28, 1 Sam. 18:10-11, Lk. 4:9 & 8:33, Matt. 17:14-18, Mk. 5:5, Lk. 8:27, etc.).

5.) Some areas can have higher concentrations of devils than others. This preference is strongly dictated by their affinity for the dead (see Mk. 5:1-10). When you combine their affinity for dead bodies, cemeteries and graven images, with their church attendance, worship of Jesus, quoting of scripture, working of miracles, prophesying and imparting of wisdom, you come away with a COUNTERFEIT CHRISTIAN CHURCH built upon a graveyard, whose altar descends into the underground into a City of the Dead (the Vatican Necropolis - see Matt. 23:27 for Christ's prophecy concerning this matter).

The Church of Dead Men's Bones

From the 2002 *National Geographic* documentary *Inside the Vatican*, narrated by actor Martin Sheen, we get the following:

IMAGE/public domain
High Altar and entrance to the tombs.

"The power of the place is inescapable and a long way from its humble ORIGINS AS A GRAVEYARD. It is the smallest sovereign nation and yet one of the most powerful. If it had a gross national product it would be measured, not in money, but in souls. ... In 1939, workers renovating the grottos beneath Saint Peter's [Basilica] *made a stunning find. Just below the floor level they discovered an ancient Roman GRAVE. It soon BECAME CLEAR that there WASN'T JUST ONE GRAVE, but AN ENTIRE CITY OF THE DEAD. After many months of digging the excavators came to a section of older GRAVES near the area underneath the HIGH ALTAR. Directly beneath the ALTAR ... they found the bones of a man."*

Do you know where the Bible reveals the highest concentration of devil spirits? In graveyards (Mk. 5:1-13, Lk. 8:26-33). Did the Lord Jesus literally prophesy of Vatican City where he said:

Continued on following page

Continued from previous page

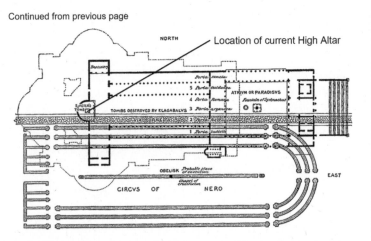

NORTH — Location of current High Altar

IMAGE/*Pagan & Christian Rome* by Rodolfo Lanciani (1892) with added location pointer
The Roman Catholic Church was purposely built over a mass graveyard.

> *"Woe unto you, scribes and Pharisees, hypocrites! for ye are like unto whited sepulchers, which indeed appear beautiful outward, but are within full of dead men's bones, and of all uncleanness." Matthew 23:27*

The evidence is difficult to deny. The Vatican Palace alone hosts 11,000 rooms, its world-class collection of art and antiquities notwithstanding. Without question, Vatican City is one of the *most outwardly beautiful places in the world*. But within, it is admittedly *"full of dead men's bones"*. If you visit the Vatican and view their most holy High Altar, you can literally descend underground beneath the altar into the *"City of the Dead"* to view the *sepulchers containing these dead men's bones*. You'd be hard-pressed to find a more perfect and literal representation of Christ's words anywhere else in the world. The Bible reveals that unclean spirits prefer to congregate in places where images are used in worship, and near the mass graves of the dead.

in the Book of Jude preach, quoted 'en to by Jesus

6.) Many assume that devils are the disembodied spirits of fallen angels. This may be true, but no direct reference is found in scripture. The Bible, in fact, gives no emphatic origin for unclean spirits, other than the inference that they once inhabited physical bodies. However, like angels, devils can inflict blindness and muteness, an ability that strongly hints towards a possible connection (see Matt. 12:22, Gen. 19:11, Matt. 9:32-33, Lk. 1:19, etc.).

7.) Just as the Lord Jesus Christ is pictured as a lamb or a lion and the Holy Spirit is pictured as a dove, devils and unclean spirits are also typified by certain animals. In general, any animal that the scriptures picture as being "unclean" is a potential candidate for this typology (see Lev. 11). Birds, especially, are used to typify spirits. Unclean spirits are usually pictured

IMAGE/Dover Pictorial Archive
Unclean spirit pictured as a black bird, speaking to a wizard (c. 1200 AD).

as scavenger birds (birds that feed on dead bodies) like vultures, eagles and such or nocturnal birds (birds that are active at night, i.e. active in the darkness) like owls. The primary animals used by the Bible to represent devils and unclean spirits are birds, serpents, scorpions and frogs. Insects also figure prominently in this typology, especially insects associated with feeding on the blood and/or dead bodies of humans or animals like maggots (worms), flies and mosquitoes (see Matt. 13:4 & 19, Mk. 4:4 & 15, Rev. 18:2, Lk. 10:17-20, 2 Cor. 11:3, Rev. 12:9 & 14-15 and Rev. 16:13-14). Science has proven that certain flies can detect a cadaver from up to four miles away. Baalzebub, another name for the Devil, means "lord of the flies". -- ? ?

THE DEVIL – Much like the subject of unclean spirits, discussing the Devil in a few short pages will only act as a crash course on the subject. Whole books have been written on the topic, but to suffice for now, we'll only touch on the high points.

If I were forced to describe the Devil in a single word, that word would undoubtedly be "counterfeit". When taken in light of the entire Bible, it is discovered that Satan not only wants to become a god, but he wants to be the complete and total substitute for God. In short, Satan wants to be God – and that's in the strictest sense of the words. Satan wants you to worship him as if he were God Himself. The world's definition of "Satanism" is much narrower than the biblical definition. Worldly Satanism is simply relegated to a cult of believers who worship a force or demonic personality known as "Satan" or subscribe to a set of self-serving beliefs which indulge the most carnal and base desires of man. The Anton Szandor LaVey form of "Satanism" did not even acknowledge the existence of a personal Devil. While the world's classification of Satanism is, without a doubt, "Satanic", it barely even touches the hem of Satan's deceptive garment, a garment that appears, more often than not, as a form of Bible Christianity. The world's form of "Satanism" would never make this claim, but we're not seeking answers from the world, we're seeking them from God's Book. The Devil has taken it upon himself to counterfeit everything that is true. He not only imitates the things of God once, but multiple times. What follows is list of 25 "things of God" of which Satan currently has (or will have) a counterfeit:

1.) He is a spiritual Father (John 8:44)

2.) He has a literal seed (Gen. 3:15)

3.) He has a begotten Son (John 17:12 & 2 Thess 2:3) ?

4.) He has a Christ (Matt. 24:24, Mk. 13:22,1 John 2:18 & 22)

5.) He has a Seat (Rev. 2:13 & 13:2)

6.) He has spiritual children (Matt. 13:38 & 1 John 3:10)

7.) He has a Church (Rev. 2:9 & 3:9)

8.) He has a Gospel (2 Cor. 11:4 & Gal. 1:8-9)

9.) He has a Spirit (2 Cor. 11:4, 1 John 4:3, etc.)

10.) He has a Jesus (2 Cor. 11:4)

11.) He has a Shepherd (Zech. 11:15-17 & John 10:12-13)

12.) He has sheep (Matt. 7:15)

13.) He has a Kingdom (Matt. 12:26, Lk. 11:18, Dan. 11:21, Rev. 17:12-13 & 17, etc.)

14.) He has a City (Rev. 14:8, 17:5 & 18, etc.)

15.) He has angels (Matt. 25:41 & Rev. 12:7-9)

16.) He has apostles (2 Cor. 11:13)

17.) He has prophets (Matt. 7:15, 24:11, Mk. 13:22, Acts 13:6, 2 Peter 2:1, 1 John 4:1, etc.)

18.) He has preachers (2 Cor. 11:4)

19.) He promotes peace (Dan. 8:25, 11:21 & 24, etc.)

20.) Has ministers of righteousness (2 Cor. 11:14-15)

21.) He quotes the scriptures (Matt. 4:5-6 & Luke 4:9-11)

22.) He works miracles (Ex. 7:22, 8:7, Matt. 24:24, Mark 13:22, Rev. 13:13-15 & 19:20, etc.)

23.) He teaches doctrine (1 Tim. 4:1)

24.) He has wisdom (Ezk. 28:17, 1 Cor. 1:21, James 3:15)

25.) He will have a World Government (Rev. 13:2-8)

The Bible clearly reveals that Satan is the king of counterfeit. His ultra-cunning methods of deception are accomplished through

IMAGES/miscellaneous sources   Various groups pulling strings behind the scenes.

To build his coming kingdom on Earth, the Devil works behind the scenes through various groups, both known and unknown, seen and unseen. There is ample evidence to show sinister forces are constantly at work (see chapter 16 for more on the Conspiracy).

outwardly good looks, good works and good words. He has angels, prophets and preachers who all act as ministers of *"righteousness"* (i.e. they perform righteous works - not unrighteous) in order to promote lies and deception which will eventually culminate in the son of Satan himself being enthroned as the literal King and God of Earth. The progression towards this final goal is subtle, and is accomplished through the puppeteering of religious and national leaders – all while looking, speaking, and acting good, of course. Satan is currently the spiritual *"god of this world"* (see 2 Cor. 4:4) and controls most (if not all) of the kingdoms of Earth (especially those that are actively engaged in building a one world government). The Devil once offered these world kingdoms to the Lord Jesus Christ with the added stipulation:

> *"... All these things will I give thee, IF thou wilt fall down and WORSHIP ME." Matthew 4:9 also see Luke 4:5-6*

This diabolical offer still stands. And as unnerving and (heaven forbid) "conspiratorial" as it may sound, TRUE Satanism is hidden in the highest echelons of the world's governments. The clear implication here is that those who currently occupy these lofty positions, in one way or another, have encountered this same offer themselves. Membership to this elite group can include kings, presidents, prime ministers and anyone associated with the highest inner workings of global nations and states. This does not mean, however, that all presidents, kings and rulers are Devil worshipers. But it does indicate that such malevolent men are those who currently control the true global reins of power. Many of these rulers are never known by the general public, remaining nameless, faceless and essentially "invisible". But they are agents who undoubtedly are subservient to those the scriptures describe as being the true rulers of this present evil world. This is an important aspect to understanding the Devil's ever-present web of conspiracy, especially those which seemingly involve an admixture of governments, occultism and the unknown (more on this later).

> *"For we wrestle not against flesh and blood, but against principalities, against powers, against THE RULERS OF THE DARKNESS OF THIS WORLD, against spiritual wickedness in high places." Ephesians 6:12*

"[3] Grace be to you and peace from God the Father, and from our Lord Jesus Christ, [4] Who gave himself for our sins, that he might deliver us from this PRESENT EVIL WORLD, according to the will of God and our Father: [5] To whom be glory for ever and ever. Amen."
Galatains 1:3-5

The Bible shows the Devil to be a fallen "cherub" and not, as it is usually assumed, a fallen "angel". As we've already seen, all cherubim are closely associated with the Throne of God. And so it is, for the original, pre-fallen position of Lucifer was that of a *"covering cherub"*, the same position represented by the golden cherubim depicted on the Ark of the Covenant:

"[17] And thou shalt make a mercy seat of pure gold: two cubits and a half shall be the length thereof, and a cubit and a half the breadth thereof. [18] And thou shalt make two cherubims of gold, of beaten work shalt thou make them, in the two ends of the mercy seat. [19] And make one cherub on the one end, and the other cherub on the other end: even of the mercy seat shall ye make the cherubims on the two ends thereof. [20] And the CHERUBIMS shall stretch forth their wings on high, COVERING THE MERCY SEAT with their wings, and their faces shall look one to another; toward the mercy seat shall the faces of the cherubims be. [21] And thou shalt put the mercy seat above upon the ark; and in the ark thou shalt put the testimony that I shall give thee. [22] And there I will meet with thee, and I will commune with thee from above the mercy seat, from between the two cherubims which are upon the ark of the testimony, of all things which I will give thee in commandment unto the children of Israel." Exodus 25:17-22

IMAGE/Dover Pictorial Archive   Doré's illustration from Milton's *Paradise Lost* (1866)

For centuries mythology and art have depicted the Devil as a sort of ruler or king over Hell. But this is not true. According to the Bible, Hell was *"prepared for the devil and his angels"*, not as a kingdom, but as a future prison (Matt. 25:41, Rev. 20:7-10). Currently, the Devil neither reside in Hell nor on the Earth. Instead, a lifeless place of outer darkness is the only true environment fit for such a fallen being. Today that place is known as "outer space" (see chapters 9 and 10 for more information).

Note that when God meets with Israel He communes from a spot known as the *"mercy seat"*. This seat, surrounded by cherubim, is a type and picture of the literal Throne of God (Ezekiel's vision). The typology is so close in fact, when King David was preparing for Solomon to build the Temple, he referred to the place for the Mercy Seat as *"the chariot of the cherubims"*.

"And for the altar of incense refined gold by weight; and gold for the pattern of the CHARIOT OF THE CHERUBIMS, that spread out their wings, and covered the ark of the covenant of the LORD." 1 Chronicles 28:18

For the true depiction of God's chariot Throne see Ezekiel chapters 1 and 10. Other references to God's flying cherubic chariot Throne include 2 Samuel 22:11, Psalms 18:10, 80:1 & 99:1. The point here is that the cherubim that cover the mercy seat with their wings are referred to as *"covering"* cherubim. The book of Ezekiel shows that sometime in the past one of these covering cherubim *"sinned"* and God vowed to *"destroy"* him.

"Thou art the anointed CHERUB THAT COVERETH; and I have set thee so: thou wast upon the holy mountain of God; thou hast walked up and down in the midst of the stones of fire. Thou wast perfect in thy ways from the day that thou wast created, till iniquity was found in thee. By the multitude of thy merchandise they have filled the midst of thee with violence, and THOU HAST SINNED: therefore I will cast thee as profane out of the mountain of God: and I will destroy thee, O COVERING CHERUB, from the midst of the stones of fire." Ezekiel 28:14-16

A *"stone of fire"* is a red-hot coal. The scriptures indicate that when Lucifer was cast *"from the midst of the stones of fire"*, this may be a reference to his removal from the coals *"between the wheels, even under the cherub"* (Ezk. 10:2).

The Bible only shows the existence of four cherubim. When added to the cherub that *"sinned"*, the total comes to five – four holy beasts and one unholy beast. Four holy cherubic beasts that surround God's Throne and worship God, and one fallen renegade beast bent on God's destruction. Because the word "beast" can be used interchangeably with the word "cherub", we find the first biblical references to Satan the Devil worded as follows:

> *"Now the SERPENT was more subtle than any BEAST of the field ... And the LORD God said unto the serpent, Because thou hast done this, thou art cursed above all CATTLE, and above every BEAST of the field; upon thy belly shalt thou go, and dust shalt thou eat all the days of thy life:" Genesis 3:1 & 14*

The Devil is a serpentine type "beast" (not a snake) that God classifies among the "cattle" (see Ezk. 1:7). Evidently, Lucifer is a different type of cherub from those currently depicted around God's Throne. None of the other cherubim are described in this manner. The scriptures are not clear on why this is so, but my guess is that it may be a POST-FALLEN CONDITION – after Lucifer sinned, he was cursed, and his physical image changed. If not, then Lucifer was the only serpentine cherub of his kind. When God cursed the Devil in the garden, Satan went from being an upright flying dragon, to being a legless flying serpent (or possibly both wingless and legless). All serpents and snakes are a picture and type of this curse.

Like the other cherubim, it is assumed that Satan also has the ability to transform his appearance into one of the four cherubic faces (man, ox, lion or eagle). The second book of Corinthians clearly testifies of this power where it reads "...*Satan himself is transformed...*" (2 Cor. 11:14). However, since the Devil is serpent-like and different from any of the other four cherubim, it is unclear what is the exact nature of his four faces – if he even retains this feature at all. The scriptures never addressed this. But the Book of the Revelation shows he is now a *"Great Red Dragon"* (Rev. 12:3). A creature which can transform itself into a humanoid, man-like being called *"an angel of light"*. Identifying the current form of the Adversary is a tricky. These multiple appearances are only rivaled by his numerous names and titles, a number equaling 6+6+6.

Count the Number of the Devil's Names

1.) The Devil (Rev. 12:9, etc.)

2.) Satan (1 Chron. 21:1, Job 1:6, Rev. 12:9, etc.)

3.) The [that old] Serpent (Gen. 3:1, Rev. 12:9, etc.)

4.) Lucifer (Isa. 14:12)

5.) The [that] Wicked One (Matt. 13:38-39, etc.)

6.) The Tempter (Matt. 4:3, 1 Thess. 3:5)

7.) The Enemy (Matt. 13:25, 28 & 39)

8.) The Adversary (1 Tim. 5:14, 1 Peter 5:8)

9.) The Accuser (Rev. 12:10)

10.) The [Great Red] Dragon (Rev. 12:9, etc.)

11.) The Prince of this World (John 12:31, etc.)

12.) The god of this World (2 Cor. 4:4)

13.) The Prince of the Power of the Air (Eph. 2:2)

14.) Prince of the Devils (Matt. 12:24 & 27)

15.) Chief of the Devils (Luke 11:15)

16.) The Father of Lies (John 8:44)

17.) The Anointed Cherub (Ezk. 28:14-16)

18.) Beelzebub (Matt. 12:24-27, Mk. 3:22-23, etc.)

NOTE: Not to be confused with Rev. 13:18 dealing with the number/name of the Antichrist (not the number of his names).

One of the most prominent devices of Satan is to steal the words of God from man (Gen. 3:1-4, Matt. 13:19, Mk. 4:15). Just as one of God's primary concerns deals with the words of a written book (see chapter 6), so too, the Devil is concerned with the words of God. If the Devil can get you to reject God's written words, either through out-and-out denial and infidelity or by counterfeiting the Holy Bible,

IMAGE/Dover Pictorial Archive   Satan replacing the Bible with a counterfeit (c. 1626 AD)

then he can ultimately block your access to the only pure truth in the Universe – the *King James Bible*. The Devil doesn't think twice about counterfeiting God's Holy Spirit. He will have no problem convincing the entire world that the son of Satan is the "son of God". And he has already destroyed the ability of most Christians to discern between the things of Satan and the things of God through his mass influx of counterfeit Bible versions. *"Yea, hath God said"* (Gen. 3:1) has been his mantra throughout the ages. If you have no access to the pure revelation of God, you have (among other things) no means of detecting Satan. If this were not enough, the Devil also commands an untold legion of angels and devils (Matt. 9:34 ,25:41 & Rev. 12:7-9); has a semblance of "omnipresence" (2 Cor. 4:4, Eph. 2:2); can "possess" people (Lk. 22:3, Acts 5:3); is a consummate man pleaser (Matt. 16:23, Mk. 8:33, Gal. 1:10); can both deceive and control large segments of the world's population (2 Cor. 4:3-4, Rev.

12:9, Job 1:12-15 & 17, etc.); and demands worship from those in high political positions (Matt. 4:9, etc.). It's no wonder the Apostle Paul refers to him as *"the god of this world"*. The Devil, indeed, wields the power of a "god", but the true God, the Creator of the Universe, will see to it that Satan has an end:

> *"And the devil that deceived them was cast into the lake of fire and brimstone, where the beast and the false prophet are, and shall be tormented day and night for ever and ever." Revelation 20:10*

Celestial Horses – As bizarre and shocking as it may sound, the Bible reveals the existence of extraterrestrial horses – supernatural creatures with the powers of flight and invisibility that are evidently impervious to fire and the adverse effects of outer space. These fascinating creatures show up on several different occasions either pulling chariots or simply with riders on their backs. With their first appearance in the second book of Kings, these incredible animals are referred to as *"horses of fire"*. Here they are seen swooping down from the sky and scooping up Elijah in a fiery chariot:

> *"And it came to pass, as they still went on, and talked, that, behold, there appeared a chariot of fire, and horses of fire, and parted them both asunder; and Elijah went up by a whirlwind into heaven. And Elisha saw it, and he cried, My father, my father, the chariot of Israel, and the horsemen thereof. And he saw him no more: and he took hold of his own clothes, and rent them in two pieces."*
> *2 Kgs 2:11-12*

On another occasion, a host of these horses exhibited their power of invisibility while hiding from the Syrian army. Elisha's servant is not able to see this phantom army until God *"opens his eyes"*:

IMAGE/public domain   The Pegasus of myth was undoubtedly inspired by heavenly horses.

"And Elisha prayed, and said, LORD, I pray thee, open his eyes, that he may see. And the LORD opened the eyes of the young man; and he saw: and, behold, the mountain was full of HORSES AND CHARIOTS OF FIRE round about Elisha." 2 Kings 6:17

And again, in the Book of Revelation we find the Lord Jesus Christ Himself astride one of these beasts with an entire Heavenly Army also following Him on celestial-horseback (see Rev. 19:11-14), a jaw-dropping sight.

Even though God's heavenly horses are not pictured with wings, the mythology of flying, winged horses like the "Pegasus" is undoubtedly inspired by ancient encounters with these creatures. The scriptures also seem to indicate that the early pagans may have worshiped these horses where we find it written:

"And he [Josiah, King of Judah] *took away the HORSES that the kings of Judah had GIVEN TO THE SUN, at the entering in of the house of the LORD, by the chamber of Nathanmelech the chamberlain, which was in the suburbs, and burned the chariots of the sun with fire."*
2 Kings 23:11

Other biblical encounters with heavenly horses are found in the books of Zechariah and Revelation. While it may be true that other supernatural-type animals exist in the Third Heaven, "celestial horses", as we've called them, remain the only such entities explicitly cited by the Bible. But other scriptures which point to the possible existence of other celestial-type animals can be found (Acts 10:11-12 & 11:5-6).

Chapter 12 Summary

This chapter has addressed the Bible's summation of "extraterrestrial life". Alien life which can exist OUTSIDE of the earth and its atmosphere. The word "alien", however, is used in the strictest sense of the word, meaning "foreigner" and not "space monsters from Mars". Modern man has been brainwashed by the words "extraterrestrial" and "alien", and simply mentioning one or the other generally conjures images not based on truth. This study was designed to help you realign your thinking with God's words. While much of the "alien life" addressed in this chapter interacts with life on Earth (the First Heaven), these life forms also dwell in or have access to the dwelling place of God (the Third Heaven). The next chapter will examine this access and list biblical examples that show space travel is not strictly limited to such things as spaceships, or so-called flying saucers and UFOs.

13

Star Treks

Many assume that alien life from distant planets frequently visits the Earth (usually depicted as highly advanced, humanoid-type creatures piloting spacecraft), but the Bible does not teach this. The previous chapter demonstrated that highly advanced, highly intelligent forms of life regularly interact with the Earth and its inhabitants (albeit many of these life forms remain invisible and/or appear identical to man). While this planet is the focus of God's attention (see Chapter 8), the Earth is also the focus of the most powerful and malevolent evil force in the Universe – Satan, the original sinner. Other heavenly activities recorded in scripture include what surprisingly could be labeled as "space travel". The term conjures ideas of high technology, including rockets, space shuttles, UFOs, flying saucers and spaceships (man-made or otherwise). But the scriptures show that space travel is nothing new. The thing that *is* new, however, is the idea that space travel requires some sort of flying craft to both propel one through space and protect one from its hazardous environment. As we'll soon see, this is not always the case.

Before we begin our examination of biblical space travel, one point needs to be clarified. If you've never really studied the Bible, you may think of the Third Heaven (the dwelling place of God) as being in another "realm" or "alternate dimension", and therefore unreachable by physical travel. You may only see Heaven as a place filled with invisible spirits and picture it as being on an alternate plane of reality. However, this is not true. While it's true that *"God is a Spirit"* (Jn. 4:24), it's also true that God is also a Man, and the Lord Jesus Christ is the *"express image of his person"* (Heb. 1:3). In other words, God is not only a Spirit, but a physical Person with a physical Body (a tripartite Being - see page 226). Have you ever considered where THE PHYSICAL BODY of the Lord Jesus Christ went after ascending into Heaven? Right now, it's physically seated at the right hand of God (Col. 3:1). How did it get there? Believe it or not, Heaven is a physical, visible, CREATED PLACE (*"In the beginning God CREATED the heaven..."* Gen. 1:1) occupied by spirits, people and other celestial beings. The fact that Heaven is filled with spirits no more makes it a "spiritual realm" or "alternate dimension" than planet Earth. Every living creature on this planet possesses a spirit. If it has no spirit, it is not alive. Therefore, the Earth is just as much a "spiritual realm" as Heaven. The difference however, is that the Third Heaven is a SINLESS land of light occupied by God Almighty (1 John 1:5), while the Earth is a FALLEN planet, buried in a black Universe, occupied by creatures under the curse of sin. But both places have spirits, and both are occupied by physical, visible, living creatures (see Chapter 12). In short, Heaven is a real place. This chapter will look at some of the people and things that have traveled (or will travel) through the Second Heaven of outer space.

Enoch is Translated

Enoch was the son of Jared, the great, great, great, grandson of Seth and the great, great, great, great grandson of Adam. The son of

Enoch was the oldest man who ever lived (Methuselah - 969 years old) and Noah was his great grandson. The Bible records of Enoch:

> *"And all the days of Enoch were three hundred sixty and five years: And Enoch walked with God: and he was not; for God took him." Genesis 5:23-24*

> *"By faith Enoch was translated that he should not see death; and was not found, because God had translated him: for before his translation he had this testimony, that he pleased God." Hebrews 11:5*

Because he *"pleased God"*, Enoch was *"translated"*. To "translate" something means to move it from one place or condition to another. The Bible says that Enoch did *"not see death"*, therefore, he was literally transported bodily from the surface of the Earth to the Third Heaven without having to die. The Bible does not say that he "ascended into heaven", but that he was simply "translated" by God. This indicates that he did not have to travel through outer space, but was instantaneously moved to Heaven. Enoch is literally, physically and bodily in Heaven (right now), walking around (right now). He's one of the people that we mentioned previously that's present in the Third Heaven with God. He's not a bodiless spirit floating around in Heaven strumming on a harp. He's a spirit which resides in the physical body of a man, whose feet are touching the ground of Heaven. Enoch is a real man, and Heaven is a real place.

The Chariot of Fire

The record of Elijah being carried to Heaven by a fiery chariot is a well known biblical event. Many New Agers and Ufologists misconstrue this account, wrongly interpreting the flying horses and chariot as a "spacecraft" of some kind. The horses and chariot are

IMAGE/Dover Pictorial Archive   Elijah is taken up into Heaven (c. 893 BC)

real, however, and as we discovered in chapter 12, appear elsewhere in the Bible. The Bible records of Elijah:

> *"And it came to pass, as they still went on, and talked, that, behold, there appeared a chariot of fire, and horses of fire, and parted them both asunder; and ELIJAH WENT UP by a whirlwind INTO HEAVEN. And Elisha saw it, and he cried, My father, my father, the chariot of Israel, and the horsemen thereof. And he saw him no more: and he took hold of his own clothes, and rent them in two pieces."* 2 Kings 2:11-12

These scriptures reveal that Elijah literally *"went up"* in a chariot *"into heaven"* while the prophet Elisha witnessed the event. In order for the chariot, horses and horsemen to leave the surface of the

Earth, travel through the sky and enter the heavens, they obviously have to be supernatural-type creatures. Elisha was later mocked by some men from Jericho who knew of the event. They jested that perhaps the Lord had simply taken Elijah up to cast him down in some valley or mountain. The men insisted a search be. Elisha finally gave in to their demands, but the body of Elijah was never found, and the reason is obvious. Although he was not *"translated"* like Enoch, the prophet Elijah *"went up"* gradually (as gradually as a *"whirlwind"*) and was carried from the Earth through the first and second heavens. Elijah is literally, physically and bodily in Heaven (right now), walking around (right now). Elijah is a real man, and Heaven is a real place.

The Missing Body of Moses

The biblical record of Moses' body being taken to heaven is a little less clear than that of Enoch and Elijah. Moses was not taken to Heaven bodily. He died first, and his body was taken later. It sounds strange, but it's scriptural. After Moses died it was God Himself who buried the body.

> *"So Moses the servant of the LORD died there in the land of Moab, according to the word of the LORD. And HE [God] BURIED HIM in a valley in the land of Moab, over against Bethpeor: but NO MAN knoweth of his sepulchre unto this day." Deut. 34:5-6*

When God buried Moses' physical body its location was never revealed. However, this "body" shows up again in the New Testament where we read the following strange account:

> *"Yet Michael the archangel, when contending with the devil he disputed about THE BODY OF MOSES, durst not bring against him a railing accusation, but said, The Lord rebuke thee." Jude 1:9*

IMAGE/Dover Pictorial Archive   Christ is Transfigured (c. 32 AD)

When the Lord Jesus Christ was transfigured on the mount, Moses and Elijah are
seen with him "in the flesh". Where had their physical bodies been before this time?
They were both present BODILY in the Third Heaven with God.

Apparently, Michael the Archangel was sent to Earth to transport
the corpse of Moses to Heaven to reunite it with Moses' spirit. I know
this sounds "far out", but when the Lord Jesus Christ and Elijah
APPEAR TOGETHER BODILY on the Mount of Transfiguration,
guess who else is standing there with them "in the flesh"? Moses:

> *"And after six days Jesus taketh Peter, James, and John*
> *his brother, and bringeth them up into an high mountain*
> *apart, And was transfigured before them: and his face*
> *did shine as the sun, and his raiment was white as the*
> *light. And, behold, there appeared unto them Moses and*
> *Elias [Elijah] talking with him." Matthew 17:1-3*

The point is, somewhere along the way the physical body of Moses had to get from the Earth to the Third Heaven. That didn't happen when Moses died. It happened some time later. We know how the body of Elijah reached the Third Heaven (2 Kings 2:11-12), so it's easy to understand how it appears with Christ on the Mount, but the body of Moses is another matter. The later appearance of Moses' physical body represents a unique case only answered by the intervention of an Archangel. As a result, Moses is literally, physically and bodily in Heaven (right now), walking around (right now). Moses is a real man, and Heaven is a real place.

The Two Witnesses

The Book of Revelation gives an amazing future account of two witnesses who will ascend up to Heaven after being killed and brought back to life. I'm not going to go into a lot of detail about who these witnesses are, but needless to say, we've already addressed them both by name. Both witness are in Heaven prior to the Great Tribulation. Both men have an ancient scriptural record of working signs and wonders, and because of that, are held in high regard by the nation of Israel (1 Cor. 1:22). They also both appear with Christ on the Mount of Transfiguration, *"standing before the God of the earth"*. One witness represents the Law; the other, the Prophets:

> *"[3] And I will give power unto my two witnesses, and they shall prophesy a thousand two hundred and threescore days, clothed in sackcloth. [4] These are the two olive trees, and the two candlesticks standing before the God of the earth. [5] And if any man will hurt them, fire proceedeth out of their mouth, and devoureth their enemies: and if any man will hurt them, he must in this manner be killed. [6] These have power to shut heaven, that it rain not in the days of their prophecy: and have*

power over waters to turn them to blood, and to smite the earth with all plagues, as often as they will. [7] And when they shall have finished their testimony, the beast that ascendeth out of the bottomless pit shall make war against them, and shall overcome them, and kill them. [8] And their dead bodies shall lie in the street of the great city, which spiritually is called Sodom and Egypt, where also our Lord was crucified. [9] And they of the people and kindreds and tongues and nations shall see their dead bodies three days and an half, and shall not suffer their dead bodies to be put in graves. [10] And they that dwell upon the earth shall rejoice over them, and make merry, and shall send gifts one to another; because these two prophets tormented them that dwelt on the earth. [11] And after three days and an half the Spirit of life from God entered into them, and they stood upon their feet; and great fear fell upon them which saw them. [12] And they heard a great voice from heaven saying unto them, Come up hither. And THEY ASCENDED UP TO HEAVEN in a cloud; and their enemies beheld them."
Revelation 11:3-12

The unique thing about Revelation's two witnesses, is that when they *"ascend up to heaven"* (Rev. 11:12), it will be both men's third trip between Heaven and Earth. They both have prior records of ascending or otherwise being taken to Heaven. During the Great Tribulation, after the Church Age ends and the Lord turns back to deal with the nation of Israel, these witnesses will also return to Earth bearing signs and wonders (1 Cor. 1:22, Deut. 4:34, Deut. 26:8, Psa. 78:10-11, Rev. 11:6). After the Antichrist's world government beheads them (Rev. 13:15 & 20:4), they will both be resurrected by God and return to the Third Heaven.

The Ascension of Christ

The clearest biblical record of a man literally departing the surface of the Earth, ascending up into the sky and finally winding-up physically in the Third Heaven is the account of the Lord Jesus Christ Himself. Christians, especially, need to think about this. For it is THIS EVENT THAT DEMONSTRATES that Heaven is literally located in a physical place *"above"* the Earth. Heaven is not in an alternate "dimension" or on another "plane of reality". Heaven is real. And although it may be located far, far, above the heavens (over 14 billion lightyears or more away from Earth, on the other side of the darkness – see chapter 10), the Lord Jesus Christ arrived there by first ascending off the surface of planet Earth. Think about it. If Heaven is not located above the Earth (and above outer space), what would be the point in ascending up into the sky to get there? There would be no point. To travel upward if your destination is not upward is totally pointless. God wouldn't do anything in vain, would He? If you had to reach a destination located to your North, would you first travel South, East or West? Of course not. Unless, of course, you didn't know where you were going. The Lord Jesus Christ knew where he was going:

> *"And when he had spoken these things, while they beheld, he was TAKEN UP; and a cloud received him out of their sight. And while they looked stedfastly toward heaven as HE WENT UP, behold, two men stood by them in white apparel; Which also said, Ye men of Galilee, why stand ye GAZING UP INTO HEAVEN? this same Jesus, which is TAKEN UP from you into heaven, shall so come in like manner as ye have SEEN HIM GO INTO HEAVEN"*
> Acts 1:9-11

Note the words *"he was taken up"*, *"he went up"*, *"gazing up"* and *"taken up from you into heaven"*. If this verse testifies of anything,

298   The Ascension of Christ

it testifies to the fact that the physical body of a man (God in the flesh), WENT UP INTO HEAVEN. One second he was standing on the ground, and the next second he was flying "up, up and away" with his arms outstretched over his head like "Superman".

> *"And he led them out as far as to Bethany, and he LIFTED UP HIS HANDS, and blessed them. And it came to pass, while he blessed them, he was parted from them, and carried UP INTO HEAVEN." Luke 24:50-51*

Not only do the written words of God show that the Lord Jesus ascended up to Heaven, but they also reveal that he'll return again to the Earth, just before his millennial reign. Jesus will return bodily to the Earth descending the heavens with an invincible army of mounted saints (see Rev. 19 and Joel 2:1-11). He flew up to Heaven once, and the Bible says he'll fly back down to the Earth. That's two complete trips through outer space – one up and one down:

> *"... Ye men of Galilee, why stand ye GAZING UP into heaven? this same Jesus, which is taken up from you into heaven, shall so COME IN LIKE MANNER as ye have SEEN HIM GO INTO HEAVEN." Acts 1:11*

> *"And I SAW heaven opened, and behold a white horse; and he that sat upon him was called Faithful and True, and in righteousness he doth judge and make war. His eyes were as a flame of fire, and on his head were many crowns; and he had a name written, that no man knew, but he himself. And he was clothed with a vesture dipped in blood: and his name is called The Word of God. And the ARMIES which were IN HEAVEN followed him upon white horses, clothed in fine linen, white and clean." Revelation 19:11-14*

IMAGE/Dover Pictorial Archive   Christ ascends up into heaven (c. 33 AD)

The ascension of Christ is one of the most solid biblical proofs showing that Heaven is literally located above the Earth.

The Lord Jesus Christ is in Heaven (right now), seated at the right Hand of God (right now). Jesus is God manifest in the flesh, and Heaven is a real place.

The residents of Heaven are not all simply vagabond spirits floating around or doing whatever bodiless spirits are supposed to do. Enoch is real. Elijah is real. Moses is real. The Lord Jesus Christ is real. Heaven really IS occupied by physical visible people. Enoch, Moses and Elijah once walked this Earth. But now their feet literally trod a much more hallowed ground – a ground unmarred by the ravages of sin.

Humans are not the only living things to travel through the open heavens, however. Practically all of the various kinds of extraterrestrial life mentioned in chapter 12 have ventured down to Earth at one time or another. The angels of God, fallen angels, unclean spirits, cherubim, celestial horses and even the Devil himself, all have made trips to this planet, and many continue to do so. The Devil's journeys, especially, are clearly described.

Space Journeys of the Devil

Popular belief teaches that Satan was cast down to the Earth after his fall and is now somehow the "King" or ruler over Hell. This idea is found nowhere in the Bible. The scriptures agree that the Devil is a fallen creature. Ezekiel says he was once "perfect" until *"iniquity was found"* in him (Ezk. 28:15). But Satan is no more a "ruler" over Hell than the Greek god Hades. The Bible says that Hell (and the future Lake of Fire) was *"prepared for the devil"* (Matt. 25:41). And that preparation has nothing to do with him ruling over a kingdom. It has to do with him BURNING in the presence of an eternal, *Consuming Fire* without a covering for his sins (Rev. 20:10). To claim that Satan

IMAGE/public domain
The Devil, as a angel of light,
standing before the Throne of God.

was cast down to the Earth at the time of his fall is some more unbiblical nonsense. Satan is not permanently "cast out" of the Third Heaven until the third "woe" of Revelation 8:13. A point of time in the FUTURE, not the past (see Rev. 12:3-12). Until that time though, the Devil has full access to the Throne Room of God, outer space and planet Earth. The book of Job testifies:

> *"Now there was a day when the sons of God came to present themselves before the LORD, and Satan came also among them. And the LORD said unto Satan, Whence comest thou? Then Satan answered the LORD, and said, From going to and fro IN THE EARTH, and from walking up and down in it." Job 1:6-7*

> *"Again there was a day when the sons of God came to present themselves before the LORD, and Satan came also among them to present himself before the LORD. And the LORD said unto Satan, From whence comest thou? And Satan answered the LORD, and said, From going to and fro IN THE EARTH, and from walking up and down in it." Job 2:1-2*

Undoubtedly, the fall of Lucifer took place many centuries before the book of Job, but here we see Satan in the Third Heaven standing *"before the Lord"* on two separate and distinct occasions. This makes it clear that he's still allowed access to God's Throne and has yet to be permanently cast out. God asks the Devil twice, *"from whence comest thou?"* And Satan gives the same answer in both instances, *"From going to and fro in the earth, and from walking up and down in it."* Note that in this answer the Devil admits that he's come *"from ... the earth"*. It appears that the Devil not only travels from the Earth to Heaven, but his trips are frequent and often. If Satan runs up to Heaven and back every time he accuses one of the saints, he must be racking up quite the frequent flier miles. He's not called *"the accuser of the brethren"* for nothing (Rev. 12:10). Other verses in Job help to illustrate this fact. In Job 1:12 and 2:7 we see Satan leaving *"the presence of the Lord"* (i.e. the Third Heaven) and the verses that follow show Satan operating back on Earth. In Job 26:13 we find this strange wording:

> *"By his spirit he* [God] *hath garnished the heavens; his hand hath formed the crooked serpent." Job 26:13*

What kind of *"serpent"* would be connected with *"the heavens"*? A flying serpent. And this flying *"crooked serpent"*, this serpent *"in the heavens"*, is both seen and named in the book of Revelation:

> *"And there was WAR IN HEAVEN: Michael and his angels fought against THE DRAGON; and THE DRAGON fought and his angels, And prevailed not; neither was THEIR PLACE found any more IN HEAVEN. And THE GREAT DRAGON was cast out, that OLD SERPENT, called the Devil, and Satan, which deceiveth the whole world: he was cast out into the EARTH, and his angels were cast out with him." Revelation 12:7-9*

Here we see Satan both in heaven and on earth within three short verses, clearly teaching that the Devil has yet to be permanently confined to any particular location. Although he does not currently "dwell" in heaven, but outer space, he is free to move about as he pleases. The Bible calls him *"the prince of the power of the air"* (Eph. 2:2) and that power undoubtedly encompasses his ability to subtly move between the three heavens undetected. Intelligent, nonhuman life does travel through outer space, and one of those life forms is a Great Red Dragon, an Old Serpent, known as *"Satan the Devil"*.

Other Flying Things

Just as the Devil travels between Heaven and Earth, so too do angels, fallen angels, cherubim and unclean spirits, as the following references reveal:

IMAGE/Dover Pictorial Archive   Michael and the Great Red Dragon.

When Michael the Archangel wars against Satan, the Great Red Dragon, and casts him out of Heaven, this takes place in the future. This flying serpent currently still has access to the Third Heaven and the Throne of God.

- Angels in Heaven - Gen. 28:12, Job 38:4-7, Matt. 18:10, Rev. 5:11, 7:11, 12:7, etc.
- Angels on the Earth - Gen. 19:1-16, Jud. 6:11-21, Num. 22:22-35, Luke 1:11-38, etc.
- Fallen Angels in Heaven - Rev. 12:7
- Fallen Angels on the Earth - Gen. 6:2-4, Rev. 9:14-15
- Cherubim in Heaven - Rev. 4:6-9, 5:6-14, 7:11, 14:3, 19:4
- Cherubim on the Earth - Ezk. 1 & 10
- Unclean Spirits in Heaven - 1 Kgs 22:21-22, 2 Chron. 18:20-21
- Unclean Spirits on the Earth - Matt. 8:28-33, Lk. 4:33-35, Acts 16:16-18, Rev. 16:14, etc.

These verses show that while some of these beings may not particularly *dwell* in the Third Heaven (especially fallen angels and unclean spirits), they can be found both in Heaven and on Earth. This indicates that *they regularly move back and forth between the two locations.* In all honesty, the Bible takes it for granted that other forms of life have visited, are visiting, or will visit the Earth, and that this EXTRATERRESTRIAL LIFE has the ability to travel through outer space and beyond. But because these travelers, for the most part, are supernatural type beings and not EVOLVED HUMANOIDS flying spaceships from other planets, many people (both saved and lost) refuse to see this for what it really is – *alien life traversing the heavens.* Those who refuse to accept this revelation are putting themselves in a position to be deceived.

For whatever reason (infidelity towards the words of God in most cases), the majority of Christians today have *disconnected the Bible from reality.* Its words have been tampered with and played with for such a long time, via corrupt manuscripts and false Bibles, that no one takes it serious anymore. It's a joke. And because such words as "aliens", "outer space" and "technology" (and other related terms) are not literally found within its pages, professing scholars and skeptics have destroyed the common man's faith in the Book. It is treated more as a fuzzy-wuzzy, "feel good book", or as a handbook on psychology that's only used to help one cope with the problems and difficulties of everyday life. What many Christians miss, however, is that THE BIBLE IS SO MUCH MORE. To downgrade the scriptures to a spiritual book of psychology, that's simply been stuffed with unknowable "symbolic and apocalyptic language", is to ignore a large chunk of the Bible's teachings. Words which the Creator has written specifically to YOU (Prov. 22:20-21, Rom. 15:4). Special revelation which you cannot get by any other means. Don't shortchange yourself by simply using the Bible to help you "feel better" when you're stressed out or feeling down. The Bible has things to teach

– doctrinal things. And many times those things and teachings can be surprising or unpleasant, but that does not make them any less true. That's why, I'm sure, that many professing Christians will be shocked at some of the findings in this book. Whether they realize it or not, they're not accustomed to relating the Bible to reality. Many prefer to "spiritualize" God's History Book. That's why it's a big deal when I say that the Bible shows that "extraterrestrial life" exists, or that "space travel" is in the Bible. Many Christians are not used to thinking of the Bible in this way. Yet, for the Christian this should be the norm. The Bible not only teaches the lost how to get saved and teaches the Christian how to have a closer walk with the Lord Jesus Christ; but it also exposes the physical, visible and invisible REALITIES of our world and the Universe (2Tim. 3:16-17).

New Jerusalem: Giant City from Space

In the book of John, the Lord Jesus Christ makes the following statement:

> "In my Father's house are many mansions: if it were not so, I would have told you. I go to prepare a place for you. And if I go and prepare a place for you, I will come again, and receive you unto myself; that where I am, there ye may be also." John 14:2-3

The place which Christ so unequivocally declared was in preparation for the saints is a place full of "mansions". The Hebrews says:

> "But now they desire a better country, that is, an heavenly: wherefore God is not ashamed to be called their God: for he hath prepared for them a city." Hebrews 11:16

> "For here have we no continuing city, but we seek one to come." Hebrews 13:14

More light on the subject reveals that this heavenly mansion being prepared is a city – *"he hath prepared for them a city"*. The Apostle John is privileged to see this magnificent prepared-city and writes:

> *"And I John saw the holy city, new Jerusalem, coming down from God out of heaven, prepared as a bride adorned for her husband." Revelation 21:2*

When the prophet Elijah was carried up to heaven he rode in the first inanimate object ever recorded to travel from Earth to the Third Heaven – a chariot. The Holy City of New Jerusalem, which descends *"down from God out of heaven"*, will be, unquestionably, the largest inanimate object to ever cross the immense distance of space. The size of this vast mobile space city is nearly large enough to house the Moon (a fitting comparison, since the Moon, biblically speaking, is a picture and type of the bride of Christ). Its exact dimensions are given in the book of Revelation:

> *"And he carried me away in the spirit to a great and high mountain, and shewed me that great city, the holy Jerusalem, descending out of heaven from God, And the city lieth foursquare, and the length is as large as the breadth: and he measured the city with the reed, twelve thousand furlongs. The length and the breadth and the height of it are equal." Revelation 21:10 & 16 For the full description read Revelation 21:10-27*

John says that New Jerusalem is *"foursquare"*, that is, it's shaped like a gigantic cube, where *"the length and the breadth and the height of it are equal"*. The dimensional breakdown looks like this:

City Length in Furlongs = 12,000 furlongs

12,000 furlongs = 7,920,000 feet

7,920,000 feet = 1,500 miles

City Length in Miles = 1,500 miles

City of New Jerusalem
Size Comparison Diagram

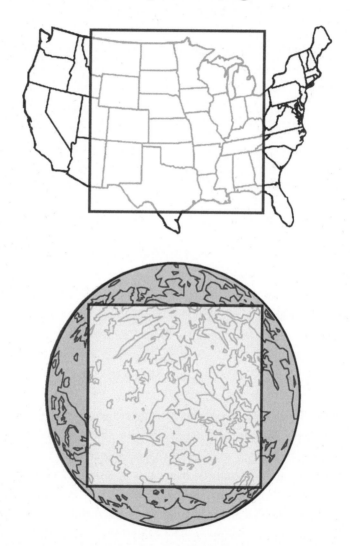

This diagram was designed to give you an approximate idea of the size of New Jerusalem as compared with America and the Moon. The massive city which descends from God out of the Third Heaven is shaped like a 1,500 mile cube. The Bible says the Apostle John saw this huge thing with his own eyes (Rev. 21:2).

In other words, New Jerusalem is a mind-blowing 1,500 miles wide by 1,500 miles high. No city on Earth even comes close to such massive dimensions. To put this in perspective, the Moon measures 2,160 miles at its equator. This means that New Jerusalem is only 660 miles smaller than Earth's Moon. If New Jerusalem were to touch down on United States soil, it would completely cover the heart of America, extending from the most southern tip of Texas to the southern edge of Canada and with east to west dimensions extending from Chattanooga, Tennessee all the way to Las Vegas, Nevada.

The Apostle Paul wrote that New Jerusalem was the spiritual "mother" of all born-again saints:

> "But Jerusalem which is above is free, which is the mother of us all." Galatians 4:26

Referring to a colossal spaceship-type city which descends through outer space as a "mother" is very interesting. Especially when you consider the fact that science fiction writers and movies have, for years, referred to giant, city-sized UFOs as "motherships". One outstanding example of science fiction mimicking a detail which the Bible revealed 1,900 years previously is seen in the popular *Star Trek* series. In 1989 the television series *Star Trek: The Next Generation* introduced a villain known as the "Borg" (short for cyborg). Composed of hundreds of cybernetic organisms (trans-humans), the Borg functioned as a single-minded "collective" and piloted a massive, 1.87 mile, cube-shaped spacecraft.

It's highly unlikely that the producers of *Star Trek* consulted the scriptures for ideas. But their so-called "Borg Cube" with its cybernetic "collective" is almost an exact duplicate of the truth presented by the Bible – an evil mirror image. The Lord Jesus Christ has prepared the giant city of New Jerusalem for his saints (John 14:2-3). And although a large untold number of saints will dwell within this city, the Bible says that each person will *"have the mind of Christ"* (see

IMAGE/©1989 CBS Studios   The *Star Trek* Borg ship is like a counterfeit New Jerusalem.

1 Cor. 2:16). That is, these individual saints will function as a holy "collective" – just like the Borg. Is this an accident? Is this another bizarre "coincidence" of science fiction? No. Regardless of what the world would have us believe, there are really no "new" ideas (Ecc. 1:10). The use of a giant cube-shaped ship by the *Star Trek* series, is simply the Devil making a lot of noise, in an attempt to both prepare and convince the world, that such an object arriving from space is EVIL. But the opposite is true. Borg or no Borg, however, the Bible still stands. And the fact remains that such a giant city will one day come (and I quote), *"down from God out of heaven"* (Rev. 21:2).

Chapter 13 Summary

We've now discovered that not only does the written word of God support the idea of intelligent life beyond Earth, but the scriptures also reveal that humans and humanoid type creatures have traveled through outer space, and some continue to do so. Both the angels of God and Satan regularly travel the heavens, moving back and fourth between the first and third heavens. The scriptures also show that inanimate objects have traveled through space in the past and will also travel there in the future. The Bible never says "aliens", "greys" or "Martians", however. This phenomenon will be addressed later in the book.

14

How to Make a Monster:
Biblical Insights on the Creation of Counterfeit Life

C hances are what you're about to read you've probably never read in any Christian book before. That's not because the scriptural proof texts aren't there, nor is it because the texts are obscure or stretched, but simply because many have failed to study the subject or to recognize the significance of scriptures which reveal the matter. Because of the rarity of the topic the reader needs to proceed with caution, relying on the Bible (and comparing scripture with scripture) as their final Authority and not any preconceived notions. This chapter is quite long because there is a lot of ground to cover. Due to the extreme nature of the subject, it is best entered before the Lord in fear, trepidation and prayer.

> "If any of you lack wisdom, let him ask of God, that giveth to all men liberally, and upbraideth not; and it shall be given him." James 1:5

> "Open thou mine eyes, that I may behold wondrous things out of thy law." Psalms 119:18

311

Life vs. Anti-life

God is the Author and Originator of life, of that fact the Bible leaves absolutely no question (Job 33:4). But many are not aware that the scriptures also reveal that we may reside in a Universe where NOT ALL LIFE FORMS are the product of His Creative Hand. While God is God, and He is sovereign, His Will is not the only will currently in operation. There is the will of the Devil and the will of man. And, for the time being, GOD ALLOWS these rebellious factions to continue. This in no way implies that if "counterfeit life forms" exist, that they are plentiful and/or numerous. It is simply being stated that, according to the Bible, such beings CAN EXIST. I know that sounds shocking, but scriptures that undergird the fact are not without number. A careful study will reveal there are (or were) a number of unique life forms whose origins, evidently,

IT WILL SCARE THE LIVING *YELL* OUT OF YOU!

HOW TO MAKE A MONSTER

SEE THE GHASTLY GHOULS IN FLAMING COLOR!

The subject of counterfeit life-creation is nothing new. Hollywood has promoted the concept for years with its monster movies.

fall outside the Will of God. That is, their existence is not a natural result of life having multiplied *"after its kind"* (Genesis 1: 21-28). The creation of these whatever-you-want-to-call-them has come about by other means.

God's will for the propagation of life is that life multiply *"after its kind"*. This is the life-producing process He originally set in motion for all life on planet Earth (see Gen. 1:21-28). Life which does not conform in some way to this initial safeguard is life OUTSIDE THE WILL OF GOD. Is such a thing possible? How? Let's just say that while I do not profess to know the exact "nuts and bolts" of how such a process works, I do know that the Bible provides evidence that supports the idea. The evidence shows that there are several instances in scripture where a life form is found that does not conform to the after-its-kind standard – it is a misfit.

The Coming of the Sons of God

The first biblical occurrence of "counterfeit life creation" shows that it can result from the union of two or more of five of the life classes created by God. More specifically, the Bible shows a joining of supernatural, angelic beings with terrestrial, Earth-bound beings:

> *"There were giants in the earth in those days; and also after that, when the SONS OF GOD CAME IN UNTO THE DAUGHTERS OF MEN, and they bare children to them, the same became mighty men which were of old, men of renown." Genesis 6:4*

In other words, the Bible shows that the *"giants"* were not a natural result of mankind reproducing *"after its kind"*. They were the product of two life forms which were never meant to be mixed: angels and men. Many Christians ardently dispute the idea that "angels" have anything to do with the passage. But the fact that the "fruit" of these unions produced whole races of super-beings, surely says that SOMETHING out of the ordinary was going on. The popular and more easily digestible rendering of the verse can be found in the 1917 C.I. Scofield Bible reference notes which state:

> *"Some hold that these 'sons of God' were the 'angels which kept not their first estate' (Jude 1:6). It is asserted that the*

speak
female
of a angel

> *title is in the O.T. exclusively used of angels. But this is*
> *an error (Isaiah 43:6). Angels are spoken of in a sexless*
> *way. No female angels are mentioned in scripture, and*
> *we are expressly told that marriage is unknown among*
> *angels (Matthew 22:30). The uniform Hebrew and*
> *Christian interpretation has been that verse Genesis 6:2*
> *marks the breaking down of the separation between the*
> *godly line of Seth and the godless line of Cain ..."*

While Mr. Scofield does not deny that the Old Testament references to *"sons of God"* refer to the angels. In the Genesis 6 instance, he rejects that scripture-with-scripture interpretation in favor of a more down-to-earth rendering. By doing this, Scofield has knowingly, or unknowingly, used scriptural sleight-of-hand in an effort to cover up the true, more unbelievable meaning of the verse. What follows is a breakdown of the errors of Scofield's private interpretation:

The Folly of the Godly Line

SCOFIELD ERROR #1: *"It is asserted that the title* [sons of God] *is in the O.T. exclusively used of angels. But this is an error (Isa.43:6)."*

CORRECTION: It is not an error. The terminology *"sons of God"* (with wording in that exact order), is only found five times in the Old Testament – EVERY SINGLE VERSE is a reference to the angel. But the exact title *"sons of God"* is used throughout the Bible to describe three distinct types of *"sons of God"* (see chapter 12, pages 262-264). Here again is that breakdown to help refresh your memory:

> **1.) The Only Begotten Son of God** - The Lord Jesus Christ (Psa. 2:7, Heb. 1:5, 1 John 4:9, etc.)
> **2.) Adopted Sons of God** - Born-again Christians (Rom. 8:14-15)

3.) Directly-Created Sons of God - Adam and the
Angels (Gen. 1:27, 2:7, Luke 3:38, Job 2:1, 38:7)

Contrary to Scofield's objections, the title *"sons of God"* (with
wording in that exact order) is EXCLUSIVELY used by the angels in
Old Testament instances:

*"Now there was a day when the SONS OF GOD came to
present themselves before the LORD, and Satan came
also among them." Job 1:6*

*"Again there was a day when the SONS OF GOD came
to present themselves before the LORD, and Satan came
also among them to present himself before the LORD."
Job 2:1*

Both verses in Job give us a window into events happening in
the Third Heaven, events otherwise unknowable without special
revelation. Satan is standing before the Throne of God, as well as
angels. Both beings the scriptures classify as *"host of heaven"*. Note
how 1 Kings and 2 Chronicles both use similar wording as Job,
showing supernatural beings standing about God's Throne – no
humans are present:

*"And he said, Hear thou therefore the word of the LORD:
I saw the LORD sitting on his throne, and all the HOST
OF HEAVEN standing by him on his right hand and on
his left." 1 Kings 22:19 & 2 Chronicles 18:18*

Job also uncovers this critical piece of information:

*"[4] Where wast thou when I laid the foundations of
the earth? declare, if thou hast understanding. [5] Who
hath laid the measures thereof, if thou knowest? or who*

hath stretched the line upon it? [6] Whereupon are the foundations thereof fastened? or who laid the corner stone thereof; [7] When the morning STARS sang together, and all the SONS OF GOD shouted for joy?" Job 38:4-7

These four verses in Job constitute the scriptural smoking gun regarding the exact identity of the Old Testament *"sons of God"*. In their context, two important facts are uncovered:

1.) God asks Job, *"WHERE WAST THOU when I laid the foundations of the earth?"* And the rhetorical answer is that Job was "nowhere". The scriptures go on to clearly show that while neither Job, nor any part of mankind, were present during this process, the *"sons of God"* were there *"when"* it happened. Job 38:7 shows them singing and shouting for joy at the time the Lord lays the Earth's foundation. In time, this places the existence of the *"sons of God"* BEFORE Genesis 1:1 – BEFORE God said: *"In the beginning God created the heaven and the earth"*.

2.) Job 38:7 also equates the title *"sons of God"* with *"stars"* (see page 259). These stars are no reference to lights in the night sky, for planetary type stars did not even exist until the fourth day of Genesis (Gen. 1:16). And planetary type stars cannot literally *"sing together"* nor *"shout for joy"*. Some may deny this (Isa. 44:23, 55:12), but why personify the singing and shouting to force the verse to mean "planetary stars", when the Bible already teaches that they DID NOT EXIST at the time, and that there are other kinds of stars who are known as *"sons of God"* which have LITERAL VOICES (Rev. 1:20).

The final two references of our Old Testament study of the words *"sons of God"*, actually constitutes the first and second mentioning of the phrase.

> *"[1] And it came to pass, when men began to multiply on the face of the earth, and daughters were born unto them,[2] That the SONS OF GOD saw the daughters of men that they were fair; and they took them wives of all which they chose. [3] And the LORD said, My spirit shall not always strive with man, for that he also is flesh: yet his days shall be an hundred and twenty years. [4] There were giants in the earth in those days; and also after that, when the SONS OF GOD came in unto the daughters of men, and they bare children to them, the same became mighty men which were of old, men of renown." Gen. 6:1-4*

These verses teach us several thing:

1.) Sons of God have the potential of being enticed and led astray due to the *"fair"* appearance of the earthly *"daughters of men"*. Note the wording of the following interesting verse dealing with spiritual headship and why the woman was created:

> *"[8] For the man is not of the woman; but the woman of the man. [9] Neither was the man CREATED FOR the woman; but the woman FOR THE MAN. [10] FOR THIS CAUSE* [because the woman was created for the man] *ought the woman to have power on her head BECAUSE OF THE ANGELS." 1 Cor. 11:8-10*

Here we see a unique warning regarding angels and their potential interest in human women. Note that the woman was not *"created for"* the angels, but explicitly *"for the man"*. The verse then admonishes the woman *"to have power on her head because of"* some strange reason connected with angels. What in the world do angels have to do with the purpose behind the creation of the woman? Nothing. The woman was not created for the angels. As a matter of fact, the word "woman" means *"taken out of Man"* – not taken out of angel (Gen. 2:18-23). But try telling that to a fallen angel.

> **2.)** Early on, when the sons of God first began to take them wives, many women probably had no idea they were mating with fallen angels. That realization probably did not occur until sometime after their offspring began to be born. I say this, because when manifesting in physical form, angels appear *identical to human men* (see pages 240-243). This means that angels could work among men incognito. I believe they used this to their advantage as a way of deceiving earth's women into a wrong relationship:

> *"Be not forgetful to entertain strangers: for thereby SOME HAVE ENTERTAINED ANGELS UNAWARES."* Hebrews 13:2

This point also helps us to understand why it was only the *"sons"* of God which took the *"daughters"* of men, and why only such a combination could produce literal giants. Genesis 6 shows there were no "daughters of God" taking the "sons of men", because there are NO FEMALE ANGELS. This means that there was ONLY ONE PLACE where the carnal lust of these supernatural creatures could be satisfied – planet Earth.

> **3.)** The angelic sons of God can sire children via human women. This is the conclusion that causes such an uproar. More will be said regarding this unsavory concept in point #2 of our rebuttal.

Isaiah 43:6 (the proof text cited by Scofield) does not use the term "sons of God", but only implies the title:

> *"[1] But now thus saith the LORD that created thee, O Jacob, and he that formed thee, O Israel, Fear not: for I have redeemed thee, I have called thee by thy name; thou art mine. [2] When thou passest through the waters, I will be with thee; and through the rivers, they shall not overflow thee: when thou walkest through the fire, thou shalt not be burned; neither shall the flame kindle upon thee. [3] For I am the LORD thy God, the Holy One of Israel, thy Saviour: I gave Egypt for thy ransom, Ethiopia and Seba for thee. [4] Since thou wast precious in my sight, thou hast been honourable, and I have loved thee: therefore will I give men for thee, and people for thy life. [5] Fear not: for I am with thee: I will bring thy seed from the east, and gather thee from the west; [6] I will say to the north, Give up; and to the south, Keep not back: bring MY SONS from far, and MY DAUGHTERS from the ends of the earth; [7] Even EVERY ONE that is CALLED BY MY NAME: for I have created HIM for my glory, I have formed HIM; yea, I have made HIM."*
> *Isaiah 43:1-6*

Citing Isaiah 43:6 as a proof text to overthrow the fact that angels are the rightful owners of the Old Testament *"sons of God"* designation is where you'll find the real error. Isaiah 43:6 does not use the title explicitly, but only implies its meaning, which is fine. But to cite the verse to show that the *"sons of God"* of Genesis 6 are "not angels", after the Old Testament provides THREE OTHER REFERENCES OF THE EXACT SAME WORDING saying they are angels, is a scriptural stretch more akin to wishful thinking. It's sloppy Bible study. By using an obscure verse, Scofield usurps the first and obvious meaning of the phrase after comparing scripture with scripture. Isaiah 43:1-6 deals with the *"sons of Jacob"*, the nation of Israel. Not any supposed "godly line from Seth". Yes, the nation of Israel are God's chosen people. And yes, the nation of Israel brought forth the Saviour. Luke traces the linage of Christ clear back to Adam. But does that make it a "godly line" (Lk. 3:23-38, Acts 7:51)? No. As a matter of fact, Israel has been riddled with sin since the day of its inception (Jer. 11:13). If you read the books of First and Second Kings and First and Second Chronicles, keeping count of all their "godly kings", you'll see that the bad far outnumber the good. There is no "godly line". This is not a condemnation, but merely an historical fact (see Neh. 9 & Rom. 11:1, 25 & 28).

SCOFIELD ERROR #2: *"Angels are spoken of in a sexless way. No female angels are mentioned in scripture, and we are expressly told that marriage is unknown among angels (Matthew 22:30)."*

CORRECTION: While brother Scofield is correct in his statement that *"no female angels are mentioned in scripture"*, his statement that *"Angels are spoken of in a sexless way"* could not be any further from the truth. The word "sexless" implies neither male nor female. We've already covered this thoroughly, but in regards to outward appearance, the Bible often uses the word "man" interchangeably with the word "angel" (see Chapter 11 & 12). So to say that angels are somehow "sexless" is nonsense. Perhaps what Scofield intended to say was, "Angels are spoken of in an *asexual* way". Asexual means to be without sex or sexual organs (I apologize for having to be so explicit). This word seems more fitting in regards to Scofield's next statement that *"marriage is unknown among angels"*. But then again, the term "asexual" would seem to negate the use of the term "male". Scofield's conclusion that *"marriage is unknown among angels"* is only a half-truth. It's true that marriage is unknown *"among angels"*, for they, being all males, cannot intermarry. But only the obedient *"angels of God in heaven"* do not marry at all.

> *"[29] Jesus answered and said unto them, Ye do err, not knowing the scriptures, nor the power of God. [30] For in the resurrection they neither marry, nor are given in marriage, but are as the ANGELS of God IN HEAVEN."* Matthew 22:29-30

> *"[24] And Jesus answering said unto them, Do ye not therefore err, because ye know not the scriptures, neither the power of God? [25] For when they shall rise from the dead, they neither marry, nor are given in marriage; but are as the ANGELS WHICH ARE IN HEAVEN."* Mark 12:24-25

> *"[34] And Jesus answering said unto them, The children of this world marry, and are given in marriage: [35] But they which shall be accounted worthy to obtain that world, and the resurrection from the dead, neither marry, nor are given in marriage: [36] Neither can they die any more: for they are equal unto the angels; and are the children of God, being the children of the resurrection."* Luke 20:34-36

Here we've quoted the supposed proof text for the belief that *"angels do not marry"* (Matt. 22:30). Also presented are the concurring verses in Mark and Luke. Although the verses are specifically speaking of the future state of born-again saints, when read carefully, several facts regarding angels can be learned:

1.) Angels are equal to *"the children of God"* (the saints) for both are labeled as *"sons of God"*.

2.) Angels neither marry nor are given in marriage AMONG THEMSELVES (because they're all males).

3.) Angels cannot die.

While these three points constitute sound Bible doctrine, Matthew and Mark point out a distinction that must be considered when correctly applying these doctrines to the angel:

"...*the angels of God in heaven."* (Matt. 22:30)

"...*the angels which are in heaven."* (Mark 12:25)

These verses can be used to teach that MARRIAGE will be unknown to glorified saints, because marriage is unknown among heavenly angels. These verses can be used to teach that DEATH will be unknown to glorified saints, because death is unknown among heavenly angels. However, the verses cannot be used to teach that marriage and death are unknown among FALLEN ANGELS, for these are the *"angels that sinned"* which are destined to *"die like men".* Why? Because the angels that sinned are the demigods and principalities that committed fornication with the daughters of men. In other words, if an angel of God in Heaven makes the decision to SIN, he forfeits his immortality. Some angels are immortal and cannot die (glorified saints are compared to *these* angels), but others which have fallen are mortal and will *"die like men"* (glorified saints are not compared to *these* angels):

"*For if God spared not the ANGELS THAT SINNED, but cast them down to hell, and delivered them into chains of darkness, to be reserved unto judgment;"* 2 Peter 2:4

"*I have said, Ye are gods; and all of you are CHILDREN OF THE MOST HIGH* [i.e. sons of God]. *But ye shall DIE LIKE MEN, and fall like one of the princes."* Psa. 82:6-7

"Then shall he say also unto them on the left hand, Depart from me, ye cursed, into everlasting fire, prepared for the devil and his angels" Matthew 25:41

For Scofield to make the blanket statement that *"marriage is unknown among angels"*, is just as wrong as painting all angels with a brush of sinless immortality. Some angels are destined to spend eternity with the Creator. Others are not. Some angels have rebelled and sided with the Devil. Others have not. Some angels have sinned and will eventually die. Others have not. Some angels have married and fathered offspring. Others have not. Generalizing into one, something which the scriptures divide is a common way to produce doctrinal error.

SCOFIELD ERROR #3: *"The uniform Hebrew and Christian interpretation has been that verse Genesis 6:2 marks the breaking down of the separation between the godly line of Seth and the godless line of Cain ..."*

CORRECTION: As stated in the rebuttal to Error #1 (page 320), there's no such scriptural example as a "godly" or "godless" line of people. Being born into a certain family line does not determine the godliness or ungodliness of a person. This is determined by the heart of the individual. Even the nation of Israel, the chosen people of God (which did not arise until 10 generations after Noah), could never be considered as a "godly" line (see Nehemiah 9 and the words of his prayer for the details). Believing such things is either scriptural ignorance, or desperate measures employed to escape the true meaning of the verse. The Bible is clear that *"all"* have sinned:

"Wherefore, as by one man sin entered into the world, and death by sin; and so death passed upon all men, for that all have sinned" Romans 5:12

"[9] ... for we have before proved both Jews and Gentiles, that they are all under sin; [10] As it is written, There is none righteous, no, not one: [11] There is none that understandeth, there is none that seeketh after God. [12] They are all gone out of the way, they are together become unprofitable; there is none that doeth good, no, not one." Romans 3:9-12

For the Scofield Bible study notes to eliminate the angelic element from Genesis 6, not only misleads the reader on the proper identity of the early *"sons of God"*, but also leaves an inexplicable mystery on how mere humans could produce a race of literal *"giants"* via the one-way marriage of supposed "godly men" with "godless women". Scofield's popular *"uniform Hebrew and Christian interpretation"* does not add up. And all the while, HE COMPLETELY IGNORES THE REALITY OF THE GIANTS. Note that Genesis 6:4 does not say that "sons of men" came in unto the "daughters of God". The Bible reveals that the bizarre offspring were ONLY SIRED by *a specific combination of a male type of being* (angel) *with a female different from itself* (human). One may choose to take the course that the giants were not the product of an abnormal union, but the catalyst behind these men becoming "renown" was not the godliness or ungodliness of their parents – it was the fact that their fathers were the original *"sons of God"* – the angels. The obvious question to Scofield's assertion is that, if the men of Genesis 6 are so "godly" why are they the instigators of the sin? That makes no sense. Wouldn't the supposed "godless women" be the ones who initiate the transgression? If the *"sons of God"* are the originators of the sin (and the verse shows that they are), then these "sons of God" (whoever they are) are NOT GODLY – but UNGODLY!

Anyone should now be able to see the folly of Scofield's reasoning. His forced, erroneous rendering of the passage produces a ludicrous conclusion – humans begetting literal giants. People choose this explanation of the verse because THEY DON'T WANT TO BELIEVE the verse's true meaning. Therefore, they'll resort to scriptural back-flips, become a Bible contortionist and make irrational statements in order to escape the verse. The Bible leaves no question that giants are real – or at least were real once upon a time. They are not only pictured as being creatures of extraordinary stature, but eventually comprise their own races and nations (this subject is thoroughly covered in the next chapter).

Having now looked at all five Old Testament references to *"sons of God"*; all three references to angels which do not marry; and having briefly examined the false theory of a godly and godless line of peoples, it is now clear to those who have ears to hear, that it was wrong for Scofield to cite Isaiah 43:6 as a supposed proof text to challenge the fact that angels are the rightful owners of the Old Testament *"sons of God"* designation. Doing so created a private interpretation for his conclusion that a supposed godly line of people married a godless line of people. Simply put, Scofield's evidence cannot be used to prove that the Genesis 6 fallen angels did not marry human women. It can only be used to prove that angels do not marry among themselves. However, if an angel does desire to copulate it must seek outside of it's own kind. Once *"men began to multiply on the face of the earth, and daughters were born unto them"*, the fallen angels recognized that not only could they now satisfy their carnal lusts, but that they appeared identical to the daughter's earthly counterpart. In their evil minds it apparently seemed like a win-win situation. But the resulting sin created the first abomination – A COUNTERFEIT LIFE FORM – the giant. The wrath of God soon followed.

Confusion & the Gods of Witchcraft

The Genesis 6 joining of angels and man was the first instance in history of the physical mixing of differing life forms. An attempt at

IMAGE/public domain   Witches riding animals

Many early illustrations depict witches riding animals on pagan "sabats" or "holy days" (some while unclothed). This means the symbolism is considered sacred to the witch. There are also other images of witches with animals too perverted to show. The scriptures make the meaning of this imagery clear (Lev. 20:15-16).

this kind of perverted union is also seen in the RELIGIOUS RITUALS which followed the advent of fallen sons of God after the Flood:

> "[22] Thou shalt not lie with mankind, as with womankind: it is abomination. [23] Neither shalt thou LIE WITH ANY BEAST to defile thyself therewith: neither shall any woman stand before a BEAST TO LIE DOWN thereto: it is CONFUSION." Leviticus 18:22-23 (also see Lev. 20:15-16)

When God called out Abram and later brought forth a nation unto Himself, Israel was commanded to abstain from such abominable practices, not only because they were sins of the worst sort, but because the Lord testified that the other nations of the world had *"committed all these things"* (Lev. 20:23). While there may be no explicit evidence showing the practice of bestiality had any effect other than the total mental and spiritual corruption of the human and animal involved, history and scripture both indicate that there may be more to this practice than merely sexual perversion. When the Lord declares judgement upon the world in Genesis 6, His wrath is not only aimed at mankind, but at the animal world as well:

> *"[6] And it repented the LORD that he had made man on the earth, and it grieved him at his heart. [7] And the LORD said, I will DESTROY MAN whom I have created from the face of the earth; BOTH MAN, and BEAST, and the creeping thing, and the fowls of the air; for it repenteth me that I have made THEM." Genesis 6:6-7*

These scriptures show that God was grieved with both man AND the animal. Why would God be grieved with the animals? What would drive Him to exact a death penalty upon the animal world? What had they done? The Bible lists several reasons for executing an animal, but ONLY ONE REASON is given for putting men and animals to death AT THE SAME TIME:

> *"[15] And if a man lie with a beast, he shall surely be PUT TO DEATH: AND ye shall SLAY THE BEAST. [16] And if a woman approach unto any beast, and lie down thereto, thou shalt KILL THE WOMAN, AND THE BEAST: they shall surely be put to death; their blood shall be upon them." Leviticus 20:15-16*

One must remember also that pre-Flood animals were not afraid of man. The ancient animals had no "natural" fear of man, but lived in harmony with him. There were no "wild" animals, and no "carnivorous" animals – meat eaters. All pre-Flood animals were herbivores – plant eaters (Gen. 1:30). The natural fear of the animal world was not instilled until after the Flood. And because of this, the ancient animals were much more susceptible to the advances of sexual deviants.

> *"[1] And God blessed Noah and his sons, and said unto them, Be fruitful, and multiply, and replenish the earth. [2] And THE FEAR OF YOU and the dread of you shall be upon every BEAST of the earth, and upon every FOWL of the air, UPON ALL that moveth upon the earth, and UPON ALL the FISHES of the sea; into your hand are they delivered. [3] Every moving thing that liveth shall be meat for you; even as the green herb have I given you all things." Genesis 9:1-3*

Realizing this, it's fair to say that the ancient animals were DIFFERENT from the "wild animals" of today. God not only changed their overall behavior towards man, but also, in many cases, their diet. The same animals which boarded the ark behaved differently soon thereafter. This means that using modern-day counterparts and saying that men and ancient animals could not reproduce, is like comparing apples with oranges. One can only guess at the outcomes of the past because the exact specimen involved can no longer be tested. ANIMALS HAVE CHANGED. Regardless, one wonders what happened before the Flood to help such an abominable practice as bestiality to later became part of SACRED RELIGIOUS RITUALS.

Witchcraft has its roots in the days following the Flood. It's first mentioned by name in the book of Samuel (1Sam. 15:23). There, it is castigated and compared with the sin of *"rebellion"*. This direct link of *"witchcraft"* with *"rebellion"* implies that it was the REBELLING ANGELS which left their first estate who introduced (or at least

Riding the Goat

IMAGES/vintage postcards

Freemasonry's goat-riding joke

For years the Masonic Lodge has had a running joke on new candidates where they're lead to believe that "riding the goat" plays a part in Masonic ritual. It doesn't. But established Lodge members like to pretend it's true, just to make new initiates sweat. Unfortunately for Masonry, the joke's on them. Blue Lodge Masons have carelessly flirted with occultism for so long, that they've become blinded to its obvious imagery. To them, it's simply a joke. To the discerning Christian it's something much worse. To illustrate the ongoing perpetration of this gag, a former church in Dundee, KY that was later converted into a Lodge, actually removed the cross from the steeple and replaced it with a goat. This building is now a local historical landmark and may be viewed on Google Maps (It's located on HWY 69, about 2-tenths of a mile south of the Dundee Fire Department).

IMAGE/Google Maps
Goat-steepled Lodge
in Dundee, KY.

IMAGES/public domain   The animal ancient animal world was different (c. 4000-2344 BC)

inspired) the concepts of sorcery and black magic. The religious practices of witchcraft may very well have come about after the Flood, but its birth was inspired by events which preceded the Flood.

Likewise, an extra-biblical study of witchcraft, compared to a biblical study of angels, will further illustrate that witchcraft is not only an attempt to counterfeit God, but also an attempt to reproduce (or call upon) the powers and abilities of angels (more is said about this in chapter 16). Perhaps it was the fallen angels and giants which corrupted the pre-Flood animal world? And perhaps the post-

Flood manifestation of bestiality was an attempt to recreate certain gods and beings which existed during the days of Noah. One point of peculiar evidence is the gods depicted by heathen religions are many times man-animal combinations: Molech the bull-man; Pan the goat-man; Dagon the Philistine fish-man; Cernunnos the Celtic stag-man; Ganesa the Hindu elephant-man; Bast the Egyptian cat-woman; Thoth the Egyptian Ibis-man; Garuda the Hindu eagle-man; Hanuman the Hindu monkey-man, and the list goes on (see pages 441-443 for an image gallery depicting these things).

Likewise, mythology is replete with monsters which the Bible identifies with *"confusion"* (the same word it links with bestiality): Medusas, griffons, basilisks, centaurs, chimeras, harpies, manticores, minotaurs, sphyinxes and many others. Most people tend to believe that the ideas for the appearance of the ancient gods and monsters were simply pulled out of thin air, or personifications of things in nature. I do not believe that. Ideas are not created in a vacuum. They're most usually inspired by something else. The original creature which outwardly appears as an amalgamation of other life forms is the cherub. This appearance is an illusion, however, for the cherub is a unique creature unto itself – not a genetic hybrid. God created the cherub directly, and did not assemble it from the parts of existing living beings. The same cannot be said of the gods of the heathen, nor the bestiary of mythology. The scriptures point to the possibility that certain of the monstrous "gods" of old, may in fact have been REAL CREATURES (or similar-looking creatures) created during the corrupt *"days of Noah"*. The later advent of bestiality and witchcraft was simply an attempt to either reproduce or worship those things which once walked the Earth. The reason many relegate the gods of old strictly to "mythology" is because when they look at history they can see no further back than post-Flood times (Gen. 9-10). But the scriptures show that the roots of such beliefs reach back unto the days before the Flood (Gen. 6).

The scriptures predict the days of Noah to return (Matt. 24:37, Lk. 17:26). Knowing that those former days contain the inspirations for certain practices in witchcraft, consider the LITERAL IMAGERY of Satan's final kingdom. The end-times city of Babylon is pictured as a woman who rides a beast – a WHORE with an ANIMAL (Rev. 17:3).

IMAGE/public domain   The Whore of Babylon riding the Beast

Revelation states that this woman will *"corrupt the earth with her fornication."* (Rev. 19:2) The first time the earth is described as *"corrupt"* is with the appearance of the fallen sons of God who helped corrupt the world with their offspring (Gen. 6). The final kingdom of the Antichrist is the last time the earth is described as corrupt. But the Lord will bring an end to this wickedness, for He will *"... kill the WOMAN, and the BEAST..."* (Lev. 20:15-16, Rev. 14:8, Rev. 18) Does such imagery imply that the mixing of different life forms will return with the rise of this kingdom? Didn't a former King of Babylon have such a dream regarding this future kingdom? (Dan. 2:43)

Jannes & Jambres: Magicians Extraordinaire

The second biblical occurrence of counterfeit life shows that it does not necessarily depend on the union of disparate species, but certain workings in the black arts may also produce a similar result.

> *"[8] And the LORD spake unto Moses and unto Aaron, saying, [9] When Pharaoh shall speak unto you, saying, Show a miracle for you: then thou shalt say unto Aaron, Take thy rod, and cast it before Pharaoh, and it shall become a serpent. [10] And Moses and Aaron went in unto Pharaoh, and they did so as the LORD had commanded: and Aaron cast down his rod before Pharaoh, and before his servants, and it became a serpent. [11] Then Pharaoh also called the wise men and the sorcerers: now the magicians of Egypt, THEY ALSO DID IN LIKE MANNER with their enchantments. [12] For they cast down every man HIS ROD, and they BECAME SERPENTS: but Aaron's rod swallowed up their rods." Exodus 7:8-12*

Having been read countless times, these verses are very familiar to the average Christian. For the most part, however, the implications of what's going on seem to have been glossed over. Many excuse the passages by stating that the Egyptian sorcerers were simply creating "illusions" or using "sleight-of-hand". But this is not what the Bible depicts. The Bible never questions or casts doubt upon these acts of occult enchantment, but rather, legitimizes them by stating; "*... the magicians of Egypt, they ALSO DID IN LIKE MANNER ... For they cast down every man his rod, and they became serpents ...*". In this instance, life was produced from preexisting material (wood). Such an event by the hands of man is recorded nowhere else in scripture. But there's no doubt in my mind as to what happened – a counterfeit miracle of life-creation was allowed to take place through the practice of sorcery and black magic. It also must be strongly stressed that THE LORD IMMEDIATELY DESTROYS these life forms. The life created by God (depicted by the serpent of Aaron's rod) overpowers and destroys the anti-life created by the satanic magicians (depicted by the serpent-rods of the Egyptian):

> *"For they cast down every man his rod, and they became serpents: but AARON'S ROD SWALLOWED UP THEIR RODS." Exodus 8:12*

This account of rods changing into serpents is not an idea of what might have happened, but a clear declaration of what did happen. But the Bible does not stop there, for in the very next chapter, we see the same thing happening again:

> *"[2] And if thou refuse to let them go, behold, I will smite all thy borders with frogs: [3] And the river shall bring forth frogs abundantly, which shall go up and come into thine house, and into thy bedchamber, and upon thy bed, and into the house of thy servants, and upon thy people, and into thine ovens, and into thy kneadingtroughs: [4] And the frogs shall come up both on thee, and upon thy people, and upon all thy servants.[5] And the LORD spake unto Moses, Say unto Aaron, Stretch forth thine hand with thy rod over the streams, over the rivers, and over the ponds, and cause frogs to come up upon the land of Egypt. [6] And Aaron stretched out his hand over the waters of Egypt; and the frogs came up, and covered the land of Egypt. [7] And THE MAGICIANS DID SO with their enchantments, and BROUGHT UP FROGS upon the land of Egypt." Exodus 8:2-7*

Note especially the wording in Exodus 8:3; *"the river shall bring forth"*, and compare it with the wording of Genesis 1:20; *"Let*

IMAGE/Foster Bible Pictures, 1897   Rods changing into serpents (c. 1487 BC)

the waters bring forth". This shows that not only did Moses and Aaron bring forth life like Genesis 1:20, so did the magicians. I'll be honest, *I don't like what these verses say or imply.* Of all the methods of counterfeit-life-creation, this, in my mind, is THE MOST DISTURBING. The passage shows that certain imitation animal life forms can be created which appear identical to that of God. The verses are frightening and difficult to reconcile, and I would prefer that they did not exist. However, as a professing Bible-believer, what am I supposed to do? Reject them? Ignore them? A genuine "heresy" is something not supported by scripture. All you need to do to illustrate that that is not the case here, is to ask yourself: *"Who created the serpents found in Exodus 7:11-12? Who created the frogs found in Exodus 8:7?"* If your answer is that the Egyptian animals were "smoke and mirrors", you're calling God a liar. But if your answer is "God", you have a problem. Nowhere in scripture do we find the Lord working with the practitioners of the black arts.

To the contrary, the Apostle Paul likened these men to those of evil, corrupt, reprobate minds who *"deceive"* and *"resist the truth"*:

> *"Now as Jannes and Jambres withstood Moses, so do these also resist the truth: men of corrupt minds, reprobate concerning the faith. But they shall proceed no further: for their folly shall be manifest unto all men, as theirs also was. ... But evil men and seducers shall wax worse and worse, deceiving, and being deceived."*
> *2 Timothy 3:8,9&13*

Both instances show that an illicit form of life was brought forth by occult magic. The Bible uses the word *"enchantments"* specifically to describe the process. Notice the word: en-CHANT-ment. To "chant" means to repeat a monotonous, rhythmic phrase, many times in unison with another person. The word "spell" and "incantation" mean basically the same. The point to notice here is that high occult arts attempt to counterfeit God by producing some effect via the SPOKEN WORD. Their goal is to be as proficient as, *"And God said ... and it was so."* (Gen. 1) However, the passages do not imply that one can simply go around zapping out snakes with a stick left and right, or popping frogs from the water like popcorn. Some measure of occult knowledge is involved – and undoubtedly *a working with unclean spirits*. This is why such practices are forbidden (Lev. 19:31, etc.). The Bible shows that God *allows* certain of the Devil's ministers to possess this miraculous ability *to a degree*. The good news is, other degrees of the ability are not allowed (Praise God):

> *"[16] And the LORD said unto Moses, Say unto Aaron, Stretch out thy rod, and smite the DUST OF THE LAND, that it may become lice throughout all the land of Egypt. [17] And they did so; for Aaron stretched out his hand with his rod, and smote the dust of the earth, and it*

> *became lice in man, and in beast; all the dust of the land became lice throughout all the land of Egypt. [18] And the magicians did so with their enchantments to bring forth lice, but THEY COULD NOT: so there were lice upon man, and upon beast. [19] Then the magicians said unto Pharaoh, THIS is the finger of God ..." Ex. 8:16-19*

The cross-reference to this counterfeit miracle can also be found in Genesis. But the Egyptians recognized it as being of God, for it could not be reproduced – dust is also connected to the creation of man:

> *"And the LORD God formed man of the DUST OF THE GROUND, and breathed into his nostrils the breath of life; and man became a living soul." Genesis 2:7*

Witchcraft is the antithesis of Christianity and all things godly. It is directly connected to working hand-in-hand with devils and unclean spirits, and out-and-out rejection of the words of God. It is the ultimate display of rebellion which seeks to replace God with oneself or another. The mantra of 20th century reprobate Aleister Crowley, one of the world's most influential occultists, and a man who practiced and taught Egyptian black magic (see chapter 16), was, *"Do what thou wilt shall be the whole of the Law,"* an idea whose origin with which we're all familiar (Isa. 14:13-14), for it reflects the mind of the author of all rebellion:

> *"For REBELLION is as the SIN OF WITCHCRAFT, and stubbornness is as iniquity and idolatry. Because thou hast REJECTED THE WORD of the LORD, he hath also rejected thee from being king." 1 Samuel 15:23*

> *"Regard not them that have familiar spirits, neither seek after wizards, TO BE DEFILED by them: I am the LORD your God." Leviticus 19:31*

"And he caused his children to pass through the fire in the valley of the son of Hinnom: also he observed times, and used enchantments, and used witchcraft, and dealt with a familiar spirit, and with wizards: he wrought much evil in the sight of the LORD, to PROVOKE HIM TO ANGER." 2 Chronicles 33:6

IMAGE/public domain A sorcerer conjuring a devil, 1648

"[10] There shall not be found among you any one that maketh his son or his daughter to pass through the fire, or that useth divination, or an observer of times, or an enchanter, or a witch, [11] Or a charmer, or a consulter with familiar spirits, or a wizard, or a necromancer. [12] For all that do these things are an abomination unto the LORD: and because of these abominations the LORD thy God doth drive them out from before thee."
Deuteronomy 18:10-12

This substitution for God not only seeks to merely usurp the position of God, but to also obtain His divine abilities. Hence, the use of spoken words (spells, enchantments, incantations, etc.) meant to manipulate the forces of nature and/or to create life: *Abracadabra, Hocus-Pocus, Open Sesame, Presto,* etc. Did you ever see a stage

IMAGE/public domain   American magician, Harry Kellar (1894)

Stage magicians have often been depicted as working in conjunction with devils and spirits, regardless of whether their acts are sleight of hand or genuine works of magic.

340 Jannes & Jambres: Magicians Extraordinaire

magician pull a rabbit out of a hat with magic wand? This is simply a subtle counterfeit of the miracles of the outstretched rod of Moses. But Moses didn't say, *"abracadabra"*, he said, *"Thus saith the Lord."*

Author, Raymond Buckland, the man responsible for introducing Gardnerian Wicca to the United States and a lifelong practitioner of the occult, states in his *Complete Book of Witchcraft*:

> *"...in Ceremonial magic, for example; when the Magician is conjuring and WORKING WITH VARIOUS ENTITIES, most of whom are decidedly antagonistic towards the Magician. Some traditions of the Craft do tend to lean towards this aspect of Ceremonial magic in their workings, for whatever reason, and DO IN FACT CONJURE VARIOUS BEINGS. But this can be dangerous."* [1]

Witchcraft is nothing to be trifled with. It is incredibly dangerous, and an overt sign of rebellion against the words of The Almighty. Yet it is more prominent in the world today than ever before. The Holy Bible and modern witchcraft both testify to the fact that some forms of life CAN BE PRODUCED by invoking certain of its practices. While the Bible does not elaborate at great length on the subject, it does teach that the Devil's wise men can at times counterfeit the signs and wonders of God, especially as seen by Moses and Aaron, and Jannes and Jambres. Many of the miracles of the Exodus will be repeated during the Great Tribulation. Seven similarities between the two events include:

1.) Both have water turning into blood.

2.) Both have boils breaking forth on man.

---

[1] Buckland, Raymond. Buckland's Complete Book of Witchcraft. St. Paul, MN: Llewellyn Publications, 1998. p155

3.) Both have fire and hail raining down from heaven.

4.) Both have supernatural darkness.

5.) Both mention "frogs".

6.) Both have a plague of locusts.

7.) Both have the creation of counterfeit life.

As Christians we must learn from these instances to educate ourselves and to teach others, lest we become *"ignorant of his devices"* (2 Cor. 2:11). The Bible also shows that where allowed, God puts reins on this ability and promptly destroys the imitation. Here's what the scriptures reveal regarding the difference between those who consult *wisdom from devils* and those who seek *wisdom from the Lord:*

> *"[3] And the king spake unto Ashpenaz the master of his eunuchs, that he should bring certain of the children of Israel, and of the king's seed, and of the princes; [4] Children in whom was no blemish, but well favoured, and SKILLFUL IN ALL WISDOM, and cunning in KNOWLEDGE, and UNDERSTANDING SCIENCE, and such as had ability in them to stand in the king's palace, and whom they might teach the learning and the tongue of the Chaldeans. [18] Now at the end of the days that the king had said he should bring them in, then the prince of the eunuchs brought them in before Nebuchadnezzar. [19] And the king communed with them; and among them all was found NONE LIKE Daniel, Hananiah, Mishael, and Azariah [i.e. Shadrach, Meshach and Abednego]: therefore stood they before the king. [20] And in ALL MATTERS OF WISDOM AND UNDERSTANDING, that the king inquired of them, he found them TEN TIMES BETTER than ALL THE MAGICIANS and ASTROLOGERS that were in all his realm."*
> *Daniel 1:3-4 & 18-20*

Alive! It's Alive! It's Alive!

"Perhaps our role on this planet is not to worship God —
but to create Him." – Arthur C. Clark, futurist & atheist

The third biblical occurrence of counterfeit life will take place during the Tribulation. In this instance, life is brought forth by raw satanic power.

> *[11] And I beheld another beast coming up out of the earth; and he had two horns like a lamb, and he spake as a dragon. [12] And he exerciseth all the power of the first beast before him, and causeth the earth and them which dwell therein to worship the first beast, whose deadly wound was healed. [13] And HE DOETH GREAT WONDERS, so that he maketh fire come down from heaven on the earth in the sight of men, [14] And deceiveth them that dwell on the earth BY MEANS OF THOSE MIRACLES which he had power to do in the sight of the beast; saying to them that dwell on the earth, that they should make an image to the beast, which had the wound by a sword, and did live. [15] And HE HAD POWER TO GIVE LIFE UNTO THE IMAGE of the beast, that the image of the beast should both speak, and cause that as many as would not worship the image of the beast should be killed." Revelation 13:11-15*

Here is another clear example of what most Christians believe to be the impossible – life created apart from God. Note the wording inspired by the Holy Spirit regarding the false prophet: *"And he had POWER TO GIVE LIFE unto the image..."*. The life presented here is an "image" (i.e. dead matter) indwelt by an unclean spirit. Perhaps this event will mark the first real-world actualization of "artificial intelligence", an event known by modern science as the "Singularity", a point in time which is marked by the emergence of sentient-like machines. A time when computer intelligence supposedly surpasses the intelligence of man. Perhaps such a future computer will be the image mentioned in Revelation 13:15, and perhaps its "intelligence" is brought forth by the spirit of the Antichrist. I'm speculating here,

IMAGE/public domain   From *The Golem*, 1899
In Jewish folklore, a Golem is dead matter (usually like dirt or clay) shaped into the image of a man and then brought to life.

but the possibility exists. Remember Ezekiel's vision of the living wheels (see pgs. 248-251)? Perhaps the spirit of the Antichrist and this image share a similar relationship – a shared spirit. A GHOST IN A MACHINE. Of course, in the end, it doesn't really matter whether the Antichrist's image is a computerized, sentient robot or simply a giant, solid, multi-metal image like that of King Nebuchadnezzar

(Daniel 3:1-6), the end result is the same. The Holy Bible reveals that the means used to *"give life unto the image of the beast"*, will be nothing less than miraculous. Life will be imparted to an inanimate, inorganic "image", and THE THING WILL COME ALIVE. Of this fact the scriptures are clear and no amount of semantical acrobatics will undo or explain away the wording:

> *"And HE HAD POWER TO GIVE LIFE UNTO THE IMAGE of the beast, that the image of the beast should both speak, and cause that as many as would not worship the image of the beast should be killed." Rev. 13:15*

If you're still on the fence about whether the creation of counterfeit life is doctrinal and believe that "only God can create life", just remember that scripture classifies the above event as a SUPERNATURAL COUNTERFEIT MIRACLE. The fact that it outwardly appears as a "work of God" IS THE WHOLE POINT (Isa. 14:13-14, 2Thess. 2:4). It will be one of the crowning achievements from the Devil's bag of wonders. If you're interested in THE crowning achievement, compare Revelation 13:12 & 17:7-8 with John 2:22 for a similar, yet more advanced working. This counterfeit wonder will be his masterwork by which he will *deceive the whole world* (Rev. 12:9 & 13:14). After bringing a dead man to life, the mad Dr. Frankenstein exclaimed; *"Now I know what it feels like to be God!"* Those are the sentiments of the Devil exactly.

Two Thousand Years of Mystical Images

> *"During the night, while complaining and praying before this crucifix, he saw the body of Christ MOVE, detach one arm from the affixing nail and reach toward him. At the same time, A VOICE CAME FROM the crucifix with great*

clarity and SPOKE both consoling and reassuring: 'Take
courage, faint-hearted one, continue the work you have
begun, I will be with you because it is my work."
– Joan Carroll Cruz, *Miraculous Images of Our Lord* [2]

It may sound double-tongued to say a professing "Christian Church" has put its official stamp of approval on numerous supernatural events involving images and idols. But this apparent spiritual paradox has flourished for centuries within the bowels of the Roman Catholic Church. The Roman Church has officially granted approval to OVER 175 EVENTS involving paintings and images which have apparently come to life, bled and/or spoken. This granting of approval, the Catholic Church claims, is the recognition that these miracles are genuine ACTS OF GOD, and not manifestations of some other unspeakable entity. Although it may seem gratuitous for Rome to attribute such miracles to "God", it is also naive, deceptive and void of any scriptural underpinnings. In the introduction to her book *Miraculous Images of Our Lady: 100 Famous Catholic Portraits & Statues*, best-selling Catholic author, Joan Carroll Cruz reassures the reader:

"The purpose of this work is to identify 100 of these
favored images and to chart their histories and the
reasons for their designation as miraculous objects.
It must be understood that the Blessed Virgin does not
perform these miracles by herself. It is ultimately our
Heavenly Father who performs the miracles according
to His holy will at the request of Our Lady." [3]

[2] Cruz, Joan Carroll. *Miraculous Images of Our Lord.* Rockford, IL: Tan Books & Publishers, Inc., 1995. p 105-106

[3] Cruz, Joan Carroll. *Miraculous Images of Our Lady.* Rockford, IL: Tan Books & Publishers, Inc., 1993. p xiii

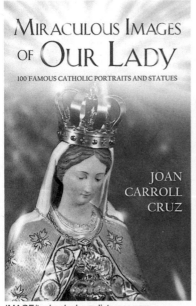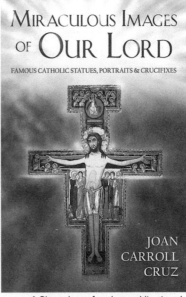

IMAGE/tanbooks.benedictpress.com   A Chronology of unclean spirits at work.

Taking a positive stand on "miraculous images", these two officially-approved Roman Catholic books thoroughly demonstrate that the Roman Catholic Church has played an active role in the approval and promotion of demonic activity for hundreds of years.

And to coax the reader further, Cruz adds:

> "It must be noted that all the images mentioned in this volume were thoroughly studied by Church authorities before ecclesiastical permission was granted for the images to be enshrined and honored in their respective churches or shrines." [4]

Miraculous Images of Our Lady goes on to document the miracles of images officially approved by the Roman Catholic Church. A partial list of these wonders includes:

---

[4] Cruz, Joan Carroll. Miraculous Images of Our Lady. Rockford, IL: Tan Books & Publishers, Inc., 1993. p xiii

- Images which have teleported
- Images which have levitated
- Images which have wept tears or blood
- Images which have healed tumors, deafness, blindness, muteness, paralysis, etc.
- Images which have controlled the weather
- Images which have raised the dead
- Images which have moved their heads or arms
- Images which have spoken

Cruz is the author of three such books detailing paranormal accounts of images, idols and paintings. All her work carries the *"Nihil Obstat and Imprimatur"* of the Roman Catholic Church, authoritatively clarifying that nothing she has written contradicts church teachings or doctrine. I have NO DOUBT that many of these accounts are true. However, if I were to concur with Catholic Church authorities and say that these miracles were "authentically from God", that would be grossly misleading. Because the word "miracle" always implies a supernatural event entailing something good (healing the sick, raising the dead, averting droughts, etc.), it is many times ASSUMED that God is the author. Such an assumption is wrong, however, according to scripture. When Joan Carroll Cruz asserts that the Catholic Church "thoroughly studied" these supposed image-induced miracles, she did not mean that Roman authorities *"...searched the scriptures daily, whether those things were so."* (Acts 17:11) Instead, Cruz means that Catholic leadership verified the miracle itself, and not scriptural proofs for the phenomena. That is, while they may have asked the question, *"Did this miracle REALLY OCCUR?"*, they somehow forgot to ask the question, *"What does the Bible say about images which manifest such powers?"*:

> *"... the church is never in a hurry to pronounce her judgments on such occurrences and that SHE ACTS WITH MAXIMUM CAUTION and PRUDENT RESERVE and is ready to affirm miracles only after positive and unquestionable proofs have been extended."* [5]

Other than verification of the miracle itself, from where the Catholic Church is receiving *"positive and unquestionable proofs"* I do not know. Its acting with *"maximum caution and prudent reserve"*, is also highly questionable. In the first place, to make the emphatic claim that the God of the Bible is the author and originator of bleeding, crying, glowing, levitating, teleporting, moving and talking images is preposterous. For those who profess the ability to interpret the scriptures to attribute such things to "God", is the height of all spiritual stupidity. Only a demon-possessed maniac, or one attempting to deceive his flock by the most outrageous means, would ever say such a thing. After all, why would God permit such nonsense after stating:

> *"Ye shall MAKE YOU NO IDOLS nor graven image, neither rear you up a standing image, neither shall ye set up any image of stone in your land, to bow down unto it: for I am the LORD your God." Leviticus 26:1*

> *"[34] They did not destroy the nations, concerning whom the LORD commanded them: [35] But were mingled among the heathen, and LEARNED THEIR WORKS. [36] And they served their IDOLS: which were a snare unto them. [37] Yea, they sacrificed their sons and their daughters unto DEVILS". Psalms 106:34-37*

---

[5] Cruz, Joan Carroll. Miraculous Images of Our Lady. Rockford, IL: Tan Books & Publishers, Inc., 1993. p 252

IMAGE/by painter Cristóbal Lozano, 1792   A Catholic image comes to life (1582 AD)

In 1582 an idol reportedly came to life. From the book *Miraculous Images of Our Lord*, popular Catholic writer Joan Carroll Cruz writes: *"Our Lord reaches out His arm to St. Camillus de Lellis..."* (p.109). Note how the author refers to a graven image as "Our Lord" (compare with Neh. 9:18 and Rev. 13:15). This represents only one of many "Church approved" paranormal events involving graven images and paintings within the Catholic Church over the past two thousand years. Such long-standing spiritual deception and gross lack of discernment, both point to the true spirit behind the supposed "Church that Christ founded".

"What say I then? that the idol is any thing, or that which is offered in sacrifice TO IDOLS is any thing? But I say, that the things which the Gentiles sacrifice, they sacrifice TO DEVILS, and not to God: and I would not that ye should have fellowship with devils." 1 Cor. 10:19-20

Despite these clear warnings, the Catholic Church insists, nay demands, that the Lord is behind the operation of its mystical images. Contrarily, God's history shows that when graven images and idols are used in worship services, they become DEMON MAGNETS – they attract unclean spirits and devils who reap the misguided worship (Psa. 106:36-38).

Many Catholic churches were birthed as a result of miraculous idols being placed in small shrines. These shrines later became "churches" due to the mass influx of "pilgrims" who sought-out the idols. In other instances, churches which enshrined the images were recognized by the Papacy and elevated to the level of "cathedral" or "minor basilica". What does this tell us about the spiritual origins of many of these establishments? Churches being founded on the basis of SENTIENT IMAGES? Does this sound like the actions of Paul or any other early Christians?

The important thing for the reader to understand here, is that the Roman Catholic Church is the largest spiritual institution the world has ever known. While on the one hand it professes to be a "Christian" establishment, trafficking in the souls of men; on the other hand it has a near 20-century history of advocating miracles which the Holy scriptures attributes to DEVILS. That's nearly 2,000 years of both promoting and ascribing supernatural, life-like qualities to dead, lifeless matter. Nearly 2,000 years of telling man that "God is at work", when the Bible shows it's the work of Satan. It's difficult to excuse such a long running record to mere spiritual incompetence. For the Bible-believing Christian, such a phenomenal precedent CANNOT BE IGNORED when dealing with counterfeit life and its prophesied rise in the future:

> *"And he had power to GIVE LIFE UNTO THE IMAGE of the beast, that the IMAGE of the beast should both SPEAK, and cause that as many as would not worship the image of the beast should be killed." (Rev.13:15)*

And the Pope said, "Amen, let's build a church around it!"

The Imagination Unchained

> *"I am enough of an artist to draw freely upon my imagination. Imagination is more important than knowledge. Knowledge is limited. Imagination encircles the world."* – Albert Einstein, catalyst for the Manhattan Project and the Atomic Bomb

The fourth and final look at counterfeit life is not named explicitly by scripture. But the verses in question can encompass an extremely wide range of mind-bending scientific techniques and knowledge all from the twisted and vain imagination of God-rejecting man. The origins of this mad type of wisdom has its roots in a world that throws off God and unites as one. A we-don't-need-God-any-more type of wisdom that seeks to reverse the God-ordained global division and polarity originally implemented at the tower of Babel. A time when God explicitly said of a godless, one-world society:

> *"And the LORD said, Behold, the people is one, and they have all one language; and this they begin to do: and now NOTHING WILL BE RESTRAINED FROM THEM, WHICH THEY HAVE IMAGINED TO DO." Genesis 11:6*

We now live in an era that parallels the time of the city and tower of Babel. With less and less hindrance from national boundaries, global

IMAGES/internet   Posters of the European Union

In 1992, the European Union published the poster on the left and the motto, *"Europe: Many tongues. One voice."* The image depicted the vision of their goal as that of Babel, with 11 inverted pentagrams (likened unto the 10 kings and the Antichrist of Rev. 17:12). The image was an immediate red flag to discerning Christians. In 2012, the poster on the right made a brief appearance. It depicts all the beliefs and religions of the EU, united under one pentagram, with the words *"EUROPE4ALL: We can all share the same star."* The EU is a template and steppingstone to world order. Its goals, symbology and ideology embody that of the globalist elite. These images make clear that it idolizes the world order at Babel and the occult pentagram star.

transportation, communication and commerce are the everyday norm. Technology and computers have reconnected the world. As nations struggle to cooperate on a political and religious level, behind the scenes manipulation (both spiritual and physical) foment wars, conflicts and tensions in an effort to control the thinking of mankind to get the masses to buy into the concept of one-worldism. While literally hundreds of quotes and proof-texts could be used to illustrate that a One World Order has been the goal of the highest political movers and shakers over the past 100 years, I'm only going to cite one quotation as an overarching example of this concept.

Once known affectionately as *"the most trusted man in America"*, late news anchor Walter Cronkite (1916-2009), earned the love and trust of Americans, becoming a news icon during his tenure as the anchor of CBS Evening News (1961-1981). However, most are unaware of Cronkite's left-leaning ambitions and his personal dream of world government. On October 19, 1999, Cronkite was awarded the Norman Cousins Global Governance Award from the World Federalists Association. Upon receiving the award, Cronkite addressed a UN assembly stating:

> *"It seems to many of us that if we are to avoid the eventual catastrophic world conflict we must strengthen the United Nations as a first step toward a world government patterned after our own government with a legislature, executive and judiciary, and police to enforce its international laws and keep the peace. To do that, of course, we Americans will have to yield up some of our sovereignty. That would be a bitter pill. It would take a lot of courage, a lot of faith in the new order. Pat Robertson has written in a book a few years ago that we should have a world government, but only when the Messiah arrives. He wrote, literally, any attempt to achieve world order before that time must be the work of the devil. Well, join me. I'm glad to sit here at the right hand of Satan."* [6]

---

[6] Joseph Farah. *Meet the Real Walter Cronkite*. WND. Joseph Farah. July 18, 2009. 28 Sept. 2012 <http://www.wnd.com/2009/07/104399/>. Also see: Jeff Fenske. *Walter Cronkite: News Anchor, or Global Propagandist?* 'I'm Glad To Sit On The Right Hand Of Satan'." tobefree - Jeff's Freedom Pages. Jeff Fenske. July 25, 2009. 28 Sept. 2012 <http://tobefree.wordpress.com/2009/07/25/walter-cronkite-news-anchor-or-global-propagandist-im-glad-to-sit-on-the-right-hand-of-satan/>. Also see: Author unknown. *Walter Cronkite Quotes*. New World Order Database. 28 Sept. 2012 <http://nwodb.com/main?e=0116>.

Were Cronkite a Bible reader, he would know that his tongue-in-cheek comment of sitting at the right hand of the Devil would not be off the mark once his desired world order arrives (Rev. 13:6-9).

Accompanying the rise in global governance is the rise in knowledge. According to the word of God, the potential for an unregenerate mankind to put into effect whatever he has *"imagined to do"* comes to fruition when he throws off God and unites as one (Gen. 11:6). The prophet Daniel spoke of the rise of this end-times knowledge where it is written:

> *"But thou, O Daniel, shut up the words, and seal the book, even to the time of the end: many shall run to and fro, and knowledge shall be increased." Daniel 12:4*

The book of Daniel was to be *"shut and sealed"* until *"the time of the end"*. When was this *"time of the end"* scheduled to arrive? During a heightened period of transportation and knowledge. The scriptures pinpoint this era by saying, *"many shall run to and fro, and knowledge shall be increased."*

The Commissioner of the US Office of Patents once said, *"Everything that can be invented has been invented."* Is this true? Surely someone like the Commissioner of US Patents would have a little more insight on the subject of expanding knowledge and its potential. Nevertheless, four short years after this informed statement was made the airplane was invented. Seventy years later man set foot on the Moon. To say that Charles H. Duell, Commissioner of the US Office of Patents (1899), was "shortsighted" would be the understatement of the millennium.

Regardless, we are now living in the most prolific period of global knowledge ever recorded. As transportation and communication become more advanced, knowledge continues to expand exponentially. Science and technology are increasing at a maddening rate with no signs of slowing down. Ralph C. Merkle, pioneer in nanotechnology and a Senior Research Fellow at the Institute for Molecular Manufacturing states:

"At some point in the future almost any infirmity that could in principle be treated is likely to be treatable in practice as well. In principle, the coming ability to arrange and rearrange molecular and cellular structure in almost any way consistent with physical law will let us repair or replace almost any tissue in the human body. Whether it's a new liver, a more vital heart, a restored circulatory system, removing some cancerous cells, or some other treatment -- at some point, nanomedicine should let us revitalize the entire human body and even revive someone who was cryopreserved today." [7]

Wikipedia, the web-based, free content encyclopedia reports;

"Despite the fact we have just entered into the 21st century, technology is being developed even more rapidly, marked progress in almost all fields of science and technology has led to massive improvements to the technology we currently possess, the rate of development in computers being only one example at which the speed of progress continues forward, leading to the speculation of a technological Singularity occurring within this century." [8]

Where has all of this knowledge come from all of a sudden? Or better yet, where is it going? Is God responsible for this global explosion in

[7] Merkle, Raph C. "Cryonics." Ralph C. Merkle. Ed. Ralph C. Merkle. 2012. Alcor Life Extension Foundation. 14 Oct. 2012 <http://merkle.com/cryo/>.

[8] Anonymous. "History of technology" Wikipedia. Wikimedia Foundation, Inc. 28 Sept. 2012 <http://en.wikipedia.org/wiki/History_of_technology>.

knowledge? Is the world seeking its wisdom from a godly source or from somewhere else? The word of God says that *"the fear of the Lord"* is the beginning of both wisdom and knowledge (Psa. 111:10, Prov. 1:7, 9:10), but, for many reasons, I think it can be justly stated that the "fear of God" has nothing to do with the proliferation of wisdom today. The scriptures show there are two types of wisdom. One type of wisdom is from God. The other is not:

> *"This wisdom descendeth not from above, but is earthly, sensual, devilish." James 3:15*

Just as ancient Israel, in a similar way, provoked the Lord to anger *"with their inventions"* (Psa. 106:29), so too, the world of today continues to push the envelope of God's tolerance with its creations. Such experimentation is bringing to pass the profound statement of Genesis 11:6, where the Lord said of a united world: *"...and now nothing will be restrained from them, which they have imagined to do"*. And one of the imaginations of today's scientific world is the creation of new life forms.

For over a hundred years man has heard the myth of so-called evolutionary "missing links". While no such links between life forms exist, science has reached the point to where it can create those links. You say, *"I don't believe scientists can create new life forms"*. But it doesn't matter what you believe. It's already being done. The remainder of this chapter will address these emerging, cutting-edge technologies, as we illustrate the fourth and final example of how to make a monster.

Secret Experiments
& the Birth of Something Beastly

> *"Never let your sense of morals get in the way of doing what's right."* - science fiction author, Issac Asimov

Many are unaware that man has been experimenting with cloning (the creation of genetically identical life forms without the benefit of sexual reproduction) for over a century. German embryologist Hans Driesch, the father of modern cloning, duplicated the first animal, a sea urchin, in 1894.[9] Other milestones on the road to cloning modernization include the cloning of tadpoles in 1952 (considered by many as the first modern cloning), and the cloning of frogs in 1962. More recently cloned animals include salamanders, mice, rabbits, kittens, sheep, pigs, calves and dogs. In 2013 it was reported that a research facility in Kobe, Japan, produced 581 clones of a single mouse, stating the mouse could *"be sequentially cloned indefinitely"*.[10] Today, cloning is growing into a mainstream business by offering clones of family pets with prices ranging between $50,000 and $100,000. The process has also been considered for reviving extinct species. The Australian-based "Lazarus Project" brought back a rare frog that went extinct in the mid-1980s. *"We are watching Lazarus arise from the dead, step by exciting step,"* the project leader said. Scientists are excited about such processes because it creates opportunities to bring back extinct species, such as the woolly mammoth, dodo and the Tasmanian tiger.[11] But cloning simply represents the tip of the iceberg in modern scientific horrors.

An online news story broke in August 2011 reporting that hybrid alligator-chickens had been created. The new creatures were more of

[9] Bellomo, Michael. *The Stem Cell Divide: The Facts, the Fiction, and the Fear Driving the Greatest Scientific, Political, and Religious Debate of Our Time.* New York, NY: AMACOM, 2006. p 134

[10] Dodson, Brian. *Starting with one mouse, scientists create 581 successive clones.*Gizmag.com. Gizmag, 16 Mar 2013. Web. 19 Mar 2013. <http://www.gizmag.com/riken-wakayama-mouse-serial-cloning-snct/26576/>.

[11] Quick, Darren. "Scientists clone extinct frog that gives birth from its mouth." Gizmag.com. Gizmag, 17 Mar 2013. Web. 19 Mar 2013. <http://www.gizmag.com/extinct-gastric-brooding-frog-cloned/26687/?utm_source=GizmagSubscribers&utm_campaign=fe8569e228-UA-2235360-4&utm_medium=email>.

IMAGE/Dover Pictorial Archive   Fake "mermaid" exhibit, 1822

An early representation of supposed human-animal hybridization is seen in this 1822 "mermaid" handbill illustration. However, the creature was really a mummified orangutan grafted to a stuffed fish.

a beakless chicken with an alligator type snout. The news story went on to say that similar genetic manipulation was in the works whereby scientists were attempting to cross chicken DNA with dinosaur DNA and create a "chickenosaurus" – a bird with dinosaur-like hands and tail. While appearing comical with the use of such terminology, the implications of such research was no laughing matter. The article further claimed the technique *"could pave the way for scientists altering DNA in the other direction and use the same process to create species better able to adapt to Earth's climate"*.[12] Note the words "create species better". That's what science thinks it can do. Create men and animals "better" than God in an attempt to compensate for the deterioration of species resulting from the curse of sin. And if this solution involves "mixing it all together" then so be it.

Another headline from July, 2011 disclosed that "secret" human-animal hybrid experiments had been underway at a UK laboratory

[12] Daily Mail Reporter. *Rewinding evolution: Scientists alter chicken DNA to create embryo with 'alligator-like' snout.* Mail Online. Ed. Danny Wheeler. Aug. 19, 2011. Associated Newspapers Limited. 28 Sept. 2012 <http://www.dailymail.co.uk/sciencetech/article-2027558/Scientists-undo-evolution-create-chicken-maniraptora-snout.html?ito=feeds-newsxml>.

since 2008. Mail Online, a UK-based internet news magazine, reported the details of the tests:

> *"Scientists have created more than 150 human-animal hybrid embryos in British laboratories. The hybrids have been produced secretively over the past three years by researchers looking into possible cures for a wide range of diseases. The revelation comes just a day after a committee of scientists warned of a nightmare 'Planet of the Apes' scenario in which work on human-animal creations goes too far. Figures seen by the Daily Mail show that 155 'admixed' embryos, containing both human and animal genetic material, have been created since the introduction of the 2008 Human Fertilisation Embryology Act. This legalised the creation of a variety of hybrids, including an animal egg fertilised by a human sperm; 'cybrids', in which a human nucleus is implanted into an animal cell; and 'chimeras', in which human cells are mixed with animal embryos."* [13]

Because evolutionism teaches that "man is an animal", science uses this theory as an excuse to create its own potpourri of life. Many scientists claim that such cross-mixing of genetics has now become inevitable, and is a NECESSARY PART of modern scientific advancement. Professor Robin Lovell-Badge, from the Medical Research Council's National Institute for Medical Research, said:

> *"The reason for doing these experiments is to understand more about EARLY HUMAN DEVELOPMENT and come up with ways of curing serious diseases, and as a scientist*

---

[13] Martin, Daniel & Caldwell, Simon. *150 human animal hybrids grown in UK labs.* Mail Online. Associated Newspapers Ltd, 22 2011. Web. 1 Nov 2012. <http://www.dailymail.co.uk/sciencetech/article-2017818/Embryos-involving-genes-animals-mixed-humans-produced-secretively-past-years.html>.

I feel there is a MORAL IMPERATIVE TO PURSUE THIS RESEARCH." [14]

Dr. Irving L. Weissman, Director of the Stanford Institute for Stem Cell Biology and Regenerative Medicine and Director of the Stanford Comprehensive Cancer Center, argued that anyone against genetic cross-mixing was actually against the saving of human lives:

> *"Anybody who puts their own MORAL GUIDANCE in the way of this biomedical SCIENCE, where they want to impose their will—not just be part of an argument— if that leads to a ban or moratorium [on man-animal hybridization] ... THEY ARE STOPPING RESEARCH that would save human lives."* [15]

In other words, to "cure serious diseases", modern science feels a "moral" obligation to make monsters. A "moral" obligation to create counterfeit life. A "moral" obligation to first destroy life in order to possibly save it. Scientists would rather dump their own "moral guidance" and be led by raw, unadulterated mad-science if it will "save human lives". They feel an overwhelming obligation to do EVIL in order to produce GOOD. If the law eventually sides with this insane reasoning, it will mean that Bible-based Christian morals would impede the "health" and "progress" of man. Regardless, the Holy Bible says:

> *"Ye shall know them by their fruits. Do men gather grapes of thorns, or figs of thistles? Even so every good*

[14] Martin, Daniel & Caldwell, Simon. *150 human animal hybrids grown in UK labs.* Mail Online. Associated Newspapers Ltd, 22 2011. Web. 1 Nov 2012. <http://www. dailymail.co.uk/sciencetech/article-2017818/Embryos-involving-genes-animals-mixed-humans-produced-secretively-past-years.html>.

[15] Mott, Maryann. "Animal-Human Hybrids Spark Controversy." National Geographic. National Geographic Society, 25 Jan. 2005. Web. 3 Mar 2013. <http:// news.nationalgeographic.com/news/2005/01/0125_050125_chimeras.html>.

tree bringeth forth good fruit; but a corrupt tree bringeth forth evil fruit." Matthew 7:16-17

"Woe unto them that call evil good, and good evil; that put darkness for light, and light for darkness; that put bitter for sweet, and sweet for bitter!" Isaiah 5:20

The Bible shows that if man truly desires to nourish himself or others with "grapes" or "figs" (a good fruit like curing diseases), then he will not go to a source which produces "thorns" and "thistles", but to a vine tree or fig tree. This is because the honest man knows that a corrupt tree (experimenting with man-animal hybridization) bringeth forth evil fruit. If you want your fruit to be evil, then you start with an evil tree.

As early as 1984 the mainstream news was reporting on the genetic hybridization of differing species. The headline of a Monday, February 27, 1984 *Time Magazine* article read, *"Crossbreeding goats and sheep"*. In the article it is learned that scientists at the Institute of Animal Physiology in Cambridge, England combined the embryos of sheep and goats; creating a completely new species, jokingly referred to as "Geep" (pronounced "jeep").[16] A January 25, 2005, *National Geographic* news article reported:

"Scientists have begun blurring the line between human and animal by producing chimeras — a hybrid creature that's part human, part animal. Chinese scientists at the Shanghai Second Medical University in 2003 successfully fused human cells with rabbit eggs. The embryos were reportedly the first human-animal chimeras successfully created. They were allowed to develop for several days

[16] Time. "Science: It's a Geep" Time Magazine. Ed. Richard Stengel. Feb. 27, 1984. Time Warner. 28 Sept. 2012 <http://www.time.com/time/magazine/article/0,9171,921546,00.html>.

in a laboratory dish before the scientists destroyed the embryos to harvest their stem cells. In Minnesota last year [2004] researchers at the Mayo Clinic created pigs with human blood flowing through their bodies. And at Stanford University in California an experiment might be done later this year [2005] to create mice with human brains. Scientists feel that,

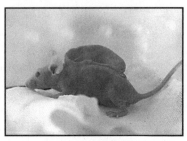

IMAGE/internet

Genetically altered mouse experiment with a human ear growing from its back.

the more humanlike the animal, the better research model it makes for testing drugs or possibly growing 'spare parts,' such as livers, to transplant into humans."[17]

Another 2005 article from the *Scientific American* reported:

"In Greek mythology, the chimera was a monster that combined the parts of a goat, a lion and a serpent. With such a namesake, laboratory-bred chimeras may sound like A BAD IDEA born of pure scientific hubris. YET they may be UNAVOIDABLE if stem cells are ever to be realized as therapies. Researchers will need to study how stem cells behave and react to chemical cues inside the body. Unless they are to do those risky first experiments in humans, THEY WILL NEED THE FREEDOM TO test in animals and thereby MAKE CHIMERAS. No one knows

[17] Mott, Maryann. "Animal-Human Hybrids Spark Controversy." *National Geographic.* Ed. Chris Johns. Jan. 25, 2005. National Geographic Society. 28 Sept. 2012 <http://news.nationalgeographic.com/news/2005/01/0125_050125_chimeras.html>.

what the consequences will be as the proportion of human cells in an animal increases. Weissman and others, for example, have envisioned one day making a mouse with fully 'humanised' brain tissue. The lawyer developmental programme and tiny size of this chimerical mouse fairly guarantee that its mental capacities would not differ greatly from those of normal mice. But what if human cells were instead put in the fetus of a chimpanzee? The BIRTH OF SOMETHING LESS BEASTLY could not be ruled out." [18]

Secret British hybridization experiments? Chickens with alligator snouts? Human rabbit eggs? Pigs with human blood? Mice with human ears and brains? As worldly wisdom continues to advance, especially in such fields like genetic science, the boundaries of what was once taboo or forbidden quickly begin to collapse. Scientists run amok, recklessly plying their profession like a two-year-old with a loaded gun. However, it's ironic that they compare their work to the mythology of the ancient Greeks. For it is an ancient form of atheistic Greek naturalism that helped lay the groundwork for such haphazard views of mankind. It taught life was simply an accident of nature and, evidently, something that can be toyed with (see chapter 2). Mankind has now come full circle. His refusal to acknowledge God's words and to listen to the lessons of history have lead him into a pit from which he will not escape. He is on the road to completely changing mankind on the genetic level. Ultimately, this will be how science offers immortality – "eternal life" in a sin-ravaged body. God is against the immortality of sinners:

[18] Rennie, John. "Human-Animal Chimeras: Some experiments can disquietingly blur the line between species." *Scientific American.* Scientific American, a Division of Nature America, Inc., 27 Jun 2005. Web. 2 Mar 2013. <http://www.scientificamerican.com/article.cfm?id=human-animal-chimeras>.

"...and now [after eating the forbidden fruit], *lest he put forth his hand, and take also of the tree of life, and eat, and LIVE FOR EVER: THEREFORE the LORD God sent him forth from the garden of Eden..." Gen. 3:22-23*

Other recent and verifiable genetic creations include genetically engineered glowing fish, cloned cats that glow in the dark and goats that produce spider-web milk.[19] Playing around with such extreme sciences creates an environment comparable to a Pandora's box that should never be opened. If these things represent current examples of genetic manipulation of which *we're being told*, what kinds of things are being created which *have not been disclosed*? While it's true that in recent years research laws have been put in place to "help regulate" such abominations, regulation is not the issue. Laws and regulations simply give license to commit such acts. The problem is that such things are going on at all. As time marches forward and laws continue to give license for the creation of monsters, future scientists who have become more acclimatized to the process will simply want the envelope pushed further. A 2011 FOX news report candidly stated:

"Extreme scenarios, such as putting brain cells into primates to create talking apes, may remain science fiction, but researchers around the world are constantly pushing boundaries." [20]

---

[19] Moss, Laura. "12 bizarre examples of genetic engineering." Mother Nature Network. MNN HOLDINGS, LLC, 27 2010. Web. 1 Nov 2012. <http://www.mnn.com/green-tech/research-innovations/photos/12-bizarre-examples-of-genetic-engineering>. To see a video of the genetically engineered glowing cloned cats visit: http://video.today.msnbc.msn.com/today/22257875#49640634

[20] Reuters. "New Rules for Making Hybrid Animal-Humans." FoxNews.com. FOX News Network, LLC, 22 Jul 2011. Web. 2 Mar 2013. <http://www.foxnews.com/scitech/2011/07/22/hybrid-animal-human-experiments-should-be-curbed-researchers-say/>.

The ISLAND *of* LOST SOULS

From the Novel by H. G. Wells

It begins where DR. JEKYLL & MR. HYDE left off! A weird, fantastic adventure with a mad doctor who discovers how to turn animals into humans—but not how to control them! On a lonely tropical island he practices his black art! Changes wild beasts into creatures whose strangely human appearance and actions hide raging animal passions! Something brand new in picture plots, with a specially selected cast, that will bring thrills to audiences and joy to exhibitors. Showmanship Plus!

IMAGE/public domain   *The Island of Lost Souls*

The Island of Lost Souls is the film adaptation of H.G. Wells' novel, *The Island of Dr. Moreau (*1896). It relates the story of a scientist who secretly experiments with the crossing of men with animals. Because evolution dictates that man's physical appearance is inconsequential, today, science sees little difference between humans and animals. The "science fiction" of H.G Wells' novel is now "science fact".

A recent article in *The Berkeley Science Review* demonstrated the mind-set of students when it argued:

> *"While these early chimeric forms were mythological constructions of disjointed body parts merged into Frankensteinesque creatures, today's chimera are a very real scientific sensation. Yet WESTERN CULTURE STILL ASSOCIATES CHIMERA WITH THE UNGODLY and unnatural. IN REALITY, NOTHING could be FURTHER FROM THE TRUTH. So ... in the future when you read scientific articles claiming exceptional work with chimeric embryos, I ADVISE YOU to remember the following: Nature made chimera first. All modern life originated from unicellular organisms ... The point is, CHIMERIC LIFEFORMS [sic] ARE EXCEEDINGLY COMMON, having originated hundreds of millions of years ago in the earliest steps of the evolutionary pathways."* [21]

According to the review, monsters and hybrid man-animal creations are okay. They're normal. After all, because of evolution, we're all just a mixed-up bunch of cells and genes which share the same origin. Animals, man, pigs, bugs, slime, what's the difference? Our physical appearances have NO REAL MEANING, so what's the big deal with playing around with the same "evolutionary processes" which created us? Nothing, so that's what we're going to do. That's the mind-set of today's college student – and the geneticist of tomorrow. Thank you dear college student for setting us straight on "reality" and the "ungodly". We're so indebted to your advanced knowledge and wisdom. All hail secular science! All hail the college education!

[21] Boatman, Liz. "Rhesus chimera: Cutting-edge science meets natural history." Berkeley Science Review Blog. University of California, Berkeley, 21 Feb 2012. Web. 2 Mar 2013. <http://sciencereview.berkeley.edu/rhesus-chimera-cutting-edge-science-meets-natural-history/>.

In 2012, the not-for-profit X Prize Foundation opened its "Jurassic Park X PRIZE" contest. The goal? To revive a species that has long been extinct in an effort to "rebuild a population".[22] Such a contest illustrates the fact that science fiction television, movies, books and periodicals can many times inspire entire generations of men and women (right or wrong) to pursue specific scientific fields (the Devil *is* slick, is he not?). Science fiction begets science fact – or at least scientific experimentation and perusal. Popular movie and sci-fi star, actor Bruce Boxleitner, said it this way:

> *"Science fiction always leads the way to science fact. As I was told by somebody at NASA, Hollywood creates the dream and then we* [science] *take that dream, and try to make it a reality."* [23]

Unfortunately, sometimes those dreams become nightmares. Back in chapter 5 we addressed how those enthused with science fiction helped put man on the Moon, an event that established the "Space Age". What event and "age" for mankind is next? What is science fiction helping man to dream about today?

Today, a simple Google search can reveal news stories of human/animal genetic manipulation all over the internet. This type of mass publicity helps negate the "shock factor" and acclimatizes the public to processes which are immoral and ungodly. Such haphazard behavior towards divinely established boundaries of human and animal life leads to confusion, and helps promote the birth of other movements whose goals are to REDEFINE LIFE and what it means to be human (or animal), their end goal being the immortalization of fallen mankind.

[22] "Jurassic Park X PRIZE." X Prize Foundation. Ed. Dr. Peter H. Diamandis. X Prize Foundation. 28 Sept. 2012 <http://www.xprize.org/prize/jurassic-park-x-prize>.

[23] Boxleitner, Bruce, perf. The TRON Phenomenon [italics]. Buena Vista Home Entertainment, Inc., 2011. DVD. 28 Sep 2012.

"Thus they changed their glory into the similitude of an ox that eateth grass. They forgat God their saviour, which had done great things in Egypt". Psa. 106:20-21

"And changed the glory of the uncorruptible God into an image made like to corruptible man, and to birds, and fourfooted beasts, and creeping things." Rom. 1:23

Man-Made Immortals & the Push for Non-Human Personhood

In September 2011, one of the first public demonstrations supporting artificial immortality took place. Lead by the Russian Transhumanist Movement, participants held signs and banners stating, *"Live 150 years"*; *"Immorality"* and *"We are against death"*.[24] What is Transhumanism? It is the merger of man and technology to such a degree that eventually the human element is no longer distinguishable from its non-human parts. It is the creation of a new, different kind of life form – a trans-human. A being that is neither man nor machine. The goal of transhumanism is to push mankind into a state of "post-humanism", including super-humans who will be physically and intellectually "above" average humans. On the road to this goal is the plan to *legally recognize all forms of sentient life*. Points 7 and 8 of the *Transhumanist Declaration* (first conceived in 1998) describe these ideals:

"(7) We advocate the WELL-BEING OF ALL SENTIENCE, including humans, NON-HUMAN ANIMALS, and ANY future ARTIFICIAL INTELLECTS, modified life forms, or

[24] Konovalenko, Maria. "The First Political Meeting on Immortality in History." Maria Konovalenko Blog. Science for Life Extension Foundation, 27 Sept. 2011. Web. 2 Mar 2013. <http://mariakonovalenko.wordpress.com/2011/09/27/the-first-political-meeting-on-immortality-in-history/>.

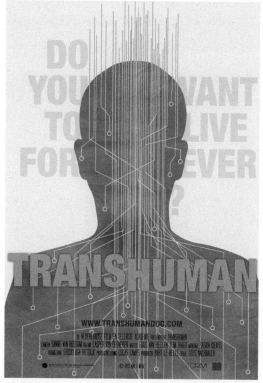

IMAGE/internet   Poster in the Transhumanism Movement

OTHER INTELLIGENCES to which TECHNOLOGICAL and SCIENTIFIC ADVANCE may give rise.

(8) We favour allowing individuals wide personal choice over how they enable their lives. This includes use of techniques that may be developed to assist memory, concentration, and mental energy; life extension therapies; reproductive choice technologies; cryonics procedures; and many other possible HUMAN MODIFICATION and ENHANCEMENT technologies." [25]

[25] Misc. Authors. "Transhumanist Declaration." Humanityplus.org. Humanity+, n.d. Web. 3 Apr 2013. <http://humanityplus.org/philosophy/transhumanist-declaration/>.

Mormon Transhumanist Association

MORMON
TRANSHUMANIST
ASSOCIATION

IMAGE/transfigurism.org   Official logo for the Mormon Transhumanist Association

Founded in 2006, the Mormon Transhumanist Association is a quasi-religious organization which seeks human transfiguration, resurrection and immortality through genetics, cybernetics and other human-body-enhancing sciences. The official *Mormon Transhumanist Affirmation* states: *"We believe that scientific knowledge and technological power are among the means ordained of God to enable such exaltation, including realization of diverse prophetic visions of transfiguration, immortality, resurrection, renewal of this world, and the discovery and creation of worlds without end."* The MTA logo is that of Ezekiel's wheel, a symbiotic life form created by God where a shared spirit resides within a machine (see Ezk. 1:20-21).

In preparation and anticipation for the future arrival of technologically advanced para-humans and super-humans, the transhumanist movement is pushing to recognize the "well-being" of animals, future artificial intelligences and "other" created intelligences. *What this means is that ANYTHING science can create in a laboratory which has what IT DEFINES as "sentient"* (life or feelings), *must eventually be given legal rights.* This includes certain animals, advanced computers, cybernetic humans and animal-human hybrids (this is the perfect kind of mind-set that will bring Rev. 13:14-15 to fruition). In the wake of this quickly-progressing movement, Yale University held a "Personhood Beyond the Human Conference" in December 2013. The self-prescribed objectives of this conference were as follows:

> *"The event will focus on PERSONHOOD FOR nonhuman ANIMALS, including great APES, CETACEANS* [whale, dolphins, etc.], *and ELEPHANTS, and will explore the evolving notions of personhood by analyzing them through the frameworks of neuroscience, behavioral science, philosophy, ethics, and law."* [26]

The conference was co-sponsored by the Nonhuman Rights Project and the Institute for Ethics and Emerging Technologies in collaboration with the Yale Interdisciplinary Center for Bioethics.

Special consideration was given to discussions of nonhuman animal personhood, both in terms of understanding the history, science, and philosophy behind personhood, and ways to protect animal interests through *the establishment of legal precedents* and by increasing public awareness.

---

[26] The 2013 Personhood Beyond the Human Conference. nonhumanrights.net. Yale University. Web. 3 Apr 2013. <http://nonhumanrights.net/about/>.

IMAGE/nonhumanrights.net   Official logo of Personhood Beyond the Human

This organization is comprised of the same kind of people who would grant "personhood" to apes, elephants and dolphins, and yet deny personhood to a child in the womb (Luke 1:44). It is a very dangerous mind-set. It opens the doors not only to the creation of "human rights" granted to human-animal hybrids, but to eventual intimate relations between the two. After all, according to Darwin and modern science, we're all one big happy family, are we not?

> *"By the close of the conference, attendees will have gained an enhanced understanding of the neurological, cognitive, and behavioral underpinnings of personhood and those traits required for such consideration; personhood theory; the history of personhood consideration and status (both in terms of philosophical and legal conceptions); and the legal hurdles and requirements for GRANTING PERSONHOOD STATUS OUTSIDE THE HUMAN SPECIES."* [27]

The Nonhuman Rights Project, a co-sponsor for the 2013 Yale conference, clearly stated their goals as well:

> *"We have come together for one clear purpose: TO BREAK THROUGH THE LEGAL WALL THAT SEPARATES HUMANS FROM NONHUMANS, thereby gaining*

---

[27] The 2013 Personhood Beyond the Human Conference. nonhumanrights.net. Yale University. Web. 3 Apr 2013. <http://nonhumanrights.net/about/>.

legal 'personhood' for nonhuman animals, beginning with some of the most intelligent animals on earth, like chimpanzees, elephants and dolphins.

The Nonhuman Rights Project is preparing to litigate the first ground-breaking legal cases intended to KNOCK DOWN THE WALL THAT SEPARATES HUMANS FROM NONHUMANS. Once this wall is breached, the first nonhuman animals on earth will gain legal 'personhood' and finally get their day in court — a day they so clearly deserve." [28]

These are Yale University intellectuals (the same crew whose 19th century colleagues endorsed the imaginary "Lunar Man-Bats"), and they're preparing to set legal precedents where MEN AND ANIMALS ARE EQUAL "PERSONS" UNDER THE LAW. This madness is what's looming on the horizon. This and transhumanism. Together, they constitute the next big "push" to help advance "equality" in a godless and perverted one-world society. Evolutionism has so poisoned science, that life no longer has any true value or demarcations. Humans, animals, computers, chimeras – they're all the same. It is confusion, and God is not its Author.

The contemporary notion of the Singularity got started with legendary science fiction writer Vernor Vinge, whose 1981 novella, *True Names,* pictured a society on the brink of this event. In a 1993 essay, *The Coming Technological Singularity,* Vinge made his vision clear when he wrote:

"...within thirty years, we will have the technological means to create superhuman intelligence. Shortly after, the human era will be ended." [29]

---

[28] "What Is The Nonhuman Rights Project?" nonhumanrightsproject.org. The Nonhuman Rights Project . Web. 3 Apr 2013. <http://www.nonhumanrightsproject. org/overview/>.

Chapter 14 Summary

This chapter has been a little lengthy, but there were several things that needed to be said. If you're finding it hard to accept, that's strictly between you and the Lord. I've simply made an attempt to gather all the pertinent verses regarding a subject that's often overlooked. In chapter 11 it was revealed that counterfeit life is one of the seven primary types of life found in scripture. Specifically, a type of life that has not been directly created by God Himself, nor been reproduced *"after its kind"*. This chapter has covered in detail the four ways which the Bible shows that such an undertaking may be achieved:

1 - By the physical union of two or more classes of life created by God (like the Genesis 6 sons of God with the daughters of men).

2 - By the working of black magic and the occult arts (like the Egyptian magicians which withstood Moses).

3 - By raw Satanic power and the synthesis of an unclean spirit into an organic or inorganic object (like the image which will come to life by the power of the Antichrist).

4 - By the escalation of worldly knowledge and the tampering with genetic codes and DNA (as a fulfillment of the prophecy of the increase of end-times knowledge).

The next chapter will be an in-depth analysis of the phenomena of giants in both the human and animal world.

---

[29] Wolens, Doug. "Singularity 101 with Vernor Vinge." Humaniy+ . H+ Magazine, 22 Apr 2009. Web. 3 Apr 2013. <http://hplusmagazine.com/2009/04/22/singularity-101-vernor-vinge/>.

15

Giants in the Earth

"There were giants in the earth in those days; and also after that..." Genesis 6:4

After having specifically examined all classifications and types of life forms created by God, namely the Creature class, the Man class, the Angelic class, the Cherubic class, the Celestial Creature class and the Symbiotic class, it was discovered in the previous chapter that certain types of life forms, evidently, fall outside of these predetermined God-ordained groups. Life falling within a seventh group deviates from being either a direct creation of God or the product of life which reproduces "after its kind". The most prominent life form found in scripture which falls into this new "Counterfeit" life class is the GIANT. This chapter will examine the scriptural and historical evidences for the existence of giants, and look at the curious anomaly of other gigantic creatures from ages past. Giant men and giant animals, what does it all mean?

Giants in the Bible

> *"[32] And they brought up an evil report of the land
> which they had searched unto the children of Israel,
> saying, The land, through which we have gone to search
> it, is a land that eateth up the inhabitants thereof; and
> all the people that we saw in it are MEN OF A GREAT
> STATURE. [33] And there we saw THE GIANTS, the
> SONS OF ANAK, which come of THE GIANTS: and we
> were in our own sight as grasshoppers, and so we were
> in their sight." Numbers 13:32-33*

Giants are real. If you're a Bible-believer, you can settle that question in your mind *right now*. The proof of giant men-like beings is without question when examined in the light of Holy Writ. They are literal, genetic misfits who first show up on this Earth around 5,885-4,360 years ago (approximately sometime between the birth of Seth and the birth of the sons of Noah - see Genesis 5 and 6). Later remnant appearances of these creatures place their average height between 9 to 12 feet tall. The height of the very first giants, however, was probably much greater. The Bible records names, races, locations, measurements and explicit physical descriptions of the beings. There is no reason to cast doubt on these verses. The word *"giant"* (singular) appears 8 times in the Bible. The word *"giants"* (plural) appears 13 times. The first mention of the word in Genesis 6:4 shows that giants are the children of the fallen *"sons of God"* and the *"daughters of men"*. Every subsequent biblical reference to giants refers to creatures of EXTREME PHYSICAL STATURE (see Num. 13:32-33, Deut. 2:10, Deut. 2:20-21, Deut. 9:1-2, 2 Sam. 21:20, 1 Chron. 20:6). Og, King of Bashan, who was *"of the remnant of giants"* and from *"the land of giants"*, had a bed that measured 13-and-a-half feet long.

Giants in the Bible: A Comparative Chart

Did giants once walk the Earth? The Bible says yes!

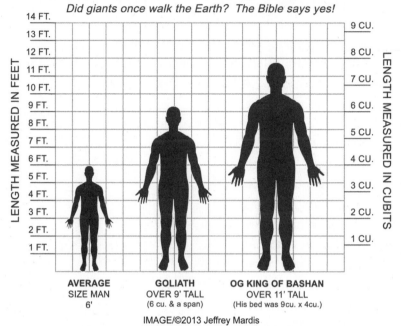

AVERAGE
SIZE MAN
6'

GOLIATH
OVER 9' TALL
(6 cu. & a span)

OG KING OF BASHAN
OVER 11' TALL
(His bed was 9cu. x 4cu.)

IMAGE/©2013 Jeffrey Mardis

"[11] For only Og king of Bashan remained of the REMNANT OF GIANTS; behold, his bedstead was a bedstead of iron; is it not in Rabbath of the children of Ammon? NINE CUBITS was the length thereof, and FOUR CUBITS the breadth of it, after the cubit of a man. [13] And the rest of Gilead, and all Bashan, being the kingdom of Og, gave I unto the half tribe of Manasseh; all the region of Argob, with all Bashan, which was called THE LAND OF GIANTS." Deuteronomy 3:11 & 13

Imagine the Creator of the Universe putting the measurements of a man's bed in the Bible. That would be a pointless and insignificant thing to do wouldn't it? Unless, of course, it revealed special information. God did not include those words as simply Bible fluff.

King Og may have been a "remnant giant", but his bed measurements put his physical height somewhere around 11 to 12 feet tall. That Bible fact is irrefutable.

The most famous biblical giant was a military champion known as "Goliath of Gath". His height is recorded at 9.9 feet tall (six cubits and a span - 1 Sam. 17:4). Also known as *"the giant in Gath"* (1Chron. 20:8), his armor alone weighed over 200 pounds (5,000 shekels of brass - 1 Sam. 17:5). Although among the shorter giants, when factoring-in the proportions of this armor-clad warrior, his immense size would have been beyond intimidating – being nearly double the height of a young David (probably around 5 to 5.5 feet tall). The Bible says that Israel was *"dismayed and greatly afraid"* at this giant's appearance (2

IMAGE/Osmar Schindler's *David & Goliath*, 1888

Sam. 17:11). The word *"giant"* is consistently used by scripture as a reference to men-like beings of great physical stature. Not simply tall men, like King Saul of Kish, who was *"higher than any of the people from his shoulders and upward"* (1 Sam. 9:2 & 10:23), but the inference is to a more radical, extreme type of height, closer to 10-13 feet or more, like Og of Bashan. The type of height that can really strike fear in the observer (see Num. 14:1-10).

While it's true that most all *"mighty men"* named in scripture are not giants, all giants in scripture are classified as *"mighty men"* (Gen.

6:4). Some mighty men are giants, some are not. Given that fact, however, the scriptures never use the word in reference to a man's reputation or social standing. According to the Bible's standards, being a person in authority does not qualify one to be labeled a *"giant"*. As a matter of fact, one of the most well-known men in all the Bible who was a *"chief among the publicans"*, would undoubtedly be labeled a *"giant"* by this modern interpretation, were it not for scripture and the immortalization of the man in a children's song. There's no question that *Zaccheaus* was a prominent leader. But this *"wee little man"* was *"little of stature"*, being nowhere near the height of a giant. Regardless of his high social status, the scriptures are careful to not classify him among those who truly qualify for the title (see Luke 19:2-3).

Biblical Names of Giants

The scriptures mention several names of giants. The naming of such creatures, especially by the Holy Bible, helps personalize them instead of simply generalizing them under the title of *"giants"*. Calling giants by name lets us know that they once personally interacted with humans.

1. Ahiman (Num. 13:22, Josh. 15:14, Jud.1:10)
2. Anak (Num. 13:22, Deut. 9:2, et.al.)
3. Goliath (1Sam. 17:4&23, 21:9 & 22:10)
4. Lahmai (1Chron. 20:5)
5. Saph (2Sam. 21:18-22 a.k.a. Sippai)
6. Sheshai (Num. 13:22, Josh. 15:14, Jud.1:10)
7. Talmai (Num. 13:22, Josh. 15:14, Jud.1:10)
8. Og (Num. 21:33, Josh. 12:4 & 13:12, et. al.)

Biblical Races of Giants

The scriptures show that the giants were a separate race of beings. This means that they were not simply "tall men" peppered

Modern map showing ancient locations of giants as outlined by scripture. Numbered locations correspond with information on pages 381-383.

throughout the various races of mankind, but were comprised of their own cultures and ethnicities.

1. Anakims (Deut. 1:28, 9:2, et.al.)

2. Emims (Gen. 14:5, Deut. 2:10)

3. Zamzummims (Gen. 14:5, Deut. 2:20)

4. Amorite (Amos 2:9, Gen. 10:6 & 15-16)

Other possible giant races include the *Rephaims, Horims, Avims* and *Caphtorims* (I did not list these races because the Bible does not *explicitly* name them as giants. But their gigantism *is* inferred, as they are listed *among the giants* of Deuteronomy. see Deut. 2:20-23). Being descendants of Ham, and Canaan directly, the "Amorites" were not pure giants. However, in order for them to reach such staggering heights, Amos 2:9 implies that the post-diluvian giants may have interbred with these early peoples (A possibility that opens a whole new can of worms – giants with humans). Needless to say, the Lord drove out the Amorites from before Israel, forbidding Israel to not make any covenants with them, lest the worship of false gods – gods from the stars – infest God's people. By the days of King Solomon, it appears the Amorites had been wiped out, as the remnant of that seed became bond servants (1 Kings 9:20-21).

Biblical Lands of Giants

The following information will correspond with the map at left. All numbers coincide with the numbers shown on the map. The image shows the ancient locations of Bible-time giants on a modern-day map. All cities and locations once occupied by giants are marked with an "x". Mt. Hermon is shown with a "mountain" symbol.

1.) **Mount Hermon** (or Mount Sion, not to be confused with "Mount Zion", Zion is in Jerusalem, the City of David, see 2Sam. 5:7, 2Kings 14:20) - The highest point in Syria

(9,232 ft) sitting on the modern Israel/Lebanon border just northwest of Ein Kinya, Israel (Josh. 12:5, Deut. 4:48, Heb. 12:18-24, Rev. 14:1, et.al)

2.) Bashan "Land of the Giants" - In modern-day Syria, around the Golan Heights (Deut. 3:13)

3.) Argob - East of the northeastern coast of the Sea of Galilee, near the modern-day Kanaf Spring (Deut. 3:13)

4.) Ashtaroth - Approx. 5 miles east of the Sea of Galilee, just north of the modern Israel/Jordan border (Josh. 12:4 & 13:12)

5.) Edrei - Near modern-day Daraa, Syria (Josh. 12:4& 13:12)

6.) Salcah (or Salchah) - the modern day city of Salkhad, Syria (Deut. 3:10, Josh. 12:4-5)

7.) Rabbath (or Rabbah) - Near modern-day Amman, Jordan, the place of King Og's 13-foot bedstead. Rabbath was not a "giant city" per se, but a city of the Ammonites, the incestuous children of Lot. The fact that Og has a bed here indicates he may have been an ally of the Ammonites or had some connection with the ancient Zamzummims (Deut. 3:11, Jer. 49:2, Gen. 19:38)

8.) Gath - About 15 miles off the cost of the Mediterranean Sea, northeast of modern-day Kiryat Gat, Israel. Gath is the home of Goliath (Josh. 11:22, 1Sam. 17:4, 2Sam. 21:20-22, et.al.)

9.) Hebron (Also known as the City of Arba, Kirjath-Arba or the Plains of Mamre) - Hebron was once known as the "City of Arba". Arba is the father of the Anakims, a race of giants which the scriptures many times use as a standard among giant races (Deut. 2:10 & 21) . The Bible names Arba not only as *"the father of Anak"*, but also as *"a great man among the Anakims"*. This points to the fact that "Arba" could actually be the name of a post-Flood, fallen son of God – an angel (Gen. 13:18, 23:2, Josh. 14:15, 15:13, et. al.).

10.) Valley of the Son of Hinnom, "Valley of the Giants" - Just outside the southern wall of the N.T. City of Jerusalem, a stronghold of Tophet and Molech (Josh 18:16, 2 Kgs. 23:10, Jer. 19:2-6, et.al.)

11.) Land of the children of Ammon - Along the eastern cost of the Salt/Dead Sea, original home of the Zamzummims (Deut. 2:18-21, Gen. 19:38)

12.) Seir - East of the southeastern cost of the Salt/Dead Sea, just east of modern Karak, Jordan, original home of the Horims (Deut. 2:12 & 22)

The primary Bible references to the lands and cities of ancient giants are contained within God's Promised Land, an approximate 150-square-mile area. The indication is that the giants somehow knew something about this area's importance to God. My guess is that *the Devil moved them to occupy the land* sometime after Abram was promised the land, but before Israel became a nation.

Having now easily demonstrated with scripture that the giants were real creatures of literal "giant" proportions, we run into a major problem. It is the reality of the giant which throws a monkey-wrench in the machinery of those who reject the angelic rendering of the

Genesis 6 *"sons of God"*. Rejecting the angels is usually followed by a rejection of the giants. However, further light of the gospel renders that explaining-way impossible. The giants were real.

One may very well reject the Genesis 6 "fallen angels" concept to explain the giants (and many do), but that does not eliminate their reality. The scriptures verify their existence. This means that the question of HOW and from WHERE such creatures originate cannot be swept under a rug. Where did the giants come from? How were whole races and nations of these beings produced if the sons and daughters of Genesis 6 were nothing more than human beings? How can one arrive at the creation of a supernatural-type being without the prior interplay of a supernatural element? Were the original giants simply the result of an explosion in birth defects among human men and women? History and medical science both show that birth defects usually cause the offspring to be WEAKER AND MORE FRAIL, not to grow more powerful and become renowned, giant *"mighty men"*. No one is arguing the fact that giants weren't genetic mutations (2 Sam. 21:20 & 1 Chron. 20:6), but they weren't simply HUMAN BEINGS with a disease or genetic defect. The merger of strange flesh was the root cause their abnormality. They were more powerful than the average human, because they *were* more than human – they were the children of the fallen sons of God.

The scriptures describe angels explicitly as being *"greater in power and might"* (2 Peter 2:11). If these greater-and-mighter beings took human women as wives, what do you suppose would happen? The only available recourse to escape the record of how the Bible's giants came into existence, is to reject the conclusions when scripture is compared with scripture. Reject the Bible's meaning of giant. Reject the Bible's names for giants. Reject the Bible's races of giants. Reject the Bible's height for giants. Reject the Bible's location for giants. Reject the Bible's evidence for giants. Just IGNORE EVERYTHING about giants to which the Bible attests. That's how you get rid of it.

"But if any man be ignorant, let him be ignorant."

1Corinthians 14:38

Giants in Medicine

Modern gigantism is associated with a disorder of the pituitary gland known as "Pituitary Gigantism", as well as the related condition of "Acromegaly" (ak-ro-MEG-uh-lee). This disorder causes an abnormal amount of growth hormone to be released into the body resulting in "gigantism". Unlike the ancient giants, who were noted for their strength and might, the Mayo Foundation for Medical Education and Research lists fatigue, muscle weakness, headaches and impaired vision as typical symptoms of those who suffer with the affliction today.[1] At the opposite end of the spectrum lies a disorder known as "Pituitary Dwarfism". This abnormality is noted as an overall diminishing in size, resulting in a proportionate dwarfing of the individual. Dwarfs not affected by this pituitary condition are usually disproportionate in size, displaying normal-sized heads, with reduced arms and legs. The scriptures recognize dwarfism as being a HUMAN DEFECT or "blemish". Dwarfs are not a separate race of beings. The fact that GIANTS ARE NOT MENTIONED on this list of "blemishes" is further proof that the Bible's giants were *something more than abnormal men*:

"[18] For whatsoever man he be that hath a BLEMISH, he shall not approach: a blind man, or a lame, or he that hath a flat nose, or any thing superfluous, [19] Or a man that is brokenfooted, or brokenhanded, [20] Or crookbacked, or a DWARF, or that hath a BLEMISH in his eye, or be scurvy, or scabbed, or hath his stones

---

[1] Mayo Clinic staff. "Acromegaly - Symptoms." Mayo Clinic. Mayo Foundation for Medical Education and Research, 3 2010. Web. 6 Nov 2012. <http://www.mayoclinic.com/health/acromegaly/DS00478/DSECTION=symptoms>.

broken; [21] No man that hath a BLEMISH of the seed of Aaron the priest shall come nigh to offer the offerings of the LORD made by fire: he hath a BLEMISH; he shall not come nigh to offer the bread of his God." Leviticus 21:18-21

These two specific flaws in human makeup (Acromegaly and Dwarfism), while rare, make it clear that such afflictions have been a REGULAR OCCURRENCE throughout history. What this means is that while the average height of man has been about 6 feet since the beginning (six being also ascribed as the biblical number for man), one can easily find human beings who break that mold due to *abnormal health conditions* of one form or another. History shows that due to sin and disease, adult *human height* fluctuates between approximately 2 and 8.5 feet tall.

The shortest human dwarfs in history have been around 1 foot, 10 inches tall. The tallest man in modern history was Robert Pershing Wadlow

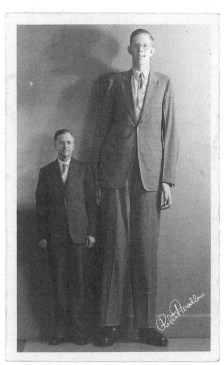

IMAGE/public domain   Robert Wadlow, 8' 11"

of Alton, Illinois. He was nearly 9 feet tall at the time of his passing in 1940 (he was 21). While not a true "giant" in the biblical sense, photos of Wadlow show his staggering size. Such images can give us

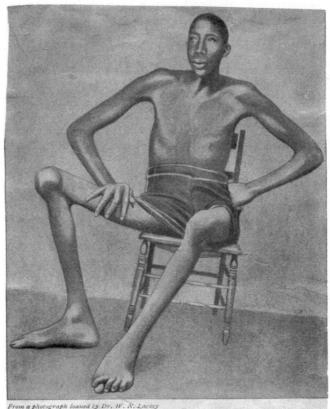

From a photograph loaned by Dr. W. R. Lackey

THE SUPERB PROPORTIONS OF A REAL GIANT
Height, 8 feet 6 inches. Died at the age of thirty-two

IMAGE/thetallestman.com   John William "Bud" Rogan
Acromegaly victim, Bud Rogan, died at age 32. He was 8' 6" and lost the
ability to walk or carry his own weight once the disease set in at age 13.
Does this sound like a *"mighty man in the earth"* to you?

a true picture of the immensity of real giants. The scriptures describe
Goliath (a remnant giant) as being 9 feet, 9 inches tall. That's nearly
a head taller than Robert Pershing Wadlow. And Goliath was neither
weak nor frail, but personally labeled as the only *"champion"* in the
entire Bible (1 Sam. 17:4, 23 & 51). He was a true giant – a monster

of a man. One can only imagine the incredible size of the early giants. Beings which, I'm guessing, averaged around 13 feet or better (thirteen being the biblical number for rebellion).

Today, the tallest man in the known world is Sultan Kosen of Mardin, Turkey. He holds the 2010-2014 *Guinness* world's record for the tallest man alive. Reportedly, he is 8 foot, 3 inches. Due to his affliction, Kosen must walk with the aid of double forearm canes, a telltale sign that Mr. Kosen is not a true giant. Unfortunately, the modern "giant" can shed no real light on the phenomenon of ancient giants. Modern "giants" are no more true giants than tall healthy men. Saul was tall, but he was not a giant:

> "[1] Now there was a man of Benjamin, whose name was Kish, the son of Abiel, the son of Zeror, the son of Bechorath, the son of Aphiah, a Benjamite, a mighty man of power. [2] And he had a son, whose name was SAUL, a choice young man, and a goodly: and there was not among the children of Israel a goodlier person than he: FROM HIS SHOULDERS AND UPWARD HE WAS HIGHER THAN ANY OF THE PEOPLE." 1 Samuel 9:1-2

The important thing to get from all this is that the Christian must be DISCERNING, and learn to discriminate between *Bible-type giants* and *humans with health issues*. There are those who would try to teach that the Bible's giants were simply human men with genetic disorders. But this argument is very weak. You're being asked to believe that when the Bible says that there *"were giants in the earth in those days"*, that this is a reference to whole races of human *"mighty men"* with acromegaly or something similar. Yet races of men are not categorized by defects. The truth is, there are giants, and then there are giants, but the two are not the same.

Giants in History

The Bible is clear that not only were giants on the Earth before the Great Flood, but *"also after that"* (Gen. 6:4). The words "also after that" being later scripturally verified by the advent of the Anakims and other races of giant men (Num. 13, Deut.2, et. al). Archaeological evidence shows that races of these things appeared again for at least several hundred years after the Flood. Most people are likewise oblivious to the fact that past generations were at least partially aware of these beings, and discoveries of their bones were reported on occasion up until about the turn of the twentieth century. In other words, as the teachings of evolutionism began to wax (around 1860), the discoveries of giant men began to wane. That is, they ceased to be reported:

> *"...early explorers, including Amerigo Vespucci, Sir Francis Drake, Coronado, De Soto, Narvaez and others, all talk about giants they encountered on their journeys. These are all documented, eyewitness sightings - which historians currently do their best to hide from the public. Archeologists often discover these large bones in graves. But these are usually dismissed as being 'mastodons' - a premise that's hard to justify given the fact that the creatures are often buried in human graves wearing battle armor along with a shield and massive sword."* [2]

Further investigation also strongly suggests that "shorter" remnant races of giants (averaging between 7 and 9 feet tall) inhabited the Americas long before the arrival of the Englishman or American Indian. Along with the oral tradition of many Native American tribes, early American county and regional history books, vintage

[2] Quayle, Stephen. *Genesis 6 Giants*. Bozeman, MT: End Time Thunder Publishers, 2002. p 190-191

diaries, and letters contained records of such findings prior to the indoctrination of evolutionary thought.[3] A February 11, 1902, *Special to the New York Times* reported:

> *"Owing to the discovery of the remains of a race of giants in Guadalupe, N.M., antiquarians and archaeologist are preparing an expedition further to explore that region. This determination is based on the excitement that exist among the people of a scope of country near Mesa Rico, about 200 miles southeast of Las Vegas, where an old burial ground has been discovered that has yielded skeletons of enormous size.*
>
> *Luciana Quintana, on whose ranch the ancient burial plot is located, discovered ... the bones of a frame [of a man] that could not have been less than 12 feet in length. The men that opened the grave said the forearm was 4 feet long and that a well preserved jaw the lower teeth ranged from the size of a hickory nut to that of the largest walnut in size. The chest of the being is reported as having the circumference of seven feet."* [4]

Another account from the January 14, 1870 issue of the *Ohio Democrat* (New Philadelphia, Ohio) stated that during an oil derrick excavation, Mr. William Thomas and Mr. Robert R. Smith, much to their shock, *"exhumed an enormous helmet of iron"* accompanied by a sword measuring *"nine feet in length"*. The article continued:

> *"... in a few hours time they had unearthed a well preserved skeleton of an enormous giant, belonging to*

[3] Hamilton, Ross. *Holocaust of Giants: What Has Happened to the Skeletons?*. Ross Hamilton, 2001. p 3-4.

[4] Zimmerman, Fritz. The Nephilim Chronicles. 2010. p 43

IMAGE/public domain   Map depicting the discovery of a giant skeleton (1619 AD)

Enlargement from a rare 17th century Argentinian map depicting the expedition of Dutch mariner Jacob Le Maire. Point "H" on the map shows where *"they found the burial site of a giant, whose bones measured between ten and eleven feet long".* (Jacques Le Maire, 1585–1616 / Willem Corneliszoon Schouten, d.1625.*Strait Through: Magellan to Cook & the Pacific.* Princeton University Library.)

> *a species of the human family which probably inhabited this and other parts of the world at that times of which the Bible speaks, when it says: 'And there were giants in those days'".*[5]

Many more accounts of the discovery of the remains of giant men has been reported across the US. Areas which have unearthed more than a few include California, Illinois, Indiana, Michigan, Minnesota, New York, Ohio, Pennsylvania, Tennessee and Wisconsin. An article appearing in the *Toronto Telegraph* (circa 1900) testifies that the phenomenon reaches into Canada as well. The paper reported the finding of a mass grave of *"two hundred skeletons nearly perfect...*

[5] Zimmerman, Fritz. The Nephilim Chronicles. 2010. p 88

The skeletons were gigantic, some of them measuring nine feet, and a few of them less than seven".[6]

When the scriptures testify that *"there were giants in the earth"*, that's exactly what it means. Their existence was not indigenous to one locale, but spread worldwide. The fossil evidence, while not exactly extensive, is also not as sparse as many would have you believe. A few of the more notable claims and finds include:

– Described as "the father of all thought in natural history in the second half of the 18th century" [7], French naturalist and cosmologist, Georges Louis Leclerc (Count de Buffon, 1707-1788) wrote that *"some giants indeed stood ten, twelve, and perhaps fifteen feet tall"*, concluding that their existence was without question.[8]

– A history of Northern England, detailing the Allerdale District of Cumbria, UK, records the findings of a giant over 13.5 feet tall, buried with a sword and battle-axe over 6 feet long.[9] *"The said gyant was buried 4 yards deep in the ground, which is now a corn field. It was 4 yards and a half long, and was in complete armour: his sword and his battle-axe lying by him. His sword was two spans broad, and more than two yards long. The head of his battle-axe a yard long, the shaft of it, all of iron, as thick as a man's thigh, and more than two yards long. His armour, sword, and battle-axe are at Mr. Sand's, of Redington (Rottington), and at Mr. Wyber's, of St. Bees."*[10]

[6] Zimmerman, Fritz. The Nephilim Chronicles. 2010. p 84

[7] Mayr, Ernst. The Growth of Biological Thought. Cambridge: Harvard, 1981. p 330

[8] DeLoach, Charles. Giants: A Reference Guide from History, the Bible, and Recorded Legend. Metuchen, NJ & London: The Scarecrow Press, 1995. p 31

– A report from the November 25, 1894 *Davenport Daily Leader* claimed a prehistoric graveyard had been recently discovered in Montpelier, France. Within that cemetery were found human skulls "measuring 28, 31 and 33 inches in circumference. The bones which were found with the skulls were also of gigantic proportions". The Paris academy claimed the remains *"belonged to a race of men between 10 and 15 feet in height"*.[11]

IMAGE/public domain
From *The World*,
Sunday, October 6, 1895

– In 1925, the bodies of eight armor-clad giants, between 8 and 9 feet tall, were unearthed by amateur archeologists at Walkerton, IN.[12]

– The skeleton of a giant standing 17 to 18 feet tall was discovered in a sepulcher in Rouen, France in 1509. Upon the tomb was affixed a copper plaque which read: *"In this tomb*

[10] Wood, Edward J. Giants & Dwarfs. London: Robson and Son, Great Northern Printing Works, 1868. p 30-31

[11] Zimmerman, Fritz. *The Nephilim Chronicles*. 2010. p 13

[12] Quayle, Stephen. *Genesis 6 Giants*. Bozeman, MT: End Time Thunder Publishers, 2002. p 195

lies the noble and puissant lord, the Chevalier Ricon de Vallemont, and his bones." [13]

Other discoveries have been recorded where the skeletons of "humans" reportedly reached 25, 30, and 36 feet or greater.[14] But such instances are cases where the bones, more often than not, are that of other large creatures which remained undiscovered at the time. One such example is the 1613 discovery of the supposed remains of a 25 foot human giant. While the bones were genuine, the discoverers fabricated a "tomb" and "complete skeleton", naming it after the legendary giant king of the Teutons, "Theutobochus Rex". The existence of the bones were verified, but were later identified as those of a mastodon.[15] Christians need to be careful in their zeal for the truth, that they do not accept every claim at face value simply because it may fall in line with scripture (like the many fake photos of supposed giant human skeletons found on the internet). There are fakes in every legitimate circle of study. Sometimes fakes are intentional, other times they're accidental, but they never help undergird truth. Scoffers and skeptics are going to reject the Bible anyhow, but it's best not to give them fuel for their fire. Besides, the Christian should never rely on his feelings or senses to tell him what's true. This is what sunk the human race in the first place (Gen. 3:6). Seeing does not equal "believing", because there's plenty in REALITY the Devil can manufacture in order to get you to believe a lie (2 Cor. 11:45-15, Rev. 13:13-15, 16:14). Instead, the Christian is to rely on God's words. We are to walk by faith not by sight (2 Cor.

---

[13] Wood, Edward J. *Giants & Dwarfs*. London: Robson and Son, Great Northern Printing Works, 1868. p 29

[14] Ibid. p 31

[15] Jacques Tissot's Brochure Entitled "DISCOURS VERITABLE DE LA VIE, MORT ET DES OS DU GEANT THEUTOBOCUSH". The Post Graduate: A Monthly Journal of Medicine and Surgery. 27. New York: 1912. p 665-679

Seeing Is Not Believing

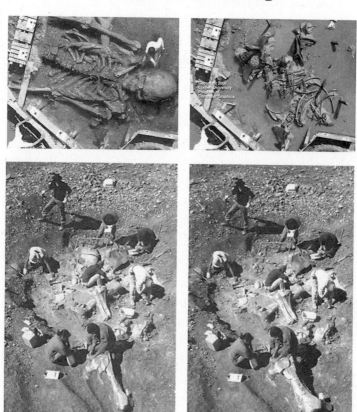

FAKE PHOTO COLUMN   **REAL PHOTO COLUMN**

From time to time a photo pops up on the internet showing archeologists excavating giant human remains. As a 20 year veteran of *Adobe Photoshop*, I know how easy it is to create a fake photograph. Christians need to be wary of relying on their eyes to tell them the truth (For more on this story visit www. answersingenesis.org).

5:7), because, on the other hand, there's plenty that we HAVEN'T SEEN that we DO believe (Heb. 11:1, 1Peter 1:7-9). Ever seen God? No. Ever seen the Lord Jesus Christ? No. Ever seen the Holy Spirit? No. Ever seen Heaven? No. Ever seen New Jerusalem? No. Ever seen the Devil? No. Ever seen the Bible's original manuscripts? No. Ever seen a lion eat straw like an ox? No. Ever seen an angel? Maybe – without realizing it (Heb. 13:2). Ever seen a unicorn, dragon or a satyr? No, no and no. In other words, if a giant were to walk up to you and shake your hand, you had better run to your Bible and check him out. If what you *see* or *hear* lines up with scripture, fine. If not, throw it out. But if you rely on your eyes to validate truth, you WILL BE DECEIVED sooner or later. The apostle Peter wrote that the written word of God was a *"more sure"* revelation than hearing a voice from heaven (2 Peter 1:17-19). Heard or seen any aliens from space lately? You better watch it!

Now that we've reviewed a little of the evidence, the obvious question arises: Where have all these giant bones, armor and weaponry gone to? Have they been hurriedly whisked away and stashed in some musty old government basement, like we find at the end of an Indiana Jones movie? Possibly. The problem is, the existence of giants – any kind of giant, man or animal – creates a real problem for the evolutionist. So, instead of openly presenting ancient artifacts that conflict with their preconceived notions of what they *want* history to teach, they simply get rid of the evidence. Find some giant human bones? Get rid of it. Find some swords and suits of armor that would fit a man 12 feet tall? Get rid of it. Do you keep digging up dinosaur bones that get bigger and bigger all the time, causing havoc for the evolutionary theory? Get rid of the stuff. Reportedly, the former director of the Bureau of Ethnology at the Smithsonian Institution, John Wesley Powell (1834-1902), was responsible for much of the early misinformation and mismanagement of archaeological findings:

"Powell and Co. likely did not purposely destroy data, though some of the precious evidence of AMERICA'S GIGANTIC PAST may have been lost or destroyed in transit. The real problem lay in the fact that these countless crates of precious truth are lost in the massive, almost legendary 'Smithsonian Warehouse', guarded by both security guards and security by obscurity." [16]

Vine Victor Deloria, Native American author, theologian and former professor at the University of Arizona's College of Law adds:

"Modern day archaeology and anthropology have nearly sealed the door on our imaginations, broadly interpreting the North American past as devoid of anything unusual in the way of great cultures characterized by A PEOPLE OF UNUSUAL DEMEANOR. The great interloper of ancient burial grounds, the nineteenth century Smithsonian Institution, created a one-way portal, through which uncounted bones have been spirited. This door and the contents of its vault are virtually sealed off to anyone, but government officials. Among these bones may lay answers not even sought by these officials concerning the deep past." [17]

Addressing the absence of the public display of some of the largest animal fossils, David Esker of DinosaurTheory.com, writes:

"Surely the public would be interested in seeing these huge bones, and yet these too are rarely seen in metropolitan

[16] - Doug Elwell, Mysterious World http://www.mysteriousworld.com/Journal/2003/Summer/Giants.

[17] Hamilton, Ross. *Holocaust of Giants: What Has Happened to the Skeletons?.* Ross Hamilton, 2001. p 3

museums. In fact, not only are many of these extremely large bones not being displayed, but curiously on at least two occasions these gigantic priceless sauropod bones have been somehow lost." [18]

Skeletal remains are not the only evidence pointing to the reality of giant men. As some of the witnesses have already testified, giant tools, weapons and armor have also been found. The Bible likewise reveals that giants left such proofs behind (Deut. 3:11, 1 Sam. 21:9).

The scriptures also testify that King Solomon levied a *"tribute of bondservice"* upon the Amorites (1 Kings 9:20-21). A race *"whose height was like the height of the cedars"* and *"strong as the oaks"* (Amos 2:9). During the construction of the House of the Lord, it's recorded that 60,000 *"strangers"* were assigned to *"bear burdens"* (2 Chron. 2:2&17). It's only logical to assume that the strongest bearers carried the heaviest burdens. A practical move of labor management and resources for the world's wisest man. It's possible that the current largest foundation stone (estimated at 500 tons) is part of King Solomon's original temple. If so, perhaps "giant labor" was utilized to lay the massive block? And if so, such scriptural insight offers evidence for the construction of other ancient monolithic structures.

The Sneaking Suspicion that Something is Amiss

Unlike the Bible's record of giant "men", until further scriptural light is given, I would never teach what you're about to read as Bible doctrine. It is merely "food for thought" in an attempt to get a better understanding of the complete picture of what happened in the past, and the alien phenomenon of today. If you're inclined to quote me on the information which follows, MAKE SURE you don't take me out of context and say I'm teaching it as "Bible doctrine". I am not. It is

---

[18] Esker, David. "The Paradox of Large Dinosaurs." DinosaurTheory.com. N.p.. Web. 3 Apr 2013. <http://www.dinosaurtheory.com/big_dinosaur.html>.

merely a possibility, and an attempt to organize and/or extrapolate upon what we've learned concerning counterfeit life thus far.

In the previous chapter we addressed the subject of bestiality, and its link with the pre-Flood world of Genesis 6, and the fallen sons of God. This link is made evident not only via *the appearance of the corrupt practices of pagan cultures* following the Flood (an observable fact - Lev. 20), but also in *the religious manifestation of many of the man-animal gods* worshiped by these cults (also an observable fact). That is, post-diluvian peoples both practiced perverted rituals with animals, and created graven images, idols and gods which strongly suggested *a prior association* with man-animal mongrels. What inspired such rituals? What caused such an antithesis against God to pop up immediately following the Flood? Could it have something to do with conditions which existed before the Flood? While pointing to the events of Genesis 6, the Bible-believing Christian says "yes".

The Bible shows that the animals of Noah's day were not "wild", but tame, having no fear of man. This difference in the ancient animal world, when added to the carnal motivations of the fallen angels and the fact that the animals were included in the global wrath of God, leads one to suspect that MUCH MORE was going on than merely the interaction of angels and men. I hesitate to say that raw bestiality was completely to blame. Even though that's a definite possibility, one can only speculate at this point. History and circumstantial evidence indicate that it certainly may have played a partial role. There's always the chance, however, that the genetic tampering may have been accomplished through other means. What I'm driving at is this: The arrival of the extraterrestrial angels brought with it a mingling which corrupted the seed of mankind. This is CLEARLY SEEN with the arrival of the GIANTS. This co-mingling produced GIGANTISM in mankind, due to *the introduction of a foreign genetic component* within the "man" life class. The evidence suggests that this alien mutation of "gigantism" may have also somehow spread to the animal world. This could also help explain why the vast majority of these GIANT CREATURES WERE NOT ABOARD Noah's ark. How this was possible exactly, I do not know. But the evidence certainly suggests *something* out of the ordinary. Before we proceed, however, I want to make clear that I am NOT suggesting that ALL the large animals of the past were a result of this genetic corruption. The Bible is very clear that at least SOME of the giant beasts of the past were created by God, AND contemporaries with early mankind:

> *"[15] Behold now BEHEMOTH, which I MADE WITH THEE; he eateth grass as an ox. [16] Lo now, his strength is in his loins, and his force is in the navel of his belly. [17] He moveth his tail like a cedar: the sinews of his stones are wrapped together. [18] His bones are as strong pieces of brass; his bones are like bars of iron." Job 40:15-18*

Job goes on to say more about the great Behemoth. But regardless of ones take on these scripture, two facts are certainly clear: (1) Behemoth was a huge animal; and (2) he was *"made with thee"*. That is, he was created during the 6 days of Genesis, and was a contemporary with Adam and the generations which follow. What this means is that SOME giant beasts were creations of God, while others may not have been. What we're concerned with examining here are the ones which "may not have been".

Mysterious Giants of the Ancient Animal World

Most are unaware that the apparent gigantism of many of the ancient animals poses a great mystery to modern science. They're not seen as simply quirks of nature, but, in many cases, as paradoxical creatures which technically should not exist. This is not taught in the public schools. And the question is rarely addressed openly, as it is an embarrassment to the scientific community. But a quick Google search of something like "Why were the dinosaurs so big?", will quickly open this unpleasant can of worms.

"One of the most cherished features of dinosaurs — their gigantism — is also one of the most mysterious. Why in the world were these animals so huge?" [19] - *National Geographic*

"The physiology behind this feat remains a mystery. Equally puzzling is the fact that dinosaurs managed to reach such big sizes … 'We don't have a good answer why dinosaurs were such big animals,' says Hans-Dieter Sues [Curator of Vertebrate Paleontology, Smithsonian]." [20] - *Discover Magazine*

"The most obvious observation about dinosaurs is that these were incredible [sic] *large animals. Kids want to know how the dinosaurs grew so large. Yet oddly enough many paleontologists would rather avoid this subject. In fact, an argument can be made that the paleontology community is attempting to hide away their largest dinosaur displays."* [21] - David Esker, College Physics Instructor/Science Researcher

"A number of commonly accepted assumptions about large dinosaurs are not compatible with scientific laws.

[19] Achenbach, Joel. "Why were dinosaurs so humongous?." *National Geographic*. National Geographic Society. Web. 3 Apr 2013. <http://ngm.nationalgeographic.com/ngm/0507/resources_who.html>.

[20] Zimmer, Carl. "Dinosaurs Why do we have so many questions about the most successful animals that ever lived?." *DISCOVER*. Kalmbach Publishing, Co, 28 Apr 2005. Web. 3 Apr 2013. <http://discovermagazine.com/2005/apr/cover

[21] Esker, David. "The Paradox of Large Dinosaurs." DinosaurTheory.com. N.p.. Web. 3 Apr 2013. <http://www.dinosaurtheory.com/big_dinosaur.html>.

For example, sauropods grazing from the tops of trees were physiologically impossible, for blood flow reasons. (A heart and circulatory system made of biological cellular tissues cannot pump blood more than about seven vertical feet above the heart, or bring blood back from legs and feet lower than about seven feet below it.)."[22] - C Johnson, Theoretical Physicist

Fortunately for the Bible-believer, we're not blinded by evolutionary thought or uniformitarian geology (the theory that geologic forces have operated uniformly from the origin of the earth to the present time). The world is a much different place today than when these creatures roamed the Earth. And we know of the cataclysmic event which can account for such differences. We know of two events as a matter of fact (Gen. 1:2 & 7:11). Before we delve into the details of our mysterious giant animals, lets first take a quick look at what the Earth and its climate were like during Noah's day. Some of these facts are backed by scripture, others are simply scientific deductions:

1.) A TROPICAL-LIKE WORLD ENVIRONMENT - It is said that this atmosphere was much more tropical-like, probably containing both more oxygen and atmospheric pressure. As a result, many things were able to grow much larger, especially plants and trees and such. Modern science believes the atmosphere of today is much the same as that of thousands of years ago. Stubbornly holding to such beliefs results in wrong conclusions and wrong answers. The consensus among creationists, however, (and a few secular scientists), is that the climate of the past was different:

[22] Johnson, C. "Sauropod Dinosaurs: Physics and Physiology." mb-soft.com. N.p., 20 Nov 1997. Web. 3 Apr 2013. <http://mb-soft.com/public/dinosaur.html>.

"The dinosaur skeletons and fleshed-out reconstructions we see in museums tower over their viewers. How and why did these massive creatures grow so monstrous? The answer is probably a lot of hot air. At least, that's what the research of Sara Decherd, a doctoral student in marine, earth and atmospheric sciences at North Carolina State University, suggests. Decherd studies the ecology of the Cretaceous period...when Earth's atmosphere contained more oxygen and more carbon dioxide and was, in her words, 'a hothouse.' She believes, and is working to demonstrate, that this richer atmosphere helped plants grow bigger and faster." [23]

2.) AN ALTERNATE LAND-TO-OCEAN RATIO - Before the first rain of the Great Flood, the scriptures tell us that the Earth was watered by *"a mist from the ground"* (Gen. 2:5). This indicates that the Earth's pre-Flood atmosphere was cloudless and more tropical-like. The fact that God placed His rainbow in the sky AFTER the Flood, also stands as strong proof that atmospheric conditions had been restructured (Gen. 9:13-16). The pre-Flood climate was not congruent to supporting rainbow phenomena. When the judgement rains of God poured from the *"windows of heaven"* (Gen. 7:11), all of that water *had to go somewhere*. This is why I believe the vast majority of our seas and oceans today are *a result of that Flood*. Because of this, it is reasonable to assume that the surface-land-to-water ratio before the Flood was much

[23] Mueller, Paul. "A Lot of Hot Air: How the Dinosaurs Grew So Monstrous." NC State University. North Carolina State University, 21 2004. Web. 30 Oct 2012. <ttp://www.ncsu.edu/news/press_releases/04_01/026.htm>

lower. Today waters cover slightly more than 70% of the Earth's surface. There's no way to know the exact pre-Flood ratio, but let's say, hypothetically, the ratio was reversed. That is, only 30% of the Earth's surface was covered by water (my guess is that the percentage was even lower).

3.) LOWER TOPOGRAPHY - It's reasonable to assume that the pre-Flood lay of the landscape was smoother and less mountainous than that of today. The voluminous, 40-day downpour (the first "rain") pummeled the land masses creating our modern mountain ranges and peaks (like when torrential rain digs its own ditches). The event literally reshaped the Earth's surface (although some of this could've also resulted from the Genesis 1:2 incident). Natural landmarks like the Grand Canyon and Mt. Everest were probably both by-products of the event. And if they existed in part previously, the devastating chaos brought about by the Great Flood, surely altered their appearance.

4.) LONGER LIFESPANS - Being closer to the first man, and less hindered by sin and disease, antediluvian peoples lived to be 700, 800, 900 years old (Gen 5 – this is also another proof against the supposed onset of "Acromegaly" in early man). However, due to the altered climate and the added baggage of sin, lifespans following the Flood dropped dramatically. Today, the age of man averages a little less than 10% of that. We are mere children in comparison – weak, sick, sin-infested children.

5.) A LARGER WORLD POPULATION - Today's worldwide population is more than 7 billion. If stacked shoulder to shoulder, that 7 billion could fill a relatively small area (like the state of Texas). The pre-Flood world

was of one language, so there may have only been a handful
of "nations" if any at all. As a result of the long lifespans,
their unhindered ability to communicate, and the much
greater land surface available, my guess is the pre-Flood
population of Earth could've easily been 10 times that
of today – 70 billion or more (the invading sons of God
would've had a heyday). The Earth was truly formed to be
"inhabited" (Isaiah 45:18).

These 5 points offer just a few insights into the world of 2400
BC. Things were much different then. Many creationists point to
the ancient atmosphere as the primary instigator of pre-Flood
gigantism. I have no doubt this is *partially* true. But it's not
completely true. The Bible shows that it does not account for ALL
types of gigantism. We know for a fact that giant "men" (or at least
men-like beings) roamed the earth during this time. We also know
that those creatures were not simply "giant humans" resulting from
a difference in climate. The physical size of humans was not affected
by the climate. It was "something else" that affected the size of man.
A supernatural "something else". An outside life form invaded the
Earth, and introduced a foreign genetic element. When mixed with
humans, this element produced a new life form – GIANTS. We can
know for a fact that the climate had no bearing on the creation of the
human-like giants, for the scriptures testify that giants were on the
Earth *"also after that"* (Gen. 6:4). That is, *"after"* the Great Flood,
"after" the pre-Flood tropical climate had disappeared.

So, on one hand we have some giants resulting from an alternate
atmosphere. And on the other hand, we have some giants resulting
from an outside genetic component. *Both scenarios are true.* And
both scenarios were in operation at the same time. The problem
is determining WHICH GIANTS were a product of which. My
proposition here is this: *Is it possible that at least SOME of the giant
creatures of the past were a product of angelic corruption and not*

climate? The only answer I have is that it is at least a possibility. The evidence that pushes this scenario into the realm of likelihood, is that the Lord pronounced sentence against the animal world as well. A gigantism produced "naturally" is not a sin, and not worthy of death. God knows this. However, *if resulting from an outside contaminant which perverted the natural order of things*, it becomes another matter altogether. As stated before, I would not teach this explicitly as Bible "doctrine". But while DIRECT scriptural evidence for believing that the fallen angels played some sort of role in the corruption of the animal world is scarce, *the implications are there*. Something DID HAPPEN to the animal world. And remember, I've stated this once before, but the scriptures give ONLY ONE instance that justifies the execution of both man and animals at the same time – BESTIALITY (see Gen. 6:7 & Lev. 20:15-16). What follows is a short list of "food for thought" dealing with certain giant creatures of the past. Was their apparent gigantism caused by climate, or something more?

1.) GIANT RATS - In 1868, the bones of a giant rat were discovered in a shipment of cave earth which had departed the island of Anguilla. The find was later verified by *The Learning Channel* (TLC) after it returned to the island over 140 years later. Fossil evidence of more giant rodents "with a wide range in sizes, from that of a dog up to that of a bear" [24], and estimated weights from 110-440 pounds, helped establish the discovery. Now labeled the *Amblyrhiza inundata* or Blunt-Toothed Giant Hutia, this beast is said to be related to the hutias indigenous to the Caribbean Islands. The average head-to-tail size of today's hutia is 9-18 inches, with weights of less than 5 pounds.

[24] Green, Bob. "Amblyrhiza Inundata: Giant Fossil Rat." Anguilla News. Anguilla News, 29 1998. Web. 27 Oct 2012. <http://news.ai/ref/amblyrhiza.html>.

However, this does not represent the largest rodents ever discovered. The 21-inch skull of *Josephoartigasia monesi* currently holds the world's record. This fossilized South American monster, originally discovered in 1987, is said to have been *"as large as a bull and as heavy as a small car"* with weights up to 1 ton.[25] A 1-ton rat would equal a rat 2000 - 4000 times the weight of today's average 1 pound to half-pound rat.

IMAGE/*Giants Against Evolution*
Plate depicting naked man fighting giant beaver

2.) GIANT BEAVERS - The skeletal remains of giant beavers reaching heights of 6 to 8.5 feet, have been found throughout North America and Canada. Known as "Castories", these creatures are comparable in size

[25] Dickinson, Boonsri. "Top 100 Stories of 2008 #79: The Ancient Rat as Big as a Bull." Discover Magazine. Kalmbach Publishing Co., 09 2008. Web. 27 Oct 2012. <http://discovermagazine.com/2009/jan/079>.

IMAGE/sculpture by Carbonneaux, 1824
Hercules fighting the giant serpent Acheloos

with the modern black bear, having 4 inch incisors and weighting between 150-485 pounds (that's 7 times larger than today's beavers).

3.) GIANT WOLVES - The only fossil evidence currently in existence for the *Andrewsarchus* is a giant 31 inch top skull. Modern paleontology still struggles with the exact placement of the creature, but the consensus is that it belonged to some type of carnivorous mammal (probably wolf-like or dog-like). Using the skull as a basis for calculating its size, estimates place the creature around 16-feet-long, 6 feet at the shoulders, and weighing 1,000-2,000 pounds. Not the kind of animal you'd want to meet down a dark alley, or anywhere else for that matter.

4.) GIANT SNAKES - For centuries, rumors have circulated regarding monster snakes. However, until the discovery of the Titanoboa in 2002, for many, those stories were regarded simply as myth and legend. Today's longest snake is the Python reticulatus. It averages around 12-17 feet long, with the world record holder measuring nearly 23 feet – a mere child alongside the Titanoboa. The Titanoboa skull alone measures over 2 feet.[26] When added to its immense body, the creature measures 45-49 feet long, weighs an estimated 2,500 lbs., and can reach 3 feet at the thickest part of its body. The monster could easily swallow a full-grown man or a large crocodile. The image at left depicting the demigod Hercules fighting a

[26] Gugliotta, Guy. "How Titanoboa, the 40-Foot-Long Snake, Was Found." Smithsonian.com. Smithsonian Institution, n.d. Web. 28 Oct 2012. <http://www.smithsonianmag.com/science-nature/How-Titanoboa-the-40-Foot-Long-Snake-Was-Found.html?c=y&page=1>.

giant serpent (while unclothed no less), could easily be an allusion to a real event (or events) of the past. Especially since the image depicts (1) gigantism, (2) public nudity (sexual perversion), and (3) a half-man, half-god. Does this imagery merely represent a myth, or is it history?

5.) GIANT REPTILES - The term "dinosaur" was coined in 1842 by the famous British paleontologist, Sir Richard Owen. Roughly translating to "terrible lizard", the dinosaur continues to capture the imagination of the 21st century, having been hijacked by modern science as a means of advancing evolutionary thought. The biblical word "dragon" was the common term used for "terrible lizard" prior to the advent of evolution. One of the things that makes dinosaurs so appealing is their tremendous size. The Sauroposeidon, while not the longest nor the heaviest reptile, is the tallest dinosaur on record. With the longest neck in the known animal world, the 60 ton Sauroposeidon would've easily towered over a five-story building. Individual vertebrae of the giant measure 4 foot in length and appear *"more like a tree trunk than part of an animal's neck."* [27] The longest verifiable giant reptile on record is known as Argentinosaurus. Hailing from Argentina, South America, this gargantuan beast is said to have stood approximately 70-feet-high, been up to 125-feet-long and weighed over 110 tons. From its foot up to the base of its stomach would've been 10-12 feet or more. As large as this is, other discoveries of partial remains suggest the largest dinosaurs have yet to be found. The

[27] Unknown. "Sauroposeidon." ZoomDinosaur.com. Enchanted Learning, 03 1999. Web. 28 Oct 2012. <http://www.enchantedlearning.com/subjects/dinosaurs/news/Sauroposeidon.shtml>.

fossil record is clear that such giant beasts once roamed the Earth in droves. If these formidable creatures have been both buried and forgotten, what other significant pieces of history remain buried by the past?

IMAGE/public domain   Replica of the giant 8 foot *Arthropleura*

6.) GIANT CENTIPEDES - Puppies and kittens are cute, sweet and cuddly, but the growth cycle of the insect is something entirely different. The Lord made most all insects relatively small. This is by design. But I've often wondered that if man was made *"in the image of God"* (Gen. 1:26), if the hideous appearance of the insect was likewise made *"in the image"* of something (demons perhaps? see Lk. 10:17-20). Many thrive in the dark, and will skitter for cover at the least sign of light. Centipedes are no exception. The largest known in the world today is the Amazonian Giant Centipede which can reach 10-12 inches in length. Its bite is poisonous, and on rare occasions has been known to kill small children. But this is nothing compared to the monstrous beasts of the past.

The Euphoberia was a giant among centipedes. It measured over 3 feet in length by about a foot wide. Its millipede cousin was even larger however – the *Arthropleura*. The largest *Arthropleura* ever discovered was 8.5 feet long by 18 inches wide. The head of the insect

Some Giant Creatures Compared with Man

Why were these creatures once so large?

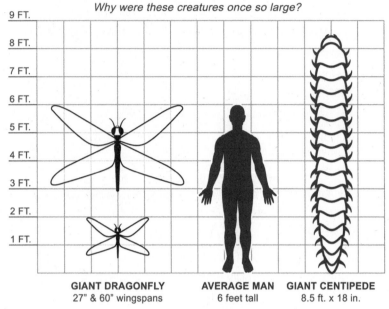

GIANT DRAGONFLY	**AVERAGE MAN**	**GIANT CENTIPEDE**
27" & 60" wingspans	6 feet tall	8.5 ft. x 18 in.

IMAGE/©2013 Jeff Mardis

would have been about as large as that of a human. Today no insects this large are know to exist (Praise the Lord).

7.) GIANT DRAGONFLIES - Paleoentomologist Frank M. Carpenter dug up a first in the world of fossilized insects, a perfectly preserved wing measuring an incredible 14 inches (1940). Today, the wing is known to belong to the giant dragonfly *Meganeuropsis americana*. It is said this large bug averaged a wingspan of around 27 inches, with a 17 inch body. Since its discovery however, specimens with 3 foot and 5 foot wingspans have also allegedly been found. Joe Taylor, the director and curator of the Mt. Blanco Fossil Museum of Crosbyton, Texas, and author of *Giants Against Evolution* writes:

"Meganeuropsis, the giant dragonfly with 36 inch wingspans found in Germany, was topped in the 1980s with the discovery in Italy of one [with] *a wing-span of 60 inches almost twice as large as the giants from Germany!"* [28]

IMAGE/wikia
Wildlife presenter, Nigel Marven, with Meganeuropsis replica.

8.) GIANT FLYING REPTILES - For the final entry into our examination of ancient giants of the animal world, we find the flying monster *Quetzalcoatlus northropi*. Named in honor of the Aztec "feathered serpent god", Quetzalcoatl, this pterosaur is the largest known animal to ever take flight. Its bat-like wings span a staggering 36-39 feet (that's larger than a Cessna 182 aircraft).[29] The skull alone is over 6 feet long. Earlier overall estimations were several feet longer, placing its potential wingspread at 50 feet. Like several of the giants previously mentioned, there are fragmentary fossils suggesting similar creatures of larger size. One of the reasons for the "downsizing" is that modern science does not believe such a large creature could ever fly (even though "nature" supposedly "evolved" to the creature the largest wings on planet Earth). Therefore,

[28] Taylor, Joe. Giants Against Evolution. 1st. Crosbyton, TX: Mt. Blanco Press, 2012. Page 124. Print. <http://www.mtblanco.com/>. AUTHOR'S NOTE: This is a good encyclopedic Christian reference regarding giants from the past.

[29] "Quetzalcoatlus northropi." National Park Service. U.S. Dept. of the Interior, Oct. 15 2012. Web. 29 Oct 2012. <http://www.nps.gov/bibe/naturescience/pterosaur.htm>.

IMAGE/Bigstockphoto.com   Replica and size approximation of *Quetzalcoatlus northropi*.

The *2010 Guinness book of World Records* lists the "Wandering Albatross" as having the largest wingspan of any modern living bird (nearly 12 feet - p 77). But the largest wingspan of any known flying creature was three to four times that wide. The flying reptile, *Quetzalcoatlus northropi*, had a wingspan of 36 to 50 feet. Its skull alone measured 6 feet long.

they shrink its size to make it more accommodating to their beliefs regarding the Earth's early climate.

9.) GIANT ANCIENT CREATURES ABOUND - Giant 16 inch/10 pound frogs; giant 5.5 foot/200 pound penguins; giant 9-foot-tall/1,100 pound "Bigfoot" Apes (*Gigantopithecus*); giant 11-foot-tall/3,500 pound bears; giant 16 foot/2.5 ton turtles; giant birds with 20-foot wingspans; giant 38 foot/8 ton crocodiles; etc.

Having now covered only a small handful of giant animals, let me ask you something. When taken into context with the Lord giving man dominion over all life on Earth (Gen. 1:26), what's PRACTICAL ABOUT THE SIZE of these creatures? When Adam named the animals (Gen. 2:19), were they all this large at the beginning, or did they somehow become larger over time? Did the shepherds of Noah's

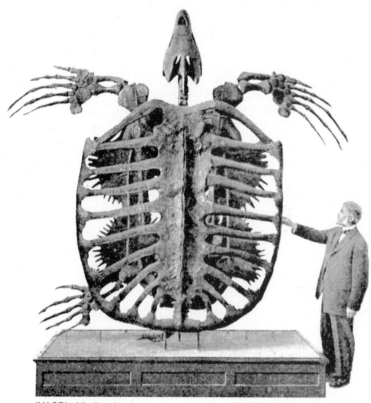

IMAGE/public domain   *Archelon* the giant turtle

day have to guard their flock from these monsters at a time when
"the earth was filled with violence" (Gen. 6:11)? One-ton rats and
wolves; 50-foot, ton-and-a-half snakes; giant 3-foot dragonflies with
reported specimen up to 5 feet? Pottery depicting men wrestling with
giant beavers? Ancient myths of demigods fighting giant serpents?
What in the world is going on? Why the vast discrepancy between
the size of animals today, and the size of animals from the ancient
past? The height of the average man has not changed. The height of
man has remained about 6 foot since the beginning (we know this
because Christ is the *"express image"* of God, and he was of average
height). It was only after the arrival and intervention of the sons of

God did the size of man change. But those changed men where not truely "men", but half-breeds. So to say that "men" were changed into giants is not entirely true – only half true.

Examples of out-of-the-ordinary giant creatures also suggests that the mingling of angels may have somehow affected the animal world. This resulted, not only in a *corrupt form of giant animal*, but the possible creation of *intelligent, man-animal creatures* later revered as "gods". Why are none of these super-sized monsters alive today? Could it be that THEY WERE PART OF THE PROBLEM? Both the Bible and the fossil record say, yes. The Bible records God's judgment on an evil and violent world where *"there were giants in the earth"* – that's a fact. The fossil record records the DEATHS OF HUNDREDS of giant creatures foreign to the world of today – that's also a fact. An issue which I believe may have helped lead to that judgement is at least partially preserved by the fossil record – GIGANTISM. Were ancient creatures killed BECAUSE they were giants – violent animals not part of the world that God originally created? Of course, as mentioned before, the Bible supports the fact that *some* of the pre-Flood large animals were created with man (Job 40:15-18), and because of that, would've been on the ark. But what about the rest?

In closing this section, I want to give you one last thing to consider. What do you get when you start with a *docile creature* which has no inherent fear of man, and then somehow mix that creature with a supernatural, rebellious being which is known to induce gigantism in earth-based life forms? Could it possibly produce *giant animal corruptions violent towards man* (see images on facing page)? Who knows, maybe the fallen sons of God had plans to eventually create an army of giants? Genesis 6 seems to indicate that they certainly started it, and those actions helped kindle the wrath of God. And a war will also culminate at a future date, and result in the heavenly casting-out of their leader and his forces (Rev. 12:7-9). Whatever the details may entail, the scriptures say of the Days of Noah:

IMAGE/Graffix Multimedia Image Services

Giant monsters attack.

Although obviously exaggerated, Hollywood is replete with stories of giant monsters ravaging the Earth. Where did this idea come from? Is it merely make-believe entertainment, or part of a forgotten history from long ago? (also see page 90)

"[11] The earth also was CORRUPT before God, and the earth was FILLED WITH VIOLENCE. [12] And God looked upon the earth, and, behold, it was corrupt; for ALL FLESH had corrupted his way upon the earth. [13] And God said unto Noah, The end of ALL FLESH is come before me; for the earth is FILLED WITH VIOLENCE THROUGH THEM; and, behold, I will destroy THEM with the earth." Genesis 6:11-13

As already noted, the scriptures prophesy for the days of Noah to return (Matt. 24:37, Lk 17:26), a time when the Earth will be *"filled with violence"* once again, and introduce the *"power...to kill...with the beasts of the earth"* (Rev.6:8).

Chapter 15 Summary

Many are unaware of the history of giants. For the most part, such beings are relegated to myth, fantasy and fairy tales. But the Bible, history, paleontology and archaeology all testify to their existence. The scriptures shows that these creatures were originally the product of angels and men. Gigantism has also manifested itself through the animal world.

Having now been introduced to the subjects of giant men, giant animals and gigantism, one may be wondering, *"What in the world does all of this have to do with space aliens?"* The Holy Bible shows the forefathers of the giants were *the first extraplanetary invaders.* Without a knowledge of that past, and the recognition that much of the same things are prophesied to happen again, Christians are left in the dark. Having this knowledge helps lay the foundation, and provides another piece to the puzzle. Specifically, *how counterfeit life is viewed and handled by the Creator.* Regardless of how that life form arose, it is always within a NEGATIVE CONTEXT. The Bible points to "genocide" as God's means of stopping the proliferation of these creatures (Gen. 6:7, 2Sam. 21:15-22, et. al.). However, a better

Ancient Creatures Denied Salvation

IMAGE/Jeff Mardis   A drowning dinosaur (c. 2344 BC)
The fossil record demonstrates that not all ancient creatures were saved.

While many creationists today are keen on showing dinosaurs boarding Noah's Ark, it is clear by simply looking out the window that many of the giants of the past did not survive. Not a single giant beast mentioned here is readily alive today. As far as we know, there are no giant rats, no giant wolves, no giant serpents, no giant dragonflies, no giant centipedes, no giant beavers, no giant flying Quetzalcoatlus', and no dinosaurs. Where are they? I believe many of these things were *deliberately drowned* (Gen. 6:13). This does not mean I'm against the depiction of dinosaurs on the ark (I believe that some were), but I believe the voluminous fossil record helps demonstrate that *many of the ancient creatures were not selected by God for salvation* (see Gen. 7:2-9). The question is – why?

description may be "XENOCIDE" – not the killing of races of human beings, but the destruction of aliens, or beings of "strange flesh". A possible inference to this concept may be found where it's written, "... *turned to flight the armies of the aliens.*" (Heb. 11:34)

The Lord not only kills the offspring resulting from such a situation, but deviants who desire to mingle themselves with a life form different than themselves are also in the crosshairs of God's wrath:

> "*Even as Sodom and Gomorrha, and the cities about them in like manner, giving themselves over to FORNICATION, and GOING AFTER STRANGE FLESH* [i.e. the angels], *are SET FORTH FOR AN EXAMPLE, suffering the vengeance of eternal fire.*" Jude 1:7

The ultimate picture of this truth is seen when Goliath (a giant who defied both God and Israel – 1Sam. 17:45) is slain by David (a type and picture of the Lord Jesus Christ - Mk. 12:35-37). It was the killing of Goliath that helped propel David into the public eye. And as far as that public was concerned, onto the throne of Israel itself (1Sam. 18:6-8). The historical event of David and Goliath is not just about a young boy who killed a big man. It's not just about the Christian "slaying the giants in their life" (i.e. facing the "big problems" of life with the help and guidance of God). While both these conclusions are true, there is a third, more literal, significance and meaning connected to the event – THE KILLING OF COUNTERFEIT LIFE. And all this happens prior to David taking the throne (compare with Rev. 19 where Christ leads and fights a battle before taking the throne).

The next chapter will culminate our studies, as we take a final look at the modern space alien phenomenon.

PART III
CHAPTERS 16 - 17

Conclusions on
Extraterrestrialism

Closing Thoughts
& Theories on the Concept

"Two possibilities exist: Either we are alone in the Universe or we are not. Both are equally terrifying."
– Arthur C. Clark, futurist, atheist

16

The Alien Riddle
Unraveled

U p to this point, we've primarily addressed biblical perspectives on the existence of alien life (chapters 6-15). Ancient and historical positions have also been examined (chapters 1-5). Not a lot has been said, however, regarding the modern phenomenon. A bizarre chronology consisting of thousands of "close encounter", "contactee" and "alien abduction" reports spanning the last century. Since that time, someone or something has convinced mankind of its existence. With such a vast array of global witnesses, every case cannot possibly be a hoax. At least SOME OF THESE WITNESSES are seeing "something" – but what? Some say they are interplanetary visitors, others believe they are figments of mass hallucination, the explanations are wide and varied. But the most important question for the Christian is: *What does the Bible say?*

So far, in an effort to explore the issue, we've seen that the Bible actually says a lot regarding both outer space and life beyond Earth. Chapters 1-15 have been provided as building blocks for understanding the phenomenon. We've scoured the scriptures in order to establish foundational elements on the subject, including: (1) life forms created by God (Chapter 11); (2) life in the heavens (Chapter 12); and (3) life which has traveled through space (Chapter 13). We've also examined the little-known subject of counterfeit life (Chapter 14), as well as the history of giants (Chapter 15). The extensive scriptural evidence accumulated thus far shows that God created a diversity of intelligent life forms. Many of these intelligent life forms dwell on Earth (man and the animals). Of the extraterrestrial-type, however, none were created for inhabiting other planets. Some of the Bible's life forms originate in the Third Heaven with God. These are the real "extraterrestrials" – angels, cherubim, seraphim and celestial horses. Other Bible life forms are shown to be illegitimate creations (giants, magician's serpents, pit locusts, the image of the Antichrist, etc.). With this information in hand, this chapter will look at the modern alien phenomenon to try and determine how and why such beings have come about, and what possible purpose their alleged existence may serve.

Fairy Tales & Science Fiction: A Conditioning of the Mind

Early in our study we discovered that the concept of extraterrestrial life has been around for millennia. Events which seeded the belief, and splintered original monotheistic standards, took place only six chapters into the Bible. Today the term "extraterrestrial" has been divorced from Bible truth, conjuring ideas of advanced, off-world technology and grotesque, demon-like creatures often referred to as "grays" or "little green men". Evolutionism, in conjunction with the modern science fiction movement and the ever evasive UFO phenomenon, has deceived many into accepting the alien as a reality.

As briefly addressed in chapter 5, these facets helped shape and solidify the modern "Extraterrestrial Hypothesis" (ETH) – the belief

1956

1958

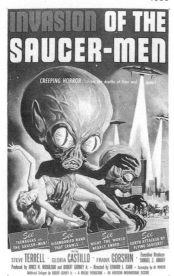

1957

1941

IMAGE/Graffix Multimedia Image Services

Early Science Fiction Movie Poster Gallery

Humanoids from space and monsters taking women

1954

1951

1956

1957

IMAGE/Graffix Multimedia Image Services

Early Science Fiction Movie Poster Gallery
Humanoids from space, giants and monsters taking women

1953

1933

1951

1955

IMAGE/Graffix Multimedia Image Services

Early Science Fiction Movie Poster Gallery
Humanoids from space, beasts and monsters taking women

that highly intelligent aliens from other planets visit, or have been visiting, the Earth.

A 2005 poll questioning 1,000 Americans regarding life on other planets, found that nearly seven out of every ten Americans support the idea - including almost half of all churchgoers.[1] A more recent 2012 poll of 1,114 Americans, found that only 17% DID NOT BELIEVE in UFOs, with 36% answering in the affirmative, and 48% being unsure. The poll also found that 79% believed the government was being less than forthcoming on its knowledge regarding UFOs. MUFON director, David MacDonald said, "We have grown up with *Star Trek*, *Star Wars* and *Battlestar Galactica*. We're at the point where we'd say, 'What planet are you from? Oh well, let's have a beer.'" [2] But this attitude of indifference should come as no real surprise, after understanding the history of Cosmic Pluralism and realizing that Hollywood has relentlessly beat us over the head with the mantra for the past sixty years, the poster art of many early black-and-white science fiction films being particularly interesting.

NOW GO VIEW
all the vintage movie posters and images on pages 89-91, 417 and 425-427.

[1] Malik, Tariq. "Most Americans Believe Alien Life is Possible, Study Shows." space. com. TechMediaNetwork.com, 31 2005. Web. 29 Nov 2012. <http://www.space. com/1150-americans-alien-life-study-shows.html>.

[2] Harish, Alon. "UFOs Exist, Say 36 Percent in National Geographic Survey." ABC News. 2012 ABC News Internet Ventures, 27 2012. <http://abcnews.go.com/ Technology/ufos-exist-americans-national-geographic-survey/story?id=16661311>.

While no one is questioning the fact that, in order to sell tickets, these posters obviously lend themselves to *sensationalism* and Hollywood *sex appeal* (i.e. pictures of monsters and scantily-clad women). That is, most assume, and in part they're right, that the main objective of these images is to MAKE MONEY. However, despite their silly and campy appearance, there is more going on here than meets the eye. The timing of their arrival was (1) right on the heels of the first science fiction boom (1930-40); (2) right on the heels of the first modern UFO sightings (1947); (3) right on the heels of Israel becoming a nation (1948); and (4) during the birth of modern man's first ventures into outer space (1950-60). While seeming to be purely a product of modern times, oddly enough, they also seem to exhibit *a knowledge of the intentions of the world's first alien invaders*. An event recorded in scripture that occurred around 4,600 years ago – *humanoids with a lust for women*. A behavior technically referred to as "xenophilia":

> *"... the sons of God saw the daughters of men that they were fair; and they took them wives of all which they chose." Genesis 6:2*

Many relate the subject of monsters in love with women to the classic fairy-tale of *Beauty and the Beast*, and the moral theme of not judging a thing by its "outward appearance", but by loving motives and intentions of the heart (Jer. 17:9). The obvious message, however, is that it's okay to love a monster – a beast.

While the moral explanation of unconditional love sounds all fuzzy and nice, it also distorts the concept of love by implying that a carnal, consensual type of love between TWO VERY DIFFERENT THINGS is always justification for such actions. Unfortunately, "love" (and more specifically in this case, the desire for physical, sensual relations) is not the litmus test for righteousness or right motives. Many people love many things, but that does not mean it's the

RIGHT KIND of love. It may be the WRONG KIND of love (adultery, fornication, homosexuality, pedophilia, bestiality, xenophilia, etc.). Sometimes this type of love can initiate one's downfall:

> *"[1] But king Solomon LOVED many strange women, together with the daughter of Pharaoh, women of the Moabites, Ammonites, Edomites, Zidonians, and Hittites; [2] Of the nations concerning which the LORD said unto the children of Israel, Ye shall not go in to them, neither shall they come in unto you: for surely they will turn away your heart after their gods: Solomon clave unto these IN LOVE." 2 Kings 11:1-2*

> *"[4] But before they lay down, THE MEN of the city, even THE MEN of Sodom, compassed the house round, both old and young, all the people from every quarter: [5] And they called unto Lot, and said unto him, Where are THE MEN which came in to thee this night? bring them out unto us, THAT WE MAY KNOW THEM. [6] And Lot went out at the door unto them, and shut the door after him, [7] And said, I pray you, brethren, DO NOT SO WICKEDLY." Genesis 19:4-7*

The fairy tale of *Beauty and the Beast* is the popular explanation for such imagery. But the literary roots of this tale reach back much further, and its historical roots even further than that. Folklorists trace the concept to Lucius Apuleius, a 2nd century Roman philosopher and author of *Metamorphoses*. Better known as *The Golden Ass*, this story relates the journeys of a man who, via black magic, accidentally changes himself into an animal. The man finds redemption through initiation into the Mystery Cult of Isis, following a lurid, trashy tale of violence, infidelity, witchcraft, pederasty and bestiality. Recognized as an highly acclaimed literary "masterpiece", this filthy account also contains a tale-within-a-tale – the mythic love story of Cupid and Psyche – the story of *marriage between a god and a mortal woman.*

So there you have it. Whether it's fairy tales, mythology or classic science fiction movies, we keep bumping into the same guilty parties. And regardless of the fact that folklorists point to "mythology" as the origins for such concepts, the Bible-believer knows better. The belief in fallen gods from beyond who marry mortal women, and the imagery of humanoid monsters, does not originate in movies or mythology, but in HISTORY.

IMAGE/public domain   *Beauty & the Beast*

Today's nonchalant attitude toward aliens is a result of having been desensitized towards a subject which the Holy Bible associates with iniquity and confusion. The point is, somebody wants us to accept this stuff. What stuff? Imagery that acclimatizes one to alien humanoids and/or the creation of counterfeit life (bestiality). Mankind is being conditioned to think a certain way. Four millennia of teachings have said these things are "gods" or super-beings from beyond. Six decades of visual indoctrination, and a constant barrage of grotesque, humanoid-type imagery, has prepared man to accept such creatures. Man is now set to welcome aliens with open arms. Or, as the MUFON director stated, to at least sit down with them over a friendly beer (Prov. 23:31).

Twinkle, Twinkle Little Star, How I Wonder What You Are

In chapter 1 we explained that the Genesis 6 *"sons of God"* were the first historical extraterrestrial visitors to planet Earth. Subsequent chapters identified these beings as *"angels"* (or more specifically, fallen angels), which the Holy Bible also typified as STARS (chapter 12). Also briefly addressed was the development of witchcraft and paganism which followed the Great Flood (chapters 1 & 14). An early religious movement whose SYMBOLISM and PRACTICES fit hand-in-glove with the advent of supernatural, god-like beings from space and the creation of counterfeit life. These details are not only reflect the Genesis 6 incident, but are equally suggested by Greek and Roman mythology, and many early science fiction movie posters of the 20th century.

One of the strongest pieces of evidence which helps equate fallen angels with ancient false gods, and in turn, links witchcraft to the worship of these beings, is the first false god mentioned by name in the Bible. Many of those familiar with Bible study, are also familiar with the "Law of First Mention". This is the observation that the "first mention" of a particular word or subject will usually set the standard for that word or subject thereafter. In this instance we have the Bible's first FALSE GOD – Molech, a name whose Hebrew spelling is "M-A-L-A-K".[3] Ironically, the Hebrew word for "angel" is also spelled "M-A-L-A-K".[4] Malak (or Molech) is associated with the STAR SYMBOL, a typology also connected with the angel. So, this first false god connected with the star, not only bears the Hebrew title of "angel", but is also connected with sodomy (sex perversion), and bestiality (a means or attempt at counterfeit-life creation):

---

[3] See *Strong's Concordance* Hebrew reference numbers for "Molech" - 4432, 4427

[4] See *Strong's Concordance* Hebrew reference numbers for "angel" - 4397

IMAGE/Foster Bible Pictures, 1897   The worship of Molech (c. 1490 BC)

Man offering his seed to the god "Molech", the first false god named by the Bible.
Molech also had a direct connection with angels and the pentagram symbol. Why
would man want to GIVE HIS SEED to a god? Where did he get THAT idea from?
Christians would do well to think long and hard on both these questions, and note the
scriptural context within which "Molech" first appears (Leviticus 18:21-25).

> *"[21] And thou shalt not let any of THY SEED pass
> through the fire to MOLECH, neither shalt thou profane
> the name of thy God: I am the LORD. [22] Thou shalt not
> lie with mankind, as with womankind: it is abomination.*

> *[23] Neither shalt thou LIE with any BEAST to defile thyself therewith: neither shall any woman stand before a BEAST TO LIE DOWN THERETO: it is confusion. [24] Defile not ye yourselves in any of these things: for in all these the nations are defiled which I cast out before you: [25] And the land is defiled: therefore I do visit the iniquity thereof upon it, and the land itself vomiteth out her inhabitants." Leviticus 18:21-25*

> *"But ye have borne the tabernacle of your MOLOCH and Chiun your images, THE STAR OF YOUR GOD, which ye made to yourselves." Amos 5:26*

> *"Yea, ye took up the tabernacle of MOLOCH, and THE STAR of your god Remphan, figures which ye made to worship them: and I will carry you away beyond Babylon." Acts 7:43*

Regardless of how modern man may use the star symbol, it is the Holy Bible which defines the origins of all such symbols. Even today, the STAR is the most prominent symbol used by the occult. *The Encyclopedia of Witches and Witchcraft* states:

> *"The pentacle, a five-pointed STAR, with a single point upright, is the MOST IMPORTANT SYMBOL of witchcraft. It is both a RELIGIOUS SYMBOL ... and a symbol of the MAGICAL CRAFT of witchcraft. A written or drawn pentacle is called a pentagram. ... In magic, the pentagram is the Witch's symbol of protection and positive power and is used to control the elemental forces."* [5]

---

[5] Guiley, Rosemary Ellen. *The Encyclopedia of Witches and Witchcraft*. New York: Facts On File, Inc., 1989. p 265.

"The four elements of nature – earth, air, fire and water – form the FOUNDATION OF NATURAL MAGIC. Modern witches and pagans revere these forces, The elements are associated with the cardinal points of the magic circle and with a HIERARCHY OF SPIRITS – who in turn are governed by HIGHER BEINGS..." [6]

Witches
Pentagram

Satanic
Pentagram

"Star of David"
Hexagram

"Elementals [are] *Low-level spirits that personify the four elements – earth, air, fire and water. The term also is applied to nature spirits, which are said to exist in all things in nature, such as animals, insects, birds, rocks and plants. RULED BY devas or ARCHANGELS (called in modern witchcraft the Lords of the Watchtowers, the Guardians or the Mighty Ones), elementals serve as the life force and may be SUMMONED BY WITCHES to assist in magic..."* [7]

As noted above, certain traditions in witchcraft make overt claims of angelic connections, labeling the powers behind their craft as "Archangels", and going so far as to name the four angels who rule the elemental quadrants: Uriel (North), Michael (South), Raphael (East) and Gabriel (West). A Google search of the words "angel magic"

---

[6] Guiley, Rosemary Ellen. *The Encyclopedia of Witches and Witchcraft.* New York: Facts On File, Inc., 1989. p 112.

[7] Ibid. p 111.

will further establish how deeply entrenched the angel is within the occult world. Although ultimately responsible for all forms of occult arts, today the [fallen] angel is particularly evident through a system known as "Enochian Magic". Organized into a working system in the 1580s, and referred to as *"the language of the angels"*, Enochian Magic claims a direct link to the beings, and teaches the seeking-out and invocation thereof.[8] This type of ceremonial magic was catapulted into modern popularity via the writings of Aleister Crowley, having strong connections to both high occult organizations the Golden Dawn and the Ordo Templi Orientis. Concerning the angel Crowley writes:

Notice how these modern occult books illustrate the importance of the angel in modern witchcraft.

"It should NEVER BE FORGOTTEN for a single moment that the CENTRAL AND ESSENTIAL WORK OF THE MAGICIAN is the attainment of the Knowledge and Conversation of THE HOLY GUARDIAN ANGEL. Once he has achieved this he must of course be left entirely in the hands of that ANGEL, who can be invariably and inevitably relied upon to LEAD HIM to the further great step—crossing of the Abyss and the attainment of the grade of Master of the Temple."[9]

Aleister Crowley (1875-1947), a Freemason and member of both the Golden Dawn and the O.T.O., was a prolific promoter of the system. He was not only one of the most influential and infamous occultists/Satanists of the 20th century, but also one of the most

Notice how these modern occult books illustrate the connections between fornication, angels and witchcraft.

perverted and morally depraved individuals to ever walk the face of this Earth. His dark teachings are nothing new, however. They're an old, old story, with roots reaching back over 4,000 years. Roots which were originally seeded by beings, which indeed, were part of a company given authority over the elements. Note the following scripture verses and the powers associated with these creatures:

Angels with Power over Air

"And after these things I saw four ANGELS standing on the four corners of the earth, HOLDING the four WINDS of the earth, that THE WIND SHOULD NOT BLOW on the earth, nor on the sea, nor on any tree." Revelation 7:1

---

[8] Greer, Mary K. "Hermetic Order of the Golden Dawn Dictionary." The Hermetic Order of the Golden Dawn. N.p.. Web. 25 Jan 2013. <http://www.hermeticgoldendawn.org/>.

[9] Crowley, Aleister. *Magic Without Tears.* New York, NY: Ordo Templi Orientis, 1954. ch 83

Angels with Power over Fire

"And the ANGEL of the LORD appeared unto him IN A FLAME OF FIRE out of the midst of a bush: and he looked, and, behold, the bush burned with fire, and the bush was not consumed." Exodus 3:2 (also see Acts 7:30)

"And another ANGEL came out from the altar, which HAD POWER OVER FIRE; and cried with a loud cry to him that had the sharp sickle, saying, Thrust in thy sharp sickle, and gather the clusters of the vine of the earth; for her grapes are fully ripe." Revelation. 14:18

"And the fourth angel poured out his vial upon the SUN; and POWER WAS GIVEN UNTO HIM to scorch men with FIRE." Revelation 16:8

Angels with Power over Water

"[3] And the second angel poured out his vial upon the SEA; and it became as the blood of a dead man: and every living soul died IN THE SEA. [4] And the third angel poured out his vial upon the RIVERS and fountains of WATERS; and they became blood. [5] And I heard THE ANGEL OF THE WATERS say, Thou art righteous, O Lord, which art, and wast, and shalt be, because thou hast judged thus. ... And the sixth angel poured out his vial upon the great RIVER Euphrates; and THE WATER thereof WAS DRIED UP, that the way of the kings of the east might be prepared." Revelation 16:3-5 & 12

"For an angel went down at a certain season into the pool, and troubled the WATER: whosoever then first after the troubling of the WATER stepped in was MADE WHOLE of whatsoever disease he had." John 5:4

Also interesting to note is where the angels of Revelation 16 are responsible for pouring their vials. One vial is poured upon the EARTH, one vial is poured into the AIR, one vial is poured into FIRE, and three vials are poured into the WATERS – earth, air, fire and water. While most all of these events have yet to come to pass, taking place thousands of years after the advent of witchcraft, *they are still instructive in the fact that THEY DEMONSTRATE THE ABILITIES OF ANGELS*, powers first recognized by man to belong to the Genesis 6 sons of God. These abilities later reflected witchcraft's ancient "Guardians" or "Mighty Ones", and admittedly comprised the cornerstone of their magic rituals and their use of the pentagram. Because the Bible's first-named false god (Molech) has a direct link to angels, the "star" symbol, and sordid sexual practices, it is now much easier to see how post-Flood polytheism and witchcraft were birthed. The imagery of their hybrid gods continued to echo these roots, and show that such beliefs helped propagate the idea of *humanoid beings from space.* In the 21st century, this concept has morphed into "evolutionary science" where students and school children are taught on a daily basis that man is made "in the image of animals", a concept repudiated by scripture:

> *"[19] They made a CALF in Horeb, and worshipped the molten image. [20] Thus they CHANGED their glory* [i.e. their God – the Root of man's origin] *into the similitude of an ox that eateth grass. [21] THEY FORGAT GOD their saviour, which had done great things in Egypt; [22] Wondrous works in the land of Ham, and terrible things by the Red Sea. [23] Therefore he said that he would DESTROY THEM, had not Moses his chosen stood before him in the breach, to turn away his WRATH, lest he should destroy them." Psalms 106:19-23*

> *"[21] Because that, when they knew God, they glorified him not as God, neither were thankful; but became vain in their imaginations, and their foolish heart was darkened. [22] Professing themselves to be wise, they became fools, [23] And CHANGED the glory of the uncorruptible GOD into an image made like to corruptible MAN, and to BIRDS, and fourfooted BEASTS, and creeping THINGS. [24] Wherefore God also gave them up to uncleanness through the lusts of their own hearts, to dishonour their own bodies between themselves: [25] Who CHANGED THE TRUTH of God into a lie, and WORSHIPPED and served the CREATURE more than the Creator, who is blessed for ever. Amen." Romans 1:21-25*

Note that the scriptures declare that claiming kinship to the animal (or mixing man in some way with the animal) is akin to FORGETTING GOD. Such a concept is always satanic. Today this type imagery is seen via "close encounters" with alleged "space aliens". The ultimate bodily representation of super-beings that are neither man nor animal, but can represent BOTH, creatures assumed by many to be evolved intelligences from far away worlds.

Close Encounters of the Counterfeit Kind

Ufology uses the designation "CE3" to describe a "Close Encounter" of the "Third Kind". It is the reporting of a visual observation of an unknown entity. For those who have allegedly witnessed them, the physical appearance of the alien has varied widely over the years. The more contemporary depiction (the 3-to-4-foot, big-headed, black-eyed, "gray") did not become a prominent icon until 1961 – fourteen years after the modern UFO phenomenon began. After over half a century of sightings, it has been concluded that all such CE3 encounters all generally fall into one of four categories [10]:

ANIMAL WORSHIP
Their god is an animal (Rom. 1:23)

GOLDEN CALF
Animal worship (Ex. 32:1-5)

DAGON
Philistine fish-man (Judges 16:23)

MOLECH
Bull-man (Lev. 18:21)

Gallery of Hybrid Gods
of the Past & Present

KERNUNNOS
The pagan Celtic stag-man

PAN
Goat-man of Witchcraft

KHNUM, BAST & ANUBIS
Egyptian man-animal gods

Gallery of Hybrid Gods
of the Past & Present

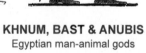

HANUMAN
The Hindu monkey-man

GANESA
The Hindu elephant-man

EVOLUTION MONKEY-MAN
Supposed "ancestor" of modern man

ALIEN - SUPER HUMANOID
Ultimate hybrid-god of the New Age

Gallery of Hybrid Gods
of the Past & Present

HUMANOID - Describes beings with an essentially human-like shape.

ANIMALIAN - Describes beings that are more animal-like than human.

ROBOTIC - Describes beings which appear more mechanical than organic.

EXOTIC - Describes the remaining 5% which cannot be classified in the first 3 groups.

The 1966-67 Point Pleasant, West Virginia "Mothman" creature, for example, was seen by over 100 eyewitnesses over a period of 13 months. This unexplained event was also accompanied by multiple sightings of strange lights in the sky and encounters with mysterious "men in black". The Mothman was very atypical in appearance, resembling a large, winged, red-eyed humanoid. To this very day, certain residents of Point Pleasant fear to talk about what they saw. Other standout examples include the 1955 Kelly, Kentucky "goblin" encounter seen by 11 witnesses; the 1947 Roswell, New Mexico "recovery of alien bodies"; the 1952 meteor-monster from Flatwoods, West Virginia; and the disturbing Allagash Wilderness abductions of 1976. And the list goes on.

Because evolution teaches that environment dictates how living things supposedly "evolve", the chances of any physical similarities between humans and extraterrestrials should be extraordinarily slim. Seth Shostak, senior astronomer at the SETI institute, states:

"In the movies they often look a lot like us -- two arms, two legs, a head, two eyes, and so forth. But really, if you go down to the local zoo, and check out the critters there,

[10] Story, Ronald. *The Encyclopedia of Extraterrestrial Encounters*. New York: New American Library, 2001. p 49.

they don't look like us. So I don't think aliens would, either. But my personal opinion is that if we find a signal ... it will be coming from a society that's more advanced than ours. So they may have already invented thinking machines. I think we're just subjecting ourselves to wishful thinking when we imagine that the aliens will be protoplasm blobs the way we are!" [11]

Another commentator has said:

"While it seems incredible that life does not exist elsewhere in the universe, it is equally incredible that it should resemble man." [12]

Despite these evolutionary-based assumptions, over 90% of all alleged sightings are HUMANOID in their appearance, a puzzle which baffles modern science. Yet such a conclusion is EXPECTED if men and/or ANGELS are somehow involved in the creative process (both men and angels are "humanoid"). Regardless of which historical close encounter you choose, however, in most cases alien life does not fit comfortably into any class of life created by God. With the exception of human-looking aliens, all modern descriptions of these creature are unconventional misfits that have no apparent DIRECT RELATIVE anywhere in Heaven or Earth. When compared with the seven life classifications found in scripture we find:

1.) Creature Class - Aliens do not belong to this group because they are not fully animal, but appear to be only PARTIALLY. Many aliens have been described as insect-

[11] Mosher, Dave. "SETI Astronomer: Aliens Probably Look Like Robots." Discovery. Discovery Communications, LLC, 23 2008. Web. 30 Nov 2012. <http://dsc.discovery.com/space/im/alien-contact-seth-shostak.html>.

[12] Story, Ronald. The Encyclopedia of Extraterrestrial Encounters. New York: New American Library, 2001. p 26.

KELLY GOBLIN
Hopkinsville/Kelly, KY - 1955

JOHANNIS ENCOUNTER
Friuli, Italy - 1947

ROSWELL CRASH
Roswell, NM - 1947

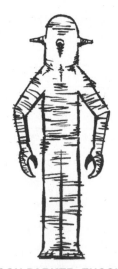

HICKSON-PARKER ENCOUNTER
Pascagoula, MS - 1973

IMAGE/©2013 Jeffrey Mardis

Despite their campy appearance, this wide range of unknown entities are depictions of actual eye-witness testimony (The Hopkinsville-Kelly, Kentucky "Goblin" is one the most credible eyewitness accounts in history). If any of these are pure fantasy, that

FLATWOODS MONSTER
Flatwoods, WV - 1952

HIGDON ENCOUNTER
Wyoming - 1974

ANDREASSON ENCOUNTER
South Ashburnham, MA - 1967

MOTHMAN ENCOUNTER
Point Pleasant, WV - 1966

IMAGE/©2013 Jeffrey Mardis

fantasy comes from the imagination of the supposed witnesses and not the author of this book. These beings have been presented here for study purposes (1Thess. 5:21), and are being treated "as if" they are actual life forms – which some may be.

like or reptile-like. But other animal-like qualities include: Monkey-like, hairy-beast-like, fish-like and cat-like.

2.) Man Class - Aliens do not belong to this group because they are not fully human, but appear to be only PARTIALLY. Most aliens are "humanoid" in appearance, with two arms, two legs and a head. Those who encounter aliens which look *identical to human men*, simply means that these are appearances of real men or fallen angels.

3.) Angelic Class - For the most part, aliens do not belong to this group because they are not fully angels, but appear to be only PARTIALLY. Most all aliens have been described as displaying some sort of supernatural ability (super intelligence, super strength, telepathy, walking through walls, invisibility, mind control, fear inducement, paralysis inducement, dimensional travel, etc.). However, those who encounter aliens which look *identical to human men*, are either appearances of real men or fallen angels.

4.) Cherubic Class - Aliens do not belong to this group because they are not cherubs. Only 5 cherubim appear in scripture, with the fifth being the fallen cherub *"Lucifer"*. The physical appearance of the cherub is described explicitly by the prophet Ezekiel. Thus far, no alien has ever matched this description.

5.) Celestial Creature - Aliens do not belong to this group because they are not Celestial Creatures. The scriptures show that these beings look *identical to* Earth-based animals. They are sinless creatures which reside only in the Third Heaven with God. The Bible lists accounts where these beings have visited Earth, but not of their own will or accord, nor via "flying saucers".

6.) Symbiotic Class - Since the Bible shows that God CREATED ONLY ONE LIFE FORM of this type, it is impossible for aliens to belong to this classification. Robot-like alien encounters may be counterfeits of this type of life, and in such cases, would belong in the "Counterfeit Class" instead.

7.) Counterfeit Class - Modern unidentified life does not fit in any of the 6 previous God-created life groups. Because of this, the "counterfeit" classification is the only group to which it can logically belong. Aliens are neither men, nor animal, nor angel, but in general, appear to be an amalgam of all three in one way or another. Like the Bible's giants (Gen. 6), conjured serpents (Ex. 7:11) and the Devil's image (Rev. 13:15), it is an illegitimate life form. The Lord always destroys such life eventually.

Many Christians today claim that aliens are "Nephilim", a conclusion drawn by casting doubt on the scripture's word "giant" and replacing it with a Hebrew transliteration. I do not agree with this change. To my knowledge, there have been no close encounters with giants which match those found in scripture, and thus no close encounter with PURE "Nephilim". The Bible describes the Nephilim as giant, men-like beings, but obviously very few modern aliens match this description. No giant, 13-foot-tall, men have been encountered departing UFOs. This means, that because of their vast discrepancy in appearance, all modern aliens cannot be classified as *pure angelic-human offspring*. To classify them as such shows a lack of scriptural adherence and a willingness to jump to conclusions.

Aliens undoubtedly have a connection with fallen angels, but their physical appearance clearly does not align with the giant men of Genesis. This indicates that SOMETHING MORE is going on. Regardless, these seven life classifications illustrate that the beings witnessed during a close encounter are not created by God. This leaves very few scriptural alternatives for their origin.

Chapter 12 briefly addressed the subject of the unclean spirits of devils. Scriptures show that such beings *currently have no physical form of their own*. Although they undoubtedly did once upon a time, death separated these beings from their bodies. The Lord Jesus Christ himself taught that these spirits are in constant search of live bodies to possess.

> *"[43] When the UNCLEAN SPIRIT is gone out of a man, he walketh through dry places, SEEKING REST, and findeth none. [44] Then he saith, I WILL RETURN into my house from whence I came out; and when he is come, he findeth it empty, swept, and garnished. [45] Then goeth he, and taketh with himself seven other spirits more wicked than himself, and they ENTER IN and DWELL THERE..." Matt. 12:43-45 (Lk. 11:24-26)*

If one studies every single Bible reference regarding unclean spirits (and similar words related to the subject), it will be discovered that there are NO INSTANCES where these spirits have manifest in bodily form. Instead, as seen by the above illustration, these wicked spirits are not at rest unless *possessing the body of another life form* – man or animal (Matt. 8:28-33, Matt. 12:43-45, Mark 5:2-13, Mark 16:9, Luke 8:2, Luke 8:27-33, Luke 11:24-26 et.al.). What better physical body for devils to inhabit, than a life form created apart from the approval and authority of God? The modern alien fits this mold perfectly. Such life forms represent nothing more than "devil suits", making the perfect home for an unclean spirit. Jacques Vallee, world-renowned ufologist, secularist and author of 12 books on UFOs, is noted as saying; *"An equally impressive parallel could be made between UFO occupants and the popular conception of demons..."* [13] Vallee is not the only researcher to arrive at this conclusion.

Journey to the Center of the Earth

"So many circumstances show the earth is hollow that the fact cannot be questioned; but its contents are not so easily determined till we look inside." – William Reed, *The Phantom of the Poles* (1906)

Like many other long-standing mysteries, the "Hollow Earth" theory has been around for a while. The most well known among these theories, is the idea that there are holes at both poles which reach into an inner world. The theory espouses that the Earth's interior supposedly hides a "Sun", and an entire civilization, undiscovered by Earth's surface. I would never go as far in making such claims. But recognizing that many such theories are often based on kernels of truth, I would go as far as the scriptures take the issue (1 Thess. 5:21). Eat the fish – leave the bones. One of the more outstanding proof texts illustrating a "hollow" type Earth inhabited by living creatures, is found in the book of Revelation:

"(1) And the fifth angel sounded, and I saw a star fall from heaven unto the earth: and to him was given the key of the BOTTOMLESS PIT. (2) And he opened the bottomless pit; and there arose a smoke out of the pit, as the smoke of a great furnace; and the sun and the air were darkened by reason of the smoke of the pit. (3) And THERE CAME

[13] Vallee, Jacques. Messengers of Deception: UFO Contacts & Cults. 2nd. ed. Daily Grail Publishing, 2008. p 14.

OUT of the smoke LOCUSTS upon the earth: and unto them was given power, as the scorpions of the earth have power. (4) And it was commanded them that they should not hurt the grass of the earth, neither any green thing, neither any tree; but only those men which have not the seal of God in their foreheads. (5) And to them it was given that they should not kill them, but that they should be tormented five months: and their torment was as the torment of a scorpion, when he striketh a man. (6) And in those days shall men seek death, and shall not find it; and shall desire to die, and death shall flee from them. (7) And the shapes of the locusts were like unto horses prepared unto battle; and on their heads were as it were crowns like gold, and their faces were as the faces of men. (8) And they had hair as the hair of women, and their teeth were as the teeth of lions. (9) And they had breastplates, as it were breastplates of iron; and the sound of their wings was as the sound of chariots of many horses running to battle. (10) And they had tails like unto scorpions, and there were stings in their tails: and their power was to hurt men five months. (11) And they had a king over them, which is the angel of the bottomless pit, whose name in the Hebrew tongue is Abaddon, but in the Greek tongue hath his name Apollyon." Revelation 9:1-11

Of all the verses in the word of God, these passages probably match the physical characteristics of the modern "space alien" better than any others. By "physical characteristics" I'm not necessarily referring to the literal appearance of the average alien, but to its physical makeup – that of a MIXED life form. The confusing makeup of the Pit Locusts coincides with the hybrid-like appearance of the modern alien (see page 252 for an illustrated concept). These verses also represent the best scriptural place to hang our hat when dealing with modern alien origins. Many assume that aliens originate from outer space. Here, however, the Bible shows that such things can come from under the ground. In other words, what we're seeing is not "extra-terrestrial" life, but "intra-terrestrial" life. Not life from OUTSIDE the Earth, but life from INSIDE the Earth. Counterfeit life arising from under ground.

Also interesting, is the fact that two outstanding characteristics are shared by the Giants of Genesis 6, the Pit Locusts, and the Horsemen Army. All three represent mongrelized non-contemporary life forms which have a STRONG CONNECTION TO ANGELS. The Giants are the children of the fallen sons of God (Gen.6:1-4); the Pit Locusts are overseen by an angelic "king" (Abaddon/Apollyon - Rev. 9:1-11); and the monstrous Horsemen Army is lead by four bound angels which will eventually be loosed (Rev. 9:14-19). All facts which seem to encourage a more LITERAL INTERPRETATION of the verses, rather than a figurative rendering. The Genesis 6 sons of God are REAL – not figurative. Abaddon the angelic king is REAL – not figurative. The four angels bound in the river Euphrates are REAL – not figurative (the fact they are imprisoned shows they are fallen). If all the angels are real, then their minions are real as well. What the Bible has just taught us is that life forms which fall OUTSIDE OF GOD'S ORDAINED PLAN FOR LIFE (life not created *"after its kind"* – see chapter 14) is connected to fallen angels – creatures in REBELLION against God. The reason I keep using the word "connected" is that while scriptures show that the ancient giants were *literally fathered* by the fallen sons of God, neither the bastard Pit Locusts nor the Horseman Army can lay claim to that fact. While this is true, these two groups, nevertheless, are lead by fallen angels. All three groups presented here, of non-contemporary life forms, are LED BY ANGELS. But only one third of that number are their LITERAL OFFSPRING. As a Bible-believing Christian, what am I

454 Journey to the Center of the Earth

to make of all this? What this is pointing us to is that the modern hybrid humanoids, which many recognize as "aliens", if real at all, are also subservient to fallen angels. *That is, in one way or another, whether they're literal offspring or not, aliens are the servants of the fallen sons of God.*

The underground home of the Pit Locusts is mankind's most unexplored environment. The volume of the Earth is estimated to be over 260 billion cubic miles (approx. 260,732,699,457 ml3). To help put this in perspective, the entire world population could easily be stacked into a space slightly larger than a single cubic mile (around 7.2 billion people in 2015). What this shows is that the interior of the Earth occupies a *massive amount* of unexplored territory.

According to the Bible, there are at least three subterranean regions: (1) Abraham's Bosom (sometimes called "Paradise"); (2) the Great Gulf; and (3) Hell.

> *"[22] And it came to pass, that the beggar died, and was carried by the angels into ABRAHAM'S BOSOM: the rich man also died, and was buried; [23] And in HELL he lift up his eyes, being in torments, and seeth Abraham afar off, and Lazarus in his bosom. [24] And he cried and said, Father Abraham, have mercy on me, and send Lazarus, that he may dip the tip of his finger in water, and cool my tongue; for I am tormented in this FLAME. [25] But Abraham said, Son, remember that thou in thy lifetime receivedst thy good things, and likewise Lazarus evil things: but now he is comforted, and thou art tormented. [26] And beside all this, between us and you there is A GREAT GULF fixed: so that they which would pass from hence to you cannot; neither can they pass to us, that would come from thence." Luke 16:22-26 (also see Lk. 23:43 & Psa. 86:13)*

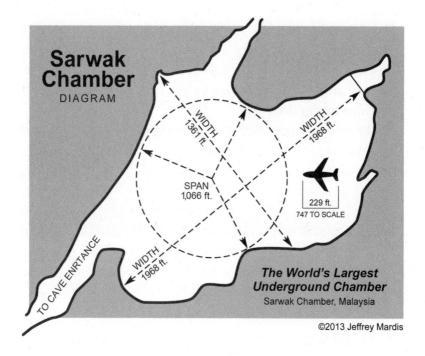

Sarwak Chamber
DIAGRAM

WIDTH
1361 ft.

WIDTH
1968 ft.

SPAN
1,066 ft.

229 ft.
747 TO SCALE

WIDTH
1968 ft.

TO CAVE ENRTANCE

The World's Largest Underground Chamber
Sarwak Chamber, Malaysia

©2013 Jeffrey Mardis

The exact sizes and locations of the once-occupied "Paradise" (Psa. 68:18, Eph. 4:8-10) and the "Great Gulf" are unknown. But undoubtedly they are hollow, cavernous type regions much like caves located near the Earth's surface. With the largest known caves and cavernous chambers being only RECENT discoveries, obviously seismic detection technology has its limits. The world's largest open cave chamber (Sarwak Chamber in Malaysia), was not discovered until 1980, with large chambers of comparable size being discovered even more recently. A sphere of 1,066 feet in circumference can fit within the largest hollow of Sarwak Chamber.[14] That's over one-fifth of a mile. In 2009 the world's largest single-passage cave was discovered in Vietnam – the Son Doong Cave. The giant Son Doong

[14] Dixon, Kevin. "Measuring Sarawak Chamber." The Mulu Caves Project. Mulu Caves Project 2009. Web. 25 Jan 2013. <http://www.mulucaves.org/wordpress/articles/measuring-sarawak-chamber>.

IMAGE/Bigstockphoto.com

The inner-Earth is the world's most unexplored territory. In spite of the technological advancements of the age, man is still discovering giant caves and caverns in the Earth. The world's largest chamber was discovered in 1980. What else lies beneath?

reaches 460 feet high by 460 feet wide. Current explorers have been blocked by "seasonal floodwaters" at the 2.8 mile mark, but plan on returning in order to complete its mapping.[15] The point is, the Earth has plenty of lost or hidden underground caves and passages. To think that modern science has discovered them all is easily disproved by recent discoveries.

The third and most infamous region, the region known as "Hell", was confirmed by seismic readings in 1926, after discovering that the Earth had a fiery liquid core. A fact revealed by scripture and the Lord Jesus Christ hundreds of years previously.

> *"For a FIRE is kindled in mine anger, and shall BURN unto the LOWEST HELL, and shall consume the earth with her increase, and SET ON FIRE the foundations of the mountains." Deuteronomy 32:22*

[15] Owen, James. "World's Biggest Cave Found in Vietnam." National Geographic. National Geographic Society, 31 01 2011. Web. 25 Jan 2013. <http://news.nationalgeographic.com/news/2009/07/090724-biggest-cave-vietnam.html>.

"And fear not them which kill the body, but are not able to kill the soul: but rather fear him which is able to destroy both soul and body IN HELL." Matthew 10:28 et. al.

"And if thine eye offend thee, pluck it out: it is better for thee to enter into the kingdom of God with one eye, than having two eyes to be cast into HELL FIRE" Mark 9:47

"[9] (Now that he ascended, what is it but that he also DESCENDED first into THE LOWER PARTS OF THE EARTH? [10] He that DESCENDED is the same also that ascended up far above all heavens, that he might fill all things.)" Eph. 4:9-10

Many have tried to deny the existence of Hell, but both science and scripture leave no room for doubt. It is a place burning with fire, located in the heart of the Earth, that's been *"prepared for the devil and his angels"* (Matt. 18:8-9 & 25:41, et. al.). Hell is also known as "the Pit". It is bottomless, consisting only of "sides" (Isa. 14:15, Ezk. 31:16). This pit can also be opened, having bars, gates and a key, but other entry points may also be possible (Job. 17:16, Jonah 2:6, Matt. 16:18, Rev. 9:1, 20:1, Num. 16:31-33). The Bible also indicates that these three subterranean regions (Paradise, the Great Gulf and Hell) will probably merge at some point, whereupon Hell will be enlarged (Isa. 5:14). At that time, this molten region will become the dreaded *"Lake of Fire"* (Rev. 19:20 & 20:10,14-15).

Much more could be said regarding these general inner-Earth regions, but Revelation 9:1-11 clearly shows that counterfeit-type life forms dwell there (or at least will dwell there at some point in the future). Like the modern alien, these mysterious man-horse-locusts are *confusing in their appearance*. When coupled with the fact that they are also *ruled by an angelic king*, the exact origin of these things immediately becomes suspect. Meaning, like the offspring of

6 sons of God, the Creator had no hand in their creation. circumstances seem to point to an illegitimate type of ___ – an origin hidden from the masses of mankind UNDER THE GROUND.

I've often wondered if the invisible elite who govern this world, and have bowed the knee to Satan (Matt. 4:9), have also made some sort of CONTACT with the beings of the inner Earth. Perhaps these men are being instructed, or are working in conjunction with the king of the Bottomless Pit (or other rulers of the darkness) and are acquiring forbidden wisdom regarding the mixing of life forms (James 3:15)? If such an end-times scenario were to take place, how would the elite go about accomplishing such extreme feats of contact, science and secrecy? Surprisingly, just as the Bible made allusions to the landing of NASA's "Eagle" on the Moon (Obad. 1:4), so too it infers of man's attempted descent into the Earth. Events which the Bible depicts as rebellious moves against God.

> "Though they DIG INTO HELL, thence shall mine hand take them; though they CLIMB UP TO HEAVEN, thence will I bring them down" (Amos 9:2)

Secrets from the Underground

> "Hide me from the SECRET COUNSEL OF THE WICKED; from the insurrection of the workers of iniquity: They encourage themselves in AN EVIL MATTER: they commune of laying snares PRIVILY; they say, Who shall see them?" Psalms 64:2&5

> "I have not spoken in SECRET, in A DARK PLACE OF THE EARTH: I said not unto the seed of Jacob, Seek ye me in vain: I the LORD speak righteousness, I declare things that are right." Isaiah 45:19

*"Can any hide himself in SECRET PLACES that I shall
not see him? saith the LORD. Do not I fill heaven and
earth? saith the LORD." Jeremiah 23:24*

When dealing with the modern theory of aliens (not the angelic invaders of Genesis 6), there are a couple of reasons why the "intra-terrestrial" concept is more conformable to scripture than the classic "extraterrestrial" concept. First, as examined in the previous section, scriptures reveal that unconventional life forms exist underground (or at least will exist there at some point in the future - Rev. 9). Secondly, in conjunction with the Bible's clear teachings on hollow, cavernous-type, inner-Earth regions, the paper trail shows that conventional technological know-how for constructing underground facilities, believe it or not, stretches back over a century and a half. This type of man-made structure (many of which are hidden from public knowledge) falls under the prophetic category that end-times knowledge shall be increased (Dan. 12:4 - for more information see the section in chapter 14 titled *The Imagination Unchained*). For the Bible-believer, these examples represent good reasons why modern aliens may originate from the inner-Earth rather than outer space. This also lends itself to the "possibility" that as rebellious-man proceeds to "dig into hell" (Amos 9:2) that he will encounter (or has already encountered/or that he has had a hand in the creation of some of) the beings which dwell there.

In chapter 12 we briefly touched on the Devil and his offer to those who would obtain true global power. The requisite was that one must first bow down and worship him (Matt. 4:9 & Lk. 4:5-6). The result would mean unsolicited "membership" in a global elite, and much closer access to the true *"rulers of the darkness of this world"* (Eph. 6:12). A secret governing setup of this type creates the perfect environment for the creation of what modern conspiracy authors have dubbed a "Breakaway Civilization". A clandestine group of elite, who have hoarded secret technology for such a long period of time, that they have become an advanced hidden civilization unto themselves (and may have headquarters on the Moon or elsewhere). Whether true or not, because of such dastardly connections to the god of this world, and motives which fall in line with bringing that *"man of sin"* to power, much of the real work of these men remains HIDDEN FROM PUBLIC VIEW (John 3:19). Secret subterranean facilities are just one way to go about fulfilling such plans.

> *"...I have noiseless methods to dig tunnels and winding*
> *secrete catacombs in order to reach a pre-planned place,*
> *even if they have to be built underneath ditches and rivers."*
> – Leonardo da Vinci, inventor, visionary (1452-1519)

Records are available to the public which demonstrate that secret underground tunnels and bases have existed in the United States since at least the early 1950s (and possibly earlier).[16] Further evidence is available to show the technology for building such facilities has existed since at least the mid-to-late 1800s. When dealing with technology, that's a long time ago. That means that this branch of knowledge has had over 160 years to advance and grow. While many may shrug their shoulders at these claims and think, "so what", this attitude does not erase the fact that (1) secret government facilities are ALWAYS constructed behind closed doors; and (2) what takes place within these facilities remains largely UNKNOWN, and under the highest levels of security. Why? With the world now on a daily march towards "unity", and the downsizing of superpower militaries, it's highly unlikely that all underground establishments are used for the buildup of arms. Dr. Richard Sauder, a recognized authority on underground and undersea bases states:

---

[16] Sauder, Richard. Underground Bases & Tunnels: What's the Government Trying to Hide? Kepton, Illinois: Adventures Unlimited Press, 1995. p 129.

"I must say the more I look into the question of clandestine underground (or secret undersea) bases, the more I am persuaded that those who build and operate them are UP TO NO GOOD. They are stealthy and DECEPTIVE. In many cases, we simply DO NOT KNOW WHAT THEY ARE DOING, or where or why they are carrying out their clandestine programs. But we do know highly secret underground facilities exist." [17]

An 1880 Tunnel Boring Machine

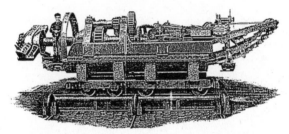

IMAGE/from the *Handbook of Mining & Tunneling Machinery*,
by Barbara Stack (John Wiley & Sons, 1982)

Many are not aware that tunnel boring machine technology is much older than both the automobile and the airplane. TBMs have been around for over a century and a half. Machines used in mining, and the construction of highways, subways, aqueducts, public retail shopping centers and other civilian projects. The world's foremost manufacturer has been in business since 1952.[18] But the birth of the technology and concept began in 1846 with the first real TBM being built in 1851.[19] The early machines, while large, were very small in comparison to the tunnelers of today. The largest TBM known to exist

[17] Sauder, Richard. Underwater & Underground Bases: Surprising Facts the Government Does Not Want You to Know! Kepton, Illinois: Adventures Unlimited Press, 2001. p 221.

[18] "Continuing to Break New Ground." The Robbins Company. Web. 11 Jan 2013. <http://www.therobbinscompany.com/about/history/>.

fig.A

fig.B

fig.C

IMAGES/public domain & shutterstock.com

The tunnel boring machine (TBM) and its affiliate industry have been around for over one hundred and sixty years, with the first practical machine being built in 1851. **Fig.A)** a giant 33 foot TBM cutterhead (the largest in the world is nearly *twice as large*. It belongs to "Big Bertha" and measures 57.5 feet in diameter, the height of a 5-story building); **Fig.B)** A modern TBM on public display in Warsaw, Poland manufactured by German Herrenknecht AG; **Fig.C)** A modern underground tunnel.

today is "Big Bertha". According to the Washington State Department of Transportation she has a 57.5 foot, 5-story-tall cutterhead, is 326 feet long, and weighs over 7,000 tons when assembled. Bertha was designed and built to dig a two-mile-long tunnel beneath downtown Seattle, Washington in the summer of 2013.[20]

Another one of the more large public jobs attributed to TBM technology was completed in May 1994. It is the longest undersea tunnel in the world and connects France with Great Britain. The twin-tube Channel Tunnel stretches 24 miles below the English Channel, and averages 14 feet below its seabed, with its deepest point at 246 feet.[21] But these everyday, mundane jobs do not include all these machines have been involved with. There exists a whole other world to which the average citizen is not privy. A world of secret government bases and tunnels hidden beneath the earth.

Since the early 1970s patents for exotic tunnel boring technologies have existed. These include research for Plasma, Electron Beam, Water Cannon, Pulsed Laser, Atomic Fusion, Flame-Jet and Nuclear Powered TBMs (among other technologies). These exotic technologies were explored not only to advance and speed-up conventional tunnel-digging capabilities, but also in an effort to eliminate tunneling waste. That is, dirt and rock removed from a hole must be put somewhere, but new technologies allowed for the incorporation of excess "muck" into the tunnel wall itself. These new

[19] Maidl, B., Schmid, L., Ritz, W. and Herrenknecht, M. (2008) Historical Development and Future Challenges, in Hardrock Tunnel Boring Machines, Wiley-VCH Verlag GmbH & Co. KGaA, Weinheim, Germany. doi: 10.1002/9783433600122. ch1

[20] "Following Bertha, the SR 99 Tunneling Machine." Washington State Department of Transportation. WSDOT. Web. 7 May 2013. <http://www.wsdot.wa.gov/Projects/Viaduct/About/FollowBertha>.

[21] "FAQ's." ChannelTunnel.co.uk. Channel Tunnel Publications. Web. 2 Feb 2013. <http://www.channeltunnel.co.uk/>.

tunneling methods saved the expense of thousands of dump-truck-loads of waste, while creating dense, glassy-smooth subterranean walls. Equally documented (and interesting) is the fact that throughout the 1980s public records show that NASA funded Los Alamos National Laboratories and Texas A&M University to develop Lunar TBMs, tunnel boring machines for use on the surface of the Moon.[22] There's an old saying that says; "out of sight - out of mind". Meaning that if you can't see it, you're not likely to think about it. What could be more secretive than experiments not only under ground, but under ground on the Moon? It's very possible that while conventional waste-creating TBMs continue to work on the more public, mainstream tunneling jobs, exotic equipment takes care of the top-secret shadow projects.[23] The Bible says there's a reason the motivators behind these projects constantly seek to remain hidden.

> *"And this is the condemnation, that light is come into the world, and men loved DARKNESS rather than light, because THEIR DEEDS WERE EVIL. For every one that doeth evil hateth the light, neither cometh to the light, lest his deeds should be reproved." John 3:19-20*

Behind the Veil of Conspiracy

I realize that because much of this stuff (hidden underground/undersea bases, monster sightings, ufos, etc.) lies on the outer edges of perceived reality, that for many, it does not constitute reality at all. For the Bible-believing Christian, however, the realms of the "invisible" are taken for granted. We not only live in an age where

[22] Sauder, Richard. Underground Bases & Tunnels: What's the Government Trying to Hide? Kepton, Illinois: Adventures Unlimited Press, 1995. p 100-102.

[23] Ibid. p 89.

the just must *"walk by faith, not by sight"* (2Cor. 5:7), but our very salvation is built upon One whom we've never seen.

> *"Jesus saith unto him, Thomas, because thou hast seen me, thou hast believed: blessed are they that HAVE NOT SEEN, and yet have believed." John 20:29*

> *"Now faith is the substance of things hoped for, the evidence of THINGS NOT SEEN." Hebrews 11:1*

> *"That the trial of your faith, being much more precious than of gold that perisheth, though it be tried with fire, might be found unto praise and honour and glory at the appearing of Jesus Christ: Whom HAVING NOT SEEN, ye love; in whom, though NOW YE SEE HIM NOT, yet believing, ye rejoice with joy unspeakable and full of glory". 1Peter 1:7-8*

And our faith is not blind, to the contrary, the scriptures show that it is built upon *"many infallible proofs"* (Acts 1:3). And yet while God may currently be unseen, He is not unreachable nor hidden.

> *"And I say unto you, Ask, and it shall be given you; seek, and ye shall find; knock, and it shall be opened unto you. For every one that asketh receiveth; and he that seeketh findeth; and to him that knocketh it shall be opened." Luke 11:9-10*

> *"God that made the world and all things therein, seeing that he is Lord of heaven and earth, dwelleth not in temples made with hands; Neither is worshipped with men's hands, as though he needed any thing, seeing he giveth to all life, and breath, and all things; And hath*

made of one blood all nations of men for to dwell on all the face of the earth, and hath determined the times before appointed, and the bounds of their habitation; That they should SEEK THE LORD, if haply they might feel after him, AND FIND HIM, though HE BE NOT FAR FROM EVERY ONE OF US". Acts 17:24-27

The Bible-believer also recognizes that there's a flip side to this aspect. A side that shows that while reachable goodness and holiness are just past the veil of the unseen, the workers of iniquity and deceit *"in high places"* are also entrenched in dark hidden places NOT WANTING TO BE FOUND.

"THEY GATHER themselves together, THEY HIDE themselves, they mark my steps, when THEY WAIT for my soul." Psalms 56:6

"Hide me from the SECRET COUNSEL of the WICKED; from the insurrection of the WORKERS OF INIQUITY: They encourage themselves IN AN EVIL MATTER: they commune of laying snares PRIVILY; they say, Who shall see them?" Psalms 64:2&5

"Yea, and all that will live godly in Christ Jesus shall suffer persecution. But EVIL MEN and SEDUCERS shall WAX WORSE AND WORSE, deceiving, and being deceived." 2Timothy 3:12-13

Paul's letter to the church at Ephesus clearly outlined the pinnacle of this dilemma (and don't forget that the Ephesians were the SAME ONES who worshipped *"the image which fell down from Jupiter"* - Acts 19:35).

"For we wrestle NOT AGAINST FLESH AND BLOOD, but against principalities, against POWERS, against the RULERS OF THE DARKNESS of this world, against SPIRITUAL WICKEDNESS in high places." Eph. 6:12

What this means, as unpalatable as it sounds in today's "free-spirited" world, is that *there's a conspiracy afoot.* A conspiracy perpetrated by the *"rulers of the darkness of this world"* (Eph. 6:12) and joined in and carried out by secret counsels of men. The Bible shows that this is not only possible, but *doctrinal.*

The word "conspiracy" is found ten times in the scriptures. And those appearances teach that the most prominent type of conspiracies are *government conspiracies.* Conspiracies committed by individuals within governments. However, there are many other conspiracies found in scripture which do not use the word explicitly, but meet all criteria necessary to its existence. The most notable of these conspiracies involve a being identified as the *"god of this world".* A god who has *"blinded the minds of them which believe not",* and is prophesied one day soon to *"deceiveth the whole world"* (2 Cor. 4:4, Rev. 12:9).

If you want to challenge a being which the scriptures identify as a "god" and try to come out "on top", that's your business. But the Holy Bible has already predicted that those who are not under the protection of the shed Blood of the Lord Jesus Christ will ultimately succumb to his beguiling will (Rev. 12:9). History proves that NO MAN challenging the prophesies of scripture can win. It is a statistical impossibility. You will lose just as sure as the Sun rises and sets (and even "more sure" than that). If we were to only deal with 48 of the scriptures which predicted the life of the Lord Jesus Christ, the mathematics which backup its validity and "odds", are represented by a number so vast (10 to the 147th power), that if such a number were represented by individual "electrons" it would comprise a universe four times the size of the known Universe.[24] And this mind-blasting, mind-numbing "number" (if you can even call it that) does not include hundreds of other prophecies in scripture. That is, despite the astronomical ODDS AGAINST IT (1 in 10 to the 147th power), the 48 prophesies concerning Christ came through on the money. In other words, the Universe itself cannot contain the proofs of scriptural Truth. If that doesn't prove a God-Intelligence is behind the Bible, then nothing does. Only a fool would ever dare chance the odds of going against a Book that has already proven itself trustworthy with such impossibilities.

Do you believe global conspiracies and deception are "impossible"? That's not what the Bible predicts. Do you believe that man evolved from ameba, and that he is a cousin of artichokes, aardvarks, asses and apes? That's not what the Bible teaches. Do you believe that Martians pilot flying saucers and that alien civilizations exist on other planets? That's not what the Bible says. Do you believe that planet Earth is inconsequential and is no more significant than a lost dust-mite in the Amazon jungle? That's not in the Bible. Do you believe in a future where "alien disclosure" will transform the galaxy into a *Star Trek*-like universe, and man will live hand-in-tentacle with his alien "brothers and sisters"? That's not what the Bible predicts. What are the odds of *your own private future theories and guesses coming to pass* when stacked up alongside a proven Book like the *King James Bible*?

> *"Heaven and earth shall pass away, but my words shall not pass away." Matthew 24:35 (Mk. 13:31 & Lk. 21:33)*

---

[24] Ruckman, Peter S. 1 in 23,000,000: Betting On the Bible & It's Historical Accuracy. Pensacola, FL: Bible Baptist Bookstore, 2001. p 80-81

Final Summary & Conclusions

After taking into consideration the 15 previous chapters, the conclusion to the origin of the belief-in, and purpose of the modern alien may be summarized as follows:

1.) THE HISTORY OF EXTRATERRESTRIAL LIFE: The history of the belief in extraterrestrial life originated with the advent of the angelic *"sons of God"* around 4,600 years ago (Gen. 6:2). At this time, the aliens were witnessed "in the flesh" and became a part of Earth's one-world, one-language society. Because they were *"greater in power and might"* (2 Peter 2:11), they were seen as "gods" walking the Earth, and their evil presence heavily influencing a young, newly-fallen mankind for the worse (Genesis 6:4-7). This meeting of strange flesh produced a form of gigantism. The fossil record shows that gigantism affected many ancient animals which are not alive today (which may or may not be a part of angelic corruption). The Bible says that the Earth was then *"filled with violence"* (Gen. 6:11-13).

2.) THE BIRTH OF WITCHCRAFT: Because the sons of God were no longer literally and visibly in their midsts, post diluvian peoples organized religions based around the fresh MEMORIES and HISTORIES of these beings and the powers they possessed. As a result, religious "polytheism" was born – the belief in many "gods". Having now discarded the belief in the one, true Creator God, this new system gave rise to: (a.) the belief in extraterrestrial life and "gods from the stars" (like Molech); (b.) the religious use of images, idols and the star symbol (pentagram, hexagram, etc.) to honor the memory of the gods.; (c.) the seeking-out of the lost wisdom of angels (the Mystery Religions); (d.) the worship of the "creature" more than the "Creator"; and (e.) eventually became known as "witchcraft". With these new beliefs in hand (and heart), early post-Flood generations attempted to recreate Earth's one-world, pre-Flood conditions under the leadership of Nimrod (Gen. 10:8-9). Their objective coalesced into a prideful *"city and tower"* which reached *"unto heaven"* in an effort to elevate man and REUNITE HIM with the gods (Gen. 11:4-6). However, God intervened in their plans (Gen. 11:5-9). The resulting linguistic dispersal created the "nations" which retained *polytheism as their core religious belief.* God later called Abram OUT OF THIS FALSE WORLD SYSTEM and brought forth a chosen people whose first command was; *"Thou shalt have no other gods before me"* (Gen. 12:1-3, Ex. 20:3). After the birth of Christianity, it became God's plan to send Christian missionaries back into these nations to witness the saving gospel of the Lord Jesus Christ.

> " *[29] Forasmuch then as we are the offspring of God, we ought not to think that the Godhead is like unto gold, or silver, or stone, graven by art and man's device. [30] And THE TIMES OF THIS IGNORANCE God winked at; BUT NOW COMMANDETH ALL MEN EVER WHERE TO REPENT: [31] Because he hath appointed a day, in the which he will judge the world in righteousness by that man whom he hath ordained; whereof he hath given assurance unto all men, in that he hath raised him from the dead." Acts 17:29-31*

> *"[9] For they themselves shew of us what manner of entering in we had unto you, and how ye TURNED TO GOD FROM IDOLS to serve the living and TRUE GOD; [10] And to WAIT FOR HIS SON FROM HEAVEN, whom he raised from the dead, even Jesus, which delivered us from the wrath to come." 1 Thessalonians 1:9-10*

The important thing to remember here is that the first extraterrestrial visitors triggered the birth of polytheistic worship and witchcraft. Today, it is for THIS VERY REASON, that the belief in extraterrestrial

UFOs and aliens circulates strongly among practitioners of the New Age and the occult.

3.) DISCERNING DISTINCTIONS: When confronted with the question of extraterrestrial life the Christian must always remember to make distinctions and divisions where the Bible makes distinctions and divisions. What this means is that we can say "Yes" to the existence of life beyond Earth, but we must say "No" to the existence of "evolved" intelligences on other planets. If this distinction is not drawn, the resulting answer will be confusing and unclear. The problem, however, is that most Christians do not know enough scripture to draw appropriate conclusions. Because of this, their discernment ends up being *"destroyed for lack of knowledge"* (Hos. 4:6).

4.) THE UNIVERSE IS NOT DESIGNED FOR LIFE – ONLY PLANET EARTH: Many people, including Christians, miss the fact that the Universe, as it is in its *current state*, is not designed for living creatures. That is, the realm just OUTSIDE the Earth's atmosphere (the Second Heaven) is not designed for human or animal habitation (see chapters 9 & 10). This is one way that we can *know* that *there is no life on other planets* (or at least that *life was never intentionlly put there* BY GOD). Regardless, people continue to believe that *"all things continue as they were from the beginning of the creation"* (2 Peter 3:4), not realizing that outer space is now purposely a REALM OF DEATH and the primary dwelling place of Satan. Whereas before outer space existed, the Earth was in direct fellowship with God, and there was only ONE Heaven. Note the wording: *"In the beginning God created the HEAVEN* [singular] *and the earth."* (Genesis 1:1). While the heavens are not currently conformable to habitation, they do, nevertheless, declare the Glory of God. They are a witness and testimony to His power. This is for the benefit of fallen man to recognize his Creator. Those who do not are willingly ignorant.

"The heavens declare the glory of God; and the firmament sheweth his handiwork." Psalms 19:1

"[5] For this they willingly are ignorant of, that by the word of God the heavens were of old, and the earth standing out of the water and in the water: [6] Whereby the world that then was, being overflowed with water, perished [see Gen. 1:2]: [7] But the heavens and the earth, which are now, by the same word are kept in store, reserved unto fire against the day of judgment and perdition of ungodly men." 2Peter 3:5-7

5.) THE MODERN ALIEN MOVEMENT IS A LIE: The modern belief that highly advanced civilizations from other planets are visiting the Earth via spacecraft is a ruse. If real, they are beings created apart from the procreative processes established for life on Earth (Gen. 1). And since they are not direct creations of God Himself, their origins must be sought from other sources. Whatever that source, the Bible reveals that *FALLEN ANGELS have some sort of connection.* Aliens are either man-made, angel-made or both (i.e. forces working in collusion). In some cases, these life forms may be part of an elaborate plot which attempts to help man *bypass the deadly effects of outer space by engineering experimental man-animal hybrids designed for deep space travel* – an ability which God has denied to man (i.e. dominion in space. See chapters 9 & 10 for further explanation). Top secret government cover stories for such attempts and failed attempts are that "alien craft have crashed" (e.g. the Roswell Crash and cover-up incident), or that "aliens are visiting the Earth". This is propaganda, and the "party line" of what mankind is SUPPOSED TO BELIEVE, while something different goes on back stage behind the scenes. If one ventures back stage, however, he will find a series of secretive inventions and plans put in place to help fallen mankind eventually reach the dwelling place of God on his own terms. Plans

IMAGES/MGM Studios Inc.   Actor Robert Culp is surgically transformed into an alien.

Has science fiction knowingly (or unknowingly) shown us a glimpse of the Devil's true plans? In a 1963 episode of *The Outer Limits* titled "The Architects of Fear", a clandestine group of elitists meet together to create an artificial threat from space. Their purpose? To push mankind into global unity.

that include *secretive life forms, secretive flying craft* and *secretive motives,* but NOT SALVATION in the shed blood of the Lord Jesus Christ. Plans from the spiritual children of the Devil, that match the aspirations of their father.

> "Ye are of your father the Devil, and the lusts of your father ye will do. ..." John 8:44

> "For thou hast said in thine heart, I WILL ASCEND into heaven, I will exalt my throne ABOVE THE STARS of God: I will sit also upon the mount of the congregation, in the sides of the north: I WILL ASCEND above the heights of the clouds; I will be like the most High." Isaiah 14:13-14

In other words, strange beings from the heavens are not invading the Earth. Strange beings from the Earth are invading the heavens. However, the "engineered astronaut" theory is not a blanket explanation for the "alien". The true final solution to the alien phenomenon question is multifaceted. The evidence shows that there are other purposes for these demoniac beings, not just human space travel by proxy. The ultimate puppeteer is Satan the Devil, and much of the alien phenomenon is used to *prepare mankind for his eventual rise to power.* Be that as it may, WE KNOW their final objectives. Much like today, and the current direction of global society, when the world was confederate at Babel man declared:

> *"And they said, Go to, let US build US a city and a tower, whose top may REACH UNTO HEAVEN; and let US make US a name, lest WE be scattered abroad upon the face of the whole earth. And the LORD came down to see the city and the tower, which the children of men builded. And the LORD said, Behold, the people is one, and they have all one language; and this they begin to do: and now nothing will be restrained from them, which they have imagined to do." Genesis 11:4-6*

Have times changed? No. More "technically advanced" maybe, but not changed. Man's unregenerate nature remains in opposition to his Creator. And unlike Genesis 6, today's world has six thousand years of sin on which to build. If you give that man more "technically advanced" computerized toys, he's simply going to devise more advanced ways to carry out the will of his father – *whether he realizes it or not* (Matt. 23:31). Unsaved man doesn't like the idea of fulfilling the will of the Devil without being a willing participant or believer. But that doesn't matter. The Bible says that the god of this world has *"BLINDED THE MINDS of them which believe not"* (2 Cor. 4:4). Their "minds" have been blinded. Their thinking process have been blinded. Their intentions (good or bad) are irrelevant.

6.) AN ULTIMATE DECEPTION: While a substantial phenomenon exists regarding both UFO and ET encounters, the Holy Bible points to a long-running, deep-seated conspiracy of a SPIRITUAL nature. A conspiracy which also manifests itself in the PHYSICAL realm, and is ultimately designed as a set up to prepare the world to receive that *"man of sin, the son of perdition"* (2Thess.

2:3). An event for the world which will seem to be nothing less than the arrival of "God Himself". The arrival of the builder and maker of the world's utopia and promised land. It will be the COUNTERFEIT KINGDOM of God on Earth.

Those who experience so-called ET visitations often report having profound changes in their spiritual thinking – *changes regarding God and man's place in the Universe*. This is nothing new. Genesis shows that the fallen sons of God, after having left *"their first estate"* (Jude 1:6), fomented the greatest global deception the world had ever seen up to that time. In this instance, the shock of their arrival **MARKED THE END OF MONOTHEISM**. Today, a constant barrage of ET images, movies and literature, and the threat of "alien disclosure" is preparing the world to receive a superior intelligence(s) from space. This future "close encounter" will be the culmination of both ancient polytheism and modern Extraterrestrialism, and trigger a *reverse effect* – **the birth of a WORLDWIDE COUNTERFEIT MONOTHEISM – the worship of Satan as God Himself!** (Rev. 13:3-7) Since the monotheism of his ancient fathers (Gen. 5), man will have come full circle, but in the wrong direction. Such an outcome is not only possible, but predicted:

> *"[3] Let no man DECEIVE YOU by any means: for that day shall not come, except there come a falling away first, and that man of sin be revealed, the son of perdition; [4] Who opposeth and exalteth himself above all that is called God, or that is worshipped; so that HE AS GOD sitteth in the temple of God, shewing himself that HE IS GOD. [9] Even him, whose coming is after the working of Satan with ALL POWER and SIGNS and LYING WONDERS, [10] And with ALL DECEIVABLENESS of unrighteousness in them that perish; because they received not the love of the truth, that they might be saved. [11] And for this cause God shall send them strong*

delusion, that they should believe a lie: [12] That they all might be damned who believed not the truth, but had pleasure in unrighteousness." 2 Thess. 2:3-4&9-12

If the first "close encounters" of Genesis 6 have taught us nothing, they at least demonstrate the fact that it is THIS TYPE OF EVENT that has the power to completely sway the world against God. It is an ultimate type of deception, and one that will come quite easily from a world which has thumbed its collective nose at God. Because man willfully rejects his Creator, *God will leave mankind to their own thoughts and devices.*

Those who think that such behavior is cruel or evil, and "not becoming of a loving God", need to remember that God *"is NOT WILLING that any should perish, but that all should come to repentance"* (2 Peter 3:9). It is God's WILL that no man be eternally lost. Hell, after all, was originally created for only *"the devil and his angels"* – not man (Matt. 25:41). But God allows man free will to make his own decisions. If that man wakes up and finds he's in a Devil's Hell, he got there by his own accord. Some may object, "But that's no choice!" Yes, it is a choice. Most men simply want their OWN CHOICES to have as good an outcome as choosing God and following HIS CHOICES. But that's not possible. The whole point of the Bible is a loving God revealing Himself to mankind, a message from God, designed to *guide mankind to the Truth.* If man rejects that Truth, he has no one to blame but himself. If the Bible reveals that the world's future looks bleak, don't curse God and die (Job 2:9), GET SAVED and THANK GOD for the revelation:

"Howbeit when he, the Spirit of truth, is come, he will GUIDE YOU INTO ALL TRUTH: for he shall not speak of himself; but whatsoever he shall hear, that shall he speak: and HE WILL SHEW YOU THINGS TO COME." John 16:13

17

How to Fly through Outer Space without a Spaceship

I f there's anything we've learned from our search of the scriptures, it's that Heaven – the home of God – is a real place. Of this fact the Bible leaves no doubt. Chapter 13 showed that there are real people walking around there as you read this sentence. This "Third Heaven" can be reached by literally departing the surface of the earth and traveling northward through space. The Lord Jesus Christ demonstrated this truth when he ascended into heaven bodily, after resurrecting himself from the grave. The written word also testifies that the Lord will return *"in like manner"* (Acts 1:11). It is for this reason that the Apostle Paul wrote:

> *"And to wait for his Son from heaven, whom he raised from the dead, even Jesus, which delivered us from the wrath to come." 1 Thessalonians 1:10*

Christians have been instructed to wait for the Lord, because one day He will return to call out his Bride (the Body of Christ) before the wrath of God is once again poured out upon the Earth – a period of time known as the "Great Tribulation" (see Matt. 24:21 & Rev. 2:22):

> *"For the Lord himself shall descend from heaven with a shout, with the voice of the archangel, and with the trump of God: and the dead in Christ shall rise first: Then we which are alive and remain shall be caught up together with them in the clouds, to meet the Lord in the air: and so shall we ever be with the Lord. Wherefore comfort one another with these words." 1 Thess. 4:16-18*

> *"For God hath not appointed us to wrath, but to obtain salvation by our Lord Jesus Christ, Who died for us, that, whether we wake or sleep, we should live together with him." 1 Thess. 5:9-10*

The Christian's Hope

This anxious awaiting for the return of the Lord Jesus Christ to receive the Church unto Himself is called the Christian's "hope". This hope is not simply a wishful desire for something that "might" or "might not" happen, but, an affirmed, established, assurance and looking-forward to an occasion that the Christian KNOWS, based on scripture, will come to pass:

> *"Beloved, NOW are we the sons of God, and it DOTH NOT YET appear what we shall be: but WE KNOW that, when he shall appear, we shall be like him; for we shall see him as he is." 1John 3:2*

This "hope" is a miraculous event in which born-again saints will receive the end of their salvation, and be transformed into "glorified" immortals capable of flight, invisibility, and other supernatural attributes (1 Cor. 15:35-58). It is at this time which the saved man will once again be restored to the full image of God. He will have a perfect spirit (the Holy Spirit), soul (the mind of Christ) and body (an incorruptable, immortal body) like Christ. In short, he will have a perfected trinity completely purged of sin:

> *"[18] For I reckon that the sufferings of this present time are not worthy to be compared with the glory which shall be revealed in us. [19] For the earnest expectation of the creature* [saved man] *WAITETH for the manifestation of the sons of God. [20] For the creature was made subject to vanity, not willingly, but by reason of him who hath subjected the same in hope, [21] Because the creature itself also shall be delivered from the bondage of corruption into the glorious liberty of the children of God. [22] For we know that the whole creation groaneth and travaileth in pain together until now. [23] And not only they, but ourselves also, which have the firstfruits of the Spirit, even we ourselves groan within ourselves, waiting for the adoption, to wit, THE REDEMPTION OF OUR BODY." Romans 8:18-23*

> *"[1] For WE KNOW that if our earthly house of this tabernacle were dissolved, we have a building of God, an house not made with hands, eternal in the heavens. [2] For in this we groan, EARNESTLY DESIRING to be clothed upon with our house which is from heaven: [3] If so be that being clothed we shall not be found naked. [4] For we that are in this tabernacle do groan, being burdened: not for that we would be unclothed, but clothed upon, that MORTALITY might be swallowed up of LIFE." 2 Corinthians 5:1-4*

The transformation of the born-again corruptible man into a glorified incorruptible immortal is identified as a great Bible "mystery" (1 Cor. 15:51). Nevertheless, we can stand on the words of God which testify to this fact. Because of this, the pitch-black, airless and deadly void of outer space will no longer be a physical obstruction. Travel between the First and Third Heavens will now be possible. Once Christ receives the Church unto Himself, they will return to the Third Heaven. At the end of the Great Tribulation, the Word of God and His glorified army of saints will return to Earth on horseback to fight against the armies and corrupt world order of Satan and his counterfeit christ (see Rev. 19:11-21 and Joel 2:1-11). The Devil will then be imprisoned in the Bottomless Pit, as the Lord Jesus Christ and His Saints reign over planet Earth for one thousand years (see Rev. 20:1-6):

> *"Blessed and holy is he that hath part in the first resurrection: on such the second death hath no power, but they shall be priests of God and of Christ, and shall reign with him a thousand years." Revelation 20:6*

Where Their Worm Dieth Not

All of this prophecy for the born-again Christian is absolutely wonderful, but persons who are spiritually lost have a future filled with nothing but unthinkable horror. For the born-again Christian, this wicked old world is *as close to Hell* as they will ever get. The Christian's "Hell" is on Earth. But for the unsaved sinner, this wicked old world is *as close to Heaven* as they will ever get. The sinner's "Heaven" is on Earth. The Bible says of the unsaved:

> *"Ye are of your father the devil, and the lusts of your father ye will do. He was a murderer from the beginning, and abode not in the truth, because there is no truth in*

him. When he speaketh a lie, he speaketh of his own: for
he is a liar, and the father of it." John 8:44

Saved people are adopted sons and *children of God* and unsaved
people are *children of the Devil.* The scriptures show that the
Christian's hope is that he will eventually be TRANSFORMED into
the image of his Father. This being the case, could it be possible that
the children of the Serpent are destined to also be conformed to the
image of their father? If it's even remotely possible that the children
of the Serpent could be changed into his image, *how would the Bible
imply this?* Consider the words of the Lord Jesus Christ where he
spoke of someone being cast into Hell:

> *"And if thy hand offend thee, cut it off: it is better for thee
> to enter into life maimed, than having two hands to go
> into hell, into the fire that never shall be quenched: Where
> THEIR WORM dieth not, and the fire is not quenched.
> And if thy foot offend thee, cut it off: it is better for thee
> to enter halt into life, than having two feet to be cast into
> hell, into the fire that never shall be quenched: Where
> THEIR WORM dieth not, and the fire is not quenched.
> And if thine eye offend thee, pluck it out: it is better for
> thee to enter into the kingdom of God with one eye, than
> having two eyes to be cast into hell fire: Where THEIR
> WORM dieth not, and the fire is not quenched."*
> *Mark 9:43-48*

*"Their worm dieth not ... their worm dieth not ... their worm
dieth not"* – not just worm, "their" worm. What could this horrible
imagery possibly mean? It means that according to the Lord Jesus
Christ, someone (or something) is being "cast into hell", and that
"someone" has a "worm" that cannot die. Today the worm is a

symbol of higher knowledge and many times is seen as a WORM eating through a piece of fruit. It was once an American tradition for many children to give their school teachers (mostly women) an apple. I wonder where that got started – *giving fruit to a woman within the context of acquiring higher knowledge.* Educated people are also often referred to as "bookworms". What does the worm have to do with wisdom and higher knowledge?

> *"Now the SERPENT was more subtil than any beast of the field which the LORD God had made. And he said unto the woman, Yea, hath God said, Ye shall not eat of every tree of the garden? And when the woman saw that the tree was good for food, and that it was pleasant to the eyes, and a tree TO BE DESIRED TO MAKE ONE WISE, she took of THE FRUIT thereof, and did eat, and gave also unto her husband with her; and he did eat."*
> *Genesis 3:1&6*

At first, it may seem like a stretch to refer to the serpent as a "worm", but not only does the Bible make the association, the name-sharing also has a long tradition in history. Both scripture and history show worms as a picture and type of serpents and dragons, and all are a picture and type of Satan. Note the word association:

> *"They shall lick the dust like a SERPENT, they shall move out of their holes like WORMS of the earth: they shall be afraid of the LORD our God, and shall fear because of thee." Micah 7:17*

But that's not all, the Bible also points out that worms are a picture of death and corruption:

> *"My flesh is clothed with WORMS and clods of dust; my skin is broken, and become loathsome." Job 7:5*

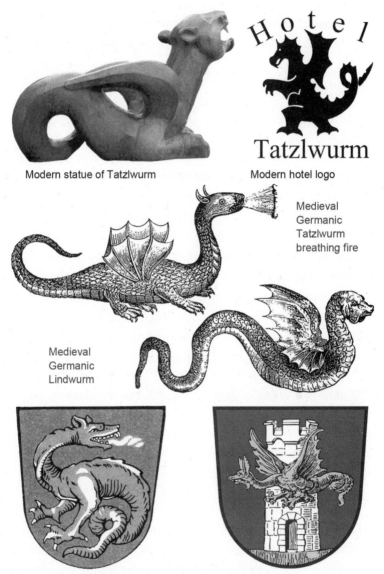

Modern statue of Tatzlwurm

Modern hotel logo

Medieval Germanic Tatzlwurm breathing fire

Medieval Germanic Lindwurm

Lindwurms in Heraldry and coats of arms

Associating the worm with a serpent or dragon not only has a long tradition in history, but can still be found in the world today. The Bible made the connection centuries earlier. The word "wurm", as found in *Lindwurm, Lindworm* and *Lindorm*, means "dragon" or "constrictor serpent". *Tatzlwurm* means "clawed dragon".

> "I have said to corruption, Thou art my father: to the
> WORM, Thou are my mother, and my sister." Job 17:14

> "They shall lie down alike in the dust, and the WORMS
> shall cover them." Job 21:26

After considering the scriptural revelation that Satan is pictured as a serpent and worm, and that the worm is a picture of death and corruption, and that Satan is the spiritual father of the unsaved, and that the Lord Jesus Christ mentions that all those cast into Hell have a "worm" which cannot die, you're free to draw your own conclusions. Clearly, this is not something you're normally going to hear in church. But that does not change the fact that these links and cross-references are strong. Are you willing to take the risk that it's all not true?

If you are not a born-again Christian, I would seriously consider getting saved right now and not dare take any chances on possibly ending up in such a nightmarish condition. Am I appealing to fear as a persuasive tool for salvation? Absolutely. There's nothing wrong with that. Many men have been moved by it. Look at what happened to Noah after the fear of the coming Great Flood spurred him to action:

> "By faith Noah, being warned of God of things not seen as
> yet, MOVED WITH FEAR, prepared an ark to the saving
> of his house; by the which he condemned the world, and
> became heir of righteousness which is by faith." Heb.11:7

If you're not born-again, an eternity in the Lake of Fire is not your only concern. You also have to contend with the likelihood that *you may very well be transformed into the image of Satan himself* (your spiritual father) where, as Jesus said, *"your worm dieth not and the fire is not quenched"*. You probably never considered this, but when the Lord Jesus Christ took the sins of the whole world upon Himself, the Bible says He was *"made to be sin"* (2 Cor. 5:21). At that time God

IMAGE/Dover Pictorial Archive   The Lord Jesus Christ shed his blood for you.

When the perfect and sinless Lord Jesus Christ died on the cross, He took upon himself the sins of every, man, woman, boy and girl who ever lived. He did this for you. You have the choice of either receiving His perfect atonement, or you can take the chance of trying to cover your sins with the filthy rags of your own self-righteousness.

forsook Christ and He cried, *"I AM A WORM AND NO MAN"* (Psa. 22:6). If this happened to the Lord Jesus Christ Himself (whether in typology or reality), what do you suppose is GOING TO HAPPEN TO YOU if you willfully reject the freely-given blood atonement of the Lord Jesus Christ? If you refuse God's free Gift, will you be *"made to be sin"* for all eternity with no way out? Possibly. But why suffer such damnation, with all of its unmentionable horrors, when Someone else has already suffered and died as the propitiation for you? (See 1 John 2:2, 4:10) Christ died and rose from the grave FOR YOU!

> *"Am I therefore become your enemy, because I tell you the truth?" Galatians 4:16*

Destination: Heaven

The true and real God is the Creator of all things (Isa. 40:25-26, 42:5, 45:12 & 18, Col. 1:16). He created the heavens with all of it's stars, planets and nebulae. He created the angels, cherubim, seraphim and watchers. He created (and named) planet Earth where he placed man and gave him dominion. And although all men are created by the same God, they are not "children of God" by right of creation. Mankind, and indeed the whole Universe, is currently under a curse. This curse, more commonly known as "sin", separates the creation from its sinless Creator. God currently resides in a land of light, but mankind lives at the bottom of a black, dark Universe under the curse of sin. God did not create all things for naught, however, and has provided a Way for lost mankind to be reunited with their Creator.

When you stand before a Holy God to be judged, God is not going to compare you with someone else to see who's "the best". We're all sinners. God is going to compare you to His only begotten, sinless, perfect Son, the Lord Jesus Christ. How do you think you measure up when compared to Jesus? If you've not claimed the Blood atonement of the Lord Jesus Christ as your own, you have absolutely no chance of escaping Hell. The door is shut and locked, and you're in forever – WORMS AND ALL. Wouldn't it have been nice if you'd gotten saved when you had the chance?

If Heaven is a real place, then Hell is a real place, too. And it's sad to say, but the majority of people will be spending their eternity there. You don't have to go, however. Why not make plans today for your free trip through outer space to be with the Creator in Heaven? God is offering it to you RIGHT NOW, why not receive it? If you recognize that you are a lost sinner and would like to find The Way back to God, follow these three simple steps:

1.) Acknowledge that the written words of God are true.

> *"Thy word is true from the beginning: and every one of thy righteous judgments endureth for ever." Psa. 119:160*

> *"Sanctify them through thy truth: thy word is truth." John 17:17*

> *"For whatsoever things were written aforetime were written for our learning, that we through patience and comfort of the scriptures might have hope." Romans 15:4*

> *"So then faith cometh by hearing, and hearing by the word of God." Romans 10:17*

The Holy Bible is God's direct revelation to man. Without the light of the preserved scriptures, man would be eternally lost and have no means of finding the truth.

2.) Admit that you are a sinner and that you cannot save yourself. Your good works cannot save you. Your religion cannot save you.

> *"But we are all as an unclean thing, and all our righteousnesses are as filthy rags; and we all do fade as a leaf; and our iniquities, like the wind, have taken us away." Isaiah 64:6*

> *"As it is written, There is none righteous, no, not one" Romans 3:10*

> *"For all have sinned, and come short of the glory of God" Romans 3:23*

> *"If we say that we have not sinned, we make him a liar, and his word is not in us." 1 John 1:10*

No human being is sinless. Even if a man could live his entire life without committing any acts of sin (and this is not possible), he would still go to Hell because his physical body remains under its curse. If you're trying to work and "earn" a right relationship with God, you can expect "wages" for your hard labor, but they will not be what you expect:

> "Now to him that worketh is the reward not reckoned of grace, but of debt. But to him that worketh not, but believeth on him that justifieth the ungodly, his faith is counted for righteousness." Romans 4:4-5

> "For the wages of sin is death; but the gift of God is eternal life through Jesus Christ our Lord." Romans 6:23

To a holy, sinless God all your "righteousnesses" (i.e. everything you do that's right) are as "filth" and cannot be accepted as payment for your sins. What you must do is receive something (or rather Someone) which God has ALREADY DECLARED TO BE RIGHTEOUS.

3.) Receive the Lord Jesus Christ as your personal Saviour.

> "But God commendeth his love toward us, in that, while we were yet sinners, Christ died for us. Much more then, being now justified by his blood, we shall be saved from wrath through him." Romans 5:8-9

> "For God so loved the world, that he gave his only begotten Son, that whosoever believeth in him should not perish, but have everlasting life. For God sent not his Son into the world to condemn the world; but that the world through him might be saved. He that believeth on him is not condemned: but he that believeth not is condemned already, because he hath not believed in the name of the only begotten Son of God." John 3:16-18

"Who his own self bare our sins in his own body on the tree, that we, being dead to sins, should live unto righteousness: by whose stripes ye were healed."
1 Peter 2:24

"Christ hath redeemed us from the curse of the law, being made a curse for us: for it is written, Cursed is every one that hangeth on a tree" Galatians 3:13

"For he hath made him to be sin for us, who knew no sin; that we might be made the righteousness of God in him."
2 Corinthians 5:21

"... and the blood of Jesus Christ his Son cleanseth us from all sin." 1 John 1:7

"That if thou shalt confess with thy mouth the Lord Jesus, and shalt believe in thine heart that God hath raised him from the dead, thou shalt be saved. For with the heart man believeth unto righteousness; and with the mouth confession is made unto salvation. For the scripture saith, Whosoever believeth on him shall not be ashamed. For there is no difference between the Jew and the Greek: for the same Lord over all is rich unto all that call upon him. For whosoever shall call upon the name of the Lord shall be saved." Romans 10:9-13

The Lord Jesus Christ IS the righteousness of God. By receiving Christ through his blood atonement, and praying in the best way you know how, you now literally "have" the righteousness required to enter Heaven. If you've followed and obeyed these steps and sincerely prayed and received the Lord Jesus Christ AS YOUR OWN personal Saviour, when God looks at you He now acknowledges:

"And the blood shall be to you for a token upon the houses where ye are: and when I see the blood, I will pass over you, and the plague shall not be upon you to destroy you ..." Exodus 12:13

By obeying God's written words and receiving the Lord Jesus Christ's blood atonement as your own, you are now a born-again Christian – an adopted *"son of God"*. Christ has become your only reliance for eternal salvation, and is your personal right of passage into the Third Heaven. The Christian's Hope is now YOUR HOPE. Glory to God!

"In whom ye also trusted, after that ye heard the word of truth, the gospel of your salvation: in whom also after that ye believed, ye were sealed with that holy Spirit of promise'. Ephesians 1:13

*I will sing the wondrous story
Of the Christ Who died for me;
How He left His home in glory
For the cross of Calvary.*

*Yes, I'll sing the wondrous story
Of the Christ Who died for me,
Sing it with the saints in glory,
Gathered by the crystal sea.*

*I was lost, but Jesus found me,
Found the sheep that went astray,
Threw His loving arms around me,
Drew me back into His way.*

Yes, I'll sing the wondrous story
Of the Christ Who died for me,
Sing it with the saints in glory,
Gathered by the crystal sea.

Soon He'll come, the Lord of Glory
Come the church His bride to claim,
And complete the wondrous story,
Come Lord Jesus come again.

Yes, I'll sing the wondrous story
Of the Christ Who died for me,
Sing it with the saints in glory,
Gathered by the crystal sea.

He will keep me till the river
Rolls its waters at my feet;
Then He'll bear me safely over,
Where my loved ones I shall meet.

Yes, I'll sing the wondrous story
Of the Christ Who died for me,
Sing it with the saints in glory,
Gathered by the crystal sea.

- I Will Sing the Wondrous Story
  Francis H. Rowley, 1886

THE END

APPENDIX A

The Bible Timeline of Early Man from Adam to Abraham

This timeline chronicles the creation, births and deaths of early man. All dates are approximate and stand on the fact that the Lord created mankind about 6,000 years ago. This means the year 4000 BC is used as the beginning for the six days of Genesis and the creation of man (Gen. 1:3-31). The ages and years of man's early ancestry, as described in Genesis chapters 5 and 11, were used as a guide to approximate these dates. This information also helps establish the dates of the events which surrounded these men, like the Great Flood, Tower of Babel, etc. Since the calendar has changed over the ages the dates are not exact – but they're close.

• **ADAM** (4000 - 3070 BC) Lived 930 years (Gen. 5:5).

• **SETH** (3870 - 2958 BC) Lived 912 years (Gen. 5:8).

• **ENOS** (3765 - 2860 BC) Lived 905 years (Gen. 5:11).

• **CAINAN** (3675 - 2765 BC) Lived 910 years (Gen. 5:14).

• **MAHALALEEL** (3605 - 2710 BC) Lived 895 years (Gen. 5:17).

• **JARED** (3540 - 2578 BC) Lived 962 years (Gen. 5:20).

• **ENOCH** (3378 - 3013 BC) Enoch never died, but was taken to Heaven by God when he was 365-years-old (Gen. 5:23).

- **METHUSELAH** (3313 - 2344 BC) Lived 969 years (Gen. 5:27).

- **LAMECH** (3126 - 2349 BC) Lived 777 years (Gen. 5:31).

- **NOAH** (2944 - 1994 BC) Lived 950 years (Gen. 9:29).

- **SHEM, HAM & JAPETH** were born around 2444 BC (Gen. 5:32).

- **ARPHAXAD** (2346 - 1908 BC) Lived 438 years (Gen. 11:13).

- **SALAH** (2311 - 1878 BC) Lived 433 years (Gen. 11:15).

- **EBER** (2281 - 1817 BC) Lived 464 years (Gen. 11:17).

- **PELEG** (2247 - 2008 BC) Lived 239 years (Gen. 11:19).

- **REU** (2217 - 1978 BC) Lived 239 years (Gen. 11:21).

- **SERUG** (2185 - 1861 BC) Lived 230 years (Gen. 11:23).

- **NAHOR** (2061 - 1955 BC) Lived 145 years (Gen. 11:25).

- **TERAH** (2126 - 1921 BC) Lived 205 years (Gen. 11:32).

- **ABRAM** (2056 - 1881 BC) lived 175 years (Gen. 25:7-8).

APPENDIX B

The Timeline of Extraterrestrialism

This timeline chronicles the most outstanding dates in the history of the belief in extraterrestrial life. Years are listed, followed by the name of the event or person, and the page on which that specific information can be found. All early Bible dates are approximate (see *Appendix A: The Bible Timeline of Early Man from Adam to Abraham* on page 493 for more information).

• **4000-2444 BC** - Arrival of the Genesis 6 fallen sons of God. The fallen angels invade Earth sometime between the fall of Adam and the Great Flood. More specifically, the New Testament seems to categorized this event within the 600 years of Noah which precede the Flood (known as "the days of Noah"). This marks the Earth's first "extraterrestrial encounter" and triggers the beginning of the end for worldwide monotheism (pg. 28)

• **2944-2344 BC** - The Days of Noah (pgs. 28-32)

• **2444 BC** - Noah is told to build an ark (pg. 28)

• **2344 BC** - The Great Flood (pg. 28)

• **2344-2130 BC** - The birth of polytheism, pagan religions and witchcraft (pg. 33)

• **2130 BC** - Tower of Babel – After the division at Babel , polytheism is seeded worldwide into newly-formed nations (pg. 34-36)

• **1981 BC** - Abram leaves the land of his pagan kindred (pg. 34)

• **590 BC** - Ezekiel's vision of God's flying Throne (pg. 266)

• **600 BC** - Philosophical "cosmic pluralism" begins around this time and is the naturalist's version of "polytheism" (pg. 43)

• **603 BC** - King Nebuchadnezzar has a dream regarding the future mingling of the *"seed of men"* (pg. 43)

• **624-545 BC** - Thales of Miletus, father of Greek philosophy and the philosophical school of naturalism (pgs. 43-44)

• **610-540 BC** - Anaximander of Miletus (pg. 44)

• **570-475 BC** - Xenophanes of Colophon (pg. 44)

• **500-428 BC** - Anaxagoras of Clazomenae (pg. 44)

• **440-370 BC** - Leucippus and Democritus formulate "Atomism", the precursor to "Evolution" (pg. 45)

• **341-270 BC** - Epicurus founds "Epicureanism". The Apostle Paul encounters these followers over 350 years later (pgs. 45-47)

• **99-55 BC** - Lucretius (pg. 47)

• **45-120 AD** - Plutarch makes a statement on Lunar life around the same time Revelation is being written (70 AD). This is the last major statement on extraterrestrial life until the Dark Ages (pgs. 49-50)

• **1401-1464 AD** - Nicholas of Cusa (pgs. 51-53)

• **1473-1543 AD** - Nicholas Copernicus introduces "Heliocentrism" (pgs. 53-54)

• **1548-1600 AD** - Giordano Bruno (pgs. 54-55)

• **1608 AD** - The telescope is invented (pg. 57)

• **1629-1695 AD** - Christian Huygens speculates on the physical appearance of alien life in his work, *Cosmotheoros* (pg. 58)

• **1688-1772 AD** - Emanuel Swedenborg integrates occultism, Spiritism, Extraterrestrialism and Christianity to create a new religious system (pgs. 59-63)

• **1780-1884 AD** - Thomas Chalmers (pg. 64)

• **1830 AD** - Joseph Smith creates Mormonism, a "Christian" cult with foundational beliefs rooted in Extraterrestrialism (pgs. 65-69)

• **1835 AD** - The *New York Sun's* lunar man-bats (pgs. 72-76)

• **1859 AD** - Charles Darwin's *The Origin of Species* is first published. These concepts soon form the bedrock for belief in the possibility of intelligent life on other planets (pg. 81)

• **1865 AD** - Jules Verne writes *From the Earth to the Moon* (pg. 80)

• **1880s - 1890s AD** - The radio is invented (pgs. 83-84)

• **1884 AD** - Scottish Presbyterian, Thomas Dick, publishes his best-selling *Celestial Scenery,* advancing the belief that God created life, not simply on planet Earth, but on all planets (pg. 79)

- **1897 AD** - H.G. Wells writes *The War of the Worlds* (pg. 80)

- **1901 AD** - H.G. Wells writes *The First Men in the Moon* (pg. 86)

- **1901 AD** - Electricity wizard, Nikola Tesla, claims that he may have received intelligent radio signals from Mars (pg. 84-85)

- **1920s-1950s AD** - The sci-fi boom begins: Pulp science fiction magazines, movie serials, motion pictures, comic books (pgs. 86-93)

- **1931 AD** - The radio telescope is invented (pg. 106)

- **1947 AD** - The first widely known UFO sighting (pg. 93)

- **1947 AD** - A "flying saucer" reportedly crashes in Roswell, New Mexico (pg. 93-94)

- **1958 AD** - NASA is formed. Many men who become part of the organization were inspired by science fiction (pgs. 95-111)

- **1959 AD** - NASA creates its first program on "Exobiology" – the search for life and its origins in outer space (pg. 108)

- **1961 AD** - The Drake Equation is formulated (pgs. 106-107)

- **1969 AD** - The United States places astronauts on the Moon – the Space Age begins (pgs. 102-105)

- **2000s AD** - The rise of "alien disclosure" movements (pg. 130)

- **2008 AD** - Vatican astronomers propose that aliens should be received as co-created "brothers and sister" (pgs. 133-137)

INDEX

E

Eagle 186, 191, 458, 496
Earth 26, 28, 30-38, 44, 47, 51,
  52, 54-58, 65, 66, 76, 79,
  80, 83, 86, 88, 90, 94,
  101, 102, 106, 111-115, 120,
  121, 123, 127-129, 132, 133,
  137-141, 153, 155, 157, 158,
  164-180, 183, 188, 190,
  191, 193-195, 198, 217-219,
  222, 232, 233, 235, 236,
  239, 241, 243, 245, 247,
  253, 257, 259, 260, 278,
  279, 288, 289, 290, 291,
  293, 294-310, 313, 316,
  318, 331, 358, 375, 376,
  389, 402-405, 410, 414,
  416, 424, 428, 432, 437,
  439, 445, 449, 451, 453-
  459, 468, 469, 471-473,
  478, 480, 486
Edrei 380, 382
Edwards, Jonathan 69
Einstein, Albert 351
Elders, Four and Twenty 269
Elements 241, 261, 424, 435, 437
Elijah 247, 286, 291, 292, 293,
  294, 295, 299, 306, 496
Elisha 247, 286, 287, 292, 293
Emims 381
Enchantments 333, 334, 336,
  337, 338
English Bibles 50
Enoch 14, 33, 36, 42, 136, 212,
  290, 291, 293, 299
Enochian Magic 436
Ephesus 37
Epicureanism 45
Epicurians 46, 49
Epicurus 41, 45, 46, 47, 112

Esker, David 397, 401
Esotericism 60, 61, 63
ET 54, 109, 126-133, 164, 394,
  474
  See also Alien,
  Extraterrestrial
ETH. *See* Extraterrestrial
  Hypothesis
European Union 352
Everest, Mount 404
Evolution 39, 81, 82, 92, 108, 111,
  114, 116, 118-121, 125, 126,
  133-136, 156, 166, 239,
  358, 366, 409, 444, 475
Evolutionary Tree 121
Evolutionism 125, 424
Exobiology 108
Exopolitics Institute 128, 129, 130
Extraterrestrial 27, 31, 32, 38, 39,
  41, 42, 49, 50, 54, 55, 57,
  58, 63, 64, 65, 72, 76-86,
  108, 110, 111, 128-130, 133,
  136, 141, 152, 156, 195, 257,
  286, 288, 300, 304, 305,
  399, 424, 432, 453, 459,
  469, 470, 471
Extraterrestrial Hypothesis 127,
  128 424
Extraterrestrialism 50, 53, 55,
  139, 421
Ezekiel 43, 162, 235, 245, 250,
  251, 265, 266, 267, 268,
  282, 283, 300, 370, 448

F

Fabric of space 185
Fairy Tales 16, 424, 428, 429,
  430, 431, 432, 433, 434,
  435, 436, 437, 438, 439

BIBLIOGRAPHY

Alnor, William M. *UFO's in the New Age: Extraterrestrial Messages & the Truth of scripture*. Grand Rapids, MI: Baker Book House, 1992.

Barnes, Jonathan. *Early Greek Philosophy*. London: Penguin Books, 2001.

Bellomo, Michael. *The Stem Cell Divide: The Facts, the Fiction, and the Fear Driving the Greatest Scientific, Political, and Religious Debate of Our Time*. New York, NY: AMACOM, 2006.

Buckland, Raymond. *Buckland's Complete Book of Witchcraft*. St. Paul, MN: Llewellyn Publications, 1998.

Bush, George. *Mesmer & Swedenborg: or, The Relation of the Developments of Mesmerism to the Doctrines & Disclosures of Swedenborg*. New York, NY: John Allen, 1847.

Catoe, Lynn E. *UFO's & Related Subjects: An Annotated Bibliography*. Washington, DC: U.S. Printing Office, 1969.

Chaikin, Andrew. *Air and Space: The National Air and Space Museum Story of Flight*. New York: The Smithsonian Institute, and Little Brown and Company Inc., 1997.

Chalmers, Thomas. *The Works of Thomas Chalmers*. D.D. Pittsburgh, PA: A. Towar, Hogan & Thompson, 1833.

Clark, Jerome. *Unexplained!*. Canton, MI: Visible Ink Press, 1999.

Copley, F.O.,(tr.), Lucretius: *On the Nature of Things*. New York: W.W. Norton & Co., 1977.

Crowe, Michael J. *The Extraterrestrial Life Debate*. Notre Dame, IN: University of Notre Dame, 2008.

Crowley, Aleister. *Magic Without Tears*. New York, NY: Ordo Templi Orientis, 1954.

Cruz, Joan Carroll. *Miraculous Images of Our Lady*. Rockford, IL: Tan Books & Publishers, Inc., 1993.

Cruz, Joan Carroll. *Miraculous Images of Our Lord*. Rockford, IL: Tan Books & Publishers, Inc., 1995.

Darling, David. *The Extraterrestrial Encyclopedia*. New York, NY: Three Rivers Press, 2000.

DeLoach, Charles. *Giants: A Reference Guide from History, the Bible, and Recorded Legend*. Metuchen, NJ & London: The Scarecrow Press, 1995.

Dick, Steven J. *The Biological Universe: The Twentieth Century Extraterrestrial Life Debate and the Limits of Science*. Cambridge, UK: Cambridge University Press, 1996.

Dobzhansky, Theodosius. *American Biology Teacher*. USA: 1973.

Epicurus, trans. Bailey, C. *Epicurus to Herodotus, in The Stoic and Epicurean Philosophers*. New York, NY: Modern Library, Whitney J. Oates, 1957.

Griggs, William N. *The Celebrated Moon Story, It's Origin And Incidents; With A Memoir Of The Author*. New York, NY: Bunnell & Price, 1852.

Guiley, Rosemary Ellen. *The Encyclopedia of Witches and Witchcraft*. New York: Facts On File, Inc., 1989.

Hamilton, Ross. *Holocaust of Giants: What Has Happened to the Skeletons?*. USA: Ross Hamilton, 2001.

Keith, Jim. *Mind Control & UFOs: Casebook On Alternative 3*. Lilburn, GA: IllumiNet Press, 1999.

Mackey, A. G. *Encyclopaedia of Freemasonry*. New York, 1929.

Maidl, B., Schmid, L., Ritz, W. and Herrenknecht, M. *Historical Development and Future Challenges, in Hardrock Tunnel Boring Machines.* Weinheim, Germany: Wiley-VCH Verlag GmbH & Co. KGaA, 2008.

Mayr, Ernst. *The Growth of Biological Thought.* Cambridge: Harvard, 1981.

Mason, S.F, *A History of the Sciences.* New York: Macmillan Pub. Co., 1962.

Pirtle, Henry. *The Kentucky Monitor: Complete Monitorial Ceremonies of the Blue Lodge.* Masonic Home, KY: Grand Lodge of Kentucky Free And Accepted Masons, 1990.

Plutarch, and Harold Cherniss. *Plutarch's Moralia. Vol. XII.* Cambridge, MA: Harvard University Press, 1976.

Quayle, Stephen. *Genesis 6 Giants.* Bozeman, MT: End Time Thunder Publishers, 2002.

Ruckman, Peter S. *1 in 23,000,000: Betting On the Bible & It's Historical Accuracy.* Pensacola, FL: Bible Baptist Bookstore, 2001.

Ruckman, Peter S. *The Christian's Handbook of Science & Philosophy.* Pensacola, FL: Bible Baptist Bookstore, 1985.

Sauder, Richard. *Underground Bases & Tunnels: What's the Government Trying to Hide?* Kepton, Illinois: Adventures Unlimited Press, 1995.

Sauder, Richard. *Underwater & Underground Bases: Surprising Facts the Government Does Not Want You to Know!* Kepton, Illinois: Adventures Unlimited Press, 2001.

Spence, Lewis. *An Encyclopedia of Occultism.* Secaucus, NJ: Citadel Press & Carol Publishing Group, 1996 [reprint of a 1920 ed].

Swedenborg, Emanual. *A Compendium of the Theological & Spiritual Writings of Emanuel Swedenborg.* Boston, NY: Crosby & Nichols, Publishers, 1853.

Story, Ronald. *The Encyclopedia of Extraterrestrial Encounters*. New
    York: New American Library, 2001.

Tesla, Nikola. Collier's Weekly. 7 Feb. 1901.

Thomas, I.D.E. *The Omega Conspiracy: Satan's Last Assault On God's
    Kingdom*. Oklahoma City OK: Hearthstone Publishing, Ltd., 1986.

Tissot, Jacques. *The Post Graduate: A Monthly Journal of Medicine and
    Surgery*. New York:1912.

Titus Lucretius Carus, trans. R. E. Latham. *On the Nature of the Universe*.
    Middlesex, England: Penguin Books, 1975.

White, Ellen G. *The Story of Patriarchs and Prophets*. Mountain View, CA;
    Pacific Press Publishing Association, 1913.

Wood, Edward J. *Giants & Dwarfs*. London: Robson and Son, Great
    Northern Printing Works, 1868.

Zimmerman, Fritz. *The Nephilim Chronicles*. USA: Fritz Zimmerman,
    2010.

ABOUT THE AUTHOR

Jeffrey W. Mardis has been a born-again Christian since April, 1979, a lifelong student of the Bible, and has been writing and researching on end-times Christian discernment issues since the late 1990s. He is founder of *Sword-In-Hand Publishing* and a member of the *Christian Small Publishers Association* (CSPA). Jeffrey resides in Campbellsville, Kentucky and has served in the graphic  design field since 1993. He is an Independent, King James Bible-Believing Baptist, and an award-winning, internationally recognized logo and trademark designer.

Also by Jeffrey W. Mardis:
Star of the King: The Christian's Guide to Learing the Identity of the Star of Bethlehem
Available from Sword-In-Hand Publishing

www.swordinhandpub.com

WHAT DWELLS BEYOND
WORDSEARCH PUZZLE

Just for fun, we've added this classic wordsearch puzzle to test your memory. All wordsearch clues may be discovered in the text, images or scripture of this book. Hidden words run forwards, backwards and diagonal. Answers on page 522.

Answers on page 522.

HIDDEN WORD CLUES:

1 - Mr. Big Bed

2 - Covers the heavens in type

3 - Lights Out

4 - Star-Man

5 - Wrote an equation for alien life

6 - Compass of the Universe

7 - First man to radio Mars

8 - NASA's Nazi rocket-man

9 - First SF magazine

10 - Second Heaven

11 - The Book

12 - What did you say?

13 - Lots-o-gods

14 - An Image fell from Here

15 - Thales of ____

16 - Paul rebuked his Followers

17 - Mr. Mermaid

18 - Wanna ride the Goat?

19 - Theory before Evolution

20 - Father of Heliocentrism

21 - The Champion

22 - Joseph Smith's World

23 - Vespertilio-homo

24 - God's chosen Nation

25 - ...which I made with thee.

26 - The Amazing ____ Man

27 - Snake Wrestler

28 - Mt. Sion

29 - North of Astaroth

30 - The Way

31 - Bird on the Moon

32 - From the Serpent's Root

33 - The Dry Land

34 - It's above the Heavens

35 - The Wind Rider

36 - The Other Witness

37 - West Virginia Sighting

38 - King of the Pit

Seek & Ye Shall Find...

```
E S U C I N R E P O C W M E K A R D N L
L L K Y T G K S P M Q R N S E C A P S D
B A M W N O U Q E M O R Z Y I B R K T K
I S Y Y L S G M Q C X T E Q J M B Z J N
B S R O E S A S M S I E H T Y L O P L W
S O B J Y N E T S H E R D M I B B T Z Z
E L M K B A H I T E R A T I A P M N A R
M O S A R E N O R L N B R A S N U Q M T
A C T G R M M N P O Y K T T K R X J G J
J J O M P E U H R R T H R Z H C A D P G
G B O L H A A T N G T S G A D D O E Z R
N N Y E R J L O S O H R G J D V P C L R
I R B B I E S U L L E N Y N W A T E R S
K R N L B A R C E I R A O M I L E T U S
G O E A M U K L M A C N L D M Z N R B T
V Y B E C C G O N T U O M S D K A R R P
Z T E I A A S G T H L G B J E A Y M Z V
Z R P S E E E T Q P E A M Z N T B Q A D
F E V G S L L Q L T S D B J D D N A D G
```

WHAT DWELLS BEYOND
WORDSEARCH PUZZLE

CLUE ANSWERS
WORDSEARCH PUZZLE

Puzzle answers with cooresponding page numbers. NOTE: Two of the clues have the same answer (6 and 33), but the word is only found once. There are 38 clues, but only 37 hidden words.

1 - Og, 377

2 - Sackcloth, 214

3 - Darkness, 197

4 - Angel, 259

5 - Drake, 107

6 - Earth, 174

7 - Tesla, 84

8 - Von Braun, 98

9 - Amazing Stories, 86

10 - Space, 182

11 - King James Bible, 144

12 - Babel, 34

13 - Polytheism, 35

14 - Jupiter, 37

15 - Miletus, 43

16 - Epicurus, 46

17 - Dagon, 441

18 - Freemasonry, 329

19 - Atomism, 45

20 - Copernicus, 54

21 - Goliath, 387

22 - Kolob, 65

23 - Man-Bat, 74

24 - Israel, 160

25 - Behemoth, 400

26 - Colossal, 90

27 - Hercules, 408

28 - Mt. Hermon, 381

29 - Argob, 380

30 - Jesus, 486

31 - Eagle, 186

32 - Cockatrice, 254

33 - Earth, 167

34 - Waters, 184

35 - Elijah, 292

36 - Moses, 295

37 - Mothman, 444

38 - Abaddon, 452

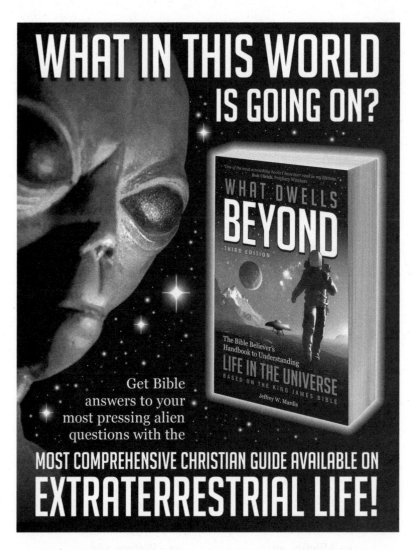

"He which testifieth these things saith,
Surely I come quickly. Amen.
Even so, come, Lord Jesus."
REVELATION 22:20